Programming Microsoft Dynamics 365 Business Central
Sixth Edition

Build customized business applications with the latest tools
in Dynamics 365 Business Central

Marije Brummel
David Studebaker
Chris Studebaker

BIRMINGHAM - MUMBAI

Programming Microsoft Dynamics 365 Business Central
Sixth Edition

Commissioning Editor: Richa Tripathi
Acquisition Editor: Chaitanya Nair
Content Development Editor: Rohit Singh
Technical Editor: Romy Dias
Copy Editor: Safis Editing
Project Coordinator: Vaidehi Sawant
Proofreader: Safis Editing
Indexer: Priyanka Dhadke
Graphics: Alishon Mendonsa
Production Coordinator: Aparna Bhagat

First published: October 2007
Second edition: November 2009
Third edition: February 2013
Fourth edition: July 2015
Fifth edition: April 2017
Sixth edition: April 2019

Production reference: 2081221

Published by Packt Publishing Ltd.
Livery Place
35 Livery Street
Birmingham
B3 2PB, UK.

ISBN 978-1-78913-779-8

www.packtpub.com

`mapt.io`

Mapt is an online digital library that gives you full access to over 5,000 books and videos, as well as industry leading tools to help you plan your personal development and advance your career. For more information, please visit our website.

Why subscribe?

- Spend less time learning and more time coding with practical eBooks and Videos from over 4,000 industry professionals

- Improve your learning with Skill Plans built especially for you

- Get a free eBook or video every month

- Mapt is fully searchable

- Copy and paste, print, and bookmark content

PacktPub.com

Did you know that Packt offers eBook versions of every book published, with PDF and ePub files available? You can upgrade to the eBook version at `www.PacktPub.com` and as a print book customer, you are entitled to a discount on the eBook copy. Get in touch with us at `service@packtpub.com` for more details.

At `www.PacktPub.com`, you can also read a collection of free technical articles, sign up for a range of free newsletters, and receive exclusive discounts and offers on Packt books and eBooks.

Contributors

About the authors

Author, programmer, consultant, project manager, presenter, evangelist, sales person, and a trainer. She has worked for Partners, ISVs, End Users, Master VARs, and Microsoft across the globe in more than 25 countries.

It's next to impossible to find someone as widely and deeply experienced as **Marije Brummel** in the Business Central community. Marije received numerous awards including the Microsoft MVP award and the NAVUG All-Star. She was chair of the Dynamics Credentialling committee and authored the official Microsoft Exam materials. She did both onsite and online readiness sessions for Microsoft when the product went through major changes, such as moving from two to three tier and the introduction of extensions.

Her biggest passion is changing the world for the better in every way possible. One of her biggest achievements was the introduction of Design Patterns into the Business Central community. She is the go-to girl when it comes to performance troubleshooting and upgrade challenges. Technologies such as the Azure stack and Web frameworks don't hold secrets in regards to Business Central.

Marije wrote a number of books and countless blog articles and YouTube videos, which influenced almost every person and project involved with Business Central. At home, she enjoys the outdoors with her dog and tries to spend as much time as possible with her kids and family. She likes shopping and traveling.

> *Working on this book with Dave and Chris has been amazing. I have been involved since the first edition and to see this book stay strong throughout the changes of the product says something about it. It has been a pleasure updating the content to the latest version of the product. I would like to thank Dave and his wife Karen for all the opportunities our friendship has brought and the lessons in life we have been able to share. Of course, I'd like to thank my wife, Dionel, and my kids for giving me the time to work on the book.*

David Studebaker has been designing and developing software since 1962 as a developer, consultant, manager, and business owner. In 1967, David coauthored the first general-purpose SPOOL system, an AT&T / IBM joint project. He has been a founding partner in several firms, most recently Studebaker Technology and Liberty Grove Software. David's publications include a decade of technical reviews for *ACM Computing Reviews* and a number of articles on shop floor data collection. David originated the Packt series of books on programming Dynamics Business Central (aka Dynamics NAV). He has a BS in mechanical engineering from Purdue University and an MBA from the University of Chicago. He is a life member of the Association for Computing Machinery.

I am grateful for the joy of working with Marije and Christopher, my coauthors. I want to thank the many special people who have provided guidance and assistance throughout my life, especially my parents. I am thankful for the love and support of my children, Becky and Chris, their spouses and children. Most of all, I am deeply grateful to Karen, my lifelong partner in marriage, family, business, and love, for her unwavering support in all things.

Chris Studebaker was a certified environmental consultant working with manufacturing facilities to meet national and state regulations before he started working with Navision in 1999. After working on regulatory reporting, data analysis, project management, and subcontractor oversight, Chris has used those skills to sell, develop, and implement NAV for the past 20 years. He has specialized in retail, manufacturing, job shop, and distribution implementations, mostly in high-user-count, high-data-volume applications. Chris acts in a consulting and training role for customers and for peer NAV professionals. He has a Bachelor of Science degree from Northern Illinois University and has done graduate work at Denmark Technical University.

This book would not have been possible without Marije and David, and I am extremely grateful for all their work. I would like to thank the many people who have mentored me through the years and am thankful for the many friendships that I've formed, both with team members and customers. The NAV world is full of supportive people, and I am thankful to my parents for introducing me to it. I would like to thank my wife, Beth, and son, Cole, for supporting my writing.

About the reviewers

Ronald E. Oates switched university majors from theatre to computer science when he discovered he had a "knack" for programming. It was a good move—in 1979, he got his first programming job as a contract programmer, developing software in COBOL, RPG II, and DEC/VAX BASIC on mainframe and mini computers. In 1986, with the advent of micro-computers, he started Productive Systems, Inc. to focus on bringing software solutions to small and mid-size businesses.

Productive Systems, Inc. became a Microsoft Partner in 1997 when the program was started. In 1999, PSI became a Navision Solution Center. Navision perfectly fit Ron's vision of solutions with existing base functionality that could be rapidly and securely modified to fit individual customer needs. Once Navision was discovered, the focus of the business was entirely Navision, then Microsoft Dynamics NAV, and now Microsoft Business Central 365.

Roberto Stefanetti is a functional and technical consultant who has worked on education and training for companies, partners, and clients. He currently works on Microsoft systems, especially ERP and related environments.

He started working on Navision in 2004, both as a developer and as a functional consultant, and he is now more involved in consulting and managing projects than in development. He has been an MVP in business application since 2016 and a Microsoft Education Influencer since 2017.

Roberto's blog is one of the most widely read in the world (with more than 1 million page visits). He has also published articles on many digital publications (such as MSDynamicsWorld, NAVUG Magazine, and others) and reviewed a number of books.

Packt is searching for authors like you

If you're interested in becoming an author for Packt, please visit authors.packtpub.com and apply today. We have worked with thousands of developers and tech professionals, just like you, to help them share their insight with the global tech community. You can make a general application, apply for a specific hot topic that we are recruiting an author for, or submit your own idea.

Table of Contents

Preface

Welcome to the worldwide community of Microsoft Dynamics Business Central developers. This is a collegial environment populated by AL developers who readily and generously share their knowledge. There are formal and informal organizations of Business Central-focused users, developers, and vendor firms scattered around the globe and active on the web. Our community continues to grow and prosper, and now includes over 110,000 user companies worldwide.

The information in this book will help you shorten your learning curve on how to program for the Business Central ERP system using the AL language, the Visual Studio integrated development environment, and their capabilities. We hope you enjoy working with Business Central as much as we have.

A brief history of Business Central

Each new version of Microsoft Dynamics Business Central (formerly NAV) is the result of inspiration and hard work, along with some good fortune and expert technical investment over the last thirty years.

The beginning

Three college friends, Jesper Balser, Torben Wind, and Peter Bang, from **Denmark Technical University** (**DTU**) founded their computer software business in 1984 when they were in their early twenties; that business was **PC Computing & Consulting** (**PC & C**), and its first product was called PC Plus.

Single-user PC Plus

PC Plus was released in 1985 with the primary goal of ease of use. An early employee said its functional design was inspired by the combination of a manual ledger journal, an Epson FX 80 printer, and a Canon calculator. Incidentally, Peter Bang is the grandson of one of the founders of Bang & Olufsen, the manufacturer of home entertainment systems par excellence.

PC Plus was a PC DOS-based, single-user system. PC Plus' design included the following features:

- An interface resembling the use of documents and calculators
- Online help
- Good exception handling
- Minimal reliance on computer resources

The PC Plus product was marketed through dealers in Denmark and Norway.

Multi-user Navigator

In 1987, PC & C released a new product, the multi-user Navigator, and a new corporate name, Navision. Navigator was quite a technological leap forward. It included the following features:

- Client/server technology
- A relational database
- Transaction-based processing
- Version management
- High-speed OLAP capabilities (SIFT technology)
- A screen painter tool
- A programmable report writer

In 1990, Navision was expanding its marketing and dealer recruitment efforts into Germany, Spain, and the United Kingdom. Also in 1990, a third version of Navigator was released. Navigator V3 was still a character-based system, albeit a very sophisticated one. If you had the opportunity to study Navigator V3.x, you would instantly recognize the roots of today's Business Central product. By V3, the product included the following features:

- A design based on object-oriented concepts
- Integrated 4GL Table, Form, and Report Design tools (the IDE)

- Structured exception handling
- Built-in resource management
- The original programming language that became C/AL, which later changed to AL
- Function libraries
- The concept of regional or country-based localization

When Navigator V3.5 was released, it also included support for multiple platforms and multiple databases. Navigator V3.5 would run on both Unix and Windows NT networks. It supported Oracle and Informix databases, as well as those developed in-house.

At about this time, several major strategic efforts were initiated. On the technical side, the decision was made to develop a GUI-based product. The first prototype of Navision Financials (for Windows) was shown in 1992. At about the same time, a relationship was established that would take Navision into distribution in the United States. The initial release in the US in 1995 was V3.5 of the character-based product, rechristened Avista for US distribution.

Navision Financials for Windows

In 1995, Navision Financials V1.0 for Microsoft Windows was released. This product had many (but not all) of the features of Navigator V3.5. It was designed for complete look-and-feel compatibility with Windows 95. There was an effort to provide the ease of use and flexibility of development of Microsoft Access. The new Navision Financials was very compatible with Microsoft Office and was thus sold as "being familiar to any Office user". Like any V1.0 product, it was quickly followed by a much improved V1.1.

In the next few years, Navision continued to be improved and enhanced. Major new functionalities, such as the following, were added:

- Customer Relation Management (CRM)
- Manufacturing (ERP)
- Advanced distribution (including Warehouse Management)

Various Microsoft certifications were obtained, providing muscle to the marketing efforts. Geographic and dealer-based expansion continued apace. By 2000, according to the Navision Annual Report of that year, the product was represented by nearly 1,000 dealers (Navision Solution Centers) in 24 countries and used by 41,000 customers located in 108 countries.

Growth and mergers

In 2000, Navision Software A/S, and its primary Danish competitor, Damgaard A/S, merged. Product development and new releases continued for the primary products of both original firms (Navision and Axapta). In 2002, the now much larger Navision Software, with all of its products (Navision, Axapta, the smaller, older C5, and XAL) was purchased by Microsoft, becoming part of the Microsoft Business Systems division along with the previously-purchased Great Plains Software business, and its several product lines. The Navision and Great Plains products all received a common rebranding to become the Dynamics product line. Navision was renamed as Dynamics NAV, and later to Business Central.

Continuous enhancement

As early as 2003, research began with the Dynamics NAV development team, planning moves to further enhance NAV and take advantage of various parts of the Microsoft product line. Goals were defined to increase integration with products such as Microsoft Office and Microsoft Outlook. Goals were also set to leverage the functional capabilities of Visual Studio Code and SQL Server, among others. All the while, there was a determination not to lose the strength and flexibility of the base product.

NAV 2009 was released in late 2008, NAV 2013 in late 2012, followed by NAV 2015 in late 2014. NAV 2017 was released in October 2016. The biggest hurdles to the new technologies have been cleared. A new user interface, the Role Tailored Client, was created as part of this renewal. NAV was tightly integrated with Microsoft's SQL Server and other Microsoft products, such as Office, Outlook, and SharePoint. Development is more integrated with Visual Studio Code and is more .NET compliant. The product is becoming more open and, at the same time, more sophisticated, supporting features such as web services access, web and tablet clients, integration of third-party controls, RDLC and Word-based reporting, and so on.

Microsoft continues to invest in, enhance, and advance Business Central. More new capabilities and features are yet to come, with the aim of building on the successes of the past. We all benefit from their work.

AL's roots

One of the first questions asked by people new to AL is often, "What other programming language is it like?". The best response is Pascal. To those unfamiliar with Pascal, the next best response would be C or C#.

At the time the three founders of Navision were attending classes at Denmark Technical University (DTU), Pascal was widely used as a preferred language not only on computer courses, but on other courses where computers were tools and software had to be written for data analyses. Some of the strengths of Pascal as a tool in an educational environment also made it an ideal model for Navision's business applications development.

Perhaps coincidentally (or perhaps not), at the same time at DTU, a Pascal compiler called Blue Label Pascal was developed by Anders Hejlsberg. That compiler became the basis for what was Borland's Turbo Pascal, which was considered the everyman's compiler of the 1980s because of its low price. Anders went with his Pascal compiler to Borland. While he was there, Turbo Pascal morphed into the Delphi language and IDE tool set under his guidance.

Anders later left Borland and joined Microsoft, where he led the C# design team. Much of the NAV-related development at Microsoft is now being done in C#. Keeping it in the family, Anders' brother, Thomas Hejlsberg, also works at Microsoft as a software architect on Business Central. Each in their own way, Anders and Thomas continue to make significant contributions to Dynamics NAV.

In a discussion about AL and Visual Studio Code, Michael Nielsen of Navision and Microsoft, who developed the original AL compiler, runtime, and IDE, said that the design criteria provides an environment that can be used without the following tasks:

- Dealing with memory and other resource handling
- Thinking about exception handling and state
- Thinking about database transactions and rollbacks
- Knowing about set operations (SQL)
- Knowing about OLAP (SIFT)

Paraphrasing some of Michael's additional comments, the goals of the language and IDE designs included:

- Allowing the developer to focus on design rather than coding, but still allowing flexibility
- Providing a syntax based on Pascal stripped of complexities, especially relating to memory management
- Providing a limited set of predefined object types and reducing the complexity and learning curve
- Implementing database versioning for a consistent and reliable view of the database
- Making the developer and end user more at home by borrowing a large number of concepts from Office, Windows, Access, and other Microsoft products

Michael is now a co-founder and partner at ForNAV. Michael and his fellow team members are all about developing high-quality reporting enhancements for Dynamics Business Central, with the goal of making working with reports easy. This is another example of how, once we're part of the Business Central community, most of us want to stay part of that community.

Who this book is for

This book is for the following:

- The business applications software designer or developer for whom the following is true:
    - Wants to become productive in Business Central Visual Code—AL development as quickly as possible
    - Understands business applications and the type of software required to support those applications
    - Has significant programming experience
    - Has access to a copy of Business Central, including the Designer granules and a standard Cronus demo database
    - Is willing to do the exercises to get hands-on experience

- The reseller manager or executive who wants a concise, in-depth view of Business Central's development environment and tool set.

- The technically knowledgeable manager or executive of a firm using Business Central that is about to embark on a significant Business Central enhancement project.
- The technically knowledgeable manager or executive of a firm considering the purchase of Business Central as a highly-customizable business applications platform.
- The experienced business analyst, consultant, or advanced student of applications software development who wants to learn more about Business Central because it is one of the most widely used, and most flexible, business application systems available.

The reader of this book does not need the following:

- Does not need to be an expert in object-oriented programming
- Does not need previous experience with Business Central, AL, or Visual Studio Code

What this book covers

Chapter 1, *Introduction to Business Central*, starts with an overview of Business Central as a business application system, which is followed by an introduction to the seven types of Business Central objects, as well as the basics of AL and Visual Studio Code. It then presents the opportunity for some hands-on work, such as defining tables, multiple page types, and reports. This chapter will close with a brief discussion of how backups and documentations are handled in Visual Studio Code.

Chapter 2, *Tables*, focuses on the foundation level of Business Central's data structure: tables and their structures. This chapter covers properties, triggers (where AL resides), field groups, table relations, and SumIndexFields. It will then present the hands-on creation of several tables in support of an example application. The chapter will also review the types of tables found in the Business Central applications.

Chapter 3, *Data Types and Fields*, will teach you about fields, the basic building blocks of Business Central's data structure. It will review the different data types in Business Central and cover all of its field properties and triggers in detail, as well as review the three different field classes.

Chapter 4, *Pages – The Interactive Interface*, reviews the different types of pages, their structures (triggers and properties), and general usage. The chapter will encourage readers to build several pages for an example application using snippets. It will also explore the different types of controls that can be used in pages. In addition, this chapter will review how and where actions are added to pages.

Chapter 5, *Queries and Reports*, teaches you about both queries and reports—two methods of extracting data for presentation to users. It will show readers how queries are constructed and some of the different ways they are utilized. It will also offer a walk-through for reporting data flow in reports, and what the different report types are. This chapter will present two Report Designers: the Visual Studio Report Designer and the Visual Studio Report Designer, and will explain how a Business Central report is constructed using both of these and in what scenarios they are best applied. This chapter will also discuss properties and triggers, before reviewing how reports can be made interactive with hands-on report creation.

Chapter 6, *Introduction to AL*, explains general object designer navigation, as well as the individual designers (table, page, and report). It will explore AL code construction, syntax, variable types, expressions, operators, and functions. The chapter will then offer a closer look at some of the more frequently used built-in functions. This chapter will wrap up with an exercise that adds AL code to a report object created in an earlier exercise.

Chapter 7, *Intermediate AL*, digs deeper into AL development tools and techniques. It will review some more advanced built-in functions, including those relating to dates and decimal calculations—both critical business application tools. This chapter will also explore AL functions that support process flow control functions, input and output, and filtering, before reviewing methods of communication between objects. Finally, this chapter offers the opportunity to practically enhance an example application.

Chapter 8, *Advanced AL Development Tools*, reviews some of the more important elements of Role's tailored user experience; in particular, the Role Center page construction. It will dig into the components of a Role Center page and how to build one. This chapter will also cover two powerful ways of connecting Business Central applications to the world outside of Business Central, using XMLports and web services. To better understand these, the chapter will not only review their individual component parts, but will also go through the hands-on effort of building an example of each one.

`Chapter 9`, *Successful Conclusions*, gives readers a detailed study of how Business Central functions are constructed, and will explain how to construct functions. This chapter will include more information about the tools and features built into AL and Visual Studio Code, as well as the new debugger. It will also review support for test-driven development, and take a look at how to integrate .NET Client Add-ins with example applications. Finally, it will review tips for design efficiency, and updating and upgrading the system, all with the goal of helping readers become more productive, high-quality Business Central developers.

To get the most out of this book

To get the maximum out of this book as a developer, the following should match you:

- Be an experienced developer
- Know more than one programming language
- Have IDE experience
- Be knowledgeable about business applications
- Be good at self-directed study

If you have these attributes, this book will help you become productive with AL and Business Central much more rapidly.

Even though this book is targeted first at developers, it is also designed to be useful to executives, consultants, managers, business owners, and others who want to learn about the development technology and operational capabilities of Dynamics 365 Business Central. If you fit into one of these, or similar, categories, start by studying Chapter 1 for a good overview of Business Central and its tools. You should then consider reviewing sections of other chapters, where specific topics may apply to your specific areas of interest.

This book's illustrations are from the W1 Cronus database, Dynamics 365 Business Central V2017.

You will need some basic tools to get the most of this book, including the following:

- A license and database that can be used for development experimentation. The ideal license is a full developer's license. If your license only contains the page, report, and table designer capabilities, you will still be able to do many of the exercises, but you will not have access to the inner workings of pages and tables and the AL code contained therein.

- A copy of the Business Central Cronus demo or test database for your development testing and study. Having a copy of a production database for examination is ideal. This book's illustrations are from the W1 Cronus database for V2017.
- The hardware and software requirements for installing and running Microsoft Dynamics Business Central can be found at `https://msdn.microsoft.com/en-us/dynamics-nav/system-requirements-for-microsoft-dynamics-nav`.

Access to other Business Central manuals, training materials, websites, and experienced associates will obviously be of benefit, but they are not required for the time spent with this book to be a good investment.

Downloading the example code files

You can download the example code files for this book from your account at `www.packtpub.com`. If you purchased this book elsewhere, you can visit `www.packtpub.com/support` and register to have the files emailed directly to you.

You can download the code files by following these steps:

1. Log in or register at `www.packtpub.com`.
2. Select the **SUPPORT** tab.
3. Click on **Code Downloads & Errata**.
4. Enter the name of the book in the **Search** box and follow the onscreen instructions.

Once the file is downloaded, please make sure that you unzip or extract the folder using the latest version of:

- WinRAR/7-Zip for Windows
- Zipeg/iZip/UnRarX for Mac
- 7-Zip/PeaZip for Linux

The code bundle for the book is also hosted on GitHub at `https://github.com/PacktPublishing/Programming-Microsoft-Dynamics-365-Business-Central-Sixth-Edition`. In case there's an update to the code, it will be updated on the existing GitHub repository.

We also have other code bundles from our rich catalog of books and videos available at `https://github.com/PacktPublishing/`. Check them out!

Downloading the color images

We also provide a PDF file that has color images of the screenshots and diagrams used in this book. You can download it here: `https://www.packtpub.com/sites/default/files/downloads/9781789137798_ColorImages.pdf`.

Conventions used

There are a number of text conventions used throughout this book.

`CodeInText` indicates code words in text, database table names, folder names, filenames, file extensions, pathnames, dummy URLs, user input, and Twitter handles. An example of this is as follows: "The `HelloWorld.al` file can be deleted immediately."

A block of code is set as follows:

```
IF Type = 'Resource' THEN No. := Resource.No.
  ELSE IF Type = 'Show' THEN No. := Radio Show.No.
    ELSE IF Type = 'Item' THEN No. := Item.No. )
```

When we wish to draw your attention to a particular part of a code block, the relevant lines or items are set in bold, as follows:

```
IF Type = 'Resource' THEN No. := Resource.No.
  ELSE IF Type = 'Show' THEN No. := Radio Show.No.
    ELSE IF Type = 'Item' THEN No. := Item.No. )
```

Any command-line input or output is written as follows:

```
$ cd css
```

Bold indicates a new term, an important word, or words that you see onscreen. For example, words in menus or dialog boxes appear in the text like this, such as "From Visual Studio Code, click on **New**, then click on **File**."

 Warnings or important notes appear like this.

 Tips and tricks appear like this.

Get in touch

Feedback from our readers is always welcome.

General feedback: Email `feedback@packtpub.com` and mention the book title in the subject of your message. If you have questions about any aspect of this book, please email us at `questions@packtpub.com`.

Errata: Although we have taken every care to ensure the accuracy of our content, mistakes do happen. If you have found a mistake in this book, we would be grateful if you could report this to us. Please visit `www.packtpub.com/submit-errata`, select your book, click on the **Errata Submission Form** link, and enter the details.

Piracy: If you come across any illegal copies of our works in any form on the internet, we would be grateful if you could provide us with the location address or website name. Please contact us at `copyright@packtpub.com` with a link to the material.

Becoming an author: If there is a topic that you have expertise in and you are interested in either writing about or contributing to, please visit `authors.packtpub.com`.

Reviews

Please leave a review. Once you have read and used this book, why not leave a review on the site that you purchased it from? Potential readers can then see and use your unbiased opinion to make purchase decisions, we at Packt can understand what you think about our products, and our authors can see your feedback on their book. Thank you!

For more information about Packt, please visit `packtpub.com`.

Introduction to Business Central

Microsoft Dynamics 365 Business Central has one of the largest installed user bases of any **enterprise resource planning** (**ERP**) system, serving over 150,000 companies and 2.5 million plus individual users, at the time of writing. The community of supporting organizations, consultants, implementers, and developers continues to grow and prosper. The capabilities of the off-the-shelf product increase with every release. The selection of add-on products and services expands both in variety and depth.

The release of Microsoft Dynamics Business Central continues its 20-plus year history of continuous product improvement. It provides more user options for access and output formatting. For new installations, Business Central includes tools for rapid implementation. For all installations, it provides enhanced business functionality and more support for ERP computing in the cloud, including integration with Microsoft Office 365.

Our goal in this chapter is to gain a big-picture understanding of Business Central. You will be able to envision how Business Central can be used by managers (or owners) of an organization to help manage activities and the resources, whether the organization is for-profit or not-for-profit. You will also be introduced to the technical side of Business Central from a developer's point of view.

In this chapter, we will take a look at Business Central, including the following topics:

- A general overview of Business Central
- A technical overview of Business Central
- A hands-on introduction to Visual Studio Code development in Business Central

Business Central – an ERP system

Business Central is an integrated set of business applications designed to service a wide variety of business operations. Microsoft Dynamics 365 Business Central is an ERP system. An ERP system integrates internal and external data across a variety of functional areas, including manufacturing, accounting, supply chain management, customer relationships, service operations, and human resource management, as well as the management of other valued resources and activities. By having many related applications well integrated, a fully-featured ERP system provides an *enter data once, use many ways* information processing toolset.

Business Central ERP addresses the following functional areas (and more):

- Basic accounting functions (for example, general ledger, accounts payable, and accounts receivable)
- Order processing and inventory (for example, sales orders, purchase orders, shipping, inventory, and receiving)
- Relationship management (for example, vendors, customers, prospects, employees, and contractors)
- Planning (for example, MRP, sales forecasting, and production forecasting)
- Other critical business areas (for example, manufacturing, warehouse management, marketing, cash management, and fixed assets)

A good ERP system, such as Business Central, is modular in design, which simplifies implementation, upgrading, modification, integration with third-party products, and expansion for different types of clients. All the modules in the system share a common database and, where appropriate, common data.

The following groupings of individual Business Central functions are based on the **Search** menu structure, which is supplemented by information from Microsoft marketing materials. The important thing is to understand the overall components that make up the Business Central ERP system:

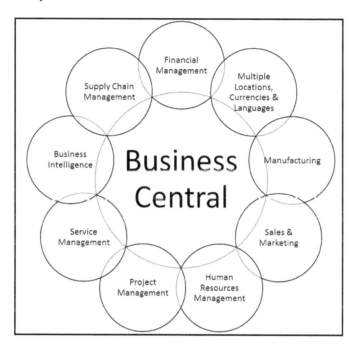

Business Central has a role tailored **User Interface** (**UI**). In Business Central, there are four instances of the **role tailored client** (**RTC**)—one each for Windows, web interaction, tablet use, and as a phone client. Generally the various clients are referred to for the most part based on where and how they are displayed (Windows, web, tablet, and so on).

 The Windows client is only available for on-premises installations.

Financial management

At the foundation of any ERP system is financial management. Irrespective of the business, the money must be kept flowing with a track of it. Business Central's financial management module contains the tools that help to manage the capital resources of the business. These include all or part of the following application functions:

- General ledger, for managing the overall finances of the firm
- Cash management and banking, for managing the inventory of financial assets
- Accounts receivable, for tracking the incoming revenue
- Accounts payable, for tracking the outgoing funds
- Analytical accounting, for analyzing the various flows of funds
- Inventory and fixed assets, for managing inventories of goods and equipment
- Multicurrency and multilingual, for supporting international business activities

Manufacturing

Business Central manufacturing is general-purpose enough to be appropriate for **Make to Stock (MTS)**, **Make to Order (MTO)**, and **Assemble to Order (ATO)**, as well as various subsets and combinations of those. Although off-the-shelf Business Central is not particularly suitable for most process manufacturing and some of the very high-volume assembly line operations, there are third-party add-on and add-in enhancements available for those applications. As with most of the Business Central application functions, manufacturing can be implemented either in a basic mode or as a fully-featured system. Business Central manufacturing includes the following functions:

- Product design (BOMs and routings), for structure management of product components and the flow management of manufacturing processes
- Capacity and supply requirement planning, for tracking the intangible and tangible manufacturing resources
- Production scheduling (infinite and finite), execution, and tracking quantities and costs, plus tracking manufacturing resources' planned use, both on a constrained and unconstrained basis

Supply chain management

Some of the functions that are categorized as part of Business Central **supply chain management** (**SCM**), such as sales and purchasing, are actively used in almost every Business Central implementation. The supply chain applications in Business Central include all or parts of the following applications:

- Sales order processing and pricing, to support the heart of every business
- Purchasing (including requisitions), for planning, entering, pricing, and processing purchase orders
- Inventory management, for managing inventories of goods and materials
- Warehouse management, including receiving and shipping, for managing the receipt, storage, retrieval, and shipment of material and goods in warehouses

As a whole, these functions constitute the base components of a system that's appropriate for distribution operations, including those that operate on an ATO basis.

Business intelligence and reporting

Although Microsoft marketing materials identify **business intelligence** (**BI**) and reporting as though it were a separate module within Business Central, it's difficult to physically identify it as such. Most of the components that are used for BI and reporting purposes are (appropriately) scattered throughout various application areas. In the words of one Microsoft document, *business intelligence is a strategy, not a product*. Functions within Business Central that support a BI strategy include the following:

- Standard reports: Distributed and ready to use by end users
- Account schedules and analysis reports: A specialized report writer for general ledger data
- Query, XMLport, and report designers: Developer tools to support the creation of a wide variety of report formats, charts, and XML and CSV files
- Analysis by dimensions: A capability embedded in many of the other tools
- Interfaces into Microsoft Office and Microsoft Office 365, including Excel-communications of data either into Business Central or out of Business Central
- RDLC report viewer: Provides the ability to present Business Central data in a variety of textual and graphic formats, including user interactive capabilities

- Interface capabilities such as Dotnet interoperability and web services: Technologies to support interfaces between Business Central and external software products
- Standard packages for Power BI: Integrated in the role center as well as dashboards

Relationship management

Business Central's **relationship management** (**RM**) functionality is definitely the *little sister* (or, if you prefer, *little brother*) of the fully featured standalone Microsoft CRM system and Dynamics 365 for Sales and Dynamics 365 for Marketing. The big advantage of Business Central RM is its tight integration with Business Central customer and sales data.

Also falling under the heading of the customer relationship module is the Business Central **service management** (**SM**) functionality. The different functionalities under RM and SM are as follows:

- **Relationship management**:
  - Marketing campaigns, to plan and manage promotions
  - Customer activity tracking, to analyze customer orders
  - To-do lists, to manage what is to be done and track what has been done
- **Service management**:
  - Service contracts, to support service operations
  - Labor and part consumption tracking, to track resources that are consumed by the service business
  - Planning and dispatching, to manage service calls

Human resource management

The Business Central human resources module is a very small module, but it relates to a critical component of the business: employees. Basic employee data can be stored and reported via the master table (in fact, you can use the **human resources** (**HR**) module to manage data about individual contractors in addition to employees). A wide variety of individual employee attributes can be tracked by the use of dimension fields:

- **Employee tracking**: Maintain basic employee description data
- **Skills inventory**: Inventory of the capabilities of employees

- **Absence tracking**: Maintain basic attendance information
- **Employee statistics**: Tracking government required employee attribute data such as age, gender, length of service

Project management

The Business Central project management module consists of the job functionality that's supported by the resources functionality. Projects can be short or long term. They can be external (in other words, billable) or internal. This module is often used by third parties as the base for vertical market add-ons (such as construction or job-oriented manufacturing). This application area includes parts or all of the following functions:

- Budgeting and cost tracking, for managing project finances
- Scheduling, for planning project activities
- Resource requirements and usage tracking, for managing people and equipment
- Project accounting, for tracking the results

A developer's overview of Business Central

From the point of view of a developer, Business Central consists of about almost six thousand potentially customizable, off-the-shelf program objects, plus the **integrated development environment** (**IDE/Visual Studio Code**) development tools that allow us to modify existing objects and create new ones.

Business Central object types

Let's start with basic definitions of the Business Central object types:

- **Table extension**: Table extensions allow for the creation of companion tables that are linked to tables defined by Microsoft in the base product or by other solutions.
- **Page customization**: Page customizations allow controls in existing pages to be modified and moved. As they are primarily a tool for use by end users, they are outside the scope of this book.
- **Page extension**: Page extensions allow controls in existing pages to be added or hidden.

- **Table**: Tables serve both to define the data structure and to contain the data records.
- **Page**: Pages are the way data is formatted and displayed appropriately for each of the client types and user roles.
- **Report**: Reports are provided for the display of data to the user in hard copy format, either on-screen (preview mode) or via a printing device. Report objects can also update data in processes with or without data display.
- **Codeunit**: Codeunits are containers for code that's been utilized by other objects. Codeunits are always structured in code segments called procedures.
- **Query**: Queries support extracting data from one or more tables, making calculations, and outputting them in the form of a new data structure. Queries can output data directly into charts, Excel, XML, and OData. They can be used as an indirect source for pages and reports.
- **XMLport**: XMLports allow for the importing and exporting of data to/from external files. The external file structure can be in XML or other file formats.
- **Profile**: Profiles allow the definition of Role Centers and group page customizations.
- **Control add-in**: Control add-in objects allow the display of HTML5 visualizations based on data from Business Central. These objects can send back events that can be used to trigger additional code.

The Visual Studio Code integrated development environment

Business Central includes an extensive set of software development tools. The Business Central development tools are accessed through Visual Studio Code. Visual Studio Code includes the **Application Language** (**AL**) compiler extension. All Business Central programming uses AL.

 When used on premises, the old development environment C/SIDE can also be used for development. To learn C/SIDE, refer to the following book: *Programming Microsoft Dynamics NAV*, 2017. The use of C/SIDE for Business Central development is discouraged by Microsoft.

The Visual Studio Code IDE is Microsoft's most popular code editor and is available for Windows, Linux, and macOS. The images used in this book will be from Windows. You can download Visual Studio Code from `https://code.visualstudio.com/`:

Visual Studio Code icons

When we open Visual Studio Code, we will see five icons. The icons appear on the left-hand side part of the screen. The icons determine the navigation part that appears on the left-hand side of your screen. If you click on an icon twice, the navigation part will be hidden and allow full screen code editing.

Explorer

The **EXPLORER** view is the default view when you open a project. It allows you to view the files in a project and select one or more files for editing. The **EXPLORER** view is shown in the following screenshot:

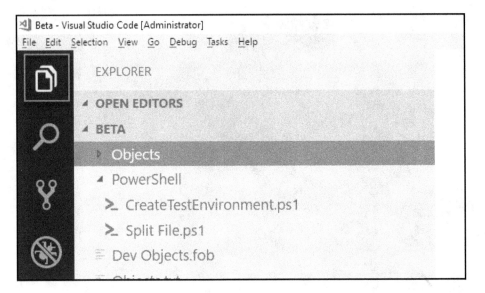

Search

The **SEARCH** view provides an advanced search and replace option within the files of your project. The **SEARCH** view is shown in the following screenshot:

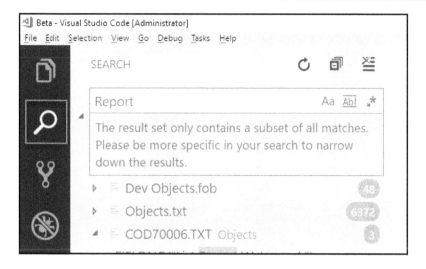

Source control

Visual Studio Code provides access to a built-in connection to **SOURCE CONTROL**. When source control is activated, all changes that are made to files are automatically tracked and displayed in this window:

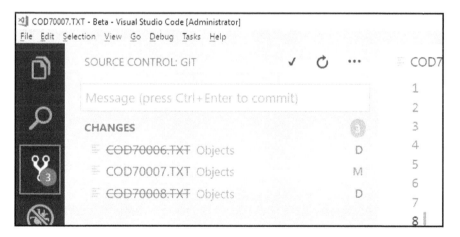

The video at `https://www.youtube.com/watch?v=NTY5VELbCWIt=22s` explains how to get started with Source Control in Visual Studio Code.

Debugger

You can connect Visual Studio Code to an active session of Business Central and use the built-in debugger to do basic troubleshooting for your code. The **DEBUG** view is shown in the following screenshot:

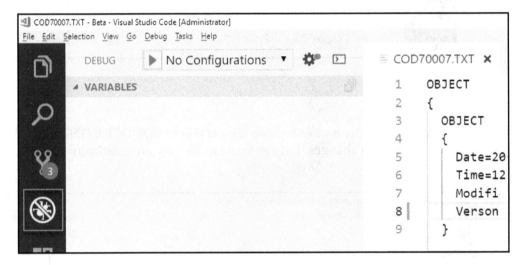

Extensions

Out-of-the-box Visual Studio Code does not understand the Business Central **AL Language** syntax. To activate the compiler, an extension needs to be installed in the **EXTENSIONS** window.

This extension, called AL language, can be downloaded from the Visual Studio Marketplace or installed directly from Visual Studio Code:

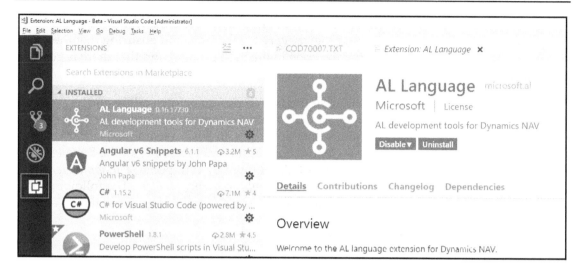

 The Visual Studio Code Marketplace can be found at `https://marketplace.visualstudio.com/`.

AL programming language

The language in which Business Central is coded is AL. A small sample of AL code within the AL Editor is shown here:

```
    1 reference
10  PROCEDURE GetSalesPrice(ExampleProduct : Record "Example Product";PersonNo : Code[20]) : Decimal;
11  var
12    ExampleProductPrice : Record "Example Product Price";
13  begin
14    WITH ExampleProduct DO
15      EXIT("Sales Price");
16
17    WITH ExampleProductPrice DO BEGIN
18      IF GET(ExampleProduct."No.", PersonNo) THEN
19        EXIT("Sales Price");
20
21      IF GET(ExampleProduct."No.") THEN
22        EXIT("Sales Price");
23    END;
24  end;
25  }
```

AL syntax is similar to Pascal syntax. Code readability is always enhanced by careful programmer attention to structure and logical variable naming, and ensuring that the process flow is consistent with that of the code in the base product and that there is good documentation both inside and outside of the code.

Good software development focuses on design before coding and accomplishing design goals with a minimal amount of code. Dynamics Business Central facilitates that approach. In 2012, a team made up of Microsoft and Business Central community members began the Business Central design patterns project. As defined by Wikipedia, *a design pattern is a general reusable solution to a commonly occurring problem*. The following links provide information on the Business Central design patterns project:

- http://blogs.msdn.com/b/nav/archive/2013/08/29/what-is-the-nav-design-patterns-project.aspx
- https://community.dynamics.com/nav/w/designpatterns/default.aspx
- https://www.packtpub.com/big-data-and-business-intelligence/learning-dynamics-nav-patterns

One of the primary goals of this project is to document patterns that exist within Business Central. In addition, new best practice patterns have been suggested as ways to solve common issues we encounter during our customization efforts. Now, when we work on Business Central enhancements, we will be aided by references to the documentation of patterns within Business Central. This allows us to spend more of our time designing a good solution using existing, proven procedures (the documented patterns) and spend less time writing and debugging code. A good reference for Business Central design and development using patterns can be found here: https://www.packtpub.com/application-development/microsoft-dynamics-nav-2013-application-design.

You can refer to the *Reusing Code* section of Business Central at https://docs.microsoft.com/en-us/previous-versions/dynamicsnav-2009/dd355277(v=nav.60).

Much of our Business Central development work is done by assembling references to previously defined objects and procedures, adding new data structures where necessary. As the tools for Business Central design and development that are provided both by Microsoft and by the Business Central community continue to mature, our development work becomes more oriented toward design and less toward coding. The end result is that we are more productive and cost-effective on behalf of our customers. Everyone wins.

Business Central object and system elements

Here are some important terms that are used in Business Central:

- **Language extension**: A file that's downloaded from the Visual Studio Code Marketplace or supplied by Microsoft. The version of the language extension in use must match the build version of Business Central with which you are working. Microsoft does a monthly update of Business Central and the language extension. There is also an insider program that allows early access before the language extension is published on the Marketplace.
- **Field**: An individual data item, defined either in a table or in the working storage (temporary storage) of an object.
- **Record**: A group of fields (data items) that are handled as a unit in many operations. Table data consists of rows (records) with columns (fields).
- **Control**: In MSDN, a control is defined as a component that provides (or enables) UI capabilities.
- **Properties**: These are the attributes of the element, such as an object, field, record, or control that define some aspect of its behavior or use. Example property attributes include display captions, relationships, size, position, and whether the element is editable or viewable.
- **Trigger**: These are mechanisms that initiate (fire) an action when an event occurs and is communicated to the application object. A trigger in an object is either empty, contains code that is executed when the associated event fires the trigger, or only contains comments (in a few cases, this affects the behavior of the trigger). Each object type, data field, control, and so on may have its own set of predefined triggers. The event trigger name begins with On, such as OnInsert, OnOpenPage, or OnNextRecord. Business Central triggers have similarities to those in SQL, but they are not the same (similarly named triggers may not even serve similar purposes). Business Central triggers are locations within objects where a developer can place comments or AL code. When we view the AL code of an object in its designer, we can see non-trigger code groups that resemble Business Central event-based triggers.
- **Procedures**: These can be defined by the developer. They are callable routines that can be accessed by other AL code from either inside or outside the object where the called function resides. When we view the AL code of an object in its designer, we can see non-trigger code groups that resemble Business Central event-based triggers. Many procedures are provided as part of the standard product. As developers, we may add our own custom procedures as needed.

- **Object numbers and field numbers**: All objects of the same object type are assigned a number that's unique within the object type. All fields within an object are assigned a number that's unique within the object (that is, the same field number may be repeated within many objects, regardless of whether it is referring to similar or different data). In this book, we will generally use comma notation for these numbers (fifty thousand is 50,000). In AL, no punctuation is used. The object numbers from 1 (one) to 50,000 and in the 99,000,000 (99 million) range are reserved for use by Business Central as part of the base product. Objects in these number ranges can be modified or deleted with a developer's license, but cannot be created. Field numbers in standard objects often start with one (1). Historically, object and field numbers from 50,000 to 99,999 are generally available to the rest of us for assignment as part of customizations that are developed in the field using a normal development license. Field numbers from 90,000 to 99,999 should not be used for new fields that have been added to standard tables as those numbers are sometimes used in training materials. Microsoft allocates ranges of object and field numbers to **Independent Software Vendor (ISV)** developers for their add-on enhancements. Some such objects (the 14 million range in North America, and other ranges for other geographic regions) can be accessed, modified, or deleted, but not created using a normal development license. Others (such as in the 37 million range) can be executed but not viewed or modified with a typical development license. The following table summarizes the object numbering practice:

Object number range	Usage
1 - 9,999	Base-application objects
10,000 - 49,999	Country-specific objects
50,000 - 99,999	Customer-specific objects
100,000 - 98,999,999	Partner-created objects
Above 98,999,999	Microsoft territory

- **Events**: Procedures can subscribe to events that are raised in the system. Business Central has both platform and manual events. Procedures can also be used to raise events.

- **Work date**: This is a date that's controlled by the user operator. It is used as the default date for many transaction entries. The system date is the date that's recognized by Windows. The work date that can be adjusted at any time by the user is specific to the workstation, and can be set to any point in the future or the past. This is very convenient for procedures such as the ending sales order entry for one calendar day at the end of the first shift, and then entering sales orders by the second shift dated to the next calendar day. There are settings to allow you to limit the range of work dates allowed. The work date can be set by clicking on the cogwheel drop-down list next to the question mark icon and selecting the **My Settings** option:

Clicking on **My Settings** in the drop-down options displays the **My Settings** screen. Here, we can enter a new **Work Date**:

Business Central functional terminology

For various application functions, Business Central uses terminology that is more similar to accounting than to traditional data processing terminology. Here are some examples:

- **Journal**: A table of unposted transaction entries, each of which represents an event, an entity, or an action to be processed. There are general journals for general accounting entries, item journals for changes in inventory, and so on.
- **Ledger**: A detailed history of posted transaction entries that have been processed, for example, the general ledger, customer ledger, vendor ledger, and item ledger. Some ledgers have subordinate detail ledgers, typically providing a greater level of quantity and/or value detail. With minor exceptions, ledger entries cannot be edited. This maintains auditable data integrity.
- **Posting**: The process by which entries in a journal are validated, and then entered into one or more ledgers.
- **Batch**: A group of one or more journal entries, posted at the same time.
- **Register**: An audit trail showing a history, by entry number ranges, of posted journal batches.
- **Document**: A formatted page such as an invoice, a purchase order, or a payment check, typically one page for each primary transaction (a page may require display scrolling to be fully viewed).

User interface

The Business Central UI is designed to be role oriented (also called role tailored). The term role oriented means tailoring the available options to fit the user-specific job tasks and responsibilities.

The first page that a user will see is the Role Center page. The Role Center page provides the user with a view of work tasks to be done; it acts as the user home page. The home Role Center page should be tailored to the job duties of each user, so there will be a variety of Role Center page formats for any installation.

Someone whose role is focused on order entry will probably see a different Role Center home page than the user whose role focuses on invoicing, even though both user roles are in what we generally think of as sales and receivables. The Business Central tailorable Role Center allows a great deal of flexibility for implementers, system administrators, managers, and individual users to configure and reconfigure screen layouts and the set of functions that are visible to a particular user.

The following screenshot is the out-of-the-box Role Center:

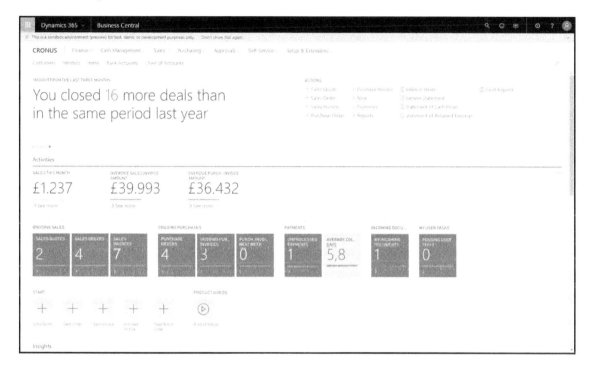

The key to properly designing and implementing any system, especially a role tailored system, is the quality of the user profile analysis that's done as the first step in requirements analysis. User profiles identify the day-to-day needs of each user's responsibilities, relative to accomplishing the business's goals. Each user's tasks must be mapped to individual Business Central functions or elements, identifying how those tasks will be supported by the system. A successful implementation requires the use of a proven methodology. It is very important that the up-front work is done and done well. The best programming cannot compensate for a bad definition of goals.

In our exercises, we will assume that the up-front work has been well done, and we will concentrate on addressing the requirements that have been defined by our project team.

Hands-on development in Business Central

One of the best ways to learn a new set of tools, like those that make up a programming language and environment, is to experiment with them. We're going to have some fun doing that throughout this book. We're going to experiment where the cost of errors (otherwise known as learning) is small. Our development work will be a custom application of Business Central for a relatively simple, but realistic, application.

We're going to do our work using the Cronus demo database that is available with all Business Central distributions and is installed by default when we install the Business Central demo system. The simplest way is to use the sandbox.

 You can find up-to-date information on getting started with Business Central sandboxes on Microsoft Docs at `https://docs.microsoft.com/en-us/dynamics365/business-central/dev-itpro/developer/devenv-sandbox-overview`.

The Cronus database contains all of the Business Central objects and a small, but reasonably complete, set of data populated in most of the system's functional application areas. Our exercises will interface very slightly with the Cronus data, but will not depend on any specific data values already there.

Business Central development exercise scenario

Our business is a small radio station that features a variety of programming, news, music, listener call-ins, and other program types. Our station call letters are WDTU. Our broadcast materials come from several sources and in several formats: vinyl records, CDs, MP3s, and downloaded digital (usually MP3s). While our station has a large library, especially of recorded music, sometimes, our program hosts (also called disc jockeys or DJs) want to share material from other sources. For that reason, we need to be able to easily add items to our playlists (the list of what is to be broadcast) and also have an easy-to-access method for our DJs to preview MP3 material.

Like any business, we have accounting and activity tracking requirements. Our income is from selling advertisements. We must pay royalties for music played, fees for purchased materials, such as prepared text for news, sports, and weather information, and service charges for our streaming internet broadcast service. As part of our licensed access to the public airwaves, a radio station is required to broadcast public service programming at no charge.

Often, this is in the form of **public service announcements** (**PSAs**), such as encouraging traffic safety or reduction in tobacco use. Like all radio stations, we must plan what is to be broadcast (create schedules) and track what has been broadcast (such as ads, music, purchased programming, and PSAs) by date and time. We bill our customers for the advertising, pay our vendors their fees and royalties, and report our public service data to the appropriate government agency.

Getting started with application design

The design for our radio station will start with a Radio Show table, a Radio Show Card page, a Radio Show List page, and a simple Radio Show List report. Along the way, we will review the basics of each Business Central object type.

When we open Visual Studio, we need to create a new project folder. This can be done using the Command Palette via **View** | **Command Palette...** or *Ctrl + Shift + P*. Then, type `AL:Go!`:

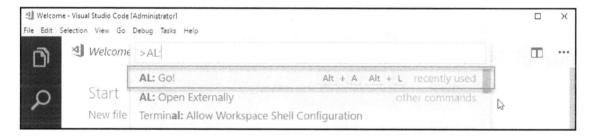

The project folder will default to your `Documents` folder if you run this on a Windows machine. We will call our project `WDTU`:

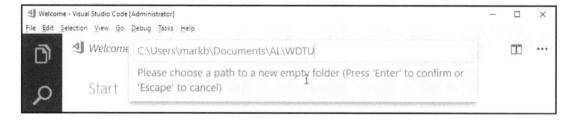

Folder structure

A folder called `WDTU` is created with some default files and subfolders. The `HelloWorld.al` file can be deleted immediately:

```
launch.json - WDTU - Visual Studio Code [Administrator]
File  Edit  Selection  View  Go  Debug  Tasks  Help

EXPLORER                          {} launch.json ✕

⌄ OPEN EDITORS                     1   {
   {} launch.json  .vscode         2       "version": "0.2.0",
⌄ WDTU                             3       "configurations": [
   ⌄ .vscode                       4           {
      {} launch.json               5               "type": "al",
   {} app.json                     6               "request": "launch",
   ≡ HelloWorld.al          1      7               "name": "Your own server",
                                   8               "server": "http://localhost",
                                   9               "serverInstance": "nav",
                                  10               "authentication": "UserPassword",
                                  11               "startupObjectId": 22,
                                  12               "startupObjectType": "Page"
                                  13           }
```

launch.json

Inside a subfolder called `.vscode`, a file is created called `launch.json` that defines the connection to your Business Central sandbox:

- `name`: For documentation purposes only. You can put the name of your project here. The content of this property does not affect the behavior.
- `server`: This contains a URL to the development endpoint of your sandbox.
- `serverInstance`: A server can have multiple instances.
- `authentication`: This can be `UserPassword`, `AAD`, or `Windows`. The default is `UserPassword`.
- `startupObjectId`: This option determines which object is executed when the project is published.
- `startupObjectType`: This allows a switch between executing a table or a page upon publishing.

app.json

The `app.json` file contains properties about your extension, such as the name and version.

All properties are explained in the Microsoft Docs (`https://docs.microsoft.com/en-us/dynamics365/business-central/dev-itpro/developer/devenv-json-files`). We will only populate the mandatory properties for now:

- `id`: This is a unique ID for your extension and is autogenerated. *Never* change this value.
- `name`: The name of your extension as it will be displayed to the user.
- `publisher`: This usually contains the name of the company or individual who owns the intellectual property of the extension.
- `version`: Your extensions can be versioned using this property. You can use this when you create a new version of the extension to determine if upgrade code needs to be executed.
- `idRange`: This tells the compiler which object numbers are to be used for this extension. You must provide a range for application object IDs in the format `"idRanges": [{"from": 50100,"to": 50200},{"from": 50202,"to": 50300}]`.

Symbol files

Before we can start creating our extension, we need to perform one more step, that is, downloading the symbol files. The compiler needs the symbol files to determine whether the dependencies are correct. The symbol files contain metadata about other extensions. To download the default symbol files from Business Central, we need to select **Al: Download Symbols** from the Visual Studio Command Palette:

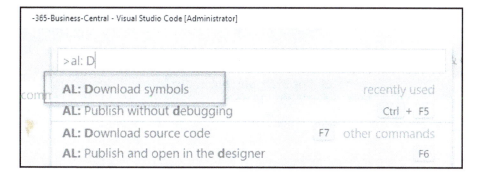

When the symbol files are downloaded, they are placed in the
`,/alpackages` folder of your project.

Application tables

Table objects are the foundation of every Business Central application. Tables contain data structure definitions, as well as properties that describe the behavior of the data, including data validations and constraints.

More business logic is required in complex applications than in simple data type validation, and Business Central allows AL code to be put in the table to control the insertion, modification, and deletion of records, as well as logic on the field level. When the bulk of the business logic is coded on the table level, it is easier to develop, debug, support, modify, and even upgrade. Good design in Business Central requires that as much of the business logic as possible resides in the tables. Having the business logic coded on the table level doesn't necessarily mean that the code resides in the table.

The Business Central online documentation recommends the following guidelines for placing AL code:

- In general, put the code in codeunits instead of on the object on which it operates. This promotes a clean design and provides the ability to reuse code. It also helps enforce security. For example, typically, users do not have direct access to tables that contain sensitive data, such as the general ledger entry table, nor do they have permission to modify objects. If you put the code that operates on the general ledger in a codeunit, give the codeunit access to the table, and give the user permission to execute the codeunit, then you will not compromise the security of the table and the user will be able to access the table.
- If you must put code on an object instead of in a codeunit, then put the code as close as possible to the object on which it operates. For example, put code that modifies records in the triggers of the table fields.

Designing a simple table

Our primary master data table will be the `Radio Show` table. This table lists our inventory of shows that are available to be scheduled.

First, create a new file in Visual Studio Code. Click on **File** | **New** and Visual Studio Code will create a new file and open the code editor window.

Each master table has a standard field for the primary key (a `Code` data type field of 20 characters called `No.`) and has standard information regarding the entity the master record represents (for example, `Name`, `Address`, and `City` for the `Customer` table, and `Description`, `Base Unit of Measure`, and `Unit Cost` for the `Item` table).

The `Radio Show` table will have the following field definitions (we may add more later on):

Field names	Definitions
No.	20-character text (code)
Radio Show Type	10-character text (code)
Name	50-character text
Run Time	Duration
Host No.	20-character text (code)
Host Name	50-character text
Average Listeners	Decimal
Audience Share	Decimal
Advertising Revenue	Decimal
Royalty Cost	Decimal

In the preceding list, three of the fields are defined as `Code` fields, which are text fields that limit the alphanumeric characters to uppercase values. `Code` fields are used throughout Business Central for primary key values. `Code` fields are used to reference or be referenced by other tables (foreign keys). `No.` will be the unique identifier in our table. We will utilize a set of standard internal Business Central functions to assign a user-defined `No.` series range that will auto-increment the value on table insertion and possibly allow for user entry (as long as it is unique in the table) based on a setup value. The `Host No.` references the standard `Resource` table, and the `Radio Show Type` field will reference a custom table that we will create to allow for flexible `Type` values.

We will have to design and define the reference properties at the field level in the table designer, as well as compile them, before the validation will work. At this point, let's just get started with these field definitions and create the foundation for the `Radio Show` table.

Creating a simple table

The easiest way to create a table the easiest way is by using snippets. To use snippets, Visual Studio Code needs to understand that our file is written in the AL language. This is simply done by saving the file with the `.al` extension. We will save our newly created file using **File** | **Save** and using a name that makes sense later. Let's use `Radio Show.al` for now:

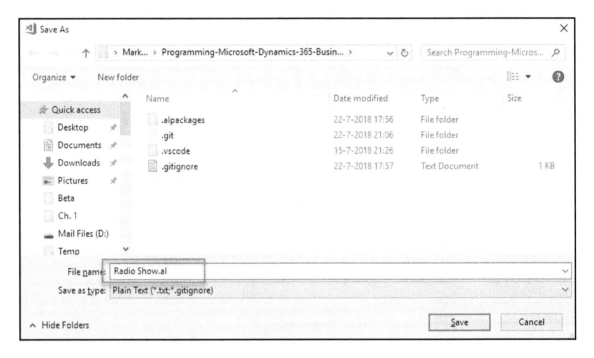

Now, we can use the snippet called `ttable`. If we type in the letters `tta`, IntelliSense will suggest this snippet:

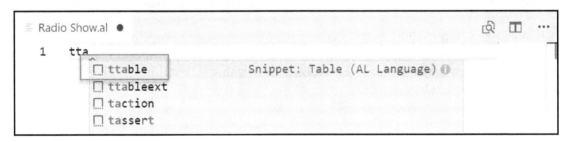

This snippet creates content for our file and sets the cursor on the place where we need to define the object ID:

```al
Radio Show.al ●
      0 references
1    table id MyTable
2    {
3        DataClassification = ToBeClassified;
4
5        fields
6        {
             1 reference
7            field(1;MyField; Integer)
8            {
9                DataClassification = ToBeClassified;
10
11           }
12       }
13
14       keys
15       {
             - reference
16           key(PK; MyField)
17           {
18               Clustered = true;
```

We will type 50100 and use *Tab* to go to the next field, object name, where we will type "Radio Show".

The snippet has already created a field with the default ID of 1. The field name is MyField and the type is Integer. We will change the name to "No." and the type to Code [20].

The next field can be field number 2. Sometimes, it is useful to leave large gaps (such as jumping from 80 to 200 or 500) when the next set of fields has a particular purpose that isn't associated with the prior set of fields.

> The fields combining the primary key can use numbers up to nine since they are very unlikely to change. If this is changed at a later date, then a substantial amount of refactoring has to be done.

The Business Central online documentation says to not leave gaps in field numbers. Based on many years of experience, we disagree. Leaving numbering gaps will allow us to add additional fields between existing fields at a later date, if necessary. The result will be data structures that are (at least initially) easier to read and understand. Once a table is referenced by other objects or contains any data, the field numbers of the previously defined fields should not be changed.

The following screenshot shows our new table definition in the table designer:

```
1    table 50100 "Radio Show"
2    {
3        fields
4        {
             0 references
5            field(1;"No."; Code[20]) {}
             0 references
6            field(10;"Radio Show Type"; Code[10]) {}
             0 references
7            field(20;"Name"; Text[50]) {}
             0 references
8            field(40;"Run Time"; Duration) {}
             0 references
9            field(50;"Host Code"; Code[20]) {}
             0 references
10           field(60;"Host Name"; Text[50]) {}
             0 references
11           field(100;"Average Listeners"; Decimal) {}
             0 references
12           field(110;"Audience Share"; Decimal) {}
             0 references
13           field(120;"Advertising Revenue"; Decimal) {}
             0 references
14           field(130;"Royalty Cost"; Decimal) {}
15       }
16   }
```

 Note that you can remove anything you don't need from the snippet. In our case, we removed the `DataClassification` and `keys` sections, the variable declaration, and triggers.

Pages

Pages provide views of data or processes that are designed for on-screen display (or exposure as web services), and also allow user data entry into the system. Pages act as containers for action items (menu options).

There are several basic types of display/entry pages in Business Central:

- List
- Card
- Document
- Journal/worksheet
- List plus
- Confirmation dialog
- Standard dialog

There are also page parts (they look and program like a page, but aren't intended to stand alone), as well as UIs that display like pages, but are not page objects. The latter user interfaces are generated by various dialog functions. In addition, there are special page types, such as **Role Center** pages and **Navigate** pages (for wizards).

Standard elements of pages

A page consists of page properties and triggers, controls, and control properties. Data controls are generally either labels displaying constant text or graphics, or containers that display data or other controls. Controls can also be buttons, action items, and page parts. While there are a few instances where we must include AL code within page or page control triggers, it is good practice to minimize the amount of code embedded within pages. Any data-related AL code should be located in the table object rather than in the page object.

List pages

List pages display a simple list of any number of records in a single table. The **Customers** list page (with its associated FactBoxes) in the following screenshot shows a subset of the data for each customer displayed. List pages/forms often do not allow you to enter or edit data. Journal/worksheet pages look like list pages, but are intended for data entry. Standard list pages are always displayed with the navigation pane on the left:

Card pages

Card pages display one record at a time. These are generally used for the entry or display of individual table records. Examples of frequently accessed card pages include **Customer Card** for customer data, **Item Card** for inventory items, and **G/L Account Card** for general ledger accounts.

Card pages have FastTabs (a FastTab consists of a group of controls, with each tab focusing on a different set of related customer data). FastTabs can be expanded or collapsed dynamically, allowing the data that's visible to be controlled by the user at any time. Important data elements can be promoted to be visible, even when a FastTab is collapsed.

Card pages for master records display all the required data entry fields. If a field is set to `ShowMandatory` (a control property that we will discuss in `Chapter 4`, *Pages – the Interactive Interface*), a red asterisk will display until the field is filled. Typically, card pages also display FactBoxes that contain summary data about related activity. Thus, cards can be used as the primary inquiry point for master records. The following screenshot is a sample of a standard customer card:

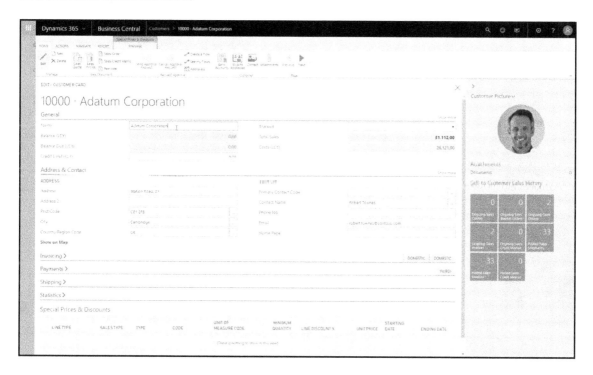

Document pages

A document page looks like a card page with one tab containing a **list part** page. An example of a document page is the **Sales Orders** page that's shown in the following screenshot. In this example, the first tab and the last four tabs are in card page format, and show **Sales Orders** data fields that have a single occurrence on the page (in other words, they do not occur in a repeating column).

The second tab from the top is in a list part page format (all fields are in repeating columns) that shows the **Sales Orders** line items. **Sales Orders** line items may include products to be shipped, special charges, comments, and other pertinent order details. The information to the right of the data entry area is related to data and computations (FactBoxes) that have been retrieved and formatted. The top FactBox contains information about the ordering customer. The bottom FactBox contains information about the item on the currently highlighted sales line:

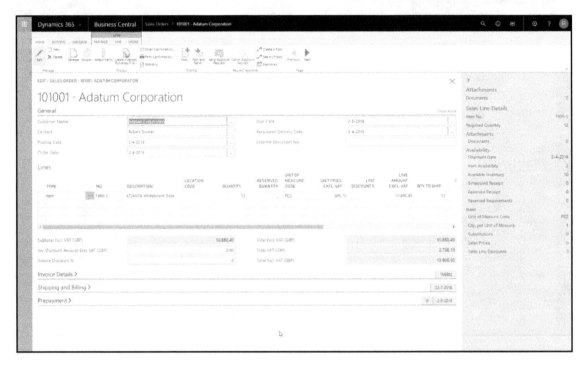

Journal/worksheet pages

Journal and worksheet pages look very much like list pages. They display a list of records in the body of the page. Many also have a section at the bottom that shows details about the selected line and/or totals for the displayed data. These pages may include a filter pane and perhaps a FactBox. The biggest difference between journal/worksheet pages and basic list pages is that journal and worksheet pages are designed to be used for data entry (though this may be a matter of personal or site preference).

An example of the **Payment Journals** page in finance is shown in the following screenshot:

Creating a list page

Now, we will create a list page for the table we created earlier. A list page is the initial page that is displayed when a user initally accesses any data table for the first time. The Business Central Development Environment has wizards (object generation tools) to help you create basic pages. Generally, after our wizard work is done, we will spend additional time in the page design tool to make the layout ready for users.

Our first list page will be the basis for viewing our `Radio Show` master records. From Visual Studio Code, click on **New**, then click on **File**. A **New Page** screen will appear. Click on **New**, type in the name of the file to be saved, and then click on **Save**. Enter the name (`Radio Show Page.al`). Now, we can use the snippet for the list pages called **tpage**:

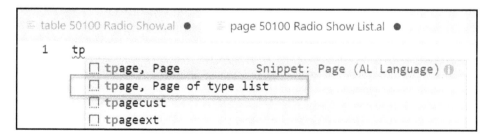

Now we will set ID to `50100` and the name to `"Radio Show List"`, and change the `SourceTable` to `"Radio Show"`, as shown in the following screenshot:

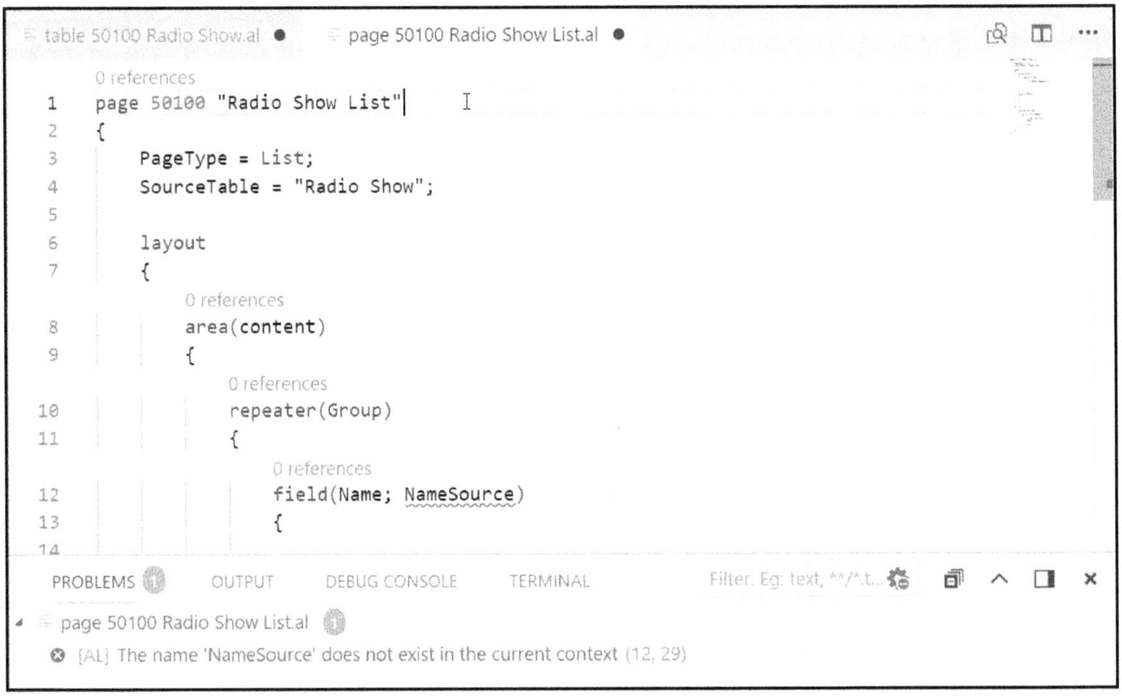

```
≡ table 50100 Radio Show.al  ●        ≡ page 50100 Radio Show List.al  ●
        0 references
   1    page 50100 "Radio Show List"|      I
   2    {
   3        PageType = List;
   4        SourceTable = "Radio Show";
   5
   6        layout
   7        {
            0 references
   8            area(content)
   9            {
                0 references
  10                repeater(Group)
  11                {
                    0 references
  12                    field(Name; NameSource)
  13                    {
  14
   PROBLEMS          OUTPUT      DEBUG CONSOLE      TERMINAL         Filter. Eg: text, **/*.t...
   ▲  ≡ page 50100 Radio Show List.al
       ⊗  [AL] The name 'NameSource' does not exist in the current context (12, 29)
```

After doing this, we can see that `NameSource` is highlighted as a problem, and the **PROBLEMS** window at the bottom of our screen tells us that `NameSource` does not exist in the context.

The reason why this problem is occurring is because of the combination of the table object and this page. We joined these objects by selecting the `Radio Show` table as `SourceTable` for this page. By joining them, the page object now has a dependency on the table object.

The next step will be to add the fields from the table to the page in the repeater. We will remove the `NameSource` field to do so.

We should also remove everything we do not need, such as FactBoxes and actions:

```
1    page 50100 "Radio Show List"
2    {
3        PageType = List;
4        SourceTable = "Radio Show";
5
6        layout
7        {
             0 references
8            area(content)
9            {
                 0 references
10               repeater(Group)
11               {
                     0 references
12                   field("No."; "No.") { ApplicationArea = Basic; }
                     0 references
13                   field("Radio Show Type"; "Radio Show Type") { ApplicationArea =
                     0 references
14                   field("Name"; "Name") { ApplicationArea = Basic; }
                     0 references
15                   field("Run Time"; "Run Time") { ApplicationArea = Basic; }
                     0 references
16                   field("Host Code"; "Host Code") { ApplicationArea = Basic; }
                     0 references
17                   field("Host Name"; "Host Name") { ApplicationArea = Basic; }
                     0 references
18                   field("Average Listeners"; "Average Listeners") { ApplicationArea
                     0 references
19                   field("Audience Share"; "Audience Share") { ApplicationArea =
                     0 references
20                   field("Advertising Revenue"; "Advertising Revenue") { Application
                     0 references
21                   field("Royalty Cost"; "Royalty Cost") { ApplicationArea = Basic; }
22
23               }
24           }
25       }
26   }
```

We can **Preview** the page by making a modification to the `launch.json` file. Change the
`startupObjectId` to `50100` and select **AL: Publish without debugging** from the
Command Palette, as shown in the following screenshot:

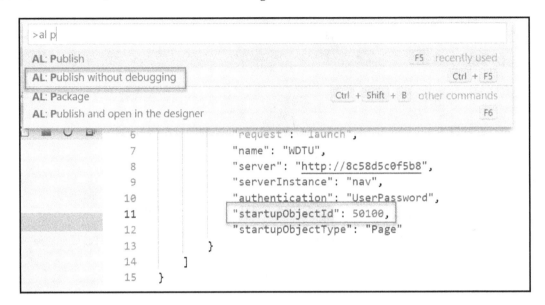

This will launch the Business Central application with our newly created page as the
startup object:

Because our table does not contain any data, we will only see a header with the name of our
page.

Creating a card page

Now, let's create a card page. The process for a card page is almost the same as for a list page, but using a different snippet. Our page number will be 50101 , and the name will be Radio Show Card:

```
1    page 50101 "Radio Show Card"
2    {
3        PageType = Card;
4        SourceTable = "Radio Show";
5        layout
6        {
             0 references
7            area(content)
8            {
                 0 references
9                group(General)
10               {
                     0 references
11                   field("No."; "No.") { ApplicationArea = Basic; }
                     0 references
12                   field("Radio Show Type"; "Radio Show Type") { ApplicationArea
                     0 references
13                   field("Name"; "Name") { ApplicationArea = Basic; }
                     0 references
14                   field("Run Time"; "Run Time") { ApplicationArea = Basic; }
                     0 references
15                   field("Host Code"; "Host Code") { ApplicationArea = Basic; }
                     0 references
16                   field("Host Name"; "Host Name") { ApplicationArea = Basic; }
                     0 references
17                   field("Average Listeners"; "Average Listeners") { ApplicationArea
                     0 references
18                   field("Audience Share"; "Audience Share") { ApplicationArea
                     0 references
19                   field("Advertising Revenue"; "Advertising Revenue") { Application
                     0 references
20                   field("Royalty Cost"; "Royalty Cost") { ApplicationArea = Basic;
21               }
22           }
23       }
24   }
```

You can copy and paste most of the definitions from the list page file, or even use **File** and **Save As** in Visual Studio Code if you find that faster or easier to use.

Let's change the `launch.json` file to this new page and publish the extension again. We can preview the page by making a modification to the `launch.json` file. Change the `startupObjectId` to `50101` and select **AL: Publish without debugging** from the Command Palette, as shown in the following screenshot:

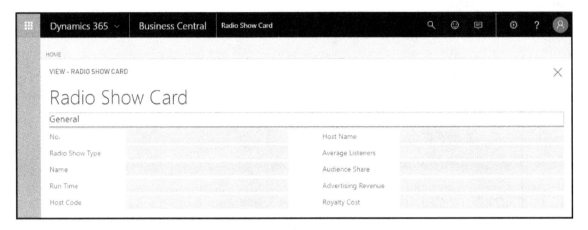

Creating some sample data

Even though we haven't added all the bells and whistles to our `Radio Show` table and pages, we can still use them to enter sample data. The **Radio Show List** page will be the easiest to use for this.

We will now revert the `launch.json` file to run the `50100` page, as originally defined, and then publish the extension. In the published window, we will click on **New** and see the following screen:

Enter the data shown in the following table so that we can see what the page looks like when it contains data. Later on, after we have added more capabilities to our table and pages, some fields will be validated, and some will be either automatically entered or available on a lookup basis. But for now, simply key in each field value. If the data we key in now conflicts with the validations we create later (such as data in referenced tables), we may have to delete this test data and enter new test data later:

No.	Radio Show Type	Description	Host Code	Host Name	Run Time
RS001	TALK	CeCe and Friends	CECE	CeCe Grace	2 hours
RS002	MUSIC	Alec Rocks and Bops	ALEC	Alec Benito	2 hours
RS003	CALL-IN	Ask Cole!	COLE	Cole Henry	2 hours
RS004	CALL-IN	What do you think?	WESLEY	Wesley Ernest	1 hour
RS005	MUSIC	Quiet Times	SASKIA	Saskia Mae	3 hours
RS006	NEWS	World News	DAAN	Daan White	1 hour
RS007	ROCK	Rock Classics	JOSEPH	Josephine Black	2 hours
RS008	TALK	Kristels Babytalks	KRIS	Kristel van Vugt	1 hour

 We will use the testability framework for automated testing later in this book. A test codeunit is provided in the downloads, but for now it is recommended to key in the data manually.

Creating a list report

To create a report, we will use the report snippet and create the 50000 `Radio Shows` report.

Open **Object Designer**, select **Report**, and click **New**. The **Report Dataset Designer** is empty when it is displayed, so we need to add a **Data Source** (table) to the first blank row.

Type 50000 or `Radio Show` into the **Data Source** column:

```
1    report 50100 "Radio Shows"
2    {
3        dataset
4        {
             0 references
5            dataitem(DataItemName; SourceTableName)
6            {
7                column(ColumnName; SourceFieldName)
8                {
9
10               }
11           }
12       }
```

If we want users to be able to execute our report from Business Central, we also need to enable a search so that they can find our report. We will do that using the `UsageCategory` and `ApplicationArea` properties.

 More information on `ApplicationArea` can be found in the Microsoft Docs at https://docs.microsoft.com/en-us/dynamics-nav/ applicationarea-property.

`UsageCategory` will determine where the report will be listed,
and `ApplicationArea` will determine the access level a user requires to be able to execute the report:

```
1    report 50100 "Radio Shows"
2    {
3        UsageCategory = ReportsAndAnalysis;
4        ApplicationArea = Basic;
5        dataset
```

 Microsoft Docs has a good up-to-date explanation of the `UsageCategory` options (https://docs.microsoft.com/en-us/dynamics365/business- central/dev-itpro/developer/devenv-al-menusuite-functionality).

The `SourceTableName` for our report is the `Radio Show` table. The columns are the fields from this table. Spaces and special characters are not allowed in column names for reports.

After selecting the columns and removing any unnecessary elements from the snippet, our report code should look as follows:

```
1   report 50100 "Radio Shows"
2   {
3       UsageCategory = ReportsAndAnalysis;
4       ApplicationArea = Basic;
5       dataset
6       {
            0 references
7           dataitem(DataItemName; "Radio Show")
8           {
9               column("No"; "No.") {  }
10              column("RadioShowType"; "Radio Show Type") {  }
11              column("Name"; "Name") {  }
12              column("RunTime"; "Run Time") {  }
13              column("HostCode"; "Host Code") {  }
14              column("HostName"; "Host Name") {  }
15              column("AverageListeners"; "Average Listeners") {  }
16              column("AudienceShare"; "Audience Share") {  }
17              column("AdvertisingRevenue"; "Advertising Revenue") {  }
18              column("RoyaltyCost"; "Royalty Cost") {  }
19
20          }
21      }
22  }
```

Generating the layout

Now that we have defined our dataset, we can create the layout. Business Central supports both RDLC, which can be edited in Visual Studio, and SQL Report Builder, and it also supports Microsoft Word.

Both layouts can be added to the report definition using the `WordLayout` and `RDLCLayout` properties:

```
1   report 50100 "Radio Shows"
2   {
3       UsageCategory = ReportsAndAnalysis;
4       ApplicationArea = Basic;
5       WordLayout = 'RadioShows.docx';
6       RDLCLayout = 'RadioShows.RDLC';
7       dataset
```

To generate the layout, we need to package our application, which can be done from the Command Palette:

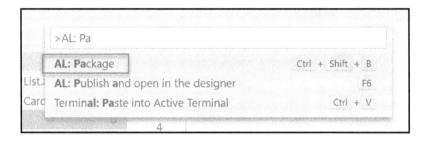

This screenshot shows the generated RDLC, which is essentially to XML syntax:

```
EXPLORER                                    RadioShows.RDLC  ✕

▲ OPEN EDITORS                         1    <?xml version="1.0" encoding="utf-8"?>
   RadioShows.RDLC                 U   2    <Report xmlns="http://schemas.microsoft.com/sqlserver/reporting/2016/01/reportde
▶ PROGRAMMING-MICROSOFT-DYNAMICS-365-BUSINES...  3    <AutoRefresh>0</AutoRefresh>
                                       4    <DataSources>
                                       5      <DataSource Name="DataSource">
                                       6        <ConnectionProperties>
                                       7          <DataProvider>SQL</DataProvider>
                                       8          <ConnectString />
                                       9        </ConnectionProperties>
                                       10       <rd:SecurityType>None</rd:SecurityType>
                                       11     </DataSource>
                                       12   </DataSources>
                                       13   <ReportSections>
                                       14     <ReportSection>
                                       15       <Body>
                                       16         <Height>2in</Height>
                                       17         <Style />
                                       18       </Body>
                                       19       <Width>6.5in</Width>
                                       20       <Page>
                                       21         <Style />
                                       22       </Page>
                                       23     </ReportSection>
                                       24   </ReportSections>
                                       25   <Code>Public Function BlankZero(ByVal Value As Decimal)
                                       26     if Value = 0 then
                                       27       Return ""
                                       28     end if
                                       29     Return Value
```

Let's see if we can run our report. To do that, we will publish our extension without
`startupObjectId`:

```
RadioShows.RDLC          {} launch.json  ×
1    {
2        "version": "0.2.0",
3        "configurations": [
4            {
5                "type": "al",
6                "request": "launch",
7                "name": "WDTU",
8                "server": "http://8c58d5c0f5b8",
9                "serverInstance": "nav",
10               "authentication": "UserPassword",
11               //"startupObjectId": 50101,
12               //"startupObjectType": "Page"
13           }
14       ]
15   }
```

In the Business Central session, we will use the searchbox and type in the word `radio`,
which will show our report:

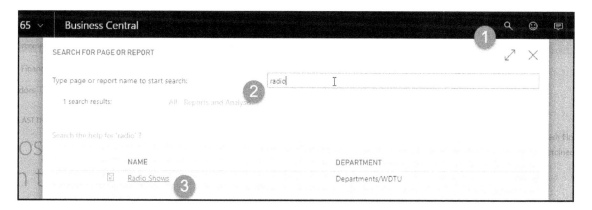

When you click on the report and select **Preview**, you should see an empty layout.

Designing the layout

In this book, we will focus on Word reports, and we will go ahead and remove the RDLC file and associated property in the report. We will use the `DefaultLayout` property to make Word the default report format choice. Next, we will right-click on the `RadioShows.docx` file and open it in Microsoft Word:

In Microsoft Word, we need to locate the **Developer** tab, which might not be visible by default. Go to **File** | **Options** | **Customize Ribbon** and select **Developer**:

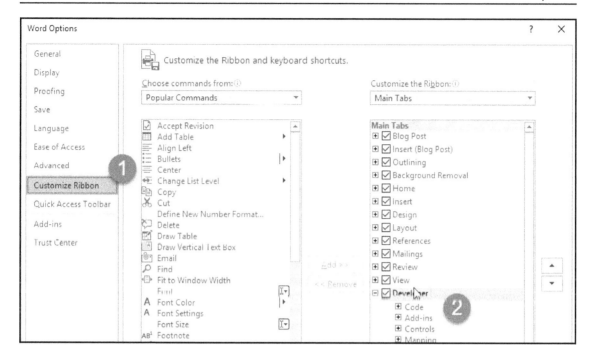

This will allow you to select **XML Mapping Pane**:

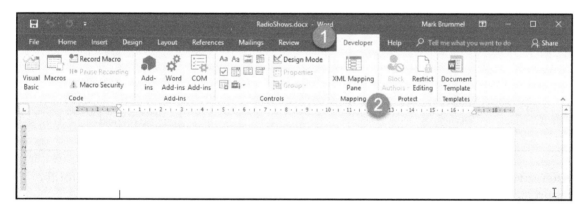

Let's create a simple list report by adding a table control to the report. We will select the middle row of the table control. Then, we will right-click on `DataItemName` and use **Insert Content Control** | **Repeating**:

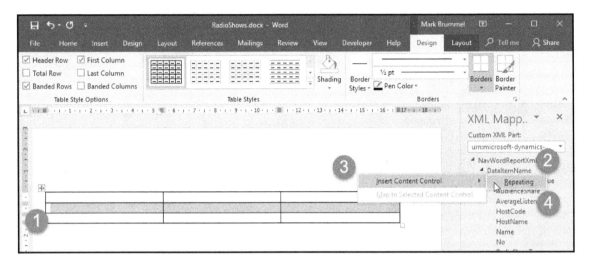

The next step is to add the fields to the rows, add captions, and, for eye candy, add a style:

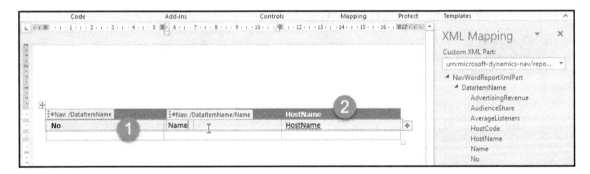

After saving the Microsoft Word document, we can publish our extension, search for the report, and select **Preview**:

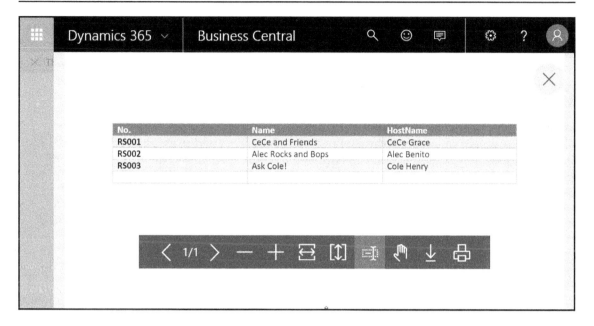

No.	Name	HostName
RS001	CeCe and Friends	CeCe Grace
RS002	Alec Rocks and Bops	Alec Benito
RS003	Ask Cole!	Cole Henry

There is much more to come. All we've done so far is scratch the surface. But by now, you should have a pretty good overview of the development process for Business Central.

You will be in especially good shape if you've been able to follow along in your own system, doing a little experimenting along the way.

Other Business Central object types

Let's finish up our introductory review of the Business Central object types.

TableExtension and PageExtension

Similar to the `Table` and `Page` objects, the table and page extension objects allow you to define fields in the database and display them to the user.

Table extensions are connected to existing tables and share the same primary key values. Fields defined in table extensions can be used on any existing page and report that uses the original table.

Page extensions allow developers to add new fields, tabs, actions, and FactBoxes to existing pages. You can also use this to hide controls.

Codeunits

A codeunit is a container for **chunks** of AL code to be called from other objects. These chunks of code are called procedures. Procedures can be called from any of the other Business Central object types that can contain AL code. Codeunits can also be exposed (published) as web services. This allows the procedures within a published codeunit to be invoked by external routines.

Codeunits are suited structurally to contain only procedures. Even though procedures could be placed in other object types, the other object types have superstructures that relate to their designed primary use, such as pages, and reports.

Codeunits act only as containers for AL coded procedures. They have no auxiliary procedures, no method of direct user interaction, and no predefined processing. Even if we are creating only one or two procedures and they are closely related to the primary activity of a particular object, and if these procedures are needed from both inside and outside of the report, the best practice is still to locate the procedures in a codeunit.

There are several codeunits being delivered as part of the standard Business Central product, which are really function libraries. These codeunits consist completely of utility routines, and are generally organized on some functional basis (for example, associated with dimensions, some aspect of manufacturing, or some aspect of warehouse management). Many of these can be found by filtering the codeunit names on the `Management` and `Mgt` strings (the same could be said for some of the tables with the `Buffer` string in their name). When we customize a system, we should create our own procedure library codeunits to consolidate our customizations and make software maintenance easier. Some developers create their own libraries of favorite special procedures, and include a procedure library codeunit in systems on which they work.

Queries

Queries are objects whose purpose is to create extracted sets of data from the Business Central database and do so very efficiently. Business Central queries translate directly into T-SQL query statements and run on the SQL Server side rather than on the Business Central Service Tier. A query can extract data from a single table or multiple tables. In the process of extracting data, a query can make different types of joins (inner join, outer join, or cross join), filter, calculate FlowFields (special Business Central calculations that are discussed in detail in `Chapter 3`, *Data Types and Fields*), sort, and create sums and averages. Queries obey the Business Central data structure business logic.

The output of a query can be a CSV file (useful for Excel charts), an XML file (for charts or external applications), or an Odata file for a web service. Queries can be published for web service access, similar to pages and codeunits. The results of a query can also be viewed by pages (as described in `Chapter 5`, *Queries and Reports)*, but are especially powerful when output to charts. With a little creativity, a query can also be used to feed data to a page or report via the use of a temporary table to hold the query results.

XMLports

XMLports is a tool for importing and exporting data. XMLports handle both XML structured data and other external text data formats. **XML (eXtensible Markup Language)** is the de facto standard for exchanging data between dissimilar systems. For example, XMLports could be used to communicate between our Business Central ERP system and our accounting firm's financial analysis and tax preparation system.

XML is designed to be extensible, which means that we can create or extend the definition as long as we communicate the defined XML format to our correspondents. There is a standard set of syntax rules to which XML formats must conform. A lot of new software uses XML. For example, the new versions of Microsoft Office are quite XML friendly. All web services communications are in the form of an exchange of XML structured data.

The non-XML text data files handled by XMLports fall into two categories. One is known as **comma-separated value** or **comma-delimited** files (they usually have a `.csv` file extension). Of course, the delimiters don't have to be commas. The other category is fixed format, in which the length and relative position of each field is predefined.

XMLports can contain AL logic for any type of appropriate data manipulation, either when importing or exporting. Functions such as editing, validating, combining, and filtering can be applied to the data as it passes through an XMLport.

Control add-ins

A control add-in allows JavaScript developers to create custom controls using plain HTML5 or jQuery. In fact, anything that creates JavaScript can be loaded into the browser, although Microsoft officially does not support frameworks like Angular and React.

Development backups and documentation

As with any system where we can do development work, careful attention to documentation and backing up our work is very important. Visual Studio Code provides a variety of techniques for handling each of these tasks.

The first area we can place documentation is in line with modified AL code. Individual comment lines can be created by starting the line with double forward slashes, //. Whole sections of comments (or commented out code) can be created by starting and ending the section with a pair of curly braces { }. Depending on the type of object and the nature of the specific changes, we should generally annotate each change inline with forward slashes rather than with curly braces wherever the code is touched so that all the changes can be easily identified by the next developer.

The best documentation resides outside of our source code. Visual Studio Code has built-in support for Git, which means that we can use any source code control system supporting that, including, but not limited to, GitHub, GitLab, or Visual Studio Team Services.

There are some great resources on how to get started with GitHub online, like the ones we mentioned earlier in this chapter. A good explanation about Git in general can be found on YouTube (`https://www.youtube.com/watch?v=tDlHCr70WUs`).

In short, when doing development in Business Central Visual Studio Code, everything we have learned earlier about good documentation practices applies. This holds true, regardless of whether the development is new work or the modification of existing logic.

 You can download the code from this book on GitHub at `https://github.com/markbrummel/Programming-Microsoft-Dynamics-365-Business-Central`.

Summary

In this chapter, we covered some basic definitions of terms related to Business Central and Visual Studio Code. We followed with an introduction to the 11 Business Central objects types (tables, table extensions, pages, page extensions, page customizations, profiles, reports, codeunits, queries, control add-ins, and XMLports). We introduced table, page, and report creation through review and hands-on use, and began a Business Central application for the programming management of the `Radio Show` WTDU. Finally, we looked briefly at the tools that we use to integrate with external entities and discussed how different types of backups and documentation are handled in Visual Studio Code. Now that we have covered the basics, we will dive into the detail of the primary object types in the next few chapters.

In the next chapter, we will focus on tables: the foundation of any Business Central system.

Questions

1. An ERP system such as Business Central includes a number of functional areas. Which of the following are part of Business Central? Choose four:
    - Manufacturing
    - Order processing
    - Planning
    - Computer Aided Design (CAD)
    - General accounting

2. Functionality in Business Central includes the following (choose three):
    - Tablet client
    - Drag and drop
    - Document emailing
    - Spellchecker
    - Mandatory fields

3. Business Central development is done in the Visual Studio Code IDE or Visual Studio. True or false?

4. Match the following table types and descriptions for Business Central:
   - Journal audit trail
   - Ledger validation process
   - Register invoice
   - Document transaction entries
   - Posting history

5. With Business Central, iPads can be used to display the RTC. True or false?

6. Which of the following describe Business Central? Choose two:
   - Customizable
   - Includes a storefront module
   - Object-based
   - C# IDE
   - Object-oriented

7. What are the Business Central object types?

8. All Business Central objects except XMLports can contain AL code. True or false?

9. Business Central includes support for publishing objects as web services. True or false?

10. The home page for a Business Central user is called what? Choose one:
    - Role Home
    - Home Center
    - Main Page
    - Role Center

11. Codeunits can be used as `startupObjectId`. True or false?

12. Microsoft Word is used in Business Central for what work? Choose one:
    - Report data definition
    - Report layout
    - Role Center design
    - Query processing

13. Codeunits are the only Business Central objects that can contain procedures. True or false?
14. Query output can be used as a data item for reports. True or false?
15. AL and Visual Studio Code are required for Business Central development. True or false?
16. Which object number range is available for assignment to customer-specific objects? Choose two:
    - 20 - 500
    - 50,000 - 60,000
    - 150,000 - 200,000
    - 50,000 - 99,999
    - 10,000 - 100,000

17. XMLports can only process XML formatted data. True or false?
18. The work date can only be changed by the system administrator. True or false?
19. A design pattern is which of the following? Choose two:
    - Reusable code
    - Stripes and plaid together
    - A proven way to solve a common problem
    - UI guidelines

20. Business Central reports are often generated automatically through the use of a wizard. True or false?

2
Tables

"If you don't know where you are going, you might wind up someplace else."

– Yogi Berra

Successful design is anticipating the anticipations of others.

– John Maynard Keynes, paraphrased

The foundation of any system is the data structure definition. In Business Central, the building blocks of this foundation are the tables and the individual data fields that the tables contain. Once the functional analysis and process definition have been completed, any new design work must begin with the data structure. For Business Central, that means the tables and their contents.

A Business Central table includes much more than just the data fields and keys. A Business Central table definition also includes data validation rules, processing rules, business rules, and logic to ensure referential integrity. These rules are in the form of properties and AL code.

 For object-oriented developers, a Dynamics Business Central table is best compared to a class with methods and properties that have been stored one-to-one as a table on SQL Server.

In this chapter, we will learn about the structure and creation of tables. Details regarding fields and the components of tables will be covered in the following chapter. In particular, we will cover the following topics:

- An overview of tables, including properties, triggers, keys, SumIndexFields, and field groups
- Enhancing our scenario application—creating and modifying tables
- Types of table—fully modifiable, content modifiable, and read-only tables

An overview of tables

There is a distinction between the table (data definition and data container) and the data (the contents of a table). The table definition describes the identification information, data structure, validation rules, storage, and retrieval of the data that is stored in the table (container). This definition is defined by its design and can only be changed by a developer. The data is the variable content that originates from user activities. The place where we can see the data being explicitly referenced, independent of the table as a definition of structure, is in the permissions setup data. In the following screenshot, the data is formally referred to as **Table Data**:

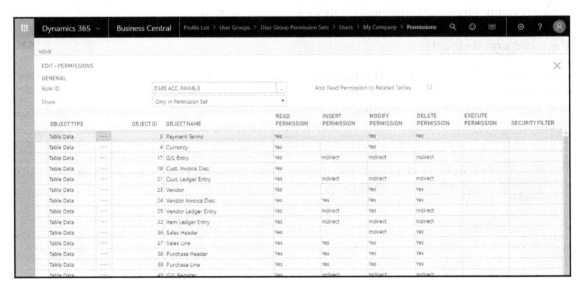

The table is not the data—it is the definition of data contained in the table. Even so, we commonly refer to both the data and the table as if they were one and the same. That is what we will do in this book.

All permanent data must be stored in a table. All tables are defined by the developer working in the development environment. As much as possible, critical system design components should be embedded in the tables. Each table should include the code that controls what happens when records are added, changed, or deleted, as well as how data is validated when records are added or changed. This includes functions to maintain the aspects of referential integrity that are not automatically handled. The table object should also include the functions that are commonly used to manipulate the table and its data, whether this be for database maintenance or in support of business logic. In the cases where the business logic is either a modification that's been applied to a standard (out-of-the-box) table or used elsewhere in the system, the code should reside in a codeunit function library and called from the table.

Visual Studio Code provides snippets for the definition of the data structure within tables. We will explore these capabilities through examples and analysis of the structure of table objects. We find that the approach of embedding control and business logic within the table object has a number of advantages:

- Clarity of design
- Centralization of rules for data constraints
- More efficient development of logic
- Increased ease of debugging
- Easier upgrading

Components of a table

A table is made up of **Fields**, **Properties**, **Triggers** (some of which may contain AL code), and **Keys**. **Fields** also have **Properties** and **Triggers**. **Keys** also have **Properties**:

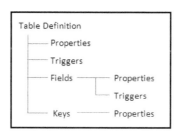

A table definition that takes full advantage of these capabilities reduces the effort that's required to construct other parts of the application. Good table design can significantly enhance the application's processing speed, efficiency, and flexibility.

A table can have the following components:

- Up to 500 fields
- A defined record size of up to 8,000 bytes (with each field sized at its maximum)
- Up to 40 different keys

Naming tables

There are standardized naming conventions for Business Central that we should follow. Names for tables and other objects should be as descriptive as possible, while kept to a reasonable length. This makes our work more self-documenting.

Table names should always be singular. The table containing data about customers should not be named `Customers`, but `Customer`. The table we created for our WDTU Radio Station Business Central enhancement was named `Radio Show`, even though it will contain data for all of WDTU's radio shows.

In general, we should always name a table so that it is easy to identify the relationship between the table and the data it contains. For example, two tables containing the transactions on which a document page is based should normally be referred to as a Header table (for the main portion of the page) and a Line table (for the line detail portion of the page). As an example, the tables underlying a **Sales Order** page are the **Sales Header** and the **Sales Line** tables. The **Sales Header** table contains all of the data that occurs only once for a **Sales Order**, while the **Sales Line** table contains all of the lines for the order.

Table numbering

There are no hard and fast rules for table numbering, except that we must only use the table object numbers that we are licensed to use. If all we have is the basic table designer rights, we are generally allowed to create tables numbered from 50,000 to 50,009 (unless our license was defined differently compared to the typical one). If we need more table objects, we can purchase licensing for table objects numbered up to 99,999. **Independent Software Vendors (ISVs)** can purchase access to tables in other number ranges.

When creating several related tables, ideally, we should assign them to numbers in sequential order. We should let common sense be our guide for assigning table numbers. It requires considerable effort to renumber tables containing data.

Table properties

The first step in studying the internal construction of a table is to open one in Visual Studio Code. We will use the `Radio Show` table we created in `Chapter 1`, *Introduction to Business Central*, to show you this.

We now have the `Radio Show` table open in Visual Studio Code, as shown in the following screenshot:

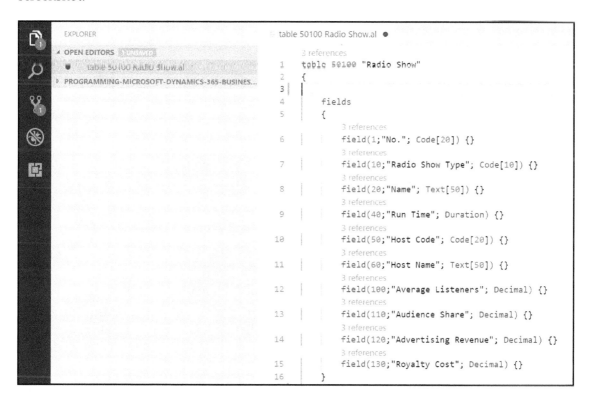

We can access the properties of a table. Place the cursor on the empty line above the fields (as shown in the preceding screenshot) and click on *Ctrl* + spacebar. If we hit *Ctrl* + spacebar while the focus is on a filled field line, we will see the properties of that field (not the table).

The options that you can see in Visual Studio Code should look as follows:

```
≡ table 50100 Radio Show.al ●
    3 references
1   table 50100 "Radio Show"
2   {
3   |
4       🔧 Caption                          Caption property ⓘ
5       🔧 CaptionML
        🔧 DataCaptionFields
6       🔧 DataClassification
        🔧 DataPerCompany
7       🔧 Description
        🔧 DrillDownPageId
8       🔧 ExternalName
        🔧 ExternalSchema
9       🔧 LinkedInTransaction
        🔧 LinkedObject
10      🔧 LookupPageId
            3 references
11      |       field(60;"Host Name"; Text[50]) {}
```

The table properties are as follows:

- `Caption`: This contains the caption that was defined for the currently selected language. The default language for Business Central is **English, US (ENU)**.
- `CaptionML`: This defines the `MultiLanguage` caption for the table. For an extended discussion on the language capabilities of Business Central, refer to the *Multilanguage Development* section (https://msdn.microsoft.com/en-us/dynamics-nav/multilanguage-development) in the online **Developer and IT Pro Help**.
- `Description`: This property is for optional documentation usage.
- `DataPerCompany`: This lets us define whether or not the data in this table is segregated by company (the default), or whether it is common (shared) across all of the companies in the database. The generated names of tables within SQL Server (not within Business Central) are affected by this choice.

- `Permissions`: This allows us to grant users of this table different levels of access (`r` for read, `i` for insert, `m` for modify, and `d` for delete) to the table data in other table objects.
- `LookupPageID`: This allows us to define what page is the default for looking up data in this table.
- `DrillDownPageID`: This allows us to define what page is the default for drilling down into the supporting detail for data that is summarized in this table.
- `DataCaptionFields`: This allows us to define specific fields whose contents will be displayed as part of the caption. For the `Customer` table, the `No.` and the `Name` will be displayed in the title bar at the top of a page showing a customer record.
- `PasteIsValid`: This property (paste is valid) determines whether users are allowed to paste data into the table.
- `LinkedObject`: This lets us link the table to an SQL Server object. This feature allows a connection, for data access or maintenance, to a non-Business Central system or an independent Business Central system. For example, a `LinkedObject` could be an independently hosted and maintained special purpose database, and hence we could offload that processing from the main Business Central system. When this property is set to `Yes`, `LinkedInTransactionProperty` becomes available. `LinkedInTransactionProperty` should be set to `No` for any linkage to a SQL Server object outside the current database. The object being linked must have a SQL Server table definition that is compatible with the Microsoft Dynamics Business Central table definition.
- `TableType`: This allows you to consume data from an OData web service, such as Dynamics CRM or an External SQL, as a table.
- `ObsoleteState`: This can be used to indicate to developers that this table will be removed in a future version.
- `ObsoleteReason`: When the `ObsoleteState` property is used, this property can be set to explain why the table has been discontinued or what will replace it.

As developers, we most frequently deal with the ID, `Name`, `LookupPageID`, `DrillDownPageID`, `Caption`, `CaptionML` (outside of the United States), `DataCaptionFields`, and `Permissions` properties. We rarely deal with the others.

Table triggers

To display the triggers with the table open in Visual Studio Code, enter the `trigger` keyword in the first line after the fields section, followed by *Ctrl* + spacebar. This is shown in the following screenshot:

```
          3 references
14    |       field(120;"Advertising Revenue"; Decimal) {}
          3 references
15    |       field(130;"Royalty Cost"; Decimal) {}
16    |    }   I
17 |  |    trigger
18    }           OnDelete
                  OnInsert
                  OnModify
                  OnRename
                  taction
```

The code contained in `trigger` is executed prior to the event represented by `trigger`. In other words, the code in the `OnInsert()` trigger is executed before the record is inserted into the table. This allows the developer a final opportunity to perform validations and to enforce data consistency such as referential integrity. We can even abort the intended action if data inconsistencies or conflicts are found.

These triggers are automatically invoked when record processing occurs as the result of user action. But when table data is changed by AL code or by a data import, the AL code or import process determines whether or not the code in the applicable trigger is executed:

- `OnInsert()`: This is executed when a new record is to be inserted in the table through the UI. (In general, new records are added when the last field of the primary key is completed and focus leaves that field. See the property in Chapter 4, *Pages – The Interactive Interface*).
- `OnModify()`: This is executed when a record is rewritten after the contents of any field other than a primary key field has been changed. The change is determined by comparing xRec (the image of the record prior to being changed) to Rec (the current record copy). During our development work, if we need to see what the *before* value of a record or field is, we can reference the contents of xRec and compare that to the equivalent portion of Rec. These variables (Rec and xRec) are system-defined variables.

- `OnDelete()`: This is executed before a record is to be deleted from the table.
- `OnRename()`: This is executed when some portion of the primary key of the record is about to be changed. Changing any part of the primary key is a rename action. This maintains a level of referential integrity. Unlike some systems, Business Central allows the primary key of any master record to be changed. This automatically maintains all of the affected foreign key references from other records.

There is an internal inconsistency in the handling of data integrity by Business Central. On the one hand, the Rename trigger automatically maintains one level of referential integrity when any part of the primary key is changed (that is, the record is **renamed**). This happens in a black box process, an internal process that we cannot see or touch.

However, if we delete a record, Business Central doesn't automatically do anything to maintain referential integrity. For example, child records could be orphaned by a deletion, that is, left without any parent record. Or, if there are references in other records back to the deleted record, they could be left with no target. As developers, we are responsible for ensuring this part of referential integrity in our customizations.

When we write AL code in one object that updates data in another (table) object, we can control whether or not the applicable table update trigger fires (executes). For example, if we were adding a record to our `Radio Show` table and used the following AL code, the `OnInsert()` trigger would fire:

```
RadioShow.INSERT(TRUE);
```

However, if we were to use either of the following AL code options instead, the `OnInsert()` trigger would not fire and none of the logic inside the trigger would be executed:

```
RadioShow.INSERT(FALSE);
```

Alternatively, you can use the following code:

```
RadioShow.INSERT;
```

The automatic black box logic enforcing primary key uniqueness will happen regardless of whether the `OnInsert()` trigger is fired.

Keys

Table keys are used to identify records and to speed up filtering and sorting. Having too few keys may result in painfully slow inquiries and reports. However, each key incurs a processing cost, because the index containing the key must be updated every time information in a key field changes. Key cost is measured primarily in terms of increased index maintenance processing. There is also additional cost in terms of disk storage space (usually not significant) and additional backup/recovery time for the increased database size (sometimes very important).

When a system is optimized for processing speed, it is critical to analyze the SQL Server indexes that are active because that is where the updating and retrieval time are determined. The determination of the proper number and design of keys and indexes for a table requires a thorough understanding of the types and frequencies of inquiries, reports, and other processing for that table.

Every Business Central table must have at least one key: the primary key. The primary key is always the first key in the key list. By default, the primary key is made up of the first field that's defined in the table. In many of the reference tables, there is only one field in the primary key, and the only key is the primary key.

Our `Radio Show` table does not have an explicit key defined, which means that Business Central defaults to the first field. If we were to explicitly define this key, we would have to declare it, as shown in the following screenshot:

```
14          field(120; "Advertising Revenue"; Decimal) { }
            3 references
15          field(130; "Royalty Cost"; Decimal) { }
16       }
17       keys
18       {
            - reference
19          key(PK; "No.") { }
20       }
21   }
```

The primary key must have a unique value in each table record. We can change the primary key to be any field, or a combination of up to 16 fields totaling up to 900 bytes, but the uniqueness requirement must be met. It will automatically be enforced by Business Central, because Business Central will not allow us to add a record with a duplicate primary key to a table.

When we add other keys, the first key remains the unique key and other keys become secondary, non-unique keys:

```
keys
{
    - reference
    key(PK; "No.") { }
    - reference
    key(Name; Name) {}
    - reference
    key(HostName; "Host Name") {}

}
```

All keys except the primary key are secondary ones. There is no required uniqueness constraint on secondary keys. There is no requirement to have any secondary keys. If we want a secondary key not to have duplicate values, our AL code must check for duplication before completing the new entry.

The maximum number of fields that can be used in any one key is 16, with a maximum total length of 900 bytes. At the same time, the total number of different fields that can be used in all of the keys combined cannot exceed 16. If the primary key includes three fields (like in the preceding screenshot), then the secondary keys can utilize up to 13 other fields (16 minus 3) in various combinations, plus any or all of the fields in the primary key. If the primary key has 16 fields, then the secondary keys can only consist of different groupings and sequences of those 16 fields.

Behind the scenes, each secondary key has the primary key appended to the backend. A maximum of 40 keys are allowed per table.

Database maintenance performance is faster with fewer fields in keys, especially the primary key. The same is true for fewer keys. This must be balanced against improved performance in processes by having the optimum key contents and choices.

Other significant key attributes include key groups and SQL Server-specific properties:

- A number of SQL Server-specific key-related parameters have been added to Business Central. These key properties can be accessed by using *Ctrl* + spacebar inside the curly braces in a key.
- The `MaintainSQLIndex` and `MaintainSIFTIndex` properties allow the developer and/or system administrator to determine whether or not a particular key or **SumIndexField Technology (SIFT)** field will be continuously maintained or whether it will be recreated only when needed. Indexes that are not maintained minimize record update time but require longer processing time to dynamically create the indexes when they are used. This level of control is useful for managing indexes that are only needed occasionally. For example, a key or SIFT index that is used only for monthly reports can be disabled, and no index maintenance processing will be done day to day. If the month end need is for a single report, that particular index will be recreated automatically when the report is run. If the month end need is for a number of reports, the system administrator might enable the index, process the reports, and then disable the index again:

```
keys
{
    Ireference
    key(PK; "No.") { }
    - reference                    Clustered          Clustered property
    key(Name; Name)     Description
    - reference                    Enabled
    key(HostName;  "H  MaintainSiftIndex
                                   MaintainSqlIndex
    }                              ObsoleteReason
}                                  ObsoleteState
                                   SqlIndex
                                   SumIndexFields
```

SumIndexFields

Dynamics Business Central, which is inherited from Dynamics NAV (formerly Navision), has a unique capability called the SIFT feature. These fields serve as the basis for FlowFields (automatically accumulating totals) and are unique to Business Central. This feature allows Business Central to provide almost instantaneous responses to user inquiries for summed data, which are calculated on the fly at runtime and are related to the SumIndexFields. The cost is primarily that of the time required to maintain the SIFT indexes when a table is updated.

Business Central maintains SIFT totals using SQL Server indexed views. An indexed view is a view that has been preprocessed and stored. Business Central creates one indexed view for each enabled SIFT key. SIFT keys are enabled and disabled through the `MaintainSIFTIndex` property. SQL Server maintains the contents of the view when any changes are made to the base table, unless the `MaintainSIFTIndex` property is set to `No`.

SumIndexFields are accumulated sums of individual fields (columns) in tables. When the totals are automatically pre-calculated, they are easy to use and provide very high-speed access for inquiries. If users need to know the total of the `Amount` values in a `Ledger` table, the `Amount` field can be attached as a SumIndexField to the appropriate keys. In another table, such as `Customer`, FlowFields can be defined as display fields that take the advantage of SumIndexFields. This gives users very rapid response for calculating a total balance amount inquiry, based on detailed ledger amounts tied to those keys. We will discuss the various data field types and FlowFields in more detail in a later chapter.

In a typical ERP system, many thousands, millions, or even hundreds of millions of records might have to be processed to give such results, which takes considerable time. In Business Central, only a few records need to be accessed to provide the requested results. Processing is fast and programming is greatly simplified.

SQL Server SIFT values are maintained through the use of SQL indexed views. By using the key property, `MaintainSIFTIndex`, we can control whether or not the SIFT index is maintained dynamically (faster response) or only created when needed (less ongoing system performance load). The AL code is the same, regardless of whether the SIFT is maintained dynamically or not.

Having too many keys or SIFT fields can negatively affect system performance for two reasons. The first, which we have already discussed, is the index maintenance processing load. The second is the table locking interference that can occur when multiple threads are requesting update access to a set of records that update SIFT values.

Conversely, a lack of necessary keys or SIFT definitions can also cause performance problems. Having unnecessary data fields in a SIFT key creates many extra entries, which affect performance. Integer fields usually create an especially large number of unique SIFT index values, and `Option` fields create a relatively small number of index values.

The best design for a SIFT index is where the fields that will be used most frequently in queries are positioned on the left-hand side of the index, in order of descending frequency of use. In a nutshell, we should be careful when designing keys and SIFT fields. While a system is in production, applicable SQL Server statistics should be monitored regularly and appropriate maintenance actions should be taken. Business Central automatically maintains a count for all SIFT indexes, thus speeding up all `Count` and `Average` FlowField calculations.

Field groups

When a user starts to enter data in a field where the choices are constrained to existing data (for example, an **Item No.**, a **Salesperson Code**, a **Unit of Measure** code, a **Customer No.**, and so on), good design dictates that the system will help the user by displaying the universe of acceptable choices. Put simply, a lookup list of choices should be displayed.

In the **Role Tailored Client** (**RTC**), the lookup display (a drop-down control) is generated dynamically when its display is requested by the user's effort to enter data in a field that references a table through the `TableRelation` property (which will be discussed in more detail in the next chapter). The format of the drop-down control is a basic list. The fields that are included in that list and their left to right display sequence are either defined by default or by an entry in the FieldGroups table.

The `fieldgroups` table is part of the Business Central table definition, much like the list of keys. In fact, the `fieldgroups` table is accessed very similar to the keys, that is, via *Ctrl* + spacebar, as shown in the following screenshot:

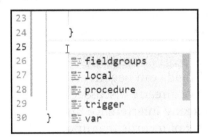

If we add `fieldgroups` for the `Radio Show` table, we can create two, which must be named `DropDown` (without a hyphen) and `Brick`:

```
    }
    fieldgroups
    {
        - reference
        fieldgroup(DropDown; "No.", Name, "Host Name") {}
        - reference
        fieldgroup(Brick; "No.", Name, "Audience Share") {}
    }
}
```

The drop-down display that's created by this particular field group is shown in the following screenshot on the **Sales Order** page. It contains fields that are in the same order of appearance as they are in the field group definition:

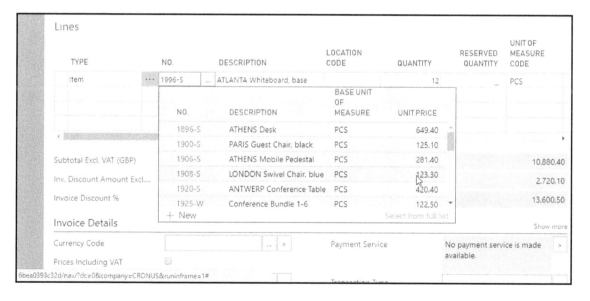

If no field group is defined for a table, the system defaults to using the primary key plus the **DESCRIPTION** field (or **NAME** field).

Bricks

In addition to the `DropDown` field group, we can also define a brick. Bricks are used differently in the web client and phone client. The brick for the **Customers** table is rendered as follows:

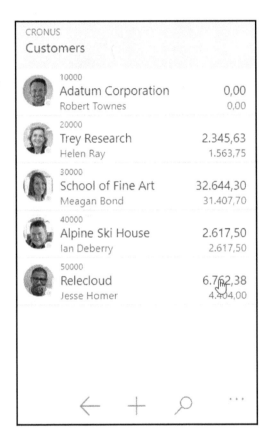

The same brick is rendered differently in the web client, as displayed in the following screenshot:

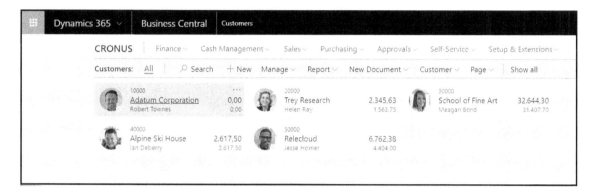

Enhancing our sample application

Now, we can take our knowledge of tables and expand our WDTU application. Our base Radio Show table needs to be added to and modified. We also need to create and reference additional tables.

Although we want to have a realistic design in our sample application, we will focus on changes that illustrate features in Business Central table design that the authors feel are among the most important. If there are capabilities or functionalities that you feel are missing, feel free to add them. Adjust the examples as much as you wish to make them more meaningful to you.

Creating and modifying tables

In Chapter 1, *Introduction to Business Central*, we created the Radio Show table for the WDTU application. At that time, we used the minimum fields that allowed us to usefully define a master record. Now, let's set properties on existing data fields, add more data fields, and create an additional data table to which the Radio Show table can refer.

Our new data fields are shown in the following layout table:

Field no.	Field name	Description
1000	Frequency	An `Option` data type (`Hourly`, `Daily`, `Weekly`, or `Monthly`) is used for the frequency of a show; `Hourly` should be used for a show segment such as news, sports, or weather that is scheduled every hour. A space/blank is used for the first option to allow a valid blank field value.
1010	PSA Planned Quantity	This is the number (stored as `Integer`) of **Public Service Announcements** (**PSAs**) to be played per show; this will be used by playlist generation and posting logic.
1020	Ads Planned Quantity	This is the number (stored as `Integer`) of advertisements to be played per show; this will be used by playlist generation and posting logic.
1030	News Required	Is headline news required to be broadcast during the show (a `Boolean`)?
1040	News Duration	This is the duration (stored as `Duration`) of the news program that's embedded within the show.
1050	Sports Required	Is sports news required to be broadcast during the show (a `Boolean`)?
1060	Sports Duration	This is the duration (stored as `Duration`) of the sports program that's embedded within the show.
1070	Weather Required	Is weather news required to be broadcast during the show (`Boolean`)?
1080	Weather Duration	This is the duration (stored as `Duration`) of the weather program that's embedded within the show.
1090	Date Filter	This is the date FlowFilter (stored as `Data Type Date` or `Data Class FlowFilter`) that will change the calculations of the flow fields based on the date filter that's applied. We will cover FlowFilters in more detail in `Chapter 3`, *Data Types and Fields*.

After we have completed our `Radio Show` table, it will look like this:

```
1    table 50100 "Radio Show"
2    {
3        fields
4        {
             6 references
5            field(1; "No."; Code[20]) { }
             3 references
6            field(10; "Radio Show Type"; Code[10]) { TableRelation = "Radio Show Type"; }
             6 references
7            field(20; "Name"; Text[50]) { }
             3 references
8            field(40; "Run Time"; Duration) { }
             3 references
9            field(50; "Host Code"; Code[20]) { }
             5 references
10           field(60; "Host Name"; Text[50]) { }
             3 references
11           field(100; "Average Listeners"; Decimal) { }
             4 references
12           field(110; "Audience Share"; Decimal) { }
             3 references
13           field(120; "Advertising Revenue"; Decimal) { }
             3 references
14           field(130; "Royalty Cost"; Decimal) { }
             0 references
15           field(1000; Frequency; Option) { }
             0 references
16           field(1010; "PSA Planned Quantity"; Integer) { }
             0 references
17           field(1020; "Ads Planned Quantity"; Integer) { }
             0 references
18           field(1030; "News Required"; Boolean) { }
             0 references
19           field(1040; "News Duration"; Duration) { }
             0 references
20           field(1050; "Sports Required"; Boolean) { }
             0 references
21           field(1060; "Sports Duration"; Duration) { }
             0 references
22           field(1070; "Weather Required"; Boolean) { }
             0 references
23           field(1080; "Weather Duration"; Duration) { }
             0 references
24           field(1090; "Date Filter"; Date) { FieldClass = FlowFilter; }
25       }
```

Next, we need to fill the `OptionMembers` property for the `Option` field called `Frequency`. This is done between the curly braces, as shown in the following screenshot:

```
14          field(120; "Advertising Revenue"; Decimal) { }
            3 references
15          field(130; "Royalty Cost"; Decimal) { }
            0 references
16          field(1000; Frequency; Option) { OptionMembers = Hourly,Daily,Weekly,Monthly; }
            0 references
17          field(1010; "PSA Planned Quantity"; Integer) { }
            0 references
18          field(1020; "Ads Planned Quantity"; Integer) { }                I
```

 TIP More information about working with the `Option` fields can be found at `https://redandbundle.com/2018/05/23/options-and-the-agony-of-choice/`.

Next, we want to define the reference table we are going to tie to the `Type` field. The table will contain a list of the available `Radio Show` types, such as `Music`, `Talk`, and `Sports`. We will keep this table very simple, with `Code` as the unique key field and `Description` as the text field. Both fields will be of the default length, as shown in the following layout. Create the new table and save it as `table 50101` with the name of `Radio Show Type`:

```
1    table 50101 "Radio Show Type"
2    {
3        fields
4        {
             0 references
5            field(1; Code; Code[20]) { }
             0 references
6            field(10; Description; Text[50]) { }
7        }
8    }
```

Before we can use this table as a reference from the `Radio Station` table, we need to create a List page that will be used for both data entry and data selection for the table. We will use a snippet to create a List page. We should be able to do this pretty quickly. Create a new file in Visual Studio Code called `page 50102 Radio Show Type.al` and start typing `tp`, then click on `tpage, Page of type list`:

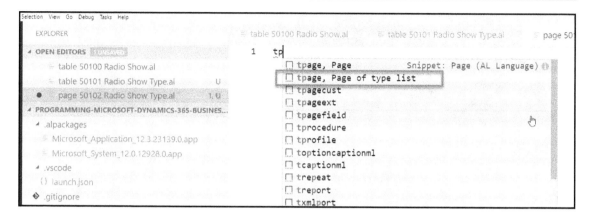

Populate the page properties with both (all) of the fields from the `Radio Show Type` table. Our designed page should look as follows:

```
1    page 50102 "Radio Show Type"
2    {
3        PageType = List;
4        SourceTable = "Radio Show Type";
5        ApplicationArea = Basic;
6        UsageCategory = Administration;
7        layout
8        {
             0 references
9            area(content)
10           {
                 0 references
11               repeater(Group)
12               {
                     0 references
13                   field(Code; Code) { ApplicationArea = Basic; }
                     0 references
14                   field(Description; Description) { ApplicationArea = Basic; }
15               }
16           }
17       }
18   }
```

Publish your solution and search for the `Radio Show Type` page. The new page will be displayed. While the page is open, enter some data (by clicking on **New**), as shown in the following screenshot:

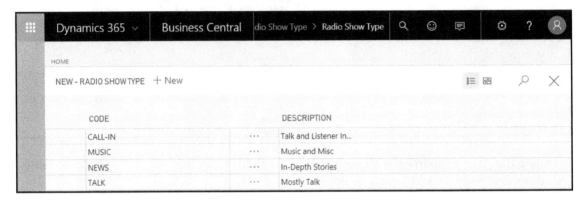

Now, we'll return to the `Radio Show Type` table and set the table's properties for `LookupPageID` and `DrillDownPageID` to point to the new page we have just created:

```
     2 references
1    table 50101 "Radio Show Type"
2    {
3        LookupPageId="Radio Show Type";
4        DrillDownPageId="Radio Show Type";
5        fields
6        {
         1 reference
7            field(1; Code; Code[20]) { }
         1 reference
8            field(10; Description; Text[50]) { }
9        }
10   }
```

Assigning a table relation property

Finally, we will open the `Radio Show` table again. This time, add the `TableRelation` property between the curly braces of the `Type` field. Connect it to our new `Radio Show Type` table:

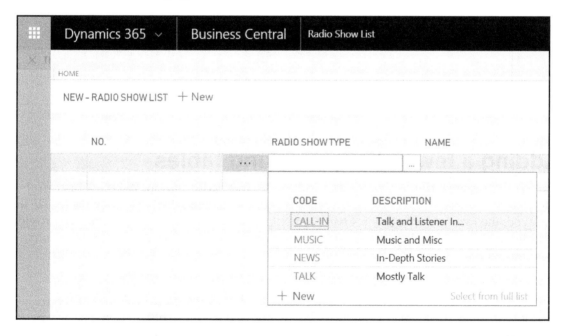

To check that the `TableRelation` **property** is working properly, we can publish and run the **Radio Show List** page again. We should highlight the **RADIO SHOW TYPE** field and click on the drop-down arrow to view the list of available entries. The following screenshot is of our **Radio Show List** page:

If all has gone according to plan, the **RADIO SHOW TYPE** field will display an assist edit image (the three dots). We will invoke the drop-down list for the `Radio Show Type` table, as shown in the preceding screenshot.

Assigning an InitValue property

Another property we can define for several of the `Radio Show` fields is `InitValue`. WDTU has a standard policy that states that news, sports, and weather should be broadcast for a few minutes at the beginning of every hour in the day. We want the `Boolean` (`true`/`false`) fields, `News Required`, `Sports Required`, and `Weather Required`, to default to `true`.

Setting the default for a field to a specific value simply requires setting the `InitValue` property to the desired value. In the case of the required Boolean fields, that value is set to `true`:

```
         0 references
17   |   field(1020; "Ads Planned Quantity"; Integer) { }
         0 references
18|  |   field(1030; "News Required"; Boolean) { InitValue = true; }
         0 references
19   |   field(1040; "News Duration"; Duration) { }
         0 references
20|  |   field(1050; "Sports Required"; Boolean) { InitValue = true; }
         0 references
21   |   field(1060; "Sports Duration"; Duration) { }
         0 references
22|  |   field(1070; "Weather Required"; Boolean) { InitValue = true; }
         0 references
23|  |   field(1080; "Weather Duration"; Duration) { }
         0 references
```

Adding a few activity-tracking tables

Our WDTU organization is a profitable and productive radio station. We track historical information about our advertisers, royalties owed, and listenership. We track the music that is played, the rates we charge for advertisements based on the time of day, and we provide a public service by broadcasting a variety of government and other public service announcements.

We aren't going to cover all of these features and functions in the following detailed exercises. However, it's always good to have a complete view of the system that we are working on, even if we are only working on one or two components. In this case, the parts of the system that aren't covered in detail in our exercises will be opportunities for you to extend your studies and practice on your own.

Any system development should start with a design document that completely spells out the goals and the functional design details. Neither system design nor project management will be covered in this book, but when we begin working on production projects, proper attention to both of these areas will be critical to success. Use of a proven project management methodology can make a project much more likely to be on time and within budget.

Based on the requirements our analysts have given us, we need to expand our application design. We started with a `Radio Show` table, one reference table (`Radio Show Type`), and pages for each of them. Earlier, we entered some test data and added a few additional fields to the `Radio Show` table (which we will not add to our pages here).

Now, we will add a supplemental table, document (header and line) tables, plus a ledger (activity history) table relating to playlist activities. Following this, we will also create some pages for our new data structures.

Our WDTU application will now include the following tables:

- `Radio Show`: This is a master list of all programs broadcast by our station.
- `Radio Show Type`: This is a reference list of possible types of radio shows.
- `Playlist Header`: This is a single instance of `Radio Show` with child data in the form of playlist lines.
- `Playlist Line`: Each line represents one of a list of items and/or duration per `Radio Show`.
- `Playlist Item Rate`: This is a list of rates for items that are played during a show, as determined by our advertising sales staff or the royalty organization we use.
- `Radio Show Entry`: This is a detailed history of all of the time spent and items played during the show, with any related royalties owed or advertisement revenue expected.
- `Listenership Entry`: This is a detailed history of estimated listenership provided by the ratings organization to which we subscribe.
- `Publisher`: This is a reference list of the publishers of content that we use. This will include music distributors, news wires, sports, and weather sources, as well as WDTU (we use material that we publish).

Remember, one purpose of this example system is for you to follow along on a hands-on basis in your own system. You may want to try different data structures and other object features. For example, you could add functionality to track volunteer activity, perhaps even detailing the type of support the volunteers provide.

For the best learning experience, you should be creating each of these objects in your development system to learn by experimenting. During the course of these exercises, it will be good if you make some mistakes and see some new error messages. That's part of the learning experience. A test system is the best place to learn from mistakes with the minimum cost.

New tables for our WDTU project

First, we need to create a `Playlist Header` table (table number `50102`), which will contain one record for each scheduled `Radio Show`:

```
1    table 50102 "Playlist Header"
2    {
3        fields
4        {
             0 references
5        |   field(1; "No."; Code[20]) { }
             0 references
6        |   field(10;"Radio Show No.";code[20]){}
             0 references
7        |   field(20;Description;Text[50]){}
             0 references
8        |   field(30;"Broadcast Date";Date) {}
             0 references
9        |   field(40;Duration;Duration){}
             0 references
10       |   field(50;"Start Time"; Time) {}
             0 references
11       |   field(60;"End Time"; Time) {}
12       }
13   }
```

Then, we will create the associated `Playlist Line` table (table number `50103`). This table will contain child records for the `Playlist Header` table. Each `Playlist Line` record represents one scheduled piece of music, advertisement, public service announcement, or embedded show within scheduled `Radio Show` that's defined in the `Playlist Header` table. `Description` for each of the option fields shows the information that needs to be entered into the `OptionMembers` property for those fields:

```
1    table 50103 "Playlist Line"
2    {
3        fields
4        {
                1 reference
5            field(1; "Document No."; Code[20]) { }
                1 reference
6            field(2; "Line No."; Integer) { }
                0 references
7            field(10; Type; Option) { OptionMembers = ,Resource,Show,Item; }
                0 references
8            field(20; "No."; Code[20]) { }
                0 references
9            field(30; "Data Format"; Option) { OptionMembers = ,Vinyl,CD,MP3,PSA,Advertisement; }
                0 references
10           field(40; Publisher; Code[10]) { }
                0 references
11           field(50; Description; Text[50]) { }
                0 references
12           field(60; Duration; Duration) { }
                0 references
13           field(70; "Start Time"; Time) { }
                0 references
14           field(80; "End Time"; Time) { }
```

Now, we'll create our `Playlist Item Rate` table. These rates include both what we charge for advertising time and what we must pay in royalties for material we broadcast:

```
1    table 50104 "Playlist Item Rate"
2    {
3        fields
4        {
                0 references
5            field(1; "Source Type"; Option) { OptionMembers = Vendor,Customer; }
                0 references
6            field(2; "Source No."; Code[20]) { }
                0 references
7            field(30; "Item No."; Code[20]) { }
                0 references
8            field(40; "Start Time"; Time) { }
                0 references
9            field(50; "End Time"; Time) { }
                0 references
10           field(60; "Rate Amount"; Decimal) { }
                0 references
11           field(70; "Publisher Code"; Code[10]) { }
12       }
13   }
```

An entry table contains the detailed history of processed activity records. In this case, the data is a detailed history of all of the `Playlist Line` records for previously broadcast shows:

```
1    table 50105 "Radio Show Entry"
2    {
3        fields
4        {
             0 references
5            field(1; "Entry No."; Integer) { }
             0 references
6            field(10; "Radio Show No."; Code[20]) { }
             0 references
7            field(20; Type; Option) { OptionMembers = ,Resource,Show,Item; }
             0 references
8            field(30; "No."; Code[20]) { }
             0 references
9            field(40; "Data Format"; Option) { OptionMembers = ,Vinyl,CD,MP3,PSA,Advertisement; }
             0 references
10           field(50; Description; Text[50]) { }
             0 references
11           field(60; Date; Date) { }
             0 references
12           field(70; Time; Time) { }
             0 references
13           field(80; Duration; Duration) { }
             0 references
14           field(90; "Fee Amount"; Decimal) { }
             0 references
15           field(100; "ACSAP ID"; Integer) { }
             0 references
16           field(120; "Publisher Code"; Code[10]) { }
17        }
18    }
```

Now, we'll create one more entry table to retain data we receive from the listenership rating service:

```
1    table 50106 "Listernership Entry"
2    {
3        fields
4        {
                 0 references
5            field(1; "Entry No."; Integer) { }
                 0 references
6            field(10; "Ratings Source Entry No."; Integer) { }
                 0 references
7            field(20; Date; Date) { }
                 0 references
8            field(30; "Start Time"; Time) { }
                 0 references
9            field(40; "End Time"; Time) { }
                 0 references
10           field(50; "Radio Show No."; Code[20]) { }
                 0 references
11           field(60; "Listener Count"; Decimal) { }
                 0 references
12           field(70; "Audience Share"; Decimal) { }
                 0 references
13           field(80; "Age Demographic"; Option) { OptionMembers = ,"0-12","13-18","19-34","35-50","51+"; }
14       }
15   }
```

Finally, we'll add the last new table definition for now, which is our Publisher table:

```
1    table 50107 Publisher
2    {
3        fields
4        {
                 0 references
5            field(1; Code; Code[20]) { }
                 0 references
6            field(10; Description; Text[50]) { }
7        }
8    }
```

New list pages for our WDTU project

Each of the new tables we have created should be supported with an appropriately named list page. As part of our WDTU project work, we should create the following pages:

- `50103`: Playlist document list
- `50105`: Playlist item rates
- `50106`: Radio show entries
- `50107`: Listenership entries
- `50108`: Publishers

Keys, SumIndexFields, and table relations in our examples

So far, we have created basic table definitions and associated pages for the WDTU project. The next step is to flesh out those definitions with additional keys, SIFT field definitions, table relations, and so on. The purpose of these are to make our data easier and faster to access, to take advantage of the special features of Business Central to create data totals, and to facilitate relationships between various data elements.

Secondary keys and SumIndexFields

The `Playlist Line` table's default primary key was `Document No.`. For the primary key to be unique for each record, another field is needed. For a Line table, the additional field is the `Line No.` field, which is incremented via AL code for each record. So, we'll change the key for table `50003` accordingly:

```
17      keys
18      {
             - reference
19   |       key(PK; "Document No.", "Line No.")
20           {
21               Clustered = true;
22           }
23      }
24
```

We know that a lot of reporting will be done based on the data in `Radio Show Ledger`. We also know that we want to do reporting on data by `Radio Show` and by the type of entry (individual song, specific advertisement, and so on). So, we will add secondary keys for each of those, including a `Date` field so that we can rapidly filter the data by `Date`. The reporting that is financial in nature will need totals of the `Fee Amount` field, so we'll put that in the `SumIndexFields` column for our new keys:

```
18      keys
19      {
            - reference
20        key(PK; "Entry No.") { Clustered = true; }
            - reference
21        key(Reporting; "Radio Show No.", Date) { SumIndexFields = "Fee Amount"; }
            - reference
22        key(Reporting2; Type, "No.", Date) { SumIndexFields = "Fee Amount"; }
23      }
```

We know that to do the necessary listenership analysis, the listenership ledger needs an additional key, combined with `SumIndexFields` for totaling listener statistics:

```
14      }
15        keys
16      {
            - reference
17        key(PK; "Entry No.") { Clustered = true; }
            - reference
18        key(Reporting; "Radio Show No.", Date,"Start Time","Age Demographic") { SumIndexFields = "Listener Count","Audience Share"; }
19      }
```

To utilize the `SumIndexFields` column we have just defined, we will need to define corresponding FlowFields in other tables. We will leave that part of the development effort for the next chapter, where we are going to discuss fields, Flowfields, and FlowFilters in detail.

Table relations

For the tables where we defined fields that are intended to refer to data in other tables for lookups and validation, we must define their relationships in the referring tables. Sometimes, these relationships are complicated and are dependent on other values within the record.

In table 50103, Playlist Line, we have the No. field. If the Type field contains Resource, then the No. field should contain Resource No.. If the Type field contains Show, then the No. field should contain Radio Show No.. Finally, if the Type field contains Item, the No. field should contain Item No.. The pseudocode (approximate syntax) for that logic can be written as follows:

```
IF Type = 'Resource' THEN No. := Resource.No. ELSE IF Type = 'Show' THEN
No. := Radio Show.No. ELSE IF Type = 'Item' THEN No. := Item.No.
```

The syntax to put in Visual Studio Code is displayed in the following screenshot:

```
8       field(20; "No."; Code[20])
9       {
10          TableRelation = IF (Type = const (Resource)) Resource."No."
11          ELSE
12          IF (Type = const (Show)) "Radio Show"."No."
13          ELSE
14          IF (Type = const (Item)) Item."No.";
15      }
```

Table 50004, Playlist Item Rate, has a similar TableRelation requirement for the Source No. field in that table. In this case, if Source Type = Vendor, then the Source No. field will refer to Vendor No., and if Source Type = Customer, then the Source No. field will refer to Customer No.:

```
8       field(20; "No."; Code[20])
9       {
10          TableRelation = IF (Type = const (Resource)) Resource."No."
11          ELSE
12          IF (Type = const (Show)) "Radio Show"."No."
13          ELSE
14          IF (Type = const (Item)) Item."No.";
15      }
```

Modifying an original Business Central table

One of the big advantages of the Business Central system development environment is the fact that we are allowed to enhance the tables that are part of the original standard product. Many package software products do not provide this flexibility. Nevertheless, with privilege comes responsibility. When we modify a standard Business Central table, we must do so carefully.

In our system, we are going to use the standard `Item` table—table 27—to store data about recordings such as music and advertisements and PSAs that we have available for broadcast. To do this, we will create a table extension, as described in `Chapter 1`, *Introduction to Business Central*. One of the new fields will be an `Option` field. Another will refer to the `Publisher` table we created earlier. When the modifications for the `Item` table design are completed, they will look as follows:

```
1   tableextension 50100 Item extends Item
2   {
3       fields
4       {
            0 references
5           field(50100; "Publisher Code"; code[10]) { }
            0 references
6           field(50101; "ACSAP ID"; Integer) { }
            0 references
7           field(50102; Duration; Duration) { }
            0 references
8           field(50103; "Data Format"; Option) { OptionMembers = ,Vinyl,CD,MP3,PSA,Advertisement; }
            0 references
9           field(50104; "MP3 Location"; text[250]) { }
10      }
11  }
```

Types of table

For this discussion, we will divide table types into three categories. As developers, we can change the definition and the contents of the first category (the fully modifiable tables). We cannot change the definition of the base fields of the second category, but we can change the contents (the content modifiable tables) and add new fields. The third category can be accessed for information, but neither the definition nor the data within is modifiable (the read-only tables).

Fully modifiable tables

The following tables are included in the fully modifiable tables category.

Master data

The master data table type contains primary data (such as customers, vendors, items, and employees). In any enhancement project, these are the tables that should be designed first because everything else will be based on these tables. When working on a modification, necessary changes to master data tables should be defined first. Master data tables always use card pages as their primary user input method. The **Customers** page is a master data table. A customer record is shown in the following screenshot:

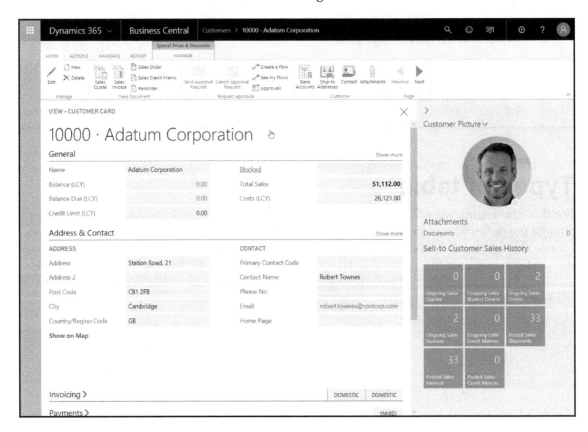

The preceding screenshot shows how the card page segregates the data into categories on different FastTabs (such as **General**, **Address & Contact**, and **Invoicing**), and includes primary data fields (for example, **Name** and **Address**) and a FlowField (**Balance (LCY)**).

Journal

The journal table type contains unposted activity detail, which is data that other systems refer to as transactions. Journals are where the most repetitive data entry occurs in Business Central. In the standard system, all journal tables are matched with corresponding template tables (one template table for each journal table). The standard system includes journals for **Sales**, **Cash Receipts**, **General Journal** entries, **Physical Inventory**, **Purchases**, **Fixed Assets**, and **Warehouse Activity**, among others.

The transactions in a journal can be segregated into batches for entry, edit review, and processing purposes. Journal tables always use worksheet pages as their primary user input method. The following screenshots show two journal entry screens. They both use the **General Journals** table, but each have quite a different appearance and are based on different pages and different templates:

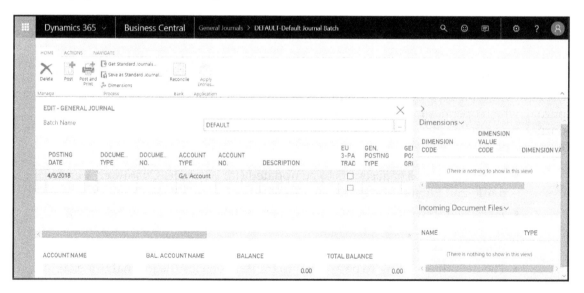

By comparing the preceding and following screenshots, we can see that the differences include not only which fields are visible, but also what logic applies to data entry defaults and validations:

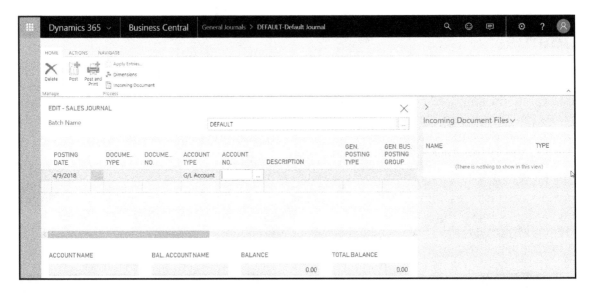

Template

The template table type operates behind the scenes, providing control information for a journal, which operates in the foreground. By using a template, multiple instances of a journal can each be tailored for different purposes. Control information that's contained in a template includes the following:

- The default type of accounts to be updated (for example, **Customer**, **Vendor**, **Bank**, and **General Ledger**)
- The specific account numbers to be used as defaults, including balancing accounts
- What transaction numbering series will be used
- The default encoding to be applied to transactions for the journal (for example, **Source Code** and **Reason Code**)
- Specific pages and reports to be used for data entry and processing of both edits and posting runs

For example, **General Journal Templates** allow the **General Journal** table to be tailored so that it can display fields and perform validations that are specific to the entry of particular transaction categories, such as **Cash Receipts**, **Payments**, **Sales**, and other transaction entry types. Template tables always use tabular pages for user input. The following screenshot shows a listing of the various **General Journal Templates** that are defined in the Cronus International Ltd. demonstration database:

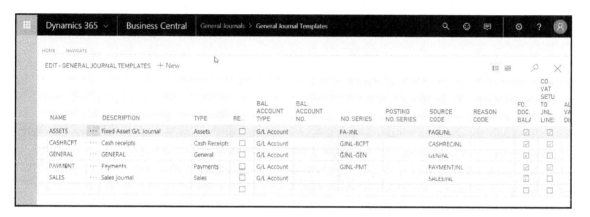

In addition to these templates, there are batch tables, which allow us to set up any number of batches of data under each journal template. The batch, template, and journal line structure provides a great deal of flexibility in the data organization and definition of required fields while utilizing a common underlying table definition (**General Journal**).

Entry tables

The entry table type contains posted activity detail, which is the data other systems call history. Business Central data flows from a journal through a posting routine into an entry. A significant advantage of Business Central entry design is the fact that Business Central allows you to retain all transaction details indefinitely. While there are routines that support the compression of the entry data (if that's even feasible), we should retain the full historical detail of all activities. This allows users to have total flexibility for historical comparative or trend data analysis.

Entry data is considered accounting data in Business Central. We are not allowed to directly enter the data into an entry or change existing data in an entry; instead, we must post to an entry. Posting is done by creating journal lines, validating the data as necessary, then posting those journal lines into the appropriate ledgers. Although we can physically force data into an entry with our developer tools, we shouldn't do so.

When used with accounting, an entry is called a **ledger entry**.

When Ledger Entry data is accounting data, we are not permitted to delete this data from an entry table. Corrections are done by posting adjustments or reversing entries. We can compress or summarize some entry data (very carefully), which eliminates detail, but we should not change anything that would affect accounting totals for money or quantities.

User views of entry data are generally done through the use of list pages. The following screenshots show a **CUSTOMER LEDGER ENTRIES** list (financially-oriented data) and an **ITEM LEDGER ENTRIES** list (quantity-oriented data). In each case, the data represents historical activity details with accounting significance. There are other data fields in addition to those shown in the following screenshots, but the fields that are shown here are representative. The users can utilize page-customization tools (which we will discuss in Chapter 4, *Pages – The Interactive Interface*) to create personalized page displays in a wide variety of ways. First, we have the **CUSTOMER LEDGER ENTRIES** list:

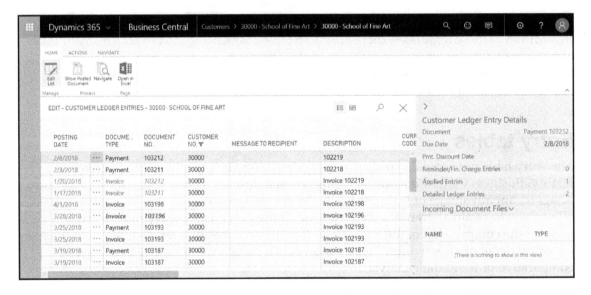

Then, we have the **ITEM LEDGER ENTRIES** list:

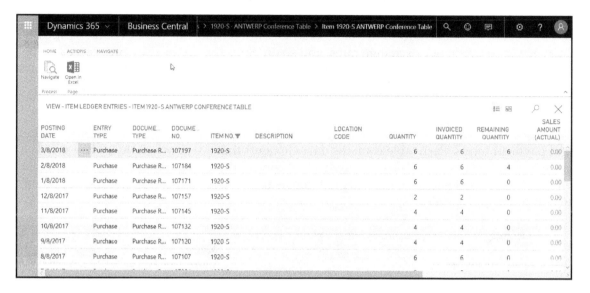

The **CUSTOMER LEDGER ENTRIES** page displays critical information such as **POSTING DATE** (the effective accounting date), **DOCUMENT TYPE** (the type of transaction), **CUSTOMER NO.**, and the **ORIGINAL** and **REMAINING AMOUNT** of the transaction. The record also contains the **ENTRY NO.**, which uniquely identifies each record. The open entries are those where the transaction amount has not been fully applied, such as an invoice amount that's not been fully paid or a payment amount that's not been fully consumed by invoices.

The **ITEM LEDGER ENTRIES** page displays similar information that's pertinent to inventory transactions. As we described previously, **POSTING DATE**, **ENTRY TYPE**, and **ITEM NO.**, as well as the assigned **LOCATION CODE** for the item, control the meaning of each transaction. Item Ledger Entries are expressed both in **QUANTITY** and **AMOUNT (VALUE)**. The open entries here are tied to the **REMAINING QUANTITY**, such as material that has been received but is still available in stock. In other words, the open entries represent current inventory. Both the Customer Ledger Entry and Item Ledger Entry tables have underlying tables that provide additional details for entries affecting values.

Subsidiary (supplementary) tables

The subsidiary (also called supplementary) table type contains lists of codes, descriptions, or other validation data. Subsidiary table examples are postal zone codes, country codes, currency codes, currency exchange rates, and so on. Subsidiary tables are often accessed by means of one of the setup menu options because they must be set up prior to being used for reference purposes by other tables. In our WDTU example, tables 50001 Radio Show Type and 50007 Publisher are subsidiary tables.

The following screenshots show some sample subsidiary tables for location, country/region, and payment terms. Each table contains data elements that are appropriate for use as a subsidiary table, plus, in some cases, fields that control the effect of referencing a particular entry. These data elements are usually entered as part of a setup process and then updated over time as appropriate:

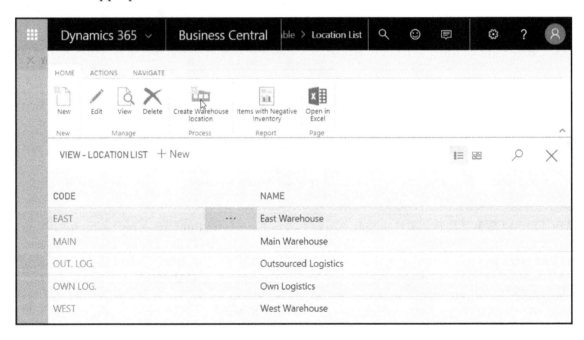

The **Location List** in the preceding screenshot is a simple validation list of the locations for this implementation. Usually, they represent physical sites, but depending on the implementation, they can also be used to segregate types of inventory. For example, locations could be refrigerated versus unrefrigerated, or there could be locations for awaiting inspection, passed inspection, and failed inspection:

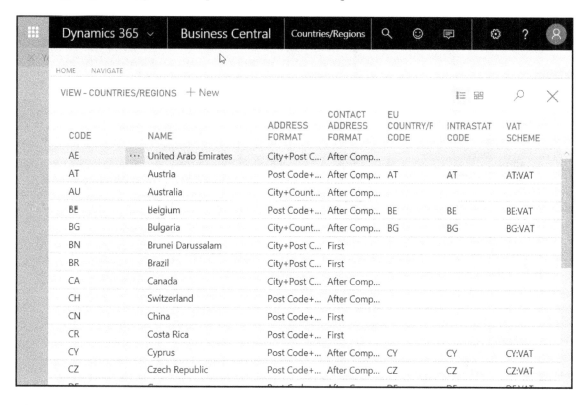

The countries/regions that are listed in the preceding screenshot are used as validation data, and define the acceptable country codes. It also provides control information for the mailing **Address Format** (general organization address) and the **Contact Address Format** (for an individual's contact address).

The **Payment Terms** table that's shown in the following screenshot provides a list of payment terms codes, along with a set of parameters that allows the system to calculate specific terms. In this set of data, for example, the **1M(8D)** code will yield payment terms that are due in a month, with a discount of 2% applied to payments that are processed within eight days of the invoice date. In another instance, **14D** payment terms will calculate the payment as being due in 14 days from the date of invoice with no discount available:

CODE	DUE DATE CALCULATION	DISCOUNT DATE CALCULATION	DISCOUNT %	CALC. PMT. DISC. ON CR. MEMO!	DESCRIPTION
10 DAYS	... 10D		0	☐	Net 10 days
14 DAYS	14D		0	☐	Net 14 days
15 DAYS	15D		0	☐	Net 15 days
1M(8D)	1M	8D	2	☐	1 Month/2% 8 days
2 DAYS	2D		0	☐	Net 2 days
21 DAYS	21D		0	☐	Net 21 days
30 DAYS	30D		0	☐	Net 30 days
60 DAYS	60D		0	☐	Net 60 days
7 DAYS	7D		0	☐	Net 7 days
CM	CM		0	☐	Current Month
COD	0D		0	☐	Cash on delivery

Register

The register table type contains a record of the range of transaction ID numbers for each batch of posted Ledger Entries. Register data provides an audit trail of the physical timing and sequence of postings. This, combined with the full details that are retained in the Ledger Entry, makes Business Central a very auditable system, because we can see exactly what activity was done and when it was done:

NO.	CREATION DATE	USER ID	SOURCE CODE	JOURNAL BATCH NAME	FROM ENTRY NO.	TO ENTRY NO.	FROM VAT ENTRY NO.
846 ⋯	8/19/2018	ADMIN	INVTPCOST		3329	3332	439
845	8/19/2018	ADMIN	INVTPCOST		3325	3328	439
844	8/19/2018	ADMIN		DEFAULT	3323	3324	438
843	8/19/2018	ADMIN		DEFAULT	3321	3322	437
842	8/19/2018	ADMIN		DEFAULT	3319	3320	436
841	8/19/2018	ADMIN		DEFAULT	3317	3318	435
840	8/19/2018	ADMIN		DEFAULT	3315	3316	434
839	8/19/2018	ADMIN		DEFAULT	3313	3314	433
838	8/19/2018	ADMIN		DEFAULT	3311	3312	432
837	8/19/2018	ADMIN		DEFAULT	3309	3310	431
836	8/19/2018	ADMIN		DEFAULT	3307	3308	430

The user views the register through a tabular page, as shown in the previous screenshot. We can see that each register entry has the **CREATION DATE**, **SOURCE CODE**, **JOURNAL BATCH NAME**, and the identifying entry number range for all of the entries in that batch. Another Business Central feature, the **NAVIGATE** function, which we will discuss in detail in Chapter 4, *Pages – The Interactive Interface*, also provides a very useful auditing tool. The **NAVIGATE** function allows the user (who may be a developer doing testing) to highlight a single Ledger Entry and find all of the other ledger entries and related records that resulted from the posting that created that highlighted entry.

Posted document

The posted document type contains the history version of the original documents for a variety of data types, such as **Sales Invoices, Purchase Invoices, Sales Shipments**, and **Purchase Receipts**. Posted documents are designed to provide an easy reference to the historical data in a format similar to what would have been stored in paper files. A posted document looks very similar to the original source document. For example, a **Posted Sales Invoice** will look very similar to the original **Sales Orders** or **Sales Invoices**. The posted documents are included in the **NAVIGATE** function.

The following screenshots show a **Sales Orders** before posting and the resulting **Posted Sales Invoice** document. Both documents are in a header/detail format, where the information in the header applies to the whole order and the information in the detail is specific to the individual order line. As part of the **Sales Orders** page, there is information being displayed to the right of the actual order. This is designed to make the user's life easier by providing related information without requiring a separate lookup action.

First, we can see that the **Sales Orders** document is ready to be posted:

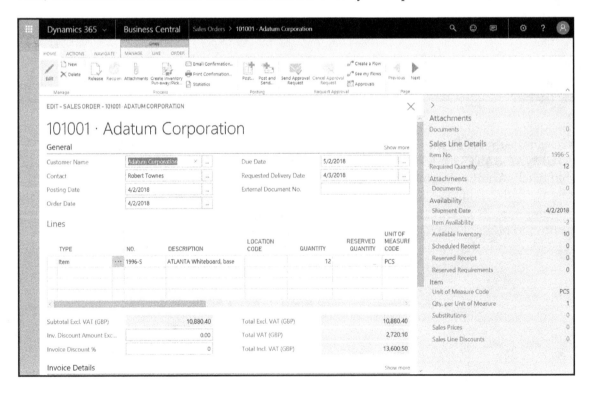

The following screenshot is that of the partial shipment **Sales Invoice** document, after the invoice was posted for the shipped goods:

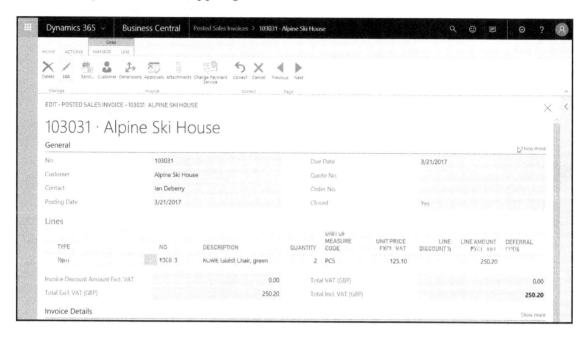

Singleton

The singleton table type contains system or functional application control information, often referred to as setup. There is one setup table per functional application area, for example, one for **Sales & Receivables**, one for **Purchases & Payables**, one for **General Ledger**, and one for **Inventory**. Setup tables contain only a single record. Since a setup table has only one record, it can have a primary key field that has no value assigned to it (this is how all of the standard Business Central setup tables are designed). The singleton table design pattern can be found at `http://blogs.msdn.com/b/nav/archive/2013/07/19/nav-design-pattern-of-the-week-single-record-setup-table.aspx`.

The **Inventory Setup** page is as follows:

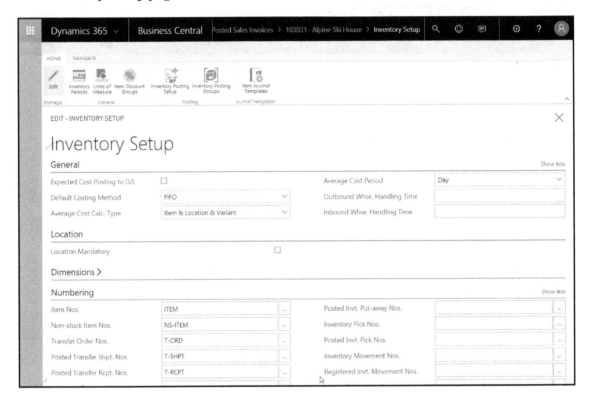

Temporary

A temporary table is used within objects to hold temporary data. A temporary table does not exist outside the instance of the object where it is defined using a permanent table as the source of the table definition. A temporary table has exactly the same data structure as the permanent table after which it is modeled.

Temporary tables are created empty when the parent object execution initiates, and they disappear along with their data when the parent object execution terminates (that is, when the temporary table variable goes out of scope).

Temporary tables are not generally accessible to users, except on a display-only basis. They can directly be the target of reports, pages, and XML ports. In general, temporary tables are intended to be work areas, and as such, are containers of data. The definition of a temporary table can only be changed by changing the definition of the permanent table on which it has been modeled.

A temporary table technique is used by advanced developers to define a new temporary table format without consuming a (paid for) licensed table slot. You can do this as follows: define the new table in an unlicensed number range. If the current production license allows for tables 50000 through 50099, assign the new layout to 50500 (for example). That layout can then be used to define a temporary table in an object. The layout cannot be used to actually store data in the database; it can only be used to provide a convenient data format design for some special intermediate process.

Content modifiable tables

The content modifiable table category includes only one table type, the system table type.

System table

The system table type contains user-maintainable information that pertains to the management or administration of the Business Central application system. System tables are created by Business Central; we cannot create system tables. However, with full developer license rights, we can modify system tables to extend their usage. With full system permissions, we can also change the data in system tables.

An example of a system table type is the User table, which contains user login information. This particular system table is often modified to define special user access routing or processing limitations. Other system tables contain data on report-to-printer routing assignments, transaction numbers to be assigned, batch job scheduling, and so on. The following are examples of system tables in which definition and content can be modified. The first three relate to system security functions:

- User: The table of identified users and their security information
- Permission Set: The table containing a list of all of the permission sets in the database

- `Permission`: The table defining what individual permission sets are allowed to do, based on object permission assignments
- `Access Control`: The table of the security roles that are assigned to each Windows login

The following tables are used to track a variety of system data or control structures:

- `Company`: The companies in this database. Most Business Central data is automatically segregated by company.
- `Chart`: This defines all of the chart parts that have been set up for use in constructing pages.
- `Web Service`: This lists the pages, queries, and codeunits that have been published as web services.
- `Profile`: This contains a list of all of the active profiles and their associated **Role Center** pages. A profile is a collection of Business Central users who are assigned to the same **Role Center**.
- `User Personalization`: In spite of its name, this table does not contain information about user personalization that has occurred. Instead, this table contains the link between the user ID and the profile ID, the language, company, and debugger controls. (A personalization is a change in the layout of a page by a user, such as adding or removing fields, page parts, restructuring menus, resizing columns, and so on. This information can be found in the `User Metadata` table.)

The following tables contain information about various system internals. Their explanation is outside the scope of this book:

- `Send-to Program`
- `Style Sheet`
- `User Default Style Sheet`
- `Record Link`
- `Object Tracking`
- `Object Metadata`
- `Profile Metadata`
- `User Metadata`

Read-only tables

There is only one table type included in the read-only table category, the virtual table type.

Virtual

The virtual table type is computed at runtime by the system. A virtual table contains data and is accessed like other tables, but we cannot modify either the definition or the contents of a virtual table. We can think of virtual tables as system data that's presented in the form of a table so that it is readily available to AL code. Some of these tables (such as the `Database File`, `File`, and `Drive` tables) provide access to information about the computing environment. Other virtual tables (such as the `Table Information`, `Field`, and `Session` tables) provide information about the internal structure and operating activities of our database. A good way to learn more about any of these tables is to create a list or card page that's bound to the table of interest. Include all of the fields in the page layout, **Save** the page, and **Run** it. We can then view the field definition and data contents of the target virtual table.

Some virtual tables (such as `Date` and `Integer`) provide tools that can be used in our application routines. The `Date` table provides a list of calendar periods (such as days, weeks, months, quarters, and years) to make it much easier to manage various types of accounting and managerial data handling. The `Integer` table provides a list of integers from -1.000.000.000 to 1.000.000.000. As we explore standard Business Central reports, we will frequently see the Integer table being used to supply a sequential count to facilitate a reporting sequence (often in a limited numeric range, such as 1 or 1 to 10).

We cannot see these tables in the list of table objects, and we can only access them as targets for pages, reports, or variables in AL code. Knowledge of the existence, contents, and usage of these virtual tables isn't useful to an end user. However, as developers, we will regularly use some of these virtual tables. There is educational value in studying the structure and contents of these tables, as well as having the ability to create valuable tools with knowledge of and by accessing one or more virtual tables.

Summary

In this chapter, we focused on the foundation level of Business Central data structure: tables and their internal structure. We worked our way through the hands-on creation of a number of tables and their data definitions in support of our WDTU application. We briefly discussed field groups and how they are used.

We identified essential table structure elements, including properties, object numbers, triggers, keys, and SumIndexFields. Finally, we reviewed the various categories of tables that can be found in Business Central.

In the next chapter, we will dig deeper into the Business Central data structure to understand how fields and their attributes are assembled to make up tables. We will also focus on what can be done with triggers. Then, we will explore how other object types use tables so that we can work toward developing a fully-featured Business Central development toolkit.

Questions

1. Which of the following is a correct description of a table in Business Central? Choose two:
    - A Business Central table is the definition of data structure
    - A Business Central table includes a built-in data entry page
    - A Business Central table can contain AL code, but that should be avoided
    - A Business Central table should implement many of the business rules of a system

2. All primary keys should contain only one data field. True or false?
3. It is possible to link a Business Central table to a table outside of the Business Central database using what property? Choose one:
    - DatabaseLink
    - ObjectPointer
    - LinkedObject
    - C# Codelet

4. System tables cannot be modified. True or false?

5. Which of the following are table triggers? Choose two:

    - `OnInsert`

    - `OnChange`

    - `OnNewKey`

    - `OnRename`

6. Keys can be enabled or disabled in executable code. True or false?

7. Because setup tables only contain one record, they do not need to have a primary key. True or false?

8. Table numbers that are intended to be used for customized table objects should only range between 5000 to 9999. True or false?

9. Which of the following tables can be modified by partner developers? Choose three:

    - Customer

    - Date

    - User

    - Item Ledger Entry

10. The drop-down display on a field lookup can be changed by modifying the table's field groups. True or false?

11. Temporary table data can be saved in a special database storage area. True or false?

12. Which of the following virtual tables are commonly used in Business Central development projects? Choose two:

    - Date

    - GPS Location

    - Integer

    - Object Metadata

13. SumIndexFields can be used to calculate totals. True or false?

14. Table permissions (for access to another table's data) include which of the following permissions? Choose three:
    - Read
    - Sort
    - Delete
    - Modify

15. The table relation property allows a field in one table to reference data in another table. True or false?
16. Tables can be created or deleted dynamically. True or false?
17. Only tables have triggers and only fields have properties. True or false?
18. Ledger Entry data in Business Central can be freely updated through either posting routines or direct data entry. True or false?
19. SQL Server for Business Central supports SIFT by which mechanism? Choose one:
    - SQL SIFT indexes
    - SQL dynamic indexes
    - SQL indexed views
    - SIFT not supported in SQL

20. Reference tables and virtual tables are simply two different names for the same type of tables. True or false?

3
Data Types and Fields

"You can't build a great building on a weak foundation. You must have a solid foundation if you're going to have a strong superstructure."

– Gordon B. Hinckley

"Perfection is achieved, not when there is nothing more to add, but rather when there is nothing more to take away."

– Antoine de Saint-Exupéry

The design of an application should begin at the simplest level, that is, with the design of the data elements. The type of data our development tool supports has a significant effect on our design. Because Business Central is designed for financially-oriented business applications, Business Central data types are financially- and business-oriented.

In this chapter, we will cover many of the data types that we will use within Business Central. For each data type, we will cover some of the more frequently modified field properties and how particular properties, such as `FieldClass`, are used to support application functionality. `FieldClass` is a fundamental property that defines whether the contents of the field is data to be processed or control information to be interpreted.

In particular, we will be covering the following topics:

- Basic definitions
- Fields
- Data types
- `FieldClass` properties
- Filtering

Basic definitions in Business Central

First, let's review some basic Business Central terminology:

- **Data type**: This defines the kind of data that can be held in a field, whether it be numeric (such as integer or decimal), text, a table `RecordID`, time, date, Boolean, and so forth. The data type defines what constraints can be placed on the contents of a field, determines the functions in which the data element can be used (not all data types are supported by all functions), and defines what the results of certain functions will be.
- **Fundamental data type**: This is a simple, single component structure consisting of a single value at any point in time, for example, a number, a string, or a Boolean value.
- **Complex data type**: This is a structure that's made up of or relates to simple data types, for example, records, program objects, such as pages or reports, **Binary Large OBjects** (**BLOBs**), `DateFormulas`, external files, and indirect reference variables.
- **Data element**: This is an instance of a data type that may be a constant or a variable.
- **Constant**: This is a data element that's explicitly defined in the code by a literal value. Constants are only modifiable during execution by a developer. All of the simple data types can be represented by constants. Examples include `MAIN` (code or text), `12.34` (decimal), and `+01-312-444-5555` (text).
- **Variable**: This is a data element that can have a value assigned to it dynamically during execution. Except for special cases, a variable will be of a single, unchanging, specific data type.

Fields

A field is the basic element of data definition in Business Central—the atom in the structure of a system. The elemental definition of a field consists of its number, its description (name), its data type, and, of course, any properties that are required for its particular data type. A field is defined by the values of its properties and the AL code contained in its triggers.

Field properties

The specific properties that can be defined for a field depend on the data type. There is a minimum set of universal properties, which we will review first. Then, we will review the rest of the more frequently used properties, some of which are data dependent and some are not. Check out the remaining properties by using Microsoft Documents.

We can access the properties of a field while viewing the table in Visual Studio Code, highlighting the field, and then clicking inside the curly braces and pressing *Ctrl* + spacebar. All of the property screenshots in this section were obtained in this way for fields within the `Radio Show` table. As we review various field properties, you will learn more if you follow along in your Business Central system using Visual Studio Code. Explore different properties and the values they can have. Use Microsoft Docs liberally for additional information and examples.

 When a property value is not explicitly set, the default value is used. It is considered a best practice to not set a property if the default value applies.

All of the fields, of any data type, have the following properties:

- `Field No.`: This is the identifier for the field within the containing table object.
- `Name`: This is the label by which AL code references the field. A name can consist of up to 30 characters, including special characters. The name can be changed by a developer at any time, and Business Central will automatically ripple that change throughout the system. If no `Caption` value has been defined, the name is used as the default caption when data from this field is displayed. Changing names that are used as literals in AL code can cause problems with some functions, such as web services and `GETFILTERS`, where the reference is based on the field name rather than the field number.
- `Caption`: This contains the defined caption for the currently selected language. It will always be one of the defined multi-language captions. The default language for a Business Central installation is determined by the combination of a set of built-in rules and the languages that are available in a specific installation of the software.

- `CaptionML`: This defines the multi-language caption for the table. It also identifies the language in use, for example, ENU for US English (as shown in the following screenshot).
- `Description`: This is an optional use property for our internal documentation.
- `Data Type`: This defines what type of data format applies to this field (for example, `Integer`, `Date`, `Code`, `Text`, `Decimal`, `Option`, and `Boolean`).
- `Enabled`: This determines whether or not the field has been activated for user generated events. The property defaults to <Yes> and is rarely changed.
- `AccessByPermission`: This determines the permission mask that's required for a user to access this field in pages or in the **user interface** (**UI**).

The following screenshot shows the properties for a field of the data type, BLOB:

```
                0 references
        field(2000; Test; Blob) {|Subtype=Bitmap; Compressed="true"}
    }                                  ⚡ Bitmap
    keys                               ⚡ Json
    {                                  ⚡ Memo
        - reference                    ⚡ UserDefined
```

The set of properties shown for a BLOB data type field is the simplest set of field properties. After the properties that are shared by all of the data types are given, the BLOB-specific properties are shown, that is, SubType and Compressed:

- `SubType`: This defines the type of data stored in BLOB and sets a filter in the import/export function for the field. The three subtype choices are `Bitmap` (for bitmap graphics), `Memo` (for text data), and `UserDefined` (for anything else). `UserDefined` is the default value.
- `Compressed`: This defines whether the data stored in BLOB is stored in a compressed format. If we want to access BLOB data with an external tool (from outside Business Central), this property must be set to `false`.

The properties of `Code` and `Text` data type fields are quite similar to one another. This is logical since both represent types of textual data, as shown in the following screenshot:

```
field(2000; Test; Code[30])
{
    InitValue = '';
    CaptionClass = '1,1';
    Editable = true;
    NotBlank = true;
    Numeric = true;
    CharAllowed = '';
    DateFormula = false;
    ValuesAllowed = '';
    SqlDataType = Varchar;
    TableRelation = Customer;
    ExtendedDatatype = Masked;
}
```

The following are some common properties between the `Code` and `Text` data types:

- `InitValue`: This is the value that the system will supply as a default when the field is initialized.
- `CaptionClass`: This can be set up by the developer to allow users to dynamically change the caption for a text box or a check box. `CaptionClass` defaults to empty. For more information, refer to *Developer and IT-pro help* (https://docs.microsoft.com/en-us/dynamics365/business-central/dev-itpro/). This is used in base Business Central in the dimensions fields.
- `Editable`: This is set to `false` when we don't want to allow a field to be edited, for example, if it is a computed or assigned value field that the user should not change. `Editable` defaults to `true`.
- `NotBlank`, `Numeric`, `CharAllowed`, `DateFormula`, and `ValuesAllowed`: Each of these allows us to place constraints on the data that can be entered into this field by a user. They do not affect data updates that are driven by application AL code.

- `SQL Data Type`: This applies to `Code` fields only. `SQL Data Type` defines what data type will be allowed in this particular `Code` field and how it will be mapped to a SQL Server data type. This controls sorting and display. Options include `Varchar`, `Integer`, `BigInteger` or `Variant`. `Varchar` is the default and causes all of the data to be treated as text. `Integer` and `BigInteger` allow only numeric data to be entered. `Variant` can contain any of a wide range of Business Central data types. In general, once set, this property should not be changed. These settings should not affect data handling that's done in SQL Server external to Business Central, but the conservative approach is not to make changes here.
- `TableRelation`: This is used to specify a relationship to data in the specified target table. The target table field must be in the primary key. The relationship can be conditional and/or filtered. The relationship can be used for validation, lookups, and data-change propagation.
- `ValidateTableRelation`: If `TableRelation` is specified, set this to `<Yes>` to validate the relation when data is entered or changed (in other words, confirm that the entered data exists in the target table). If `TableRelation` is defined and this property is set to `<No>`, the automatic table referential integrity will not be maintained.

 Caution: Application code can be written that will bypass this validation.

- `ExtendedDataType`: This property allows for the optional designation of an extended data type, which automatically receives special formatting and validation. Type options include an email address, URL, phone number, report filter, progress bar ratio, or masked entry (as dots). An action icon may also be displayed, as shown in the following screenshot, where there are three fields with `ExtendedDataType` defined:

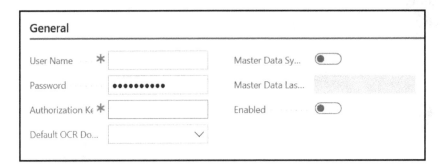

Let's take a look at the properties of two more data types, `Decimal` and `Integer`, especially those properties related to numeric content:

- `DecimalPlaces`: This sets the minimum and maximum number of decimal places (min:max) for storage and for display in a `Decimal` data item. The default is 2 <2:2>, the minimum is 0, and the maximum is 255.

- `BlankNumbers`, `BlankZero`, and `SignDisplacement`: These can be used to control the formatting and display of the data field on a page. `BlankNumbers` and `BlankZero` means that all fields of the chosen values are to be displayed as blank. `SignDisplacement` allows data positioning to be shifted for negative values.

- `MinValue` and `MaxValue`: When set, these constrain the range of data values that are allowed for user entry. The range that's available depends on the field data type.

- `AutoIncrement`: This allows for the definition of one `Integer` field in a table to automatically increment for each record that's entered. When this is used, which is not often, it is almost always to support the automatic updating of a field that's used as the last field in a primary key, hence enabling the creation of a unique key. Use of this feature does not ensure a contiguous number sequence. When the property is set to `true`, the automatic functionality should not be overridden in code:

```
field(2000; Test; Decimal)
{
    DecimalPlaces=0;
    BlankNumbers=DontBlank;
    BlankZero=true;
    SignDisplacement=1;
    MinValue=0;
    MaxValue=10;
    AutoIncrement=true;
}
```

The properties for an `Option` data type are similar to those of other numeric data types. This is reasonable because `Option` is stored as an integer, but there are also `Option`-specific properties:

- `OptionMembers`: This details the text interpretations for each of the stored integer values contained in an `Option` field

- `OptionCaption` or `OptionCaptionML`: These serve the same captioning and multi-language purposes as caption properties for other data types

Internally, options are stored as integers that are tied to each option's position in `OptionMembers`, starting with position 0, 1, 2, and so on. `OptionMembers` and `OptionCaption` are shown in the following screenshot:

```
field(1000; Frequency; Option)
{
    OptionMembers = Hourly,Daily,Weekly,Monthly;
    OptionCaptionML = ENU = 'Hourly,Daily,Weekly,Monthly';

}
```

Field triggers

To view the field triggers, let's look at our `50100` `"Radio Show"` table. Add the following triggers to the `No.` field within the curly braces:

```
1    table 50100 "Radio Show"
2    {
3        fields
4        {
             7 references
5            field(1; "No."; Code[20]) {
6                trigger OnValidate()
7                begin
8
9                end;
10               trigger OnLookup()
11               begin
12
13               end;
14           }
```

Each field has two triggers, the `OnValidate()` trigger and the `OnLookup()` trigger, which function as follows:

- `OnValidate()`: The AL code in this trigger is executed whenever an entry is made by the user. The intended use is to validate that the entry conforms to the design parameters for the field. It can also be executed under program control through use of the `VALIDATE` function (which we will discuss later).

- `OnLookup()`: Lookup behavior can be triggered by clicking on the lookup arrow in a field, as shown in the following screenshot:

- If the field's `TableRelation` property refers to a table, then the default behavior is to display a drop-down list to allow for the selection of a table entry to be stored in this field. The list will be based on `Field Groups` that have been defined for the table. We may choose to override that behavior by coding different behavior for a special case. We must be careful, because any entry whatsoever in the body of an `OnLookup()` trigger, even a comment line, will eliminate the default behavior of this trigger.

Field events

Instead of placing your business code in the `OnValidate` trigger of a field, you can also subscribe to system generated events. For each field, we can subscribe to the `OnBeforeValidate` event and the `OnAfterValidate` event. These events are triggered, as their name suggests, before and after the code we place in the `OnValidate` trigger.

Subscribing to these events can be useful to avoid making modifications to the objects that are shipped by Microsoft so that future updates are easier to implement and merging code is prevented.

More information about events in Dynamics Business Central can be found on MSDN: `https://docs.microsoft.com/en-us/dynamics365/business-central/dev-itpro/developer/devenv-events-in-al`.

Data structure examples

Some good examples of tables in the standard product to review for particular features are as follows:

- `Table 18 Customer` has a variety of data types and field classes. This table contains some fairly complex examples of AL code in the `Triggers` table. A wide variety of field property variations can be seen in this table as well.

- Table 14 Location and Table 91 User Setup both have good examples of OnValidate trigger AL code, as do all of the primary master tables (Customer, Vendor, Item, Job, and so on).

Field numbering

The number of each field within its parent table object is the unique identifier that Business Central uses internally to identify that field. We can easily change a field number when we are initially defining a table layout, but after other objects, such as pages, reports, or codeunits, reference the fields in a table, it becomes difficult to change the number of referenced fields. Deleting a field and reusing its field number for a different purpose is not a good idea and can easily lead to programming confusion.

We cannot safely change the definition of, re-number, or delete a field that has data present in the database easily. The same can be said for reducing the defined size of a field to less than the largest size of the data that's already present in that field. However, if we force the change, the force function will override the system's built-in safeguards. This action can truncate or delete data.

When we add new fields to standard Business Central product tables (those shipped with the product), the new field numbers must be in the 50,000 to 99,999 number range, unless we have been explicitly licensed for another number range. Field numbers for fields in new tables that we create may be anything from 1 to 999,999,999.

When a field representing the same data element appears in related tables (for example, Table 37 Sales Line and Table 113 Sales Invoice Line), the same field number should be assigned to that data element for each of the tables. Not only is this consistent approach easier for reference and maintenance, but it also supports the TRANSFERFIELDS function. TRANSFERFIELDS permits the copying data from one table's record instance to another table's record instance by doing record to record mapping based on the field numbers.

If we plan ahead and number the fields logically and consistently from the beginning of our design work, we will create code that's easier to maintain. It's a good idea to leave frequent gaps in field number sequences within a table. This allows for easier insertion of new fields numerically adjacent to related, previously defined fields. In turn, that makes it easier for the next developer to understand the modification's data structure.

See *Object Numbering Conventions* in Microsoft Docs for additional information.

Field and variable naming

In general, the rules for naming fields (data elements in a table) and variables (data elements within the working storage of an object) are the same, and we will discuss them on that basis. Information on this can be found in the released *C/AL Coding Guidelines* at `https://community.dynamics.com/nav/w/designpatterns/156.cal-coding-guidelines`, including a *How do I* video.

Variables in Business Central can either be global (with a scope across the breadth of an object) or local (with a scope only within a single function). Variable names should be unique within the sphere of their scope.

Uniqueness includes not duplicating reserved words or system variables. Refer to the *AL Reserved Words* list in the *Developer and IT pro help* for more information.

 Avoid using any word as a variable name that appears as an uppercase or capitalized word in either the *Developer and IT-pro help* or any of the published Business Central technical documentation. For example, we shouldn't use the words `page` or `image` as variable names.

Variable names in Business Central are not case-sensitive. There is a 128-character length limit on variable names (but still a 30-character length limit on field names in tables). Variable names can contain all ASCII characters, except for control characters (ASCII values 0 to 31 and 255) and the double quote (ASCII value 34), as well as some Unicode characters that are used in languages other than English. Characters outside the standard ASCII set (0-127) may display differently on different systems.

 Note that the compiler won't tell us that an asterisk (`*`, ASCII value 42) or question mark (`?`, ASCII value 63) cannot be used in a variable name. However, because both the asterisk and the question mark can be used as wildcards in many expressions, especially filtering, neither one should be used in a variable name.

The first character of a variable name must be a letter from *A* to *Z* (upper or lowercase) or an underscore (_, ASCII value 95), that is, unless the variable name is enclosed in double quotes when it is referenced in code (and such names should be avoided). Alphabets other than the 26-character English alphabet may interpret the ASCII values as characters other than *A* to *Z* and may include more than 26 characters. A variable name's first character can be followed by any combination of legal characters.

If we use any characters other than the *A-Z* alphabet, numerals, and underscore, we must surround our variable name with double quotes each time we use it in AL code (for example, Cust List, which contains an embedded space, or No, which contains a period).

> See *Naming Conventions* in the *Developer and IT-pro help* for additional AL variable naming guidance.

Data types

In this section, we are going to segregate the data types into several groups. First, we will look at fundamental data types and then complex data types.

Fundamental data types

Fundamental data types are the basic components from which the complex data types are formed. They are grouped into Numeric, String, and Date/Time data types.

Numeric data

Just like other systems, Business Central supports several numeric data types. The specifications for each Business Central data type are defined for Business Central, independent of the supporting SQL Server database rules. But some data types are stored and handled somewhat differently from a SQL Server point of view than the way they appear to us as Business Central developers and users. For more details on the SQL Server-specific representations of various data elements, refer to the *developer and IT pro help*. Our discussion will focus on the Business Central representation and handling for each data type.

The various numeric data types are as follows:

- `Integer`: This is an integer number ranging from -2.147.483.646 to +2.147.483.647.
- `Decimal`: This is a decimal number in the range of +/- 999.999.999.999.999,99. Although it is possible to construct larger numbers, errors such as overflow, truncation, or loss of precision might occur. In addition, there is no facility to display or edit larger numbers.
- `Option`: This is a special instance of an integer, stored as an integer number ranging from 0 to +2.147.483.647. An `Option` data type is normally represented in the body of our AL code as an option string. We can compare an `Option` data type to an integer in AL rather than using the option string, but that's not good practice because it eliminates the self-documenting aspect of an option field.
- `OptionMembers`: This is a set of choices listed in a comma-separated string, one of which is chosen and stored as the current option. Since the maximum length of this string is 250 characters, the practical maximum number of choices for a single option is less than 125. The currently selected choice within the set of options is stored in the option field as the ordinal position of that option within the set. For example, the selection of an entry from the option string of red, yellow, blue would result in the storing of 0 (red), 1 (yellow), and 2 (blue). If red were selected, 0 would be stored in the variable, and if blue were selected, 2 would be stored. Quite often, an option string starts with a blank to allow an effective choice if none has been chosen. An example of this (blank, `Hourly`, `Daily`, `Monthly`) is as follows:

```
field(1000; Frequency; Option)
{
    OptionMembers = Hourly,Daily,Weekly,Monthly;
    OptionCaptionML = ENU = 'Hourly,Daily,Weekly,Monthly';

}
```

- `Boolean`: A `Boolean` variable is stored as 1 or 0, which in AL code is programmatically referred to as `True` or `False`. Boolean variables may be displayed as yes or no (language dependent), *P* or blank, or `True` or `False`.

- `BigInteger`: This is an 8-byte integer as opposed to a 4-byte integer. `BigIntegers` are for very big numbers (from -9.223.372.036.854.775.807 to 9.223.372.036.854.775.807).
- `Char`: This is a numeric code between 0 and 65,535 (hexadecimal `FFFF`) representing a single 16-bit Unicode character. `Char` variables can operate either as text or as numbers. Numeric operations can be done on `Char` variables. `Char` variables can also be defined with individual text character values. `Char` variables cannot be defined as permanent variables in a table, only as working storage variables within AL objects.
- `Byte`: A single 8-bit ASCII character with a value of 0 to 255. Byte variables can operate either as text or as numbers. Numeric operations can be done on `Byte` variables. `Byte` variables can also be defined with individual text character values. `Byte` variables cannot be defined as permanent variables in a table, only as working storage variables within AL objects.
- `Action`: This is a variable that's returned from a `PAGE RUNMODAL` function or `RUNMODAL (Page)` function that specifies what action a user performs on a page. Possible values are `OK`, `Cancel`, `LookupOK`, `LookupCancel`, `Yes`, `No`, `RunObject`, and `RunSystem`.
- `ExecutionMode`: This specifies the mode in which a session is running. The possible values are `Debug` and `Standard`.

String data

The following are the data types that are included in `String` data:

- `Text`: This contains any string of alphanumeric characters. In a table, a `Text` field can be from 1 to 250 characters long. In working storage within an object, a `Text` variable can be any length if there is no length defined. If a maximum length is defined, it must not exceed 1,024. Business Central does not require a length to be specified, but if we define a maximum length, it will be enforced. When calculating the length of a record for design purposes (relative to the maximum record length of 8,000 bytes), the full defined field length should be counted.

- Code: Help says the length constraints for Code variables are the same as those for text variables, but the AL editor enforces limits of 1 to 250 characters in length. All of the letters are automatically converted into uppercase when data is entered into a Code variable; any leading or trailing spaces are removed.

- TextBuilder: Allows for easy string manipulation, such as Append, Replace, and Length.

 You can find more details on the TextBuilder class in Microsoft Docs: https://docs.microsoft.com/en-us/dynamics365/business-central/ dev-itpro/developer/api/textbuilder-class.

Date/Time data

Date/Time data display is region-specific; in other words, the data is displayed according to local standards for date and time display. The following are the data types that are included in Date/Time data:

- Date: This contains an integer number, which is interpreted as a date ranging from January 1, 1754 to December 31, 9999. A **0D** (**numeral zero, letter D**) represents an undefined date (stored as a SQL Server DateTime field), which is interpreted as January 1, 1753. According to the *developer and IT pro help*, Business Central supports a date of 1/1/0000 (presumably as a special case for backward compatibility, but not supported by SQL Server).

A **date constant** can be written as the letter **D**, preceded by either six digits in the format *MMDDYY* or eight digits as *MMDDYYYY* (where *M* for month, *D* for day, and *Y* for year). For example, *011917D* or *01192017D* both represent January 19, 2017. Later, in DateFormula, we will find *D* interpreted as day, but here, the trailing *D* is interpreted as the date (data type) constant. When the year is expressed as *YY* rather than *YYYY*, the century portion (in this case, 20) is 20 if the two-digit year is from 00 to 29, or 19 if the year is from 30 through 99.

Business Central also defines a special date called a **closing date**, which represents the point in time between one day and the next. The purpose of a closing date is to provide a point at the end of a day, after all of the real date and time-sensitive activity is recorded, that is, the point when accounting closing entries can be recorded.

Closing entries are recorded, in effect, at the stroke of midnight between two dates—this is the date of closing of accounting books and has been designed like this so that you can include or not include, at the user's option, closing entries in various reports. When sorted by date, the closing date entries will get sorted after all of the normal entries for a day. For example, the normal date entry for December 31, 2017 would display as 12/31/17 (depending on the date format masking), and the closing date entry would display as C12/31/17. All of the C12/31/17 ledger entries would appear after all normal 12/31/17 ledger entries. The following screenshot shows three 2018 closing date entries mixed with normal entries from January 1st, 2019 (this data is from the CRONUS demo. The 2018 closing entries have an opening **Entry** description showing that these were the first entries for the demo data in the respective accounts. This is not a normal set of production data):

POSTING DATE	DOCUMENT TYPE	DOCUMENT NO.	G/L ACCOUNT NO.	DESCRIPTION	GEN. POSTING TYPE	GEN. BUS. POSTING GROUP	GEN. PROD. POSTING GROUP	AMOUNT	BAL. ACCOUNT TYPE
C12/31/2018		START	5840	Opening Entry				-4,518.40	G/L Account
C12/31/2018		START	5920	Opening Entry				-45,552.00	G/L Account
C12/31/2018		START	3120	Opening Entry				-488,329.71	G/L Account
1/1/2019	Invoice	108017	1320	Order 106015	Purchase	DOMESTIC	MISC	30,000.00	G/L Account
1/1/2019	Invoice	108017	5630	Order 106015				7,500.00	G/L Account
1/1/2019	Invoice	108017	5410	Order 106015				-37,500.00	G/L Account
1/1/2019	Payment	108017	2940	Order 106015				-37,500.00	Vendor
1/1/2019	Payment	108017	5410	Order 106015				37,500.00	Bank Account
1/1/2019	Invoice	108018	1220	Order 106018	Purchase	DOMESTIC	MISC	6,600.00	G/L Account

Let's discuss a few parameters in detail:

- `Time`: This contains an integer number, which is interpreted on a 24-hour clock, in milliseconds plus 1, from 00:00:00 to 23:59:59:999. A 0T (numeral zero, letter T) represents an undefined time and is stored as 1/1/1753 00:00:00.000.
- `DateTime`: This represents a combined date and time, stored in **Coordinated Universal Time (UTC)**, and always displays local time (that is, the local time on our system). `DateTime` fields do not support Business Central closing dates. `DateTime` is helpful for an application that needs to support multiple time zones simultaneously. `DateTime` values can range from January 1, 1754 00:00:00.000 to December 31, 9999 23:59:59.999, but dates earlier than January 1, 1754 cannot be entered (don't test with dates late in 9999 as an intended advance to the year 10000 won't work). Assigning a date of 0DT yields an undefined or blank `DateTime`.

- `Duration`: This represents the positive or negative difference between two `DateTime` values, in milliseconds, stored as `BigInteger`. Durations are automatically output in the text format: *DDD* days *HH* hours *MM* minutes *SS* seconds.

Complex data types

Each complex data type consists of multiple data elements. For ease of reference, we will categorize them into several groups of similar types.

Data structure

The following data types are in the data structure group:

- **File**: This refers to any standard Windows file outside the Business Central database. There is a reasonably complete set of functions to allow a range of actions, including creating, deleting, opening, closing, reading, writing, and copying data files. For example, we could create our own Business Central routines in AL to import or export data to or from a file that had been created by some other application.

  With the three tier architecture of Business Central, business logic runs on the server, not the client. We need to keep this in mind whenever we are referring to local external files, because they will be on the server by default. Use of **Universal Naming Convention** (**UNC**) paths can make this easier to manage.

- **Record**: This refers to a single data row within a Business Central table that consists of individual fields. Quite often, multiple variable instances of a record (table) are defined in working storage to support a validation process, allowing access to different records within the table at one time in the same function.

Objects

Page, report, codeunit, query, and XMLport each represent an object data type. Object data types are used when there is a need for a reference to an object or a function in another object. Some examples of this are as follows:

- Invoking a report or an XMLport from a page or a report
- Calling a function for data validation or processing is coded as a function in a table or a codeunit

Web services

To work with web services, Business Central supports a set of HTTP, XML, and JSON variables. Documentation on these types can be found in the Microsoft Docs: `https://docs.microsoft.com/en-us/dynamics365/business-central/dev-itpro/developer/devenv-restapi-overview`.

DotNet

Business Central supports using .NET in on premises installations.

DotNet allows for the definition of a variable for .NET Framework interface types within an assembly. This supports the access of .NET Framework type members, including methods, properties, and constructors from AL. These can be members of the global assembly cache or custom assemblies.

Input/output

The following are the input/output data types:

- `Dialog`: This supports the definition of a simple UI window without the use of a page object. Typically, `Dialog` windows are used to communicate processing progress or to allow a brief user response to a go/no-go question, although the latter could result in bad performance due to locking. There are other user communication tools as well, but they do not use a `Dialog` type data item.
- `InStream` and `OutStream`: These allow you to read from and write to external files, `BLOB` data type's, and objects of the automation and DotNet data types.

DateFormula

`DateFormula` provides the definition and storage of a simple, but clever, set of constructs to support the calculation of runtime-sensitive dates. `DateFormula` is stored in a non-language dependent format, hence supporting multi-language functionality. `DateFormula` is a combination of the following:

- Numeric multipliers (for example, 1, 2, 3, 4, and so on)
- Alpha time units (all must be uppercase)
- *D* for a day
- *W* for a week
- *WD* for the day of the week, that is, day 1 through day 7 (either in the future or in the past, not today); Monday is day 1, and Sunday is day 7
- *M* for calendar month
- *Y* for year
- *CM* for current month, *CY* for current year, and *CW* for current week
- Math symbols interpretation: + (plus), that is, *CM + 10D* means the current month end plus 10 days (in other words, the 10th of next month), and - (minus), that is, (-*WD3*), which means the date of the previous Wednesday (the third day of the past week)
- Positional notation (*D15* means the 15th day of the month and *15D* means 15 days)

Payment terms for invoices supports full use of `DateFormula`. All `DateFormula` results are expressed as a date based on a reference date. The default reference date is the system date, not the work date.

Here are some sample `DateFormulas` and their interpretations (displayed dates are based on the US calendar) with a reference date of July 10, 2017, a Friday:

- *CM*: The last day of the current month, 07/31/15
- *CM + 10D*: The 10th of next month, 08/10/15
- *WD6*: The next sixth day of the week, 07/11/15
- *WD5*: The next fifth day of the week, 07/17/15
- *CM - M + D*: The end of the current month minus one month plus one day, 07/01/15
- *CM - 5M*: The end of the current month minus five months, 02/28/15

Let's take the opportunity to use the `DateFormula` data type to learn a few Business Central development basics. We will do so by experimenting with some hands-on evaluations of several `DateFormula` values. We will create a table to calculate dates using `DateFormula` and reference dates.

Go to **File** | **New** | **Save**. Save the file with the name: `table 50140 Date Formula`. Type in `ttable` (with two t's) and give the table an ID of `50140` and a name of `Date Formula`. After we've finished this test, we will save the table for later testing:

```
1    table 50140 "Date Formula"
2    {
3        fields
4        {
             1 reference
5        |   field(1; "Primary Key"; Code[10]) { }
             3 references
6        |   field(10; "Reference for Date Calculation"; Date) { }
             3 references
7 |      |   field(20; "Date Formula to Test"; DateFormula) { }
             2 references
8        |   field(30; "Date Result"; Date) { }
9        }
```

Now, we will add some simple AL code to our table so that, when we enter or change either `Reference Date` or the `DateFormula` data, we can calculate a new result date.

At the bottom of the file, we delete the triggers that were generated by the snippet and create a new procedure. The name of the procedure is `CalculateNewDate`:

```
local procedure CalculateNewDate()
begin
    "Date Result" := CalcDate("Date Formula to Test", "Reference for Date Calculation");
end;
```

Notice that our new procedure was defined as a LOCAL function. This means that it cannot be accessed from another object unless we change it to a global procedure.

Because our goal now is to focus on experimenting with `DateFormula`, we will not go into detail explaining the logic we are creating.

The logic we're going to code follows: when an entry is made (new or changed) in either the Reference Date field or in the Date Formula to Test field, invoke the CalculateNewDate function to calculate a new Date Result value based on the entered data.

First, we will create the logic within our new function, CalculateNewDate(), to evaluate and store Date Result based on the DateFormula and Reference Date fields that we enter into the table.

Just copy the AL code exactly, as shown in the following screenshot, and save the table:

```
field(1; "Primary Key"; Code[10]) { }
3 references
field(10; "Reference for Date Calculation"; Date)
{
    trigger OnValidate()
    begin
        CalculateNewDate;
    end;
}
3 references
field(20; "Date Formula to Test"; DateFormula)
{
    trigger OnValidate()
    begin
        CalculateNewDate;
    end;
}
2 references
field(30; "Date Result"; Date) { }
```

If you get an error message of any type when you close and save the table, you probably didn't copy the AL code exactly as it is shown in the preceding screenshot (this is shown again in the following code to make it easy to copy):

```
CalculateNewDate;
"Date Result" := CalcDate("Date Formula to Test","Reference for Date
Calculation");
```

This code will cause the CalculateNewDate() function to be called via the OnValidate trigger when an entry is made in either the Reference for Date Calculation or Date Formula to Test fields. The function will place the result in the Date Result field. The use of an integer value in the redundantly named primary key field allows us to enter any number of records into the table (by manually numbering them 1, 2, 3, and so forth).

Let's experiment with several different date and date formula combinations. We will access the table via a simple page, as shown in the following screenshot:

```
page 50140 "Date Formula"
{
    PageType = List;
    ApplicationArea = All;
    UsageCategory = Administration;
    SourceTable = "Date Formula";

    layout
    {
        0 references
        area(Content)
        {
            0 references
            repeater(GroupName)
            {
                0 references
                field("Primary Key"; "Primary Key") { ApplicationArea = All; }
                0 references
                field("Reference for Date Calculation"; "Reference for Date Calculation") { ApplicationArea = All; }
                0 references
                field("Date Formula to Test"; "Date Formula to Test") { ApplicationArea = All; }
                0 references
                field("Date Result"; "Date Result") { ApplicationArea = All; }
            }
        }
    }
}
```

If we build and publish the extension, we can run the page from the search option.

Enter a primary key value of 1 (one). In `Reference for Date Calculation`, enter either an uppercase or lowercase T for today, the system date. The same date will appear in the `Date Result` field, because at this point no date formula has been entered. Now, enter 1D (numeral 1 followed by uppercase or lowercase letter *D*; C/SIDE will take care of making it upper case) in the `Date Formula to Test` field. We will see that the contents of the `Date Result` field has changed to be one day beyond the date in the `Reference for Date Calculation` field.

Now, for another test entry—let's start with 2 in the primary key field. Again, enter the letter T (for today) in the `Reference Date for Calculation` field, and enter the letter W (for week) in the `Date Formula to Test` field. We will get an error message telling us that our formulas should include a number. Make the system happy and enter 1W. We'll now see a date in the `Date Result` field that is one week beyond our system date.

Set the system's work date to a date in the middle of a month (remember, we discussed setting the work date in `Chapter 1`, *Introduction to Business Central*). Start another line with the number 3 as the primary key, followed by `W` (for work date) in the `Reference Date for Calculation` field. Enter `cm` (or `CM`, `cM`, or `Cm`—it doesn't matter) in the `Date Formula to Test` field. Our result date will be the last day of our work date month. Now, enter another line using the work date, but enter a formula of `-cm` (the same as before, but with a minus sign). This time, our result date will be the first day of our work date month. Notice that the `DateFormula` logic handles month end dates correctly, even including leap years. Try starting with a date in the middle of February 2016 to confirm that:

PRIMARY KEY	REFERENCE FOR DATE CALCULATION	DATE FORMULA TO TEST	DATE RESULT
1	2/1/2017	1D	2/2/2017
2	2/1/2017	1W	2/8/2017
3	3/10/2017	CM	3/31/2017
4	3/10/2017	-CM	3/1/2017
5	2/15/2016	CM	2/29/2016

Enter another line with a new primary key. Skip over the `Reference Date for Calculation` field and just enter `1D` in the `Date Formula to Test` field. What happens? We get an error message stating that **You cannot base a date calculation on an undefined date**. In other words, Business Central cannot make the requested calculation without a reference date. Before we put this function into production, we want our code to check for a reference date before calculating. We could default an empty date to the system date or the work date and avoid this particular error.

The preceding and following screenshots show different sample calculations. Build on these sample calculations and then experiment more on your own:

PRIMARY KEY	REFERENCE FOR DATE CALCULATION	DATE FORMULA TO TEST	DATE RESULT
1	2/1/2017	1D	2/2/2017
2	2/1/2017	1W	2/8/2017
3	3/10/2017	CM	3/31/2017
4	3/10/2017	-CM	3/1/2017
5	2/15/2016	CM	2/29/2016
6	2/15/2017	CM	2/28/2017
7	4/6/2017	1M	5/6/2017
8	4/6/2017	-1M	3/6/2017
9	9/3/2017	-1W-1D	8/26/2017
10	8/26/2017	1W+1D	9/3/2017
42	3/10/2017	-1W	3/3/2017
55	1/15/2017	-CM-1D	12/31/2016
56	1/15/2017	-1Y-CM	1/1/2016

We can create a variety of different algebraic date formulas and get some very interesting and useful results. One Business Central user business has due dates for all invoices of the 10th of the next month. The invoices are dated on the dates they are actually printed, at various times throughout the month. But by using `DateFormula` of *CM + 10D*, each invoice due date is always automatically calculated to be the 10th of the next month.

Don't forget to test with `WD` (weekday), `Q` (quarter), and `Y` (year), as well as `D` (day), `W` (week), and `M` (month). For our code to be language-independent, we should enter the date formulas with < > delimiters around them (for example, `<1D+1W>`). Business Central will translate the formula into the correct language codes using the installed language layer.

Although our focus for the work we just completed was the `DateFormula` data type, we've accomplished a lot more than simply learning about that one data type:

- We created a new table just for the purpose of experimenting with an AL feature that we might use. This is a technique that comes in handy when we are learning a new feature, trying to decide how it works or how we might use it.
- We put some critical `OnValidate` logic into the table. When data is entered in one area, the entry is validated and, if valid, the defined processing is done instantly.
- We created a common routine as a new `LOCAL` function. That function is then called from all of the places to which it applies.
- Finally, and most specifically, we saw how Business Central tools make a variety of relative date calculations easy. These are very useful in business applications, many aspects of which are date centered.

References and other data types

The following data types are used for advanced functionality in Business Central, and sometimes support an interface with an external object:

- `RecordID`: This contains the object number and primary key of a table.
- `RecordRef`: This identifies a record/row in a table. `RecordRef` can be used to obtain information about the table, the record, the fields in the record, and the currently active filters on the table.
- `FieldRef`: This identifies a field in a table, hence allowing access to the contents of that field.

- KeyRef: This identifies a key in a table and the fields in that key.

   Since the specific record, field, and key references are assigned at runtime, RecordRef, FieldRef, and KeyRef are used to support logic that can run on tables that aren't specified at design time. This means that one routine built on these data types can be created to perform a common function for a variety of different tables and table formats.

- Variant: This defines variables that are typically used for interfacing with Automation and DotNet objects. Variant variables can contain data of various AL data types for passing an Automation or DotNet object, as well as external Automation data types that cannot be mapped to AL data types.

- TableFilter: This is for variables that can only be used for setting security filters from the Permissions table.

- Transaction Type: This has optional values of UpdateNoLocks, Update, Snapshot, Browse, and Report, which define SQL Server behavior for a Business Central report or XMLport transaction from the beginning of the transaction.

- BLOB: This can contain either specially formatted text, a graphic in the form of a bitmap, or other developer-defined binary data that's up to 2 GB in size. **Binary Large Objects** (**BLOBs**) can only be included in tables; they cannot be used to define working storage variables. See the *Developer and IT-pro help* for additional information.

- BigText: This can contain large chunks of text up to 2 GB in size. BigText variables can only be defined in the working storage within an object, but are not included in tables. BigText variables cannot be directly displayed or seen in the debugger. There is a group of special functions that can be used to handle BigText data. See *developer and IT pro help* for additional information.

   To handle text strings in a single data element greater than 250 characters in length, use a combination of BLOB and BigText variables.

- GUID: This is used to assign a unique identifying number to any database object. A **Globally Unique Identifier** (**GUID**) is a 16-byte binary data type that is used for the unique global identification of records, objects, and so on. The GUID is generated by an algorithm that was developed by Microsoft.
- TestPage: This is used to store a test page that is a logical representation of a page that does not display a UI. Test pages are used when you're performing Business Central application testing using the automated testing facility that is part of Business Central.

Data type usage

About 40% of the data types we talked about previously can be used to define the data that's stored either in tables or in working storage data definitions (that is, in a global or local data definition within an object). Two data types, BLOB and TableFilter, can only be used to define table stored data, not working storage data. About 60% of these data types can only be used for working storage data definitions.

The following list shows which data types can be used for table (persisted) data fields and which ones can be used for working storage (variable) data:

Table data types	Working storage data types
	Action
BigInteger	• BigInteger • BigText
BLOB	
Boolean	• Boolean • Byte • Char
Code	• Code • Codeunit
Date	Date
DateFormula	DateFormula
DateTime	DateTime
Decimal	• Decimal • Dialog • DotNet
Duration	Duration

Enum	• Enum • ExecutionMode • FieldRef • File
GUID	• GUID • HttpClient • HttpContent • HttpHeaders • HttpRequestMessage • HttpResponseMessage • InStream
Integer	• Integer • JsonArray • JsonObject • JsonToken • JsonValue • KeyRef • Notification
Media	
MediaSet	
Option	• Option • Outstream • Page • Query • Record
RecordID	• RecordID • RecordRef • Report
TableFilter	
	TestPage
Text	Text
	TextBuilder
Time	Time
	TransactionType
	Variant
	XMLport

FieldClass property options

Almost all data fields have a `FieldClass` property. `FieldClass` has as much effect on the content and usage of a data field as the data type does and, in some instances, more. In the next chapter, we'll cover most of the field properties, but we'll discuss the `FieldClass` property options now.

FieldClass – Normal

When `FieldClass` is `Normal`, the field will contain the type of application data that's typically stored in a table, which is the content we would expect based on the data type and various properties.

FieldClass – FlowField

FlowFields must be dynamically calculated. FlowFields are virtual fields that are stored as metadata; they do not contain data in the conventional sense. FlowField contains the definition of how to calculate (at runtime) the data that the field represents and a place to store the result of that calculation. Generally, the `Editable` property for FlowField is set to `No`.

Depending on the `CalcFormula` method, this could be a value, a reference lookup, or a `Boolean` value. When the `CalcFormula` method is `Sum`, `FieldClass` connects a data field to a previously defined `SumIndexField` in the table defined in `CalcFormula`. FlowField processing speed will be significantly affected by the key configuration of the table being processed. While we must be careful not to define extra keys, having the right keys defined will have a major effect on system performance, and thus on user satisfaction.

A FlowField value is always 0, blank, or `false`, unless it has been calculated. If FlowField is displayed directly on a page, it is calculated automatically when the page is rendered. FlowFields are also automatically calculated when they are the subject of predefined filters as part of the properties of a data item in an object (this will be explained in more detail in Chapter 5, *Pages – The Interactive Interface*, when we talk about reports and Chapter 8, *Intermediate AL*, when we talk about XMLports). In all other cases, `FlowField` must be forced to calculate using the AL `RecordName.CALCFIELDS(FlowField1, [FlowField2],...)` function or by using the `SETAUTOCALCFIELDS` function. This is also true if the underlying data is changed after the initial display of a page (that is, `FlowField` must be recalculated to take a data change into account).

Because FlowField does not contain actual data, it cannot be used as a field in a key; in other words, we cannot include FlowField as part of a key. Also, we cannot define a FlowField that is based on another FlowField, except in special circumstances.

When a field has its `FieldClass` set to `FlowField`, another directly associated property becomes available—`CalcFormula`. `CalcFormula` is the place where we can define the formula for calculating `FlowField`. On the `CalcFormula` property line, there is an ellipsis button. Clicking on that button will bring up the following:

```
FieldClass = FlowField;
CalcFormula = average ("Listernership Entry"."Listener Count"
where ("Radio Show No." = field ("No.")));
```

Use *Ctrl + Spacebar* to show the seven `FlowField` methods:

```
FieldClass = FlowField;
CalcFormula =   ("Listernership Entry"."Listener Count"
where ("Radio  ≣ average
               ≣ count
               ≣ exist
ferences       ≣ lookup
ld(110; "Audien≣ max
ferences       ≣ min
ld(120; "Advert≣ sum
```

The seven FlowFields are described in the following table:

FlowField method	Field data type	Calculated value as it applies to the specified set of data within a specific column (field) in a table
Sum	Decimal	The sum total
Average	Decimal	The average value (the sum divided by the row count)
Exist	Boolean	Yes or no / true or false—does an entry exist?
Count	Integer	The number of entries that exist
Min	Any	The smallest value of any entry
Max	Any	The largest value of any entry
Lookup	Any	The value of the specified entry

The `Reverse Sign` control allows us to change the displayed sign of the result for the `Sum` and `Average` `FlowField` types only; the underlying data is not changed. If `Reverse Sign` is used with the `FlowField` type, `Exist`, it changes the effective function to *does not exist*.

The last, but by no means the least significant, component of the `FlowField` calculation formula is the `Table` filter in the `where` clause:

```
FieldClass = FlowField;
CalcFormula =  ("Listernership Entry"."Listener Count"
where ("Radio Show No." = ("No.")));
               I               ≣ const
                               ≣ field
erences                        ≣ filter
```

The left part of the `where` clause contains a field in the linked table where the right part links to a field in this table, `const`, or `filter`. These choices are described in the following table:

Filter type	Value	Filtering action	OnlyMax—Limit	Values—Filter
const	A constant that will be defined in the `Value` field	Uses the constant to filter for equally valued entries		
filter	A filter that will be spelled out as a literal in the `Value` field	Applies the filter expression from the `Value` field		
field	A field from the table within which the FlowField exists	Uses the contents of the specified field to filter for equally valued entries	False	

| | | If the specified field is a FlowFilter and the `OnlyMaxLimit` parameter is true, then the FlowFilter range will be applied on the basis of only having `MaxLimit`, that is, having no bottom limit. This is useful for the date filters for balance sheet data. (For an example, see *Field 31 - Balance at Date in Table 15 - G/L Account*) | True | |
| | | Causes the contents of the specified field to be interpreted as a filter (For an example, see *Field 31 - Balance at Date in Table 15- G/L Account for an example*) | True or false | True |

FieldClass – FlowFilter

FlowFilters control the calculation of FlowFields in the table (when the FlowFilters are included in the `CalcFormula`). FlowFilters do not contain permanent data, but instead contain filters on a per user basis, with the information stored in that user's instance of the code being executed. A `FlowFilter` field allows a filter to be entered at a parent record level by the user (for example, G/L Account) and applied (through the use of FlowField formulas, for example) to constrain what child data (for example, G/L entry records) is selected.

`FlowFilter` allows us to provide flexible data selection functions to users. The user does not need to have a full understanding of the data structure that's used in apply filtering in intuitive ways to both the primary data table and also to subordinate data. Based on our AL code design, FlowFilters can be used to apply filtering on multiple tables, whether this be from a subordinate to a parent table. Of course, it is our responsibility as the developers to make good use of this tool. As with many AL capabilities, a good way to learn more is by studying standard code, as designed by the Microsoft developers of Business Central, and then experimenting.

A number of good examples on the use of FlowFilters can be found in the `Customer` (table 18) and `Item` (table 27) tables. In the `Customer` table, some of the FlowFields that are using FlowFilters are `Balance`, `Balance (LCY)`, `Net Change`, `Net Change (LCY)`, `Sales (LCY)`, and `Profit (LCY)`, where **LCY** stands for **Local Currency**. The `Sales (LCY)` `FlowField` `FlowFilter` usage is shown in the following screenshot:

```
field(66; "Balance Due"; Decimal)
{
    AutoFormatExpression = "Currency Code";
    AutoFormatType = 1;
    CalcFormula = Sum ("Detailed Cust. Ledg. Entry".Amount
    WHERE ("Customer No." = FIELD ("No."),
    "Initial Entry Due Date" = FIELD (UPPERLIMIT ("Date Filter")),
    "Initial Entry Global Dim. 1" = FIELD ("Global Dimension 1 Filter"),
    "Initial Entry Global Dim. 2" = FIELD ("Global Dimension 2 Filter"),
    "Currency Code" = FIELD ("Currency Filter")));
    Caption = 'Balance Due';
    Editable = false;
    FieldClass = FlowField;
}
```

Similarly constructed FlowFields that use FlowFilters in the `Item` table include `Inventory`, `Net Invoiced Qty.`, `Net Change`, and `Purchases (Qty.)`, as well as others.

Throughout the standard code, there are FlowFilters in most of the master table definitions, which includes date filters and global dimension filters (global dimensions are user-defined codes that facilitate the segregation of accounting data by groupings such as divisions, departments, projects, customer type, and so on). Other FlowFilters that are widely used in the standard code are related to inventory activity such as `Location Filter`, `Lot No. Filter`, `Serial No. Filter`, and `Bin Filter`.

The following screenshot shows two fields from the `Customer` table, both with a data type of `Date`. The first field in the screenshot is the `Last Date Modified` field (`FieldClass` is not defined), while the last field in the screenshot is the `Date Filter` field (`FieldClass` of `FlowFilter`):

```
1 reference
field(54; "Last Date Modified"; Date)
{
    Caption = 'Last Date Modified';
    Editable = false;
}
32 references
field(55; "Date Filter"; Date)
{
    Caption = 'Date Filter';
    FieldClass = FlowFilter;
}
```

FlowFields and FlowFilter for our application

In our application, we have decided to have several FlowFields and FlowFilters in `Table 50000 Radio Show`. The reason for these fields is to provide instant analysis for individual shows based on the detailed data stored in subordinate tables. In `Chapter 2`, *Tables*, we showed table `50000` with fields 100 through 130 and 1,090, but didn't provide any information on how those fields should be constructed. Let's go through that construction process now. Here's how fields 100 through 130 and 1,090 should look when we open table `50000` in the table designer. If you didn't add these fields as described in `Chapter 2`, *Tables*, in the *Creating and modifying tables* section, do that now:

```
field(1; "No."; Code[20]) { }
3 references
field(10; "Radio Show Type"; Code[10]) { TableRelation = "Radio Show Type"; }
6 references
field(20; "Name"; Text[50]) { }
3 references
field(40; "Run Time"; Duration) { }
3 references
field(50; "Host Code"; Code[20]) { }
5 references
field(60; "Host Name"; Text[50]) { }
3 references
field(100; "Average Listeners"; Decimal) { }
4 references
field(110; "Audience Share"; Decimal) { }
3 references
field(120; "Advertising Revenue"; Decimal) { }
3 references
field(130; "Royalty Cost"; Decimal) { }
0 references
field(1000; Frequency; Option)
```

The following five fields will be used for statistical analysis for each radio show:

- **Field 100—Average Listeners**: The average number of listeners, as reported by the ratings agency
- **Field 110—Audience Share**: The percentage of the station's total estimated listening audience per time slot
- **Field 120—Advertising Revenue**: The sum total of the advertising revenue generated by show

- **Field 130—Royalty Cost**: The sum total of the royalties incurred by the show by playing copyrighted material
- **Field 1090—Date Filter**: A filter to restrict the data that's calculated for the preceding four fields

To begin with, we will set the calculation properties for the first FlowField, `Average Listeners`:

```
field(100; "Average Listeners"; Decimal)
{
    Editable = false;
    FieldClass = FlowField;
    CalcFormula = average ("Listernership Entry"."Listener Count"
    where ("Radio Show No." = field ("No."), Date = field("Date Filter")));
}
```

Set the `Editable` property to `No`.

The following fields will be used for statistical analysis:

- For field `110`, `Audience Share`, repeat the procedure we just went through, but for field, select `Audience Share` from the `Listenership Entry` field list. Our result should be as follows:

```
field(110; "Audience Share"; Decimal)
{
    Editable = false;
    FieldClass = FlowField;
    CalcFormula = average ("Listernership Entry"."Audience Share"
    where ("Radio Show No." = field ("No."), Date = field ("Date Filter")));
}
```

- For fields `120—Advertising Revenue` and `130—Royalty Cost`, the `FlowField` calculation is a sum with multiple fields that have filters applied.

- For Advertising Revenue, make the method Sum; for table enter, Radio Show Ledger; and set field to Fee Amount:

```
field(120; "Advertising Revenue"; Decimal)
{
    Editable = false;
    FieldClass = FlowField;
    CalcFormula = sum ("Radio Show Entry"."Fee Amount"
    where (
        "Radio Show No." = field ("No."),
        "Data Format" = filter (Advertisement)
        ));
}
```

- Advertisement is an available value of the DataFormat field (data type option). If, in the Radio Show entry, we had typed a value that was not an Option value, such as Commercial, an error message would have displayed, showing us what the available Option choices are:

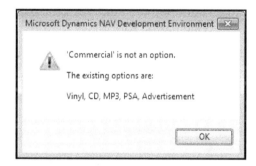

We can use this feature as a development aid when we don't remember what the option values are. We can enter a known incorrect value (such as xxx), press *F11* to compile, and find out all of the correct option values.

Let's start with the compilation:

1. Click **OK** on the **Table Filter** form and **OK** again on the **Calculation Formula** form.
2. Start Royalty Cost in the same way (**method** is Sum), all of the way through the table (table 50005) and **Field** choices in the **Calculation Formula** form. Click on the **Assist Edit** button for the table filter. Just like we did previously, fill in the first **Field** row with a value of **Date**, the **Type** with **FIELD**, and the **Value** with **Date Filter**.

3. Fill in the second row by setting **Field** to Format and **Type** to **FILTER**. In the **Value** column, enter Vinyl|CD|MP3. This means that we will filter for all of the records where the **Format** field contains a value equal to Vinyl, CD, or MP3 (the pipe symbol is translated to the Boolean **OR**). As a result, this FlowField will sum up all of the Fee Amount values that have a **Format** option selected as Vinyl, CD, or MP3, and a date satisfying the **Date Filter** that's specified in the Radio Show table:

4. The last field we will define in this exercise is the Date Filter field. We have already been referencing this Radio Show table field as a source of a user-defined date selection to help to analyze the data for listenership, payable, and revenue, but we haven't defined the field yet. This one is much easier than FlowFields because no calculation formula is required:

```
field(1090; "Date Filter"; Date) { FieldClass = FlowFilter; }
```

Filtering

Filtering is one of the most powerful tools within Business Central. Filtering is the application of defined limits on the data that is to be considered in a process. When we apply a filter to a Normal data field, we only view or process records where the filtered data field satisfies the limits defined by the filter. When we apply a filter to FlowField, the calculated value for that field will only consider data that satisfies the limits defined by the filter.

Filter structures can be applied in at least three different ways, depending on the design of the process:

- The first way is for the developer to fully define the filter structure and the value of the filter. This might be done in a report that's designed to show information on only a selected group of customers, such as those with an unpaid balance. The Customer table would be filtered to report only on customers who have an outstanding balance greater than zero.

- The second way is for the developer to define the filter structure, but allow the user to fill in the specific value to be applied. This approach would be appropriate in an accounting report that has to be tied to specific accounting periods. The user would be allowed to define what periods are to be considered for each report run.
- The third way is the ad hoc definition of a filter structure and value by the user. This approach is often used for the general analysis of ledger data, where the developer wants to give the user total flexibility in how they slice and dice the available data.

It is common to use a combination of the different filtering types. For example, the report we previously mentioned that lists only customers with an open balance (via a developer-defined filter) could also allow the user to define additional filter criteria. If the user wants to see only euro currency customers, they would filter on the customer currency code field.

Filters are an integral part of the implementation of both FlowFields and FlowFilters. These flexible, powerful tools allow the Business Central designer to create pages, reports, and other processes that can be used under a wide variety of circumstances. In most competitive systems, standard user inquiries and processes are quite specific. The Business Central AL toolset allows us to have relatively generic user inquiries and processes, and then allows the user to apply filtering to generate results that fit their specific needs.

The user will see `FlowFilter` filtering referred to as filter totals by onscreen. The application of filters and ranges may give varying results, depending on Windows settings or the SQL Server collation setup. A good set of examples of filtering options and syntax can be found in the *developer and IT pro help* in the section titled *Entering criteria in filters*.

Experimenting with filters

Now, it's time to do some experimenting with filters. We want to accomplish a couple of things through our experimentation. First, we want to get more comfortable with how filters are entered; and second, we want to see the effects of different types of filter structures and combinations. If we had a database with a large volume of data, we could also test the speed of filtering on fields in keys and on fields not in keys. However, the amount of data in the basic CRONUS database is small, so any speed differences will be difficult to see in these tests.

We could experiment on any report that allows filtering. A good report for this experimentation is the **Customer/Item** list. This reports which customer purchased what items. The **Customer/Item** list can be accessed on the role tailored client **Actions** menu via **Reports | Customer | Customer/Item Sales**.

When we initially run **Customer/Item Sales**, we will see just three data fields listed for the entry of filters on the `Customer` table and the `Value Entry` table, as shown in the following screenshot:

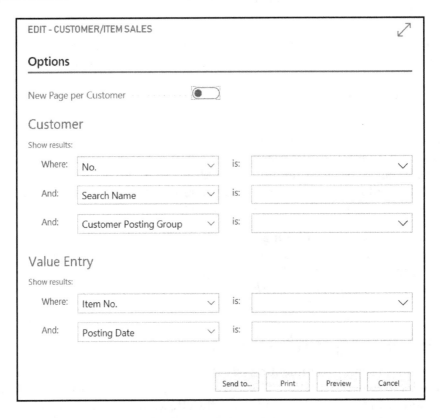

For both **Customer** and **Value Entry**, these are the fields that the developer of this report determined should be emphasized. If we run the report without entering any filter constraints at all and just use the standard Cronus data, the first page of the report will resemble the following:

Customer/Item Sales

Period:
CRONUS International Ltd.
All amounts are in LCY

| | | | | | Total | 71,612.44 | 3,986.42 | 15,084.09 | 21.1 |

Item No.	Description	Invoiced Quantity	Unit of Measure	Amount	Discount Amount	Profit	Profit %
01445544 - Progressive Home Furnishings							
1928-S	AMSTERDAM Lamp	14	PCS	498.41	0.00	109.21	21.90
1988-W	CALGARY Whiteboard, yellow	1	PCS	877.32	97.48	168.72	19.20
1972-S	MUNICH Swivel Chair, yellow	1	PCS	123.30	0.00	27.20	22.10
Progressive Home Furnishings				1,499.03	97.48	305.13	20.40
10000 - The Cannon Group PLC							
1968-S	MEXICO Swivel Chair, black	3	PCS	351.40	18.50	63.10	18.00
1996-S	ATLANTA Whiteboard, base	7	PCS	6,029.56	317.34	1,079.16	17.90
1964-W	INNSBRUCK Storage Unit/G.Door	10	PCS	2,920.00	0.00	1,206.00	41.30
70011	Glass Door	5	PCS	361.50	0.00	177.00	49.00
The Cannon Group PLC				9,662.46	335.84	2,525.26	26.10

20000 - Selangorian Ltd.

If we want to print information only for customers whose names begin with the letter A, our filter will be very simple and similar to the following screenshot:

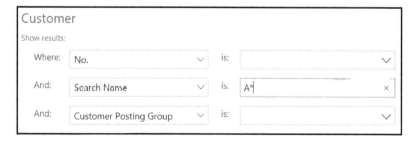

The resulting report will be similar to the following screenshot, showing only the data for the two customers on file whose names begin with the letter A:

Customer/Item Sales

Sunday, September 23, 2018
Page 1 / 1
DESKTOP-AHMVIT0\MARKB

Period:
CRONUS International Ltd.
All amounts are in LCY

Customer: Search Name: A*

Total				6,914.20	588.89	2,191.67	31.7

Item No.	Description	Invoiced Quantity	Unit of Measure	Amount	Discount Amount	Profit	Profit %
32656565 - Antarcticopy							
1968-S	MEXICO Swivel Chair, black	4	PCS	493.20	0.00	108.80	22.10
1960-S	ROME Guest Chair, green	7	PCS	875.70	0.00	193.20	22.10
1976-W	INNSBRUCK Storage Unit/W.Door	5	PCS	1,152.45	128.05	399.45	34.70
70011	Glass Door	1	PCS	61.45	10.84	24.55	40.00
Antarcticopy				2,582.80	138.89	726.00	28.10
49633663 - Autohaus Mielberg KG							
1976-W	INNSBRUCK Storage Unit/W.Door	17.57126	PCS	4,050.00	450.00	1,403.77	34.70
1896-S	ATHENS Desk	0	PCS	0.00	0.00	0.00	0.00
1906-S	ATHENS Mobile Pedestal	1	PCS	281.40	0.00	61.90	22.00
Autohaus Mielberg KG				4,331.40	450.00	1,465.67	33.80

Total				6,914.20	588.89	2,191.67	31.7

If we want to expand the customer fields so that we can apply filters, we can access the full list of other fields in the customer table. We can either click on the drop-down symbol next to a filter field that is not already in use or click on the **Add Filter** button to add a new filter field with drop-down list access. Notice that the lists are in alphabetical order, based on their field names:

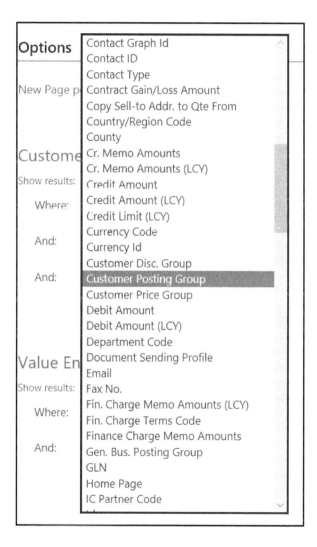

From these lists, we can choose one or more fields and then enter filters on those fields. If we chose **Territory Code**, for example, then the request page would look similar to what's shown in the following screenshot. If we clicked on the lookup arrow in the **Filter** column, a screen would pop up, allowing us to choose from data items in the related table, which, in this case, is **Territories**:

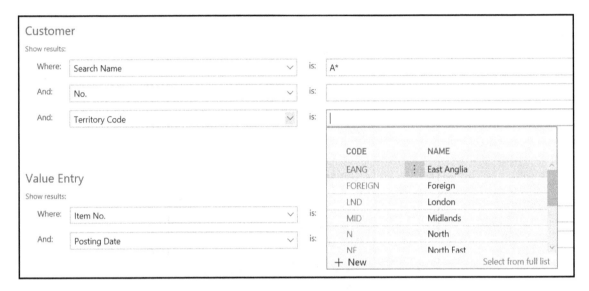

This particular request page has FastTabs for each of the two primary tables in the report. Click on the **Value Entry** FastTab to filter on the item related data. If we filter on the **Item No.** for item numbers that contain the letter W, the report will look similar to the following:

Customer/Item Sales

Period:
CRONUS International Ltd.
All amounts are in LCY

Customer: Search Name: A*
Value Entry: Item No.: *W*

Total		5,202.45	578.05	1,803.22	34.7

Item No.	Description	Invoiced Quantity	Unit of Measure	Amount	Discount Amount	Profit	Profit %
32656565 - Antarcticopy							
1976-W	INNSBRUCK Storage Unit/W.Door	5	PCS	1,152.45	128.05	399.45	34.70
Antarcticopy				1,152.45	128.05	399.45	34.70
49633663 - Autohaus Mielberg KG							
1976-W	INNSBRUCK Storage Unit/W.Door	17.57126	PCS	4,050.00	450.00	1,403.77	34.70
Autohaus Mielberg KG				4,050.00	450.00	1,403.77	34.70
Total				5,202.45	578.05	1,803.22	34.7

If we want to see all of the items containing either the letter W or the letter S, our filter would be *W* | *S*. If we made the filter, W | S, then we would only get entries that are exactly equal to W or to S because we didn't include any wildcards.

You should go back over the various types of filters we discussed and try each one and try them in combination. Get creative! Try some things that you're not sure will work and see what happens. Explore a variety of reports or list pages in the system by applying filters to see the results of your experiments. A good page to apply filters on is the customer list (**Sales | Customers**). This filtering experimentation process is safe (you can't hurt anything or anyone) and is a great learning experience.

Accessing filter controls

When a page such as the customer list is opened, the filter section at the top of the page looks as follows. On the upper-left corner is a place to enter multiple-field filters. This is called **Search**, but the result will be a multi-column filter:

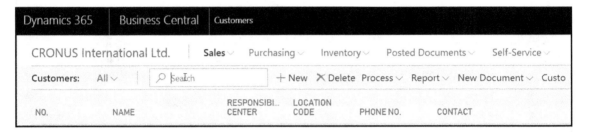

If we click on the **All** button with the chevron button in the upper-left corner to expand the **Filter** pane, the result will look similar to the following. This filter display includes an additional filtering capability, **Filter list by:**, which allows for the entry of filters for the filter totals by type:

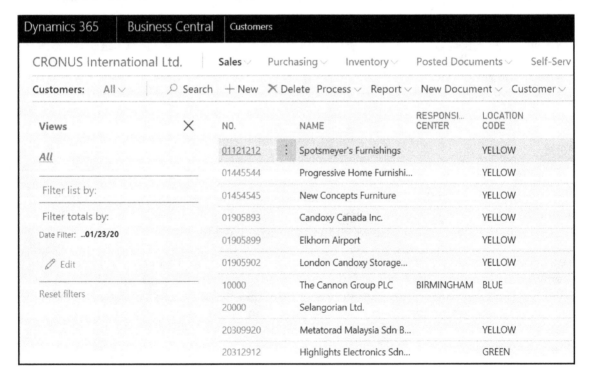

If we apply a filter, the traditional filter icon will appear on the column with a filter, as shown in the following screenshot:

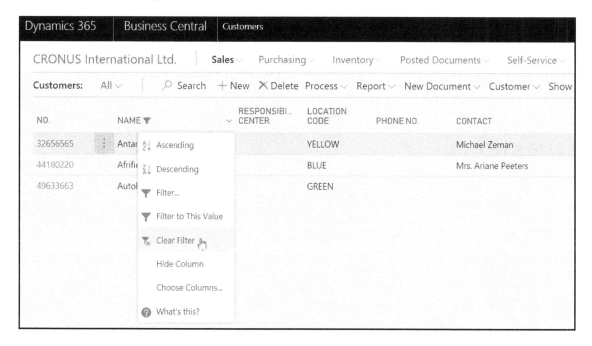

If we click on the filter icon, we can clear the filter. We can also select **Filter to This Value**, which will add a filter with the value of the currently selected row.

Summary

In this chapter, we focused on the basic building blocks of Business Central data structure: fields and their attributes. We reviewed the types of data fields, properties, and trigger elements for each type of field. We walked through a number of examples to illustrate most of these elements, though we have postponed exploring triggers until later, when we have more knowledge of AL. We covered data type and FieldClass properties, which determine what kind of data can be stored in a field.

We reviewed and experimented with the date calculation tool, which gives AL an edge in business applications. We discussed filtering, how filtering is considered as we design our database structure, and how users will access data. Finally, more of our Business Central Radio Show application was constructed.

In the next chapter, we will look at the many different types of pages in more detail. We'll put some of that knowledge to use to further expand our example Business Central application.

Questions

1. The maximum length for an AL field name or variable name is 250 characters long. True or false?

2. The table relation property defines the reference of a data field to a table. The related table data field must be one of the following:

   - In any key in the related table
   - Defined in the related table, but not in a key
   - In the primary key in the related table
   - The first field in the primary key in the related table

3. How many of the following field data types support storing application data such as names and amounts—1, 2, 3, or 4?

   - FlowFilter
   - Editable
   - Normal
   - FlowField

4. The ExtendedDataType property supports the designation of all but one of the following data types for displaying an appropriate action icon (choose the one that isn't supported):

   - Email address
   - Website URL
   - GPS location
   - Telephone number
   - Masked entry

5. One of the following is not a `FlowField` method (choose one):

   - Median
   - Count
   - Max
   - Exist
   - Average

6. It is important to have a consistent, well planned approach to field numbers, especially if the application will use the `TransferFields` function. True or false?

7. Field filters and limit totals cannot be used at the same time. True or false?

8. Which property is used to support the multi-language feature of Business Central (choose one)?

   - Name
   - CaptionML
   - Caption
   - LanguageRef

9. Which of the following are field triggers (choose two)?

   - OnEntry
   - OnValidate
   - OnDeletion
   - OnLookup

10. Which of the following are complex data types (choose three)?

    - Records
    - Strings of text
    - DateFormula
    - DateTime data
    - Objects

11. Every table must have a primary key. A primary key entry can be defined as unique or duplicates allowed, based on a table property. True or false?

12. Text and Code variables can be any length:

    - In a memory variable (working storage)—true or false?
    - In a table field—true or false?

13. FlowField results are not stored in the Business Central table data. True or false?

14. The following two filters are equivalent. True or false?

    - (*W50?|I?5|D*)
    - (I?5) OR (D*) OR (*W50?)

15. Limit totals apply to FlowFilters. True or false?

16. All data types can be used to define data both in tables and in working storage. True or false?

17. DateFormula alpha time units include which of the following (choose two):

    - C for century
    - W for week
    - H for holiday
    - CM for current month

18. FlowFilter data is stored in the database. True or false?

19. Option data is stored as alpha data strings. True or false?

20. Which of the following are numeric data types in Business Central (choose two)?

    - Decimal
    - Option
    - Hexadecimal
    - BLOB

21. Which of the following act as wildcards in Business Central (choose two)?

    - Decimal point (.)
    - Question mark (?)
    - Asterisk (*)
    - Hash mark (#)

Pages - The Interactive Interface

4

"Design is not just what it looks like and feels like. Design is how it works."

– Steve Jobs

"True interactivity is not about clicking on icons or downloading files, it's about encouraging communication."

– Ed Scholssberg

Pages are Business Central's object type for interactively presenting information. The page rendering routines that paint the page on the target display handle much of the data presentation details. This allows a variety of clients to be created by Microsoft, such as a web browser resident client, the Windows RTC client, and a universal client that can be used on all devices, such as phones, tablets, and other platforms (iPad, Android, and Windows). **Independent Software Vendors (ISVs)** have created mobile clients and even clients targeted by devices other than video displays.

One of the benefits of page technology is the focus on the user experience rather than the underlying data structure. As always, the designer/developer has the responsibility of using the tools to their best effect. Another advantage of Business Central pages is the flexibility they provide the user for personalization, allowing them to tailor what is displayed and how it is organized.

In this chapter, we will explore the various types of pages offered by Business Central. We will review many options for format, data access, and tailoring pages. We will also learn about the page designer tools and the inner structures of pages.

We will cover the following topics:

- Page design and structure overview
- Types of pages
- Page designer
- Page components
- Page controls
- Page actions
- WDTU page enhancement exercises

Page design and structure overview

Pages serve the purpose of input, output, and control. They are views of data or process information designed for onscreen display only. They are also user data entry vehicles.

Pages are made up of various combinations of controls, properties, actions, triggers, and AL code, which are briefly explained here:

- **Controls**: These provide the users with ways to view, enter, and edit data; choose options or commands; initiate actions; and view status.
- **Properties**: These are attributes or characteristics of an object that define its state, appearance, or value.
- **Actions**: These are menu items that may be icons.
- **Triggers**: These are predefined functions that are executed when certain actions or events occur.

The internal structure of a page maps to a tree structure, some of which is readily visible in the page designer display while the rest is in the background.

Page design guidelines

Good design practice dictates that enhancements integrate seamlessly with the existing software, unless there is an overwhelming justification for being different. When we add new pages or change existing pages, the changes should have the same look and feel as the original pages, unless the new functionality requires significant differences. This consistency not only makes the user's life easier, it makes support, maintenance, and training more efficient.

There will be instances where we will need to create a significantly different page layout in order to address a special requirement. Maybe we will need to use industry-specific symbols, or we will need to create a screen layout for a special display device. Perhaps, we will create a special dashboard display to report the status of work queues. Even when it will be different, we should continue to be guided by the environment and context in which our new work will operate.

Business Central page structure

Let's take a look at what makes up a typical page in the Business Central web client. The page in the following screenshot includes a list page at its core (the content area):

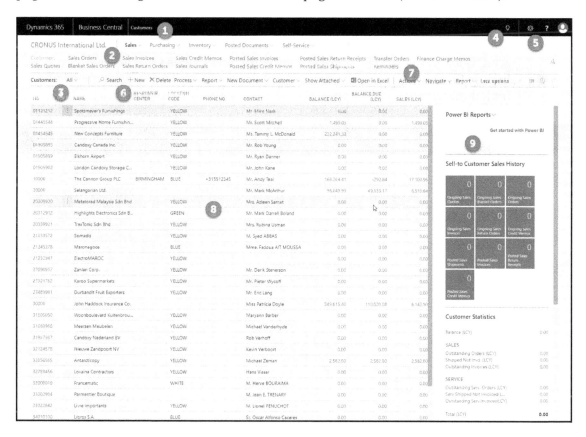

Here is a brief description of all of these options:

- The title bar (**1**) displays page caption and product identification.
- The company indicator (**2**) acts as a home button. It allows the user to navigate to the Role Center or to refresh the Role Center depending on where the user is at the moment of using the link:

- The filter button is where the user controls the filtering to be applied to the page display.
- If we click on the down-facing arrowheads in the filter button, child menu options will be displayed in a drop-down list, as shown in the following screenshot. The same list of options subordinate to **Sales Orders** is displayed both in the drop-down menu from the filter button and in the detailed list of options in the navigation pane:

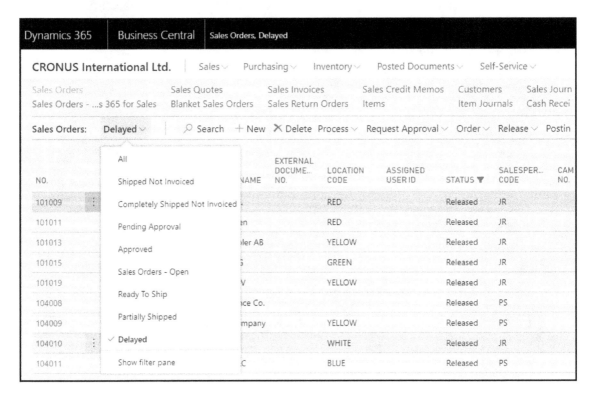

- The search field (**4**) allows users to find pages, reports, or views based on the object's name (full or partial):

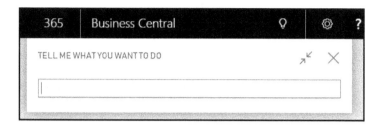

- The settings button (**5**) provides access to a general set of menu options. It provides access to some basic application information and administration functions, as shown in the following screenshot:

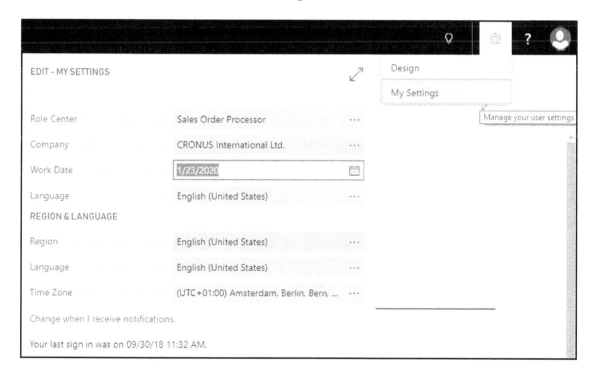

- The ribbon (**6**) contains shortcut icons to actions. These same commands will be duplicated in other menu locations, but are in the ribbon for quick and easy access. The ribbon can be collapsed (made not visible) or expanded (made visible) under user control.

- The navigation pane (**7**) contains menu options based on the active Role Center, which is tied to the user's login.
- The content area (**8**) is the focus of the page. It may be a Role Center, a list page, or a department menu list.
- The FactBox pane (**9**) can appear on the right side of certain page types, such as card, list, List Plus, document, navigate, or worksheet. A FactBox can only display a Card Part, list part, system part, or a limited set of predefined charts. FactBoxes can provide no-click and one-click access to related information about the relevant data in the content area.

Types of pages

Let's review the types of pages available for use in an application. Then, we will create several examples for our WDTU `Radio Station` system.

Each time we work on an application design, we will carefully need to consider which page type is best to use for the functionality we are creating. Types of pages available include Role Center, HeadlinePart, list, card, List Part, Card Part, List Plus, document, worksheet, navigate page, ConfirmationDialog, and StandardDialog. Pages can be created and modified by the developer and can be personalized by the administrator, superuser, or user.

Role Center page

Users are each assigned a Role Center page as their home page in Business Central—the page where they land when first logging into Business Central. The purpose of a Role Center page is to provide a task-oriented home base that focuses on the tasks that the user typically needs in order to do his/her job on a day-to-day basis. Common tasks for any user should be no more than one or two clicks away.

The standard Business Central distribution includes predefined Role Center pages, including generic roles such as the bookkeeper, sales manager, and production planner. Some of the provided Role Centers are richly featured and have been heavily tailored by Microsoft as illustrations of what is possible. On the other hand, some of the provided Role Centers are only skeletons, acting essentially as placeholders.

It is critical to understand that the provided Role Center pages are intended to be templates, not final deliverables.

Central to each Role Center page is the activities area. The activities area provides the user with a visual overview of their primary tasks. Within the activities area are the cues. Each blue cue icon (containing a document symbol) represents a filtered list of documents in a particular status, indicating an amount of work to be handled by the user. The grey cue icons (with no document symbol) display a calculated value.

The following screenshot shows a Role Center page for the user role profile of a sales order processor:

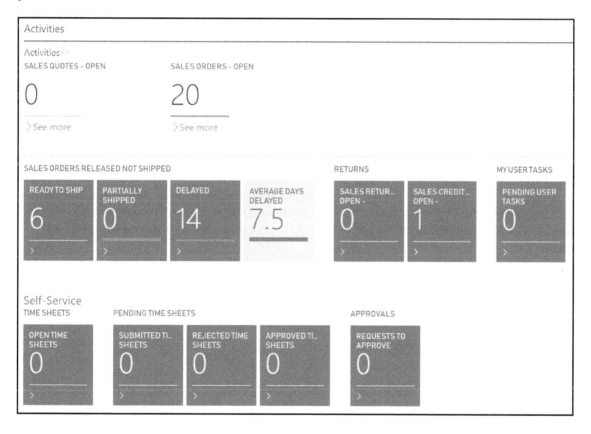

HeadlinePart page

HeadlinePart pages are embedded in the Role Center similar to activities. The part is designed to give the user insight into how the company is performing using the most important **Key Performance Indicators** (**KPIs**). As an option, machine learning can be used to provide predictive analytics:

INSIGHT FROM LAST WEEK

The largest posted sales invoice was for kr114,729

List page

List pages are the first pages accessed when choosing any menu option to access data. This includes all of the entries under the buttons on the navigation pane. A list page displays a list of records (rows), one line per record, with each displayed data field in a column.

When a list page is initially selected, it is not editable. When we click on the vertical dots an entry in a list, either an editable card page or an editable list page entry is displayed. Examples of this latter behavior are the reference table pages, such as **postcodes**, **territories**, and **languages**. A list page can also be used to show a list of master records to allow the user to visually scan through the list of records or to easily choose a record on which to focus.

List pages may optionally include FactBoxes. Some Business Central list pages, such as customer ledger entries, allow editing of some fields (for example, invoice due dates) and not of other fields.

The following screenshot shows a typical list page—the **Items** list page:

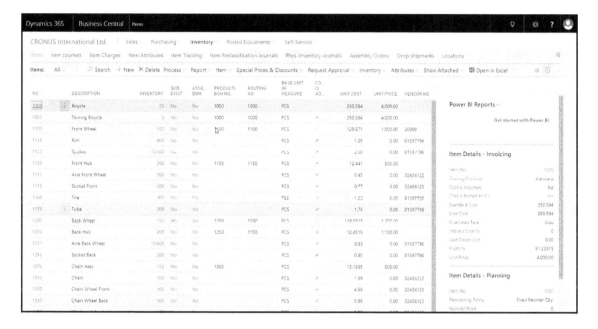

Card page

Card pages display and allow updating of a single record at a time. Card pages are used for master tables and setup data. Complex cards can contain multiple FastTabs and FactBoxes, as well as display data from subordinate tables. For example, a card page image for the **Customer Card**, page 21, follows with the **General** and **Shipping** FastTab expanded and the other FastTabs (**Address & Contact**, **Invoicing**, and **Payments**) collapsed:

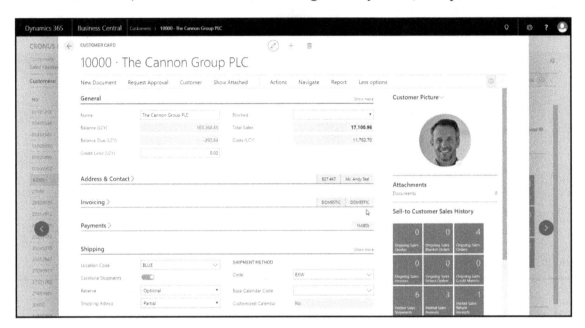

Document page

Document (task) pages have at least two FastTabs in a header/detail format. The FastTab at the top contains the header fields in a card style format, followed by a FastTab containing multiple records in a list style format (a List Part page). Some examples are **Sales Orders**, **Sales Invoices**, **Purchase Orders**, **Purchase Invoices**, and **Production Orders**. The document page type is appropriate whenever we have a parent record tied to subordinate child records in a one-to-many relationship. A document page may also have FactBoxes. An example, the **SALES ORDER** document page follows with two FastTabs expanded and four FastTabs collapsed:

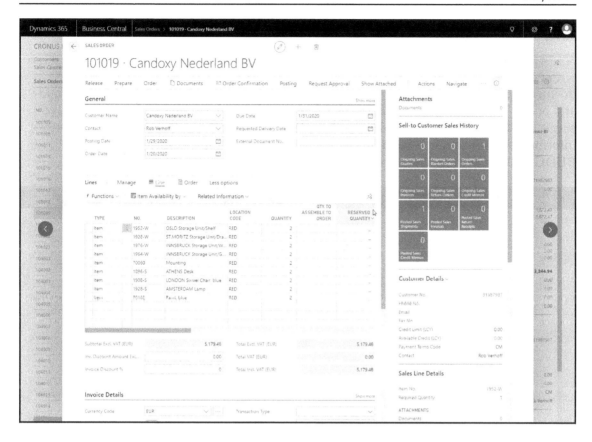

FastTabs

FastTabs, as shown in the preceding **CUSTOMER CARD** and **SALES ORDER** screenshots, are collapsible/expandable replacements for traditional left-to-right form tabs. FastTabs are often used to segregate data by subject area on a card page or a document page. In the preceding screenshot, the **General** and **Lines** FastTabs are expanded and the remaining FastTabs are collapsed. Individually-important fields can be promoted so that they display on the FastTab header when the tab is collapsed, allowing the user to see this data with minimal effort. Examples appear on the **Sales Orders** collapsed **Invoice Details** and **Prepayment** FastTabs. Promoted field displays disappear from the FastTab header when the FastTab is expanded.

List Plus page

A List Plus page is similar in layout to a document page as it will have at least one FastTab with fields in a card type format and one FastTab with a list page format. Unlike a document page, a List Plus page may have more than one FastTab with card format fields and one or more FastTabs with a list page format, while a document page can only have a single list style subpage. The card format portion of a List Plus page often contains control information determining what data is displayed in the associated list, such as in page 113, **BUDGET**, which is shown in the following screenshot:

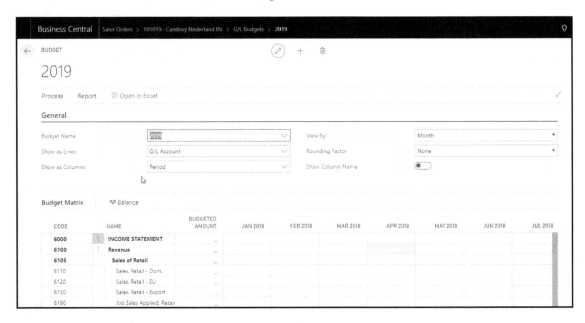

A List Plus page may also have FactBoxes. Other examples of List Plus pages are page 155, **Customer Sales**, and page 157, **Item Availability by Periods**.

Worksheet (journal) page

Worksheet pages are widely used in Business Central to enter transactions. The worksheet page format consists of a List page style section showing multiple record lines in the content area, followed by a section containing either additional detail fields for the line in focus or containing totals. All of the journals in Business Central use worksheet pages. Data is usually entered into a journal/worksheet by keyboard entry, but in some cases via a batch process.

The following screenshot shows a worksheet page, **Sales Journals**—page 253:

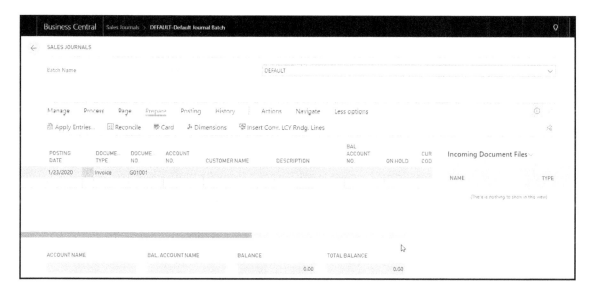

ConfirmationDialog page

This is a simple display page embedded in a process. It is used to allow a user to control the flow of a process. A sample ConfirmationDialog page is shown in the following screenshot:

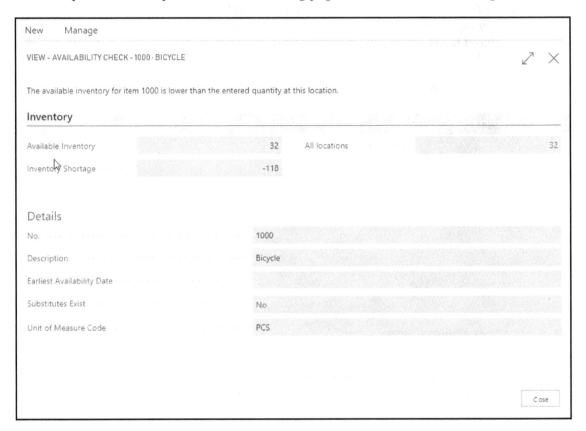

StandardDialog page

The StandardDialog page is also a simple page format to allow the user to control a process, such as **Copy Tax Setup** (page 476). The StandardDialog page allows the entry of control data, such as that shown in the following screenshot:

Navigate page

The primary use of the **navigate** page type in Business Central is as the basis for some wizard pages. With Business Central, Microsoft introduced a new application feature called **Assisted Setup**. This feature uses many wizard pages. A wizard page consists of multiple user data entry screens linked together to provide a series of steps necessary to complete a task. The following screenshot shows assisted email setup:

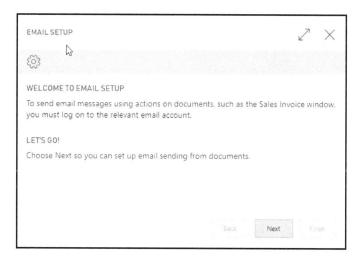

Navigate function

The **navigate function** has been a very powerful and unique feature of Business Central since the 1990s. Somewhat confusingly, in Business Central, the navigate function is implemented using the worksheet page type, not the navigate page type, which was used in earlier Business Central releases.

The navigate page (page 344) allows the user, who may be a developer operating in user mode, to view a summary of the number and type of posted entries having the same document number and posting date as a related entry or as a user-entered value. The user can drill down to examine the individual entries. Navigate is a terrific tool for tracking down related posted entries. It can be productively used by a user, an auditor, or even a developer. A sample **NAVIGATE** page is shown in the following screenshot:

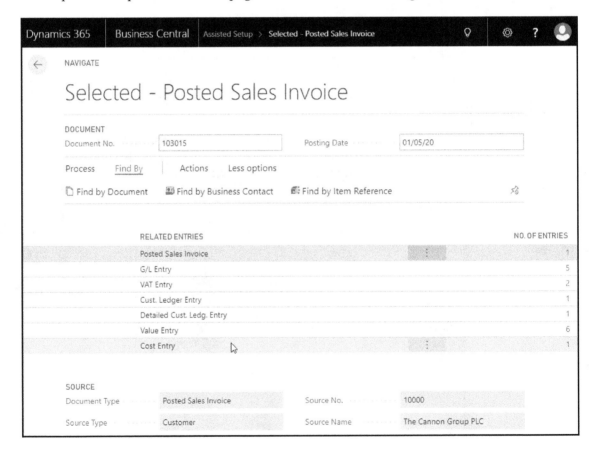

Request page

A **request page** is a simple page that allows the user to enter information to control the execution of a report or XMLport object. Request pages can have multiple FastTabs, but can only be created as part of a report or XMLport object. All request page designs will be similar to the following screenshot for the Item **PRICE LIST** (report 715) request page:

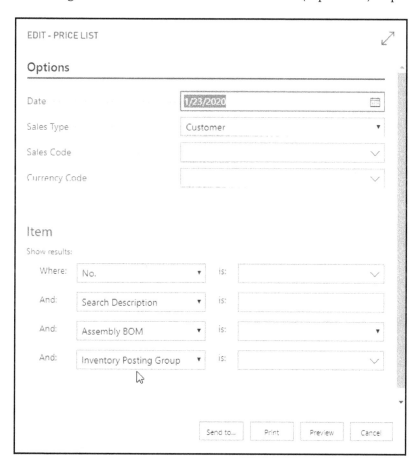

Page parts

Several of the page types we have reviewed so far contain multiple panes, with each pane including special purpose parts. Let's look at some of the component page parts available to the developer.

Some page parts compute the displayed data on the fly, taking advantage of **FlowFields** that may require considerable system resources to process the FlowField calculations. As developers, we must be careful about causing performance problems through overuse of such displays.

FactBox area

The **FactBox** area can be defined on the right side of certain page types, including card, list, List Plus, document, and worksheet. A FactBox area can contain page parts (Card Part or List Part), chart parts, and system parts (notes, MyNotes, or record links). A variety of standard Card Parts, List Parts, and charts that can be used in FactBoxes are available. System parts cannot be modified. All of the others can be enhanced from the standard instances, or new ones may be created from scratch.

Card Parts and List Parts

Card Parts are used for FactBoxes that don't require a list. Card Parts display fields or perhaps a picture control. (Business Central Help contains an example of including a .NET add-in within a FactBox to display a chart). An example of the **Customer Statistics** FactBox (page 9,082—**Customer Statistics** Factbox) is shown in the following screenshot:

Customer Statistics	
Balance (LCY)	13,732.60
SALES	
Outstanding Orders (LCY)	143,011.80
Shipped Not Invd. (LCY)	0.00
Outstanding Invoices (LCY)	0.00
SERVICE	
Outstanding Serv. Orders (LCY)	0.00
Serv Shipped Not Invoiced(L...	0.00
Outstanding Serv.Invoices(LCY)	0.00
Total (LCY)	**156,744.40**
Credit Limit (LCY)	0.00
Overdue Amounts (LCY) as of...	0.00
Total Sales (LCY)	13,732.60
Invoiced Prepayment Amoun...	0.00

List Parts are used for FactBoxes that require a list. A list is defined as columns of repeated data. No more than two or three columns should appear in a FactBox list. The following screenshot shows the three column **My Items** FactBox List Part (page 9,152):

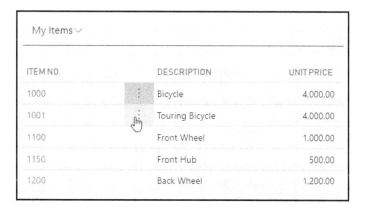

Charts

The Business Central distribution includes a charting capability that is based on a control add-in created with .NET code written outside of AL and integrated into Business Central. An example is the **Trailing Sales Orders** chart in a Factbox page part (page 760) that appears in the **Order Processor Role Center** (page 9,006). The following screenshot is of that chart:

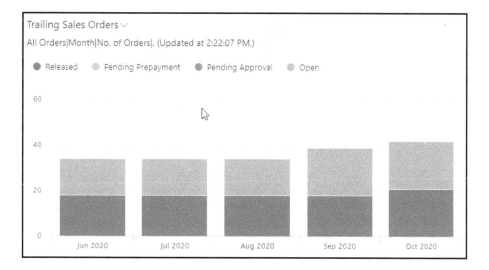

The *Cash Flow Chart Example* article (`https://docs.microsoft.com/en-us/previous-versions/dynamicsnav-2016/hh169415(v=nav.90)`) in the Business Central *Developer and IT-pro* help describes how to create charts using the chart control add-in.

Page names

Card pages are named similarly to the table with which they are associated, with the addition of the word "Card," for example, Customer table and Customer Card, Item table and Item Card, Vendor table and Vendor Card.

List pages are named similarly to the table with which they are associated. List pages that are simple not-editable lists have the word "List" associated with the table name, for example, Customer List, Item List, and Vendor List. For each of these, the table also has an associated card page. Where the table has no associated card page, the list pages are named after the tables, but in the plural format, for example, Customer Ledger Entry table and Customer Ledger Entries page, Check Ledger Entry table and Check Ledger Entries page, Country/Region table and Countries/Regions page, and Production Forecast Name table and Production Forecast Names page.

The single-record setup tables that are used for application control information throughout Business Central are named after their functional area, with the addition of the word "Setup." The associated Card page should also be, and generally is, named similarly to the table, for example, General Ledger Setup table and General Ledger Setup page, Manufacturing Setup table and Manufacturing Setup page, and so on.

Journal entry (worksheet) pages are given names tied to their purpose, with the addition of the word "Journal." In the standard product, several journal pages for different purposes are associated with the same table. For example, the Sales Journal, Cash Receipts Journal, Purchases Journal, and Payments Journal all use the General Journal Line table as their source table (they are different pages all tied to the same table).

If there is a header and line table associated with a data category, such as **Sales Orders**, the related page and subpage ideally should be named to describe the relationship between the tables and the pages. However, in some cases, it's better to tie the page names directly to the function they perform rather than the underlying tables. An example is the two pages making up the display called by the Sales Order menu entry—the **Sales Orders** page is tied to the `Sales Header` table, and the Sales Order subform page is tied to the `Sales Line` table. The same tables are involved for the Sales Invoice page and **Sales Invoice** subform page.

The use of the word subform rather than subpage, as in Sales Invoice subform, is a leftover from previous versions of Business Central, which had forms rather than pages. We are hopeful Microsoft will eventually fix this historical artifact and rename these pages subpages.

Sometimes, while naming pages, we will have a conflict between naming pages based on the associated tables and naming them based on the use of the data. For example, the menu entry Contacts invokes a main page/subpage named Contact Card and Contact Card subform. The respective tables are the Contact table and the **Contact Profile Answer table**. The context usage should take precedence in the page naming as was done here.

In-client designer

The in-client designer is accessed from within the web client, through **Settings | Design**. The page designer can be opened from anywhere in the application, but its use may be limited in some areas:

Designer

When we are in design mode and click on any part, it will highlight the section, as you can see in the following screenshot:

We can proceed to select a specific control within the section and choose to remove it:

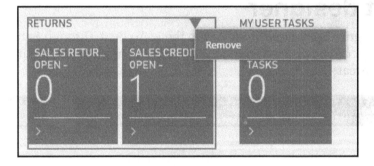

If we select a FastTab, we can change the name, for example, to **Customer**.

When we click on the more button in the designer and select **+ Field**, we will get a list of controls that can be added to the page, which we can drag and drop into the page:

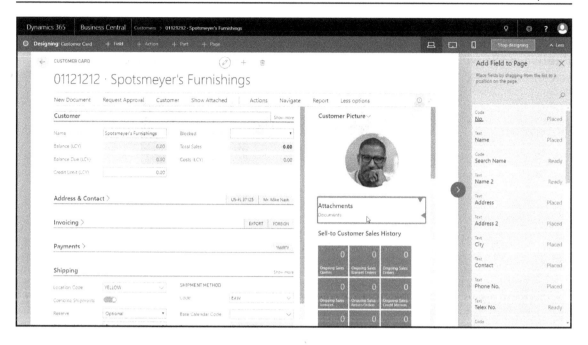

When we move the **Name 2** field into the newly renamed **Customer** tab, we can drop it right under the **Name** field:

Once we have done all of the work that is feasible within the in-client designer, we will click on **Stop designing**. The in-client designer will ask for an **Extension Name** and **Publisher**. We will select **Download Code** and click **Save**, as shown in the following screenshot:

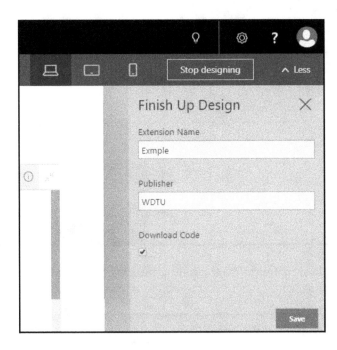

In the web browser (in our case, Google Chrome), a downloaded ZIP file will pop up that we have to save somewhere on our local computer:

The next step is to unzip the file into a folder and look at the contents. With a little bit of luck, you will recognize the structure as an extension that we can open in Visual Studio Code:

Name	Type	Compressed size	Password ...	Size	Ratio	Date modified
.vscode	File folder					
app.json	JSON File	1 KB	No	3 KB	66%	30-9-2018 14:53
PageExtension50100.al	AL File	1 KB	No	1 KB	24%	30-9-2018 14:53
PageExtension50101.al	AL File	1 KB	No	1 KB	40%	30-9-2018 14:53

When we open the extension in Visual Studio Code, we see that each page we changed using the in-client designer has a file. If we open the file that is related to the customer card, in our case, `PageExtension50101.al`, we can see exactly what we did. We can see the modification of the `General` tab and the adding of the `Name 2` field:

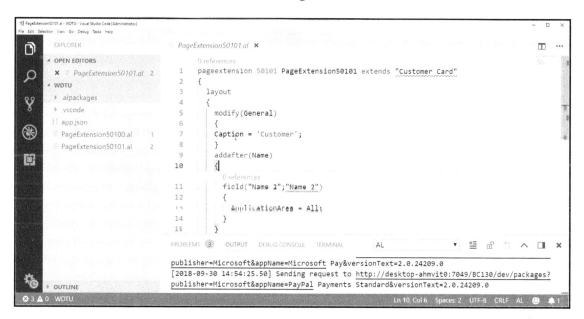

 Using the in-client designer together with Visual Studio Code is a great way to learn the technical notation (syntax) for page modification.

Page components

All pages are made up of certain common components. The basic elements of a page object are the page triggers, page properties, controls, control triggers, and control properties.

Page triggers

The following screenshot shows page triggers. The **Help** section's **Page and Action Triggers** provides good general guidance to the events that cause each page trigger to fire. Note that the **OnQueryClosePage** trigger isn't related to any query object action:

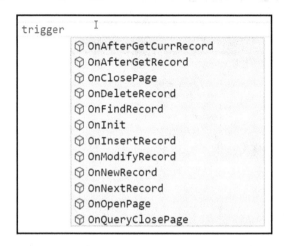

In general, according to best practices, we should minimize the AL code placed in page triggers, putting code in a table or field trigger or calling a codeunit library function instead. However, many standard pages include a modest amount of code supporting page-specific filter or display functions. When we develop a new page, it's always a good idea to look for similar pages in the standard product and be guided by how those pages operate internally. Sometimes, special display requirements result in complex code being required within a page. It is important that the code in a page be used only to manage the data display, not for data modification.

To execute AL code in pages, you can also use events. Each page object automatically generates events that you can subscribe to. Using events is preferred when adding code to page objects shipped by Microsoft to avoid any merge challenges when Microsoft changes the page in a new release.

Page properties

We will now look at the properties of the **Radio Show List** page we created earlier. The list of available page properties is the same for all page types. The values of those properties vary considerably from one page to another, even more from one page type to another. The following screenshot shows a subset of the possible properties using *Ctrl* + spacebar in our `Radio Show List` **page** (page 50100):

```
 1  page 50100 "Radio Show List"
 2  {
 3      PageType = List;
 4      SourceTable = "Radio Show";
 5      ApplicationArea = Basic;
 6      UsageCategory = Lists;
 7
 8
 9   🔧 CaptionML
     🔧 CardPageId
10   🔧 ChangeTrackingAllowed
11   🔧 DataCaptionExpression
     🔧 DataCaptionFields
12   🔧 DelayedInsert
13   🔧 DeleteAllowed
     🔧 Description
14   🔧 Editable
     🔧 EntityName
15   🔧 EntitySetName
```

We can see that many of these properties are still in their default condition (they are not shown in bold letters). The following are the properties with which we are most likely to be concerned:

- `Caption` and `CaptionML`: This is the page name to be displayed, depending on the language option in use.
- `Editable`: This determines whether or not the controls in the page can be edited (assuming the table's editable properties are also set to `Yes`). If this property is set to `Yes`, the page allows the individual control to determine the appropriate editable property value.
- `Description`: This is for internal documentation only.

- `Permissions`: This is used to instruct the system to allow the users of this page to have certain levels of access (`r` to read, `i` to insert, `m` to modify, and `d` to delete) to the table data in the specified table objects. For example, users of page 499 (**Available - Sales Lines**) are allowed to only read or modify (permissions for `Sales Line` equal to `rm`) the data in the `Sales Line` table.

> Whenever defining special permissions, be sure to test with an end-user license. In fact, it's always important to test with an end-user license.

- `PageType`: This specifies how this page will be displayed using one of the available ten page types: Role Center, card, list, List Plus, Worksheet, Confirmation Dialog, Standard Dialog, Navigate page, Card Part, List Part.
- `CardPageID`: This is the ID of the card page that should be launched when the user double-clicks on an entry in the list. This is only used on List pages.
- `RefreshOnActivate`: When this is set to `Yes`, it causes the page to refresh when the page is activated. This property is unsupported by the web client.
- `PromotedActionCategoriesML`: This allows changing the language for promoted `ActionCategories` from the default English (ENU) to another language or to extend the number of promoted `ActionCategories` from the standard three options—**New**, **Process**, and **Reports**—to add up to seven more categories. See the **Help** section, *How to: Define Promoted Action Categories Captions for the Ribbon*.
- `SourceTable`: This is the name of the table to which the page is bound.
- `SourceTableView`: This can be utilized to automatically apply defined filters and/or open the page with a key other than the primary key.
- `ShowFilter`: This is set to `No` to make the filter pane default to `Not Visible`. The user can still make the filter pane visible.
- `DelayedInsert`: This delays the insertion of a new record until the user moves focus away from the new line being entered. If this value is `No`, then a new record will automatically be inserted into the table as soon as the primary key fields are completed. This property is generally set to `Yes` when `AutoSplitKey` (see following) is set to `Yes`. It allows complex new data records to be entered with all of the necessary fields completed.
- `MultipleNewLines`: When set to `Yes`, this property supposedly allows the insertion of multiple new lines between existing records. However, it is set to `No` in the standard order forms from Microsoft. This indicates that this property is no longer active in Business Central.

- `SaveValues`: If set to `Yes`, this causes user-specific entered control values to be retained and redisplayed when the page is invoked another time.
- `AutoSplitKey`: This allows for the automatic assignment of a primary key, provided the last field in the primary key is an integer; there are rare exceptions to this, but we won't worry about them in this book. This feature enables each new entry to be assigned a key so it will remain sequenced in the table following the record appearing above it. Note that `AutoSplitKey` and `DelayedInsert` are generally used jointly. On a new entry, at the end of a list of entries, the trailing integer portion of the primary key, often named `Line No`, is automatically incremented by 10,000 (the increment value cannot be changed). When a new entry is inserted between two previously existing entries, their current key-terminating integer values are summed and divided by two (hence, the term `AutoSplitKey`) with the resultant value being used for the new entry key-terminating integer value. Because 10,000 (the automatic increment) can only be divided by two and rounded to a non-zero integer result 13 times, only 13 new automatically numbered entries can be inserted between two previously recorded entries by the `AutoSplitKey` function.
- `SourceTableTemporary`: This allows the use of a temporary table as the source table for the page. This can be very useful where there is a need to display data based on the structure of a table, but not using the table data as it persists in the database. Examples of such application usage are in page 634—**Chart of Accounts Overview** and page 6510—**Item Tracking Lines**. Note that the temporary instance of the source table is empty when the page opens up, so our code must populate the temporary table in memory.

Inheritance

One of the attributes of an object-oriented system is the inheritance of properties. While Business Central is object based rather than object oriented, the properties that affect data validation are inherited. Properties such as decimal formatting are also inherited. If a property is explicitly defined in the table, it cannot be less restrictively defined elsewhere.

Controls that are bound to a table field will inherit the settings of the properties that are common to both the field definition and the control definition. This basic concept applies to inheritance of data properties, beginning from fields in tables to pages and reports, and then from pages and reports to controls within pages and reports. Inherited property settings that involve data validation cannot be overridden, but all others can be changed. This is another example of why it is generally best to define the properties in the table for consistency and ease of maintenance, rather than defining them for each instance of use in a page or a report.

WDTU page enhancement – part 1

Before we move on to learn about controls and actions, let's do some basic enhancement work on our WDTU Radio Show application. In Chapter 1, *Introduction to Business Central*, in the *Getting started with application design* section, we created several minimal pages, and later added new fields to our Radio Show master table (table 50100). We'll now enhance the Radio Show's list and card page to include those added fields.

Because our previous page development work resulted in simple pages, we have the opportunity to decide whether we want to start with a new page snippet and replace our original pages or use the page designer to modify the original pages. If we had done any significant work on these pages previously in the page designer, the choice to go right to the page designer would be easy. Let's do a quick evaluation to help us to make our decision. First, let's take a look at the existing **Radio Show List** page:

We want to compare the list of fields that exist in the source table (Radio Show—50100) to what we see is already in the page. If there are only a couple of fields missing, it will be more efficient to do our work in the page designer. The quickest way to inspect the fields of the source table is to use the **Open to the Side** option in the list available from the drop-down menu when clicking on a file in Visual Studio Code, as shown in the following screenshot:

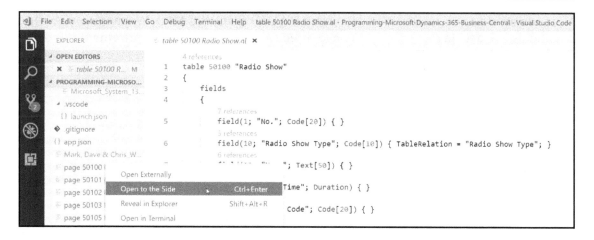

This allows us to compare the page fields and table fields side-by-side and examine whether only a few fields are missing:

Note that the `Date Filter` field cannot be placed on the page. This is a virtual field that is meant for users to limit totals by using the filter pane.

Next, we want to also create a new layout for **RADIO SHOW CARD**. When we review the data fields, we decide that we should have three FastTabs: **General**, **Requirements**, and **Statistics**. As before, the **Date Filter** field should not be on the page. After we have generated, compiled, and saved our new **RADIO SHOW CARD**, it will look like this:

RADIO SHOW CARD	⟋ + 🗑		
RS001			
Show Attached			⤢
General			
No.	RS001	Frequency	0
Radio Show Type	TALK	Host Code	CECE
Name	CeCe and Friends	Host Name	CeCe Grace
Run Time	2 hours		
Requirements			
PSA Planned Quantity	0	Sports Required	⬤
Ads Planned Quantity	0	Sports Duration	
News Required	⬤	Weather Required	⬤
News Duration		Weather Duration	
Statistics			
Average Listeners	0.00	Advertising Revenue	0.00
Audience Share	0.00	Royalty Cost	0.00

Our final step at this point is to connect the **RADIO SHOW CARD** to the **Radio Show List** page, so that when the user double-clicks on a list entry, the card page will be invoked, showing the list-selected entry. This is a simple matter of adding `CardPageId` to the list of properties. Fill in that property with either the name (`Radio Show Card`) or object ID number (`50101`) of the target card, then save, compile, and run it:

```
page 50100 "Radio Show List"
{
    PageType = List;
    SourceTable = "Radio Show";
    ApplicationArea = Basic;
    UsageCategory = Lists;
    CardPageId = "Radio Show Card";

    layout
    {
```

We should see a ribbon with both **Edit** and **Edit List**, as shown in the following screenshot:

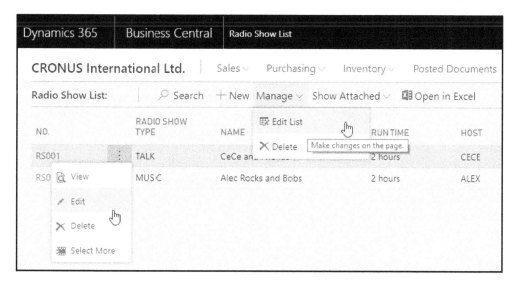

Clicking on **Edit** will bring up **Radio Show Card**. Clicking on **Edit List** will make the line in the list editable in place within the List page. If we don't want the user to be able to edit within the list, we should change the List page property from **Editable** to **No**, and the **Edit List** option will not be available, as shown in the following screenshot:

Dynamics 365	Business Central	Radio Show List				

CRONUS International Ltd. | Sales ∨   Purchasing ∨   Inventory ∨   Posted Documents ∨   Self-Service ∨

Radio Show List: 🔍 Search   + New   ✕ Delete   Show Attached ∨   📊 Open in Excel

NO.	RADIO SHOW TYPE	NAME	RUN TIME	HOST CODE	HOST NAME
RS001	⋮ TALK	CeCe and Friends	2 hours	CECE	CeCe Grace
RS002	MUSIC	Alec Rocks and Bobs	2 hours	ALEX	Alec Benito

Page controls

Controls on pages serve a variety of purposes. Some controls display information on pages. This can be data from the database, static material, pictures, or the results of an AL expression. Container controls can contain other controls. **Group** controls make it easy for the developer to handle a set of contained controls as a group. A FastTabs control also makes it easy for the user to consider a set of controls as a group. The user can make all of the controls on FastTabs visible or invisible by expanding or collapsing the FastTabs. The user also has the option to show or not to show a particular FastTab as a part of the page customizing capability. The **Help** section's **Pages Overview** and **How to: Create a Page** provide good background guidance on the organization of controls within page types for Business Central.

The following screenshot from the page designer shows all of the data controls on `page 5600 "Fixed Asset Card"`. The first column, `Expanded`, is a + or –, indicating whether the section is expanded or not. Type and subtype define how this control is interpreted by the RTC:

```
page 5600 "Fixed Asset Card"
{
  layout
  {
    area(Content)
    {
      group(General)
      {
        field("No.";"No.")
        {
        }
        field(Description;Description)
        {
        }
        group(Control34)
        { ...
        }
        field("FA Location Code";"FA Location Code")
        {
        }
        field("Budgeted Asset";"Budgeted Asset")
        {
        }
        field("Serial No.";"Serial No.")
        {
        }
        field("Main Asset/Component";"Main Asset/Component")
        {
        }
        field("Component of Main Asset";"Component of Main Asset")
```

The page's control structure can be seen in the indented format shown in the preceding screenshot. The container controls define the primary parts of the page structure. The next level of structure is the `group` control level. In this page, those are the general, depreciation book, and maintenance groups, each of which represents a FastTab. Indented under each `group` control are the `field` controls.

The **FIXED ASSET CARD** page, including the action ribbon, is displayed in the following screenshot:

Control types

There are four primary types of page controls: container, group, field, and part. Container, group, and field controls are used to define the content area of pages. Part controls are used to define FactBoxes and embedded subpages. When designing pages that may be used by different client types, such as the web client, we need to be aware that some controls operate differently or are not supported in all clients. Each customized page should be thoroughly tested in each client environment where it may be used.

Container controls

Container controls can be one of three subtypes: `ContentArea`, `FactBoxArea`, or `RoleCenterArea`. Container controls define the root-level primary structures within a page. All page types start with a container control. The `RoleCenterArea` container control can only be used on a Role Center page type. A page can only have one instance of each container subtype.

group controls

The `group` controls provide the second level of structure within a page. The `group` controls are the home for fields. Almost every page has at least one `group` control. The following screenshot from `page 5600 Fixed Asset Card`, with all of the `group` controls collapsed, shows two container controls and three `group` controls. Also showing is a page `part` control that displays a page `part` as a FastTab:

```
page 5600 "Fixed Asset Card"
{
  layout
  {
    area(Content)
    {
      group(General)
      { ...
      }
      group("Depreciation Book")
      { ...
      }                                    I
      part(DepreciationBook;"FA Depreciation Books Subform")
      {
      }
      group(Maintenance)
      { ...
      }
    }
    area(FactBoxes)
    {
      part(FixedAssetPicture;"Fixed Asset Picture")
```

The properties of a `group` control are shown in the following screenshot:

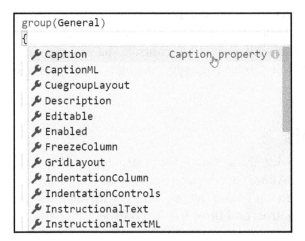

Several of the `group` control properties are particularly significant because of their effect on all of the fields within the group.

- `Visible`: This can be TRUE or FALSE, defaulting to TRUE. The `Visible` property can be assigned a Boolean expression, which can be evaluated during processing. This allows to dynamically change the visibility of a group of fields during the processing, based on some variable conditions (dynamic processing must occur in either the `OnInit`, `OnOpenPage`, or `OnAfterGetCurrRecord` trigger, and the variable must have its `IncludeInDataSet` property set to `Yes`).

- `Enabled`: This can be TRUE or FALSE, defaulting to TRUE. The `Enabled` property can be assigned a Boolean expression to allow dynamically changing the enabling of a group of fields.

- `Editable`: This can be TRUE or FALSE, defaulting to TRUE. The `Editable` property can be assigned a Boolean expression to allow dynamically changing the editability of a group of fields.

- GroupType: This can be one of the five choices: group, repeater, cuegroup, FixedLayout, or GridLayout. The GroupType property is visible on the page designer screen in the column headed SubType (see the preceding page designer screenshot):
  - group: This is used in card type pages as the general structure for fields, which are then displayed in the sequence in which they appear in the page designer group.
  - repeater: This is used in List-type pages as the structure within which fields are defined and then displayed as repeated rows.
  - cuegroup: This is used for Role Center pages as the structure for the actions that are the primary focus of a user's work day. cuegroup are found in page parts, typically having the word Activities in their name and included in Role Center page definitions. The following screenshot shows two cuegroup instances defined in the page designer:

```
page 9060 "SO Processor Activities"
{
  layout
  {
    area(Content)
    {
      cuegroup("For Release")
      { ...
      }
      cuegroup("Sales Orders Released Not Shipped")
      { ...
      }
      cuegroup(Returns)
      { ...
      }
      cuegroup("Document Exchange Service")
```

These two `cuegroup` instances are shown displayed in the following Role Center screenshot:

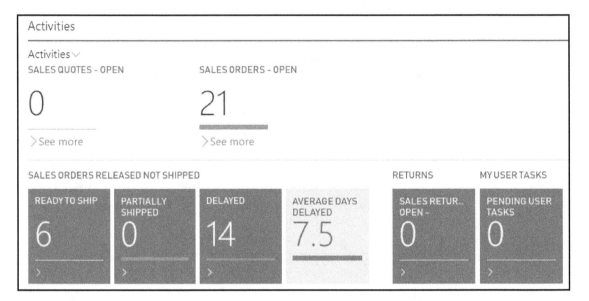

- `FixedLayout: GroupType` is used at the bottom of list pages, following a `repeater` group. The `FixedLayout` group typically contains totals or additional line-related detail fields. Many journal pages, such as page 39—**General Journal**, page 40—**Item Journal**, and page 201—**Job Journal** have `FixedLayout` groups. The item **JournalFixedLayout** group only shows `Item Description`, which is also available in a repeater column, but can easily display other fields as well. A `FixedLayout` group can also display a lookup or calculated value, like many of the statistics pages, for example, page 151—**Customer Statistics** and page 152—**Vendor Statistics**.
- `GridLayout: GroupType` provides additional formatting capabilities to layout fields, row by row, column by column, spanning rows or columns, and hiding or showing captions. Page 970—**Time Sheet Allocation** contains an example of the `GridLayout` use. To learn more about the `GridLayout` use, search `Help` for `Gridlayout`.

- `IndentationColumnName` and `IndentationControls`: These properties allow a group to be defined in which fields will be indented, as shown in the following screenshot of the **Chart of Accounts** page. Examples of pages that utilize the indentation properties include page 16—**Chart of Accounts** and page 18—**G/L Account List**:

Chart of Accounts

NO.	NAME	NET CHANGE	BALANCE	INCOME/...
1000	**BALANCE SHEET**	--	--	Balance She.
1002	**ASSETS**	--	--	Balance She.
1003	**Fixed Assets**	--	--	Balance She.
1005	**Tangible Fixed Assets**	--	--	Balance She.
1100	**Land and Buildings**			Balance She.
1110	Land and Buildings	1,479,480.60	1,479,480.60	Balance She.
1120	Increases during the Year	147.73	147.73	Balance She.
1130	Decreases during the Year	--	--	Balance She.
1140	Accum. Depreciation, Buildings	-526,620.38	-526,620.38	Balance She.
1190	**Land and Buildings, Total**	953,007.95	953,007.95	Balance She.
1200	**Operating Equipment**	--	--	Balance She.
1210	Operating Equipment	582,872.18	582,872.18	Balance She.
1220	Increases during the Year	25,116.00	25,116.00	Balance She.

- `FreezeColumnID`: This freezes the identified column and all of the columns to the left, so they remain in a fixed position while the columns to the right can scroll horizontally. This is like freezing a pane in an Excel worksheet. Users can also freeze columns as part of the personalization.
- `ShowAsTree`: This works together with the indentation property. `ShowAsTree` allows an indented set of rows to be expanded or collapsed dynamically by the user for easier viewing. Example pages that use this property are page 583—**XBRL Taxonomy Lines**, page 634—**Chart of Accounts Overview**, and page 5522—**Order Planning**.

Field controls

All field controls appear in the same format in the page designer. The `SubType` column is empty and the `SourceExpr` column contains the data expression that will be displayed.

All of the field control properties are listed for each field, but individual properties only apply to the data type for which they make sense. For example, the `DecimalPlaces` property only applies to fields where the data type is decimal. The following is a subset screenshot of the properties for field controls:

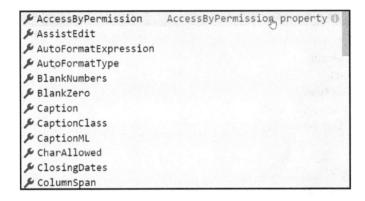

We'll review the field control properties that are more frequently used or that are more significant in terms of effect, as follows:

- `Visible`, `Enabled`, and `Editable`: These have the same functionality as the identically named group controls, but they only apply to individual fields. If the group control is set to `FALSE`, either statically (in the control definition within the page) or dynamically by an expression evaluated during processing, the group control's `FALSE` condition will take precedence over the equivalent field control setting. Precedence applies in the same way at the next, higher levels of identically named properties at the page level, and then at the table level. For example, if a data field is set to non-editable in the table, that setting will take precedence over (override) other settings in a page, control group, or control.
- `HideValue`: This allows the value of a field to be optionally displayed or hidden, based on an expression that evaluates to `TRUE` or `FALSE`.
- `CaptionandCaptionML`: These define the caption that will be displayed for the field (in English or the current system language if not English).
- `ShowCaption`: This is set to `Yes` or `No`; it determines whether or not the caption is displayed.

- `MultiLine`: This must be set to `TRUE` if the field is to display multiple lines of text.
- `OptionCaption` and `OptionCaptionML`: These set the text string options that are displayed to the user. The captions that are set as page field properties will override those defined in the equivalent table field property. The default captions are those defined in the table.
- `DecimalPlaces`: This applies to decimal fields only. If the number of decimal places defined in the page is smaller than that defined in the table, the display is rounded accordingly. If the field definition is the smaller number, it controls the display.
- `Width`: This allows setting a specific field display width—a number of characters. This is especially useful for the `SubType` control of `GridLayout`.
- `ShowMandatory`: This shows a red asterisk in the field display to indicate a required (mandatory) data field. `ShowManadatory` can be based on an expression that evaluates to `TRUE` or `FALSE`. This property does not enforce any validation of the field. Validation is left to the developer.
- `ApplicationArea`: This allows us to hide controls based on the Application Area feature, which was introduced in Business Central.

> This blog entry explains how the Application Area property is implemented by Microsoft. You can check it out by clicking on the following link: `https://marijebrummel.blog/2016/11/19/nav2017-applicationarea-the-mistery-of-disapearing-controls/`.

- `QuickEntry`: This allows the field to optionally receive focus or be skipped, based on an expression that evaluates to `TRUE` or `FALSE`.
- `AccessByPermission`: This determines the permission mask required for a user to view or access this field.
- `Importance`: This controls the display of a field. This property only applies to individual (non-repeating) fields located within a FastTab. Importance can be set to `Standard` (the default), `Promoted`, or `Additional`, which are briefly described here:
    - `Standard`: This is the normal display. Implementations of the rendering routines for different targets may utilize this differently.
    - `Promoted`: If the property is set to `Promoted` and the page is on a collapsed FastTab, then the field contents will be displayed on the FastTab line. If the FastTab is expanded, the field will display normally.

- *Additional*: If the property is set to `Additional` and the FastTab is collapsed, there is no effect on the display. If the FastTab is expanded, then the user can determine whether or not the field is displayed by clicking on the show more fields or show fewer fields display control in the lower-right corner of the FastTab.

- `RowSpan` and `ColumnSpan`: These are used in conjunction with the `GridLayout` controls as layout parameters.

- `ControlAddIn`: When the field represents a control add-in, this contains the name and public token key of the control add-in.

- `ExtendedDatatype`: This allows a text field to be categorized as a special data type. The default value is `None`. If `ExtendedDatatype` is selected, it can be any one of the following data types:

  - `Phone No.`: This displays a regionally appropriate phone number format.

  - `URL`: This displays a formatted URL.

  - `E-MailFilter`: This is used on reports.

  - `Ratio`: This displays a progress bar.

  - `Masked`: This fills the field with bold dots in order to mask the actual entry. The number of masking characters displayed is independent of the actual field contents. The contents of a masked field cannot be copied. If `ExtendedDatatype` is set with `Phone No.`, `URL`, or `E-Mail` data, an active icon is displayed on the page following the text field, providing access to call the phone number, access the URL in a browser, or invoke the email client. Setting `ExtendedDatatype` will also define the validation that will automatically be applied to the field.

  - `Person`: This allows rendering an image as a person in the web client.

  - `Resource`: This is not used, according to Microsoft.

- `Image`: This allows the display of an image on a cue for a field control in a `cuegroup` control. It only applies to a `cuegroup` field of an integer data type. If no image is wanted, choose a value of `None`.

Page part controls

Page parts are used for FactBoxes and subpages. Many of the properties of page parts are similar to the properties of other Business Central components and operate essentially the same way in a page part as they operate elsewhere. Those properties include ID, Name, Visible, Enabled, Editable, Caption, CaptionML, ToolTip, ToolTipML, and Description.

Other properties that are specific to the page part controls are as follows:

- SubPageView: This defines the table view that applies to named Subpage as shown in the following screenshot of part:

```
part(Subpage;"Example Document Subpage")
{
    SubPageLink="Document No."=FIELD("No.");
}
```

- SubPageLink: This defines the fields that link to the subpage and the link that is based on a constant, a filter, or another field. This is also shown in the preceding screenshot.
- ProviderID: This contains the ID of another page part control within the current page. This enables us to link a subordinate part to a controlling parent part. For example, page 42—**Sales Order** uses this property to update **Sales Line** FactBox by defining a **ProviderID** link from FactBox to the **Sales Lines** FastTab.
- PartType: This defines the type of part to be displayed in a FactBox. There are three options, and each option also requires another related property to be defined as follows:

PartType option	Required property
Page	PagePartID
System	SystemPartID
Chart	ChartPartID

The properties are further explained as follows:

- `PagePartID`: This must contain the page object ID of a FactBox part if `PartTypeOption` is set to `Page`.
- `SystemPartID`: This must contain the name of a predefined system part if `PartTypeOption` is set to `System`. The factavailable choices are: `Outlook`, `Notes`, `MyNotes`, and `RecordLinks`.
- `ChartPartID`: This must contain a chart ID if `PartTypeOption` is set to `Chart`. The chart ID is a link to the selected entry in the chart table (the `2000000078` table number).

- `UpdatePropagation`: This allows us to update the parent page from the child (subordinate) page. A value of `Subpage` updates the subpage only. A value of both will cause the parent page to be updated and refreshed at the same time as the subpage.

 The Business Central chart control add-in provides significant additional charting capability. Information can be found in the **Help** section, *Displaying Charts Using the Chart Control Add-In* (`https://msdn.microsoft.com/en-us/library/hh167009(v=nav.90).asp x`).

Page control triggers

There are five triggers for each field control. The container, `group`, and `part` controls do not have associated triggers. The following screenshot shows page control triggers:

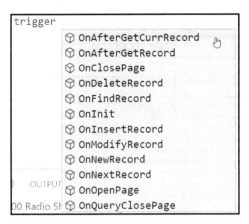

The guideline for the use of these triggers is the same as the guideline for page triggers—if there is a choice, don't put AL code in a control trigger. Not only will this make our code easier to upgrade in the future, but it will also make it easier to debug, and it will be easier for the developer following us to decipher our changes.

Bound and unbound pages

Pages can be created as **bound** (associated with a specific table) or **unbound** (not specifically associated with any table). Typically, a card or list page will be bound, but the Role Center pages will be unbound. Other instances of unbound pages are rare. Unbound pages may be used to communicate status information or initiate a process. Examples of unbound pages are page 476—**Copy Tax Setup** and page 1040—**Copy Job**, both of which have a `PageType` property of `StandardDialog`.

WDTU page enhancement – part 2

Now that we have an additional understanding of page structures, let's do a little more enhancing of our **WDTU** application pages. We've decided that it will be useful to keep track of specific listener contacts, a fan list. First, we will need to create a table of fan information that we will save as `Table` with ID as `50110` and name it `Radio Show Fan`, which will look like the following screenshot:

```
1    table 50110 "Radio Show Fan"
2    {
3        DataClassification = ToBeClassified;
4
5        fields
6        {
             0 references
7            field(1; "No."; Code[20]) { }
             0 references
8            field(10; "Radio Show No."; Code[20]) { }
             0 references
9            field(20; Name; Text[50]) { }
             0 references
10           field(30; "E-Mail"; Text[250]) { }
             0 references
11           field(40; "Last Contacted"; Date) { }
12       }
13   }
```

We want to be able to review the fan list as we scan the list, `Radio Show List`. This requires adding a FactBox area to the `50000` page. In turn, that requires a page part that will be displayed in the FactBox. The logical sequence is to create the page part first, then add the FactBox to the `50000` page. Because we just want a simple List Part with three columns, we can use the page wizard to create our page part, which we will save as `Page 50110 - Radio Show Fan Factbox. ListPart`, including just the `Name`, `Email`, and `Last Contacted` fields. The following screenshot shows the new page snippets:

```
1 tpa|
   □ tpage, Page                    Snippet: Page (AL Language) ⓘ
   □ tpage, Page of type API
   □ tpage, Page of type list
```

Next, we will use the page designer to add a FactBox area to the `50100` page, populate the FactBox area with our page part—the `50110` page, and set the properties for the page part to link to the highlighted record in the **Radio Show List** page as shown in the following screenshot:

```
25                    field("Royalty Cost"; "Royalty Cost") { ApplicationArea = Basic; }
26
27              }
28           }
          0 references
29        area(FactBoxes)
30        {
             0 references
31           part(Fans; "Radio Show Fan Factbox")
32           {
33              ApplicationArea = Basic;
34              SubPageLink = "Radio Show No." = field ("No.");
35           }
36        }
```

If we run the `50100` page, we should see something like the following screenshot:

Before finishing this part of our enhancement effort, we will create a list page that we can use to view and maintain the data in the `50110` table in the future (assign it as the `50111` page—`Radio Show Fans`).

One other enhancement we can do now is promote some fields in **RADIO SHOW CARD** so they can be seen when FastTabs are collapsed. All we have to do is choose the fields we want to promote and then change the page control property of **Importance** to **Promoted**. If we chose the fields and promote `No.`, `Radio Show Type`, `Name`, and `Avg. Listener Share`, our card with collapsed FastTabs will look like the following screenshot; we don't have any listener share data yet:

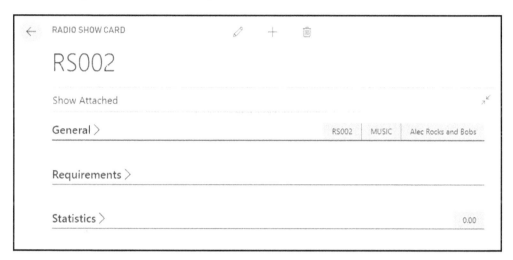

Page actions

Actions are the menu items of Business Central. Action menus can be found in several locations. The primary location is the ribbon appearing at the top of most pages. Other locations for actions are the navigation pane, Role Center, `cuegroups`, and the action menu on FactBox page parts.

Action designer, where actions are defined, is accessed from the page designer form by searching the actions part. When we search for this section on the **Fixed Asset** page (the 5600 page), we will see a list of actions, which are shown in the following screenshot as they appear in action designer:

```
actions
{
    area(Navigation)
    {
        group("Fixed &Asset")
        { …
        }
        group("Main Asset")
        { …
        }
        group(Insurance)
        {
            action("Total Value Ins&ured")
            {
            }
        }
        group(History)
        {
            action("Ledger E&ntries")
            {
            }
            action("Error Ledger Entries")
            {
            }
            action("Main&tenance Ledger Entries")
```

The associated ribbon tabs for the preceding page action list are as follows:

- First, the **Process** tab, as you can see in the following screenshot:

| Process | Report | Show Attached | | Actions | Navigate | Report | Less options |

📎 Attachments   📈 Statistics   ♗ Dimensions   🗟 Maintenance Registration

- Second, the **Actions** tab is shown in this screenshot:

| Process | Report | Show Attached | | Actions | Navigate | Report | Less options |

☑ Acquire   📄 Copy Fixed Asset...

- Third, the **Navigate** tab is shown in the following screenshot:

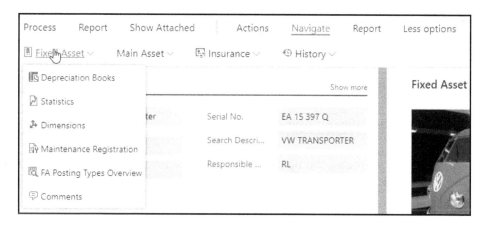

- Finally, the **Report** tab is shown here:

There are two default ribbon tabs created for every ribbon: **Process** and **Actions**. Which actions appear by default is dependent on the page type.

Actions defined by the developer appear on a ribbon tab and in the tab submenu section based on a combination of the location of the action in the page actions structure and on the property settings of the individual action. There are a lot of possibilities, so it is important to follow some basic guidelines, some of which are listed here:

- Maintain the look and feel of the standard product wherever feasible and appropriate.
- Put the actions on the **Process** tab that are expected to be used most.
- Be consistent in organizing actions from tab to tab and page to page.
- Provide the user with a complete set of action tools, but don't provide so many options that it's hard to figure out which one to use.

Page action types and subtypes

Page action entries can have one of three types: `area`, `group`, or `action`. At this time, separators don't seem to have any effect in the rendered pages. A page action type uses the following indented hierarchical structure:

Action types	Description
`area`	Primary action grouping
`group`	Secondary action grouping
`action`	Action
`group`	Secondary groups can be set up within an action list for drop-down menus of actions (a tertiary level)
`action`	The indentation indicates this is part of a drop-down menu
`action`	Action

An `area` action line type can have one of four subtype values, as shown in the following screenshot:

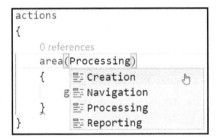

Those action options display in different sections of the ribbon as follows:

- Actions in `ReportsSubType` will appear on the ribbon in a **Reports** tab
- Actions in `NavigationSubType` will appear on the ribbon in a **Navigate** tab
- Actions in `ProcessingSubType` will appear on the ribbon in a **Process** tab
- Actions in `CreationSubType` will appear on the ribbon in a **New** tab

Action groups

Action groups provide a submenu grouping of actions within the assigned tab. In the following screenshot, the page preview is highlighting the **Main Asset** submenu, which is the caption for the associated **ActionGroup**. In **RelatedInformationActionContainer**, we can see the other **ActionGroup**, **Fixed Asset**, **Insurance**, and **History** matching the submenu groups on the ribbon's **Navigate** tab:

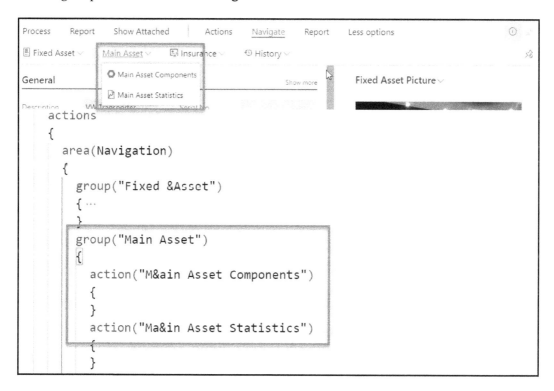

The following are the `group` properties:

- `Caption`: This is displayed in the action designer.
- `Visible` and `Enabled`: These are `TRUE` or `FALSE`, defaulting to `TRUE`. These properties can be assigned Boolean expressions, which can be evaluated during processing.
- `CaptionML`: This is the action name displayed, depending on the language option in use.
- `ToolTip` and `ToolTipML`: This is for a helpful display for the user.

- Description: This is for internal documentation.
- Image: This can be used to assign an icon to be displayed. The icon source is the Activity Button Icon Library, which can be viewed in detail in the *Developer and IT-Pro* help:

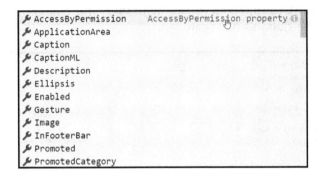

The following are the action properties shown in the preceding screenshot:

- Caption: This is displayed in the Action Designer.
- CaptionML: This is the action name displayed, depending on the language option in use.
- Visible and Enabled: These are TRUE or FALSE, defaulting to TRUE. These properties can be assigned Boolean expressions, which can be evaluated during processing.
- RunPageMode: This can be View (no modification), Edit (the default), or Create (new).
- ToolTip and ToolTipML: These are for a helpful display for the user.
- Description: This is for internal documentation.
- ApplicationArea: This allows us to hide controls based on the Application Area feature introduced in Business Central.
- Image: This can be used to assign an icon to be displayed. The icon source is the Action Icon Library.
- Promoted: If Yes, show this action in the ribbon **Home** tab.
- PromotedCategory: If Promoted is Yes, this defines the category in the **Home** tab in which to display this action.
- PromotedIsBig: If Promoted is Yes, this indicates whether the icon is to be large (Yes) or small (No—the default).

- `Ellipsis`: If `Yes`, this displays an ellipsis after the caption.
- `ShortCutKey`: This provides a shortcut key combination for this action.
- `RunObject`: This defines which object to run to accomplish the action.
- `RunPageView`: This defines the table view for the page being run.
- `RunPageLink`: This defines the field link for the object being run.
- `RunPageOnRec`: This defines a linkage for the run object to the current record.
- `InFooterBar`: This places the action icon in the page footer bar. This only works on pages with `PageType` of `NavigatePage`.
- `Gesture`: This allows an action to be executed, swiping left or right using the universal client.

To summarize a common design choice, individual ribbon actions can be promoted to the ribbon process tab based on two settings. First, set the `Promoted` property to `Yes`. Second, set the `PromotedCategory` property to define the category on the **Home** tab where the action is to be displayed. This promotion results in the action appearing twice in the ribbon, once where defined in the action structure hierarchy and once on the **Home** tab. See the preceding screenshot for example settings assigning the **Depreciation Books** action to the `Process` category in addition to appearing in the **Fixed Assets** category on the **Navigation** tab.

Navigation pane button actions

In the navigation pane, on the left side of the web client display, there is a home button where actions can be assigned as part of the Role Center page definition. The navigation pane definition is part of the Role Center. When defining the actions in a Role Center page, we can include a group of actions in an **Area** group with **Embedding**. These actions will be displayed in the main menu on the navigation pane.

Additional navigation pane buttons can also easily be defined in a Role Center page action list. First, define an area with subtype of sections. Each group defined within this area will define a new navigation pane's **Activity** button. The following screenshot is a combination image showing the RTC for the **Sales Orders** processor Role Center on the left (focused on the navigation pane) and the Action Designer contents that define the embedded buttons on the top.

The actions showing on the right that aren't visible in the navigation pane on the left are in submenus indicated by the small outline arrowheads to the far-left of several entries, including **Sales Order** and **Sales Quotes**. Business Central will automatically do some of this grouping for us based on the pages referenced by the actions, including CueGroup actions:

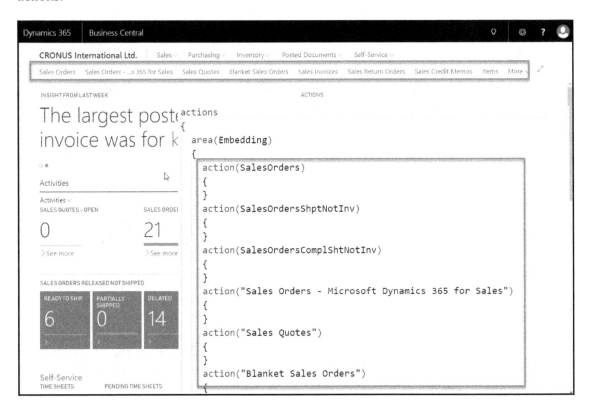

Actions summary

The primary location where each user's job role based actions should appear is the navigation pane. The Role Center action list provides detailed action menus for the **Home** button and any appropriate additional navigation pane button. Detailed page/task specific actions should be located in the ribbon at the top of each page.

As mentioned earlier, a key design criterion for the Business Central web client is for a user to have access to the actions they need to get their job done; in other words, to tailor the system to the individual user roles. Our job as developers is to take full advantage of all of these options and make life easier for the user. In general, it's better to go overboard in providing access to useful capabilities than to make the user search for the right tool or use several steps in order to get to it. The challenge is to not clutter up the first-level display with too many things, but still have the important user tools no more than one click away.

Learning more

The following section gives a description of several excellent ways to learn more about pages.

Patterns and creative plagiarism

When we want to create new functionality, the first task is to obviously create functional specifications. Once those are in hand, we should look for guidelines to follow. Some of the sources that are readily available are listed here:

- The Business Central Design Patterns Wiki (`https://community.dynamics.com/nav/w/designpatterns/default.aspx`)
- AL Coding Guidelines, as used internally by Microsoft in the development of Business Central application functionality (`https://community.dynamics.com/nav/w/designpatterns/156.cal-coding-guidelines.aspx`)
- Blogs and other materials available in the Microsoft Dynamics Business Central community (`https://community.dynamics.com/nav/default.aspx`)
- Design Patterns on Marije Brummel's blog (`https://marijebrummel.blog/category/nav-architecture-patterns-code/design-patterns/`)
- The Business Central system itself as distributed by Microsoft

It's always good to start with an existing pattern or object that has capabilities similar to our requirements and study the existing logic and the code. In many lines of work, the term plagiarism is a nasty term. However, when it comes to modifying an existing system, plagiarism is a very effective research and design tool. This approach allows us to build on the hard work of the many skilled and knowledgeable people who have contributed to the Business Central product. In addition, this is working software. This eliminates at least some of the errors we would make if starting from scratch.

The book *Learning Dynamics Business Central Patterns* explains in depth how to implement Design Patterns in Dynamics Business Central (`https://www.packtpub.com/big-data-and-business-intelligence/lea rning-dynamics-nav-patterns`).

When designing modifications for Business Central, studying how the existing objects work and interact is often the fastest way to create new working models. We should allocate some time both for studying the material in the Business Central Design Patterns Wiki and for exploring the Business Central CRONUS demonstration system.

Search through the **CRONUS demonstration system** (or an available production system) in order to find one or more pages that have the feature we want to emulate (or a similar feature). If there are both complex and simple instances of pages that contain this feature, we should concentrate our research on the simple instance first. Make a test copy of the page. Read the code. Use the page preview feature. Run the page. Make a minor modification. Preview again; then run it again. Continue this until our ability to predict the results of changes eliminates surprises or confusion.

Experimenting on your own

If you have followed along with the exercises so far in this book, it's time for you to do some experimenting on your own. No matter how much information someone else describes, there is no substitute for personal hands-on experience. You will combine things in a new way from what was described here. You will either discover a new capability that you would not have learned otherwise or you will have an interesting problem to solve. Either way, the result will be significantly more knowledge about pages in Business Central.

Don't forget to make liberal use of the help information while you are experimenting. A majority of the available detailed Business Central documentation is in the help files that are built into the product. Some of the help material is a bit sparse, but it is being updated on a frequent basis. In fact, if you find something missing or something that you think is incorrect, please use the **documentation feedback** function built into the Business Central help system. The product team responsible for help pays close attention to the feedback they receive and use it to improve the product. Hence, we will all benefit from your feedback.

Experimentation

Start with the blank slate approach because that allows you to focus on specific features and functions. Because we've already gone through the mechanical procedures of creating new pages of the card and list types and using the page designer to add controls and modify control properties, we won't detail those steps here. However, as you move the focus for experimentation from one feature to another, you may want to review what was covered in this chapter.

Let's walk through some examples of experiments you could do now, then build on as you get more adventuresome. Each of the objects you create at this point should be assigned into an object number range that you are reserving for testing. Follow these steps:

1. Create new `Table 50050` (try using `50009` if your license won't allow `50050`). Do this by opening table `50104` in Visual Studio Code, and then save it as `50050` with the name `Playlist Item Rate Test`.
2. Create a List page for `Table 50050` with at least three or four fields.
3. Enter a few test records into `Table 50050`, such as `Playlist`, `Item`, `Rate`, and `Test`. This can done by running the page.
4. Change the `Visible` property of a field by setting it to `False`.
5. Save and run the page.
6. Confirm that the page looks as expected. Go into edit mode on the page. See whether the field is still invisible.
7. Use the page in-client designer feature in order to add the invisible field; also remove a field that was previously visible. Exit the designer. View the page in various modes, such as view, edit, new, and so on.
8. Go back into Visual Studio Code and design the page again.
9. One or two at a time, experiment with setting the **Editable**, **Caption**, **ToolTip**, and other control properties.
10. Don't just focus on text fields. Experiment with other data types as well. Create a text field that is 200 characters long. Try out the **MultiLine** property.
11. After you get comfortable with the effect of changing individual properties, try changing multiple properties to see how they interact.

When you feel you have thoroughly explored individual field properties in a list, try similar tests in a card page. You will find that some of the properties have one effect in a list, while they may have a different (or no) effect in the context of a card (or vice versa). Test enough to find out. If you have some "*Aha!*" experiences, it means that you are really learning.

The next logical step is to begin experimenting with the group level controls. Add one or two to the test page, then begin setting the properties for that control, again experimenting with only one or two at a time, in order to understand very specifically what each one does. Do some experimenting to find out which properties at the group level override the properties at the field level and which ones do not override them.

Once you've done group controls, do part controls. Build some FactBoxes using a variety of the different components that are available. Use the system components and some chart parts as well. There is a wealth of prebuilt parts that come with the system. Even if the parts that are supplied aren't exactly right for the application, they can often be used as a model for the construction of custom parts. Remember that using a model can significantly reduce both the design and the debugging work when doing custom development.

After you feel that you have a grasp of the different types of controls in the context of cards and lists, consider checking out some of the other page types. Some of those won't require too much in the way of new concepts. Examples of these are the List Plus, List Parts, Card Parts, and, to a lesser extent, even document pages.

You may now decide to learn by studying samples of the page objects that are part of the standard product. You could start by copying an object, such as page 22—`Customer List`, to another object number in your testing range and then begin to analyze how it is put together and how it operates. Again, you should tweak various controls and control properties in order to see how that affects the page. It's a good idea to back up your work one way or another before making additional changes. An easy way to back up individual objects is to use Git and create multiple branches. The restore method is to go back to a previous branch.

Another excellent learning option is to choose one of the patterns that has a relationship with the area about which you want more knowledge. If, for example, you are going to create an application that has a new type of document, such as a radio program schedule, you should study the document pattern. You might also want to study create data from templates pattern. At this point, it has become obvious that there are a variety of sources and approaches to supplement the material in this text.

Summary

You should now be relatively comfortable in the navigation of Business Central and with the use of Visual Studio Code. You should be able to use the page snippets as an advanced beginner. If you have taken full advantage of the various opportunities to create tables and pages, both with our guidance and experimentally on your own, you are beginning to become a Business Central developer.

We have reviewed different types of pages and worked with some of them. We reviewed all of the controls that can be used in pages and have worked with several of them. We also lightly reviewed page and control triggers. We've had a good introduction to page designing and a significant insight into the structure of some types of pages. With the knowledge gained, we have expanded our WDTU application system, enhancing our pages for data maintenance and inquiry.

In the next chapter, we will learn about the Business Central Query and Report Designer. We will dig into the various triggers and controls that make up reports. We will also perform some query and report creation work to better understand what makes them tick and what we can do within the constraints of the query and report designer tools.

Questions

1. Once a page has been developed using the Page Snippet, the developer has very little flexibility in the layout of the page. True or False?
2. Actions appear on the Role Center screen in several places. Choose two:
    - Address bar
    - Ribbon
    - Filter pane
    - Navigation pane
    - Command bar

3. A user can choose their Role Center when they log in. True or false?
4. An action can only appear in one place in the ribbon or in the navigator pane. True or false?

5. When developing a new page, the following page part types are available. Choose two:
    - Chart part
    - Map part
    - Social part
    - System part

6. All page design and development is done within the Visual Studio Code. True or false?

7. Document pages are for word processing. True or false?

8. Two activity buttons are always present in the Navigation Pane. Which of the following two are those?
    - Posted documents
    - Departments
    - Financial management
    - Home

9. The filter pane includes "Filter list by" and "Filter totals by" options. True or false?

10. The AL code place in pages should only be to control display characteristics, not to modify data. True or false?

11. Inheritance is the passing of property definition defaults from one level of object to another. If a field property is explicitly defined in a table, it cannot be less restrictively defined for that field displayed on a page. True or false?

12. Which of the following are true about the control property importance? Choose two:
    - Applies only to card and Card Part pages
    - Can affect FastTab displays
    - Has three possible values: Standard, Promoted, and Additional
    - Applies to decimal fields only

13. FactBoxes are delivered as part of the standard product. They cannot be modified nor can new FactBoxes be created. True or False?

14. RTC Navigation Pane entries always invoke which one of the following page types?
    - Card
    - Document
    - List
    - Journal/worksheet

15. The page preview tool can be used as a drag and drop page layout design tool. True or false?

16. Some field control properties can be changed dynamically as the object executes. Which ones are they? Choose three:
    - `Visible`
    - `HideValue`
    - `Editable`
    - `Multiline`
    - `DecimalPlaces`

17. Which property is normally used in combination with the `AutoSplitKey` property? Choose one:
    - `SaveValues`
    - `SplitIncrement`
    - `DelayedInput`
    - `MultipleNewLines`

18. Ribbon tabs and menu sections are predefined in Business Central and cannot be changed by the developer. True or false?

19. Inheritance between tables and pages operates two ways—tables can inherit attributes from pages and pages can inherit from tables. True or false?

20. For the purpose of testing, pages can be run directly from the Visual Studio Code. True or false?

5
Queries and Reports

"Data helps solve problems."

– Anne Wojcicki

"The greatest value of a picture is when it forces us to notice what we never expected to see."

– John Tukey

In Microsoft Dynamics 365 Business Central, reports and queries are two ways to extract and output data for the purpose of presentation to a user (reports can also modify data). Each of these objects use tools and processes that are Business Central-based and work on data extraction (XMLports, which can also extract and modify data, will be covered in Chapter 8, *Advanced AL Development Tools*). In this chapter, we will focus on understanding the strengths of each of these tools and when and how they might be used. We will cover the Business Central side of both queries and reports in detail to describe how to obtain the data we need to present to our users. We will cover output formatting and consumption of that data in less detail. There are currently no Wizards available for either query building or report building, and therefore we must do this step by step using programming tools and our skills as designers and developers.

We will cover the following topics in this chapter:

- Queries and reports
- Report components—overview
- Report data flow
- Report components—detail
- Creating and modifying reports

Queries

Reports have always been available in Business Central as a data retrieval tool. Reports are used to process and/or manipulate the data through the `INSERT`, `MODIFY`, or `DELETE` functions, with the option of presenting the data in a formatted, printable format. In older versions, data selection could only be done using AL code or DataItem properties to filter individual tables as datasets, and to perform loops to find the data that's required for the purpose. Then, the `query` object was created with performance in mind. Instead of multiple calls to SQL to retrieve multiple datasets which would then be manipulated in AL, Queries allow us to utilize familiar Business Central tools to create advanced **T-SQL** queries.

A Business Central developer can utilize the new `query` object as a source of data both in Business Central and externally. Some of the external uses of Business Central queries are as follows:

- A web service source for SOAP and OData
- Feeding data to external reporting tools, such as Excel, SharePoint, and SSRS

Internally, Business Central queries can be used as follows:

- A direct data source for charts.
- As providers of data to which Cues (displayed in Role Centers) are bound. See Microsoft Docs: *Walkthrough: Creating a Cue Based on a Normal Field and a Query* (`https://docs.microsoft.com/en-us/dynamics-nav/walkthrough--creating-a-cue-based-on-a-normal-field-and-a-query`).
- As a dataset variable in AL to be accessed by other object types (reports, pages, codeunits, and so on). See `https://docs.microsoft.com/en-us/dynamics-nav/read-function--query-` for guidance on using the `READ` function to consume data from a query.

Query objects are more limited than SQL stored procedures. Queries are more similar to a SQL view. Some compromises in the design of query functionality were made for better performance. Data manipulation is not supported in queries. Variables, subqueries, and dynamic elements, such as building a query based on selective criteria, are not allowed within the `query` object.

The closest SQL Server objects that queries resemble are SQL views. One of the new features that allow Business Central to generate advanced T-SQL statements is the use of **SQL joins**. These include the following join methods for two tables, A and B:

- **Inner**: This query compares each row of table A with each row of table B to find all the pairs of rows that satisfy the join criteria.
- **Full outer**: This join does not require each record in the two joined tables to have a matching record so that all records from both A and B will appear at least once.
- **Left outer join**: In this join, every record from A will appear at least once, even if matching B is not found.
- **Right outer join**: In this join, every record from B will appear at least once, even if matching A is not found.
- **Cross join**: This join returns the Cartesian product of the sets of rows from A and B. The Cartesian product is a set made up of rows that includes the columns of each row in A, along with the columns of each row in B for a number of rows; in other words, it includes the columns of the rows in A, plus those in B.

Note that union join, which joins all records from A and B without the join criteria, is not available at this time.

Building a simple query

Sometimes, it is necessary to quickly retrieve detailed information from one or more ledgers that may contain hundreds of thousands to many millions of records. The `query` object is the perfect tool for such data selection as it is totally scalable and can retrieve selected fields from multiple tables at once. The following example (using Cronus data) will show the aggregated quantity per bin of lot-tracked items in stock. This query can be presented to a user by means of either a report or a page:

1. We will define the logic we need to follow and the data that's required to support that logic, and then we will develop the query. It is necessary to know what inventory is in stock, which also contains a lot number. This is accomplished using the **Item Ledger Entry** table.
2. However, the **Item Ledger Entry** record does not contain any bin information. This information is stored in the **Warehouse Ledger Entry** table.

3. The **Location Code**, **Item No.**, and **Lot No.** columns are used to match the **Item Ledger Entry** and **Warehouse Ledger Entry** records to make sure that the correct items are selected.

4. To determine which bins are designated as pick bins, the **Bin Type** records that are marked as **Pick** is equal to `True` need to be matched with the bins in **Warehouse Ledger Entry**.

5. Lastly, **Quantity** on each **Warehouse Entry** needs to be summed per **Location Code**, **Zone Code**, **Bin Code**, **Item No.**, and **Lot No.** to show the amount that's available in each bin.

Now that we have defined the necessary logic and data sources, we can create the desired `query` object, as follows:

1. In Visual Studio Code, we create a new `.al` file called `query 50100 "Lot Avail. by Bin"`. We use the snippet `query` and select `normal` query.

2. Now, we define the primary DataItem. The first DataItem is the `Item Ledger Entry` table. We can use IntelliSense to find the correct table.

3. After defining the first DataItem, we will add columns. `column` is a field from the DataItem table that will be output as an available field from the query dataset. The other `Type` option is `Filter`, which allows us to use the source `column` as a filter and does not output this `column` in the dataset. Use IntelliSense to add the `Item No.` and `Lot No.` fields under `Item Ledger Entry`, as shown in the following screenshot:

```
≡ query 50100 Lot Avail. by Bin.al  ●

       0 references
 1    query 50100 "Lot Avail. by Bin"
 2    {
 3
 4        elements
 5        {
              0 references
 6            dataitem(Item_Ledger_Entry; "Item Ledger Entry")
 7            {
                  0 references
 8                column(Item_No; "Item No.") { }
                  0 references
 9                column(Lot_No; "Lot No.") { }
10            }
11        }
```

5. The next DataItem we need is the `Warehouse_Entry` table. We must join it to the `Item Ledger Entry` by filling in the `DataItemLink` property. Link the `Location Code, Item No.`, and `Lot No.` fields between the two tables, as shown in the following screenshot:

```
 8             column(Item_No; "Item No.") { }
               0 references
 9             column(Lot_No; "Lot No.") { }
               0 references
10             dataitem(Warehouse_Entry; "Warehouse Entry")
11             {
12                 DataItemLink = "Location Code" = Item_Ledger_Entry."Location Code",
13                             "Item No." = Item_Ledger_Entry."Item No.",
14                             "Lot No." = Item_Ledger_Entry."Lot No.";
15             }
```

The following steps will define the rest of the DataItems, columns, and filters for this query:

1. Select `Entry No., Location Code, Zone Code, Bin Code`, and `Quantity` as columns under the `Warehouse Entry` DataItem.

2. Add a `Bin` table as the next DataItem.

3. Set the DataItem Link between the `Bin` and `Warehouse Entry` as the `Bin` table `Code` field linked to the `Bin Code` field for the `Warehouse Entry` table.

4. Add the `BinType` table as the last DataItem for this query. Create a DataItem link between the `Bin Type` table's `Code` field and the `Bin` table's `Bin Type Code` field.

5. Set the DataItem filter as `Pick = CONST(true)` to only show the quantities for bins that are enabled for picking.

6. For the dataset that's returned by the query, we will only want the total quantity per combination of the `Location`, `Zone`, `Bin`, `Item`, and `Lot number`. For the column where `Quantity` is in the `Warehouse Entry` DataItem, set the `Method Type` column to `Totals`. The `Method` will default to `Sum` and the columns above `Quantity` will be marked with `Group By` checked. This shows the grouping criteria for the aggregation of the `Quantity` field, as shown in the following screenshot:

```al
query 50100 "Lot Avail. by Bin"
{
    QueryType = Normal;
    elements
    {
        dataitem(Item_Ledger_Entry; "Item Ledger Entry")
        {
            column(Item_No; "Item No.") { }
            column(Lot_No; "Lot No.") { }
            dataitem(Warehouse_Entry; "Warehouse Entry")
            {
                DataItemLink = "Location Code" = Item_Ledger_Entry."Location Code",
                               "Item No." = Item_Ledger_Entry."Item No.",
                               "Lot No." = Item_Ledger_Entry."Lot No.";
                column(Entry_No; "Entry No.") { }
                column(Location_Code; "Location Code") { }
                column(Zone_Code; "Zone Code") { }
                column(Bin_Code; "Bin Code") { }
                column(Sum_Quantity; Quantity) { Method = Sum; }
                dataitem(Bin; Bin)
                {
                    DataItemLink = Code = Warehouse_Entry."Bin Code";
                    dataitem(Bin_Type; "Bin Type")
                    {
                        DataItemLink = Code = Bin.Code;
                        DataItemTableFilter = Pick = CONST (true);
                    }
                }
            }
        }
```

This query can be utilized internally in Business Central as an indirect data source in a page or a report object. Although DataItems in pages and reports can only be database tables, we can define a query as a variable, and then use the query dataset result to populate a temporary `SourceTable`. In a page, we set the `SourceTableTemporary` property to `Yes` and then load the table via AL code located in the `OnOpenPage` trigger.

In our example, we use the `Warehouse Entry` table to define our temporary table because it contains all the fields in the `query` dataset. In the `Page Properties`, we set the `SourceTableTemporary` to `Yes` (if we neglect marking this table as temporary, we are quite likely to corrupt the live data in the `Warehouse Entry` table). In the `OnOpenPage` trigger, the query object (`LotAvail`) is filtered and opened. As long as the query object has a dataset line available for output, the query column values can be placed in the temporary record variable and are available for display, as shown in the following screenshot. Because this code is located in the `OnOpenPage` trigger, the temporary table is empty when this code begins execution. If the code were to be invoked from another trigger, the `Rec.DELETEALL` statement would be needed at the beginning to clear any previously loaded data from the table:

```al
page 50141 Lot Avail. by Bin.al  ●
 1    page 50141 "Lot Avail. by Bin"
 2    {
 3        PageType = List;
 4        SourceTable = "Warehouse Entry";
 5        SourceTableTemporary = true;
 6        UsageCategory = Lists;
 7        layout {
 8            area(content) {
 9                repeater(Group) {
10                    field("Item No."; "Item No.") { ApplicationArea = Basic; }
11                    field("Location Code"; "Location Code") { ApplicationArea = Basic; }
12                    field("Bin Code"; "Bin Code") { ApplicationArea = Basic; }
13                    field("Serial No."; "Serial No.") { ApplicationArea = Basic; }
14                    field(Quantity; Quantity) { ApplicationArea = Basic; }
15        }}}
16        trigger OnOpenPage()
17        var
18            LotAvail: Query "Lot Avail. by Bin";
19        begin
20            LotAvail.Open;
21            while LotAvail.Read do begin
22                Init;
23                "Item No." := LotAvail.Item_No;
24                "Location Code" := LotAvail.Location_Code;
25                "Bin Code" := LotAvail.Bin_Code;
26                Quantity := LotAvail.Sum_Quantity;
27                Insert;
28            end;
29        end;
30    }
```

As the query dataset is read, the temporary record dataset will be displayed on the page, as shown in the following screenshot:

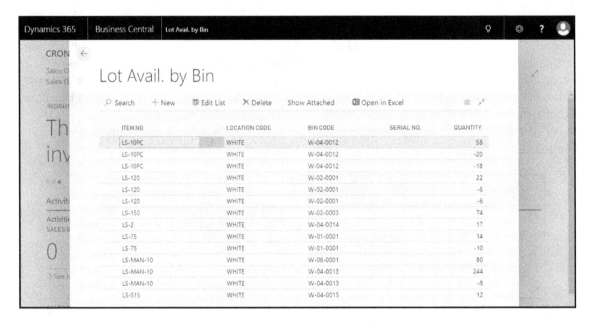

When a query is used to supply data to a report, the `Temporary` property is defined to control stepping through the query results. Before the report read loop begins, the query is filtered and invoked so that it begins processing. As long as the `query` object continues to deliver records, the `Temporary` DataItem will continue looping. At the end of the `query` output, the report will proceed to its `OnPostDataItem` trigger processing, just as though it had completed processing a normal table rather than a query created dataset. This approach is a faster alternative to a design that would use several FlowFields, particularly if those FlowFields were only used in one or two periodic reports.

A similar approach to using a query to supply data to a report is described in Marije Brummel's blog *Tip #45* (`https://marijebrummel.blog/2015/03/24/tip-45-nav2015-report-temporary-property/`).

Query and query component properties

There are several query properties we should review. Their descriptions follow.

Query properties

The properties of the `query` object can be accessed by highlighting the first empty line after the object name and clicking on *Ctrl* + spacebar. The properties of the query we created earlier will look like this:

```
query 50100 "Lot Avail. by Bin"
{
    QueryType = Normal;

    🔧 APIGroup                    APIGroup property ℹ
    🔧 APIPublisher
    🔧 APIVersion
    🔧 Caption
    🔧 CaptionML
    🔧 Description
    🔧 EntityName
    🔧 EntitySetName
    🔧 OrderBy
    🔧 Permissions
    🔧 ReadState
    🔧 TopNumberOfRows
```

We'll review three of these properties:

- `OrderBy`: This provides the capability to define a sort, data column by column, and ascending or descending, giving the same result as if a key had been defined for the query result, but without the requirement for a key.
- `TopNumberOfRows`: This allows for the specification of the number of data rows that will be presented by the query. A blank or 0 value shows all rows. Specifying a limit can make the query complete much faster. This property can also be set dynamically from the AL code.
- `ReadState`: This controls the state (committed or not) of data that is included and the type of lock that is placed on the data read.

DataItem properties

A query line can be one of three types: DataItem, `column`, and `filter`. Each has its own property set:

```
dataitem(Bin; Bin)
{
    DataItemLink = Code = Warehouse_Entry."Bin Code";
    |              I
    🔧 DataItemTableFilter  DataItemTableFilter property ⓘ
    🔧 Description
    🔧 SqlJoinType
```

Again, we'll review a selected subset of these properties:

- `SqlJoinType`: If enabled by the `DataItemLinkType` property, this property allows the specification of one of five different SQL join types (inner, left outer, right outer, full outer, or cross join). More information is available in the Help sections. Look for the `SqlJoinType` property and *SQL Advanced Options for Data Item Link Types*.
- `DataItemTableFilter`: This provides the ability to define filters that will be applied to the DataItem.

Column properties

The following screenshot is a `column` property screen showing the `Bin Code` column for our simple query:

```
column(Bin_Code; "Bin Code") { }
column(Sum_Quantity; Quantity)    🔧 Caption         Caption property ⓘ
dataitem(Bin; Bin)                🔧 CaptionML
{                                 🔧 ColumnFilter
    DataItemLink = Code = Wareh   🔧 Description
    dataitem(Bin_Type; "Bin Typ   🔧 Method
    {                             🔧 ReverseSign
```

The properties shown in the preceding screenshot are as follows:

- `Method`: Can be `Sum`, `Count`, `Avg`, `Min`, `Max`, `Day`, `Month`, or `Year`. The result in the column will be based on the appropriate computation. See the *Help* section for `Method Property` for more information.
- `ReverseSign`: This reverses the sign of the column value for numeric data.

- `ColumnFilter`: This allows us to apply a filter to limit the rows in the query result. Filtering here is similar to, but more complicated than, the filtering rules that apply to `DataItemTableFilter`. Static `ColumnFilters` can be dynamically overridden and can also be combined with `DataItemTableFilters`. See the *Help* section for the `ColumnFilter` property for more detailed information.

Reports

Some consider the standard library of reports that's provided in the Business Central product distribution from Microsoft to be relatively simple in design and limited in its features. Others feel that the provided reports satisfy most needs because they are simple, but flexible. Their basic structure is easy to use. They are made much more powerful and flexible by taking advantage of Business Central's filtering and SIFT capabilities. There is no doubt that the existing library can be used as a foundation for many of the special reports that customers require to match their own specific business management needs.

The fact is that Business Central's standard reports are basic. To obtain more complex or more sophisticated reports, we must use features that are part of the product or feed processed data for external reporting tools such as Excel. Through creative use of these features, many different types of complex report logic may be implemented.

We'll create our reports in this book with Microsoft Word. We'll examine the data flow of a standard report and the concept of reports, which will be used for processing only (with no printed or displayed output).

What is a report?

A **report** is a vehicle for organizing, processing, and displaying data in a format that's suitable for outputting to the user. Reports may be displayed on-screen in **Preview** mode, output to a file in Word, Excel, or PDF format (or, when appropriately designed, output in HTML, CSV, or XML format), emailed to a user (or other consumers of this information), or printed to hard-copy—the old-fashioned way. All of the report screenshots in this book were taken from **Preview** mode reports.

Once generated, the data contents of a report are static. When a Business Central report is output in **Preview** mode, the report can have interactive capabilities. Those capabilities only affect the presentation of the data; they do not change the actual data that's included in the report dataset. Interactive capabilities include dynamic sorting, visible/hidden options, and detail/summary expand/collapse functions. All of the specifications for the data selection criteria for a report must be done at the beginning of the report run, before the report view is generated. Business Central also allows dynamic functionality so that you can drill down into the underlying data, drill through to a page, and even drill through into another report.

In Business Central, report objects can be classified as processing only, such as report `795 Adjust Cost - Item Entries`, by setting the correct report property, that is, by setting the `ProcessingOnly` property to `Yes`. A processing only report will not display data to the user—it will simply process and update data in the tables. Report objects are convenient to use for processing because the report's automatic **read-process-write** loop and the built-in request page reduce coding that would otherwise be required. A report can add, change, or delete data in tables, regardless of whether the report is processing only or a typical report that generates output for viewing.

In general, reports are associated with one or more tables. A report can be created without being externally associated with any table, but that is an exception. Even if a report is associated with a particular table, it can freely access and display data from other referenced tables.

Four Business Central report designers

Any Business Central report design project uses at least two Report Designer tools. The first is the Report Designer, which is part of the Visual Studio Code development environment. The second is the developer's choice of Visual Studio, the SQL Server Report Builder, Microsoft Word. Refer to the Microsoft Dynamics 365 Business Central development environment requirements for more information about the choice of tools for handling RDLC report layouts for Business Central. We must also be careful to make sure that we obtain the proper version of the report tool and that it's compatible with the Business Central version we are using. The SQL Server Report Builder is installed by default during the Business Central system's installation. There is also a free version of Visual Studio, the Community Edition, which is available at
`https://msdn.microsoft.com/en-us/visual-studio-community-vs.aspx`.

For our work, we will use a combination of Visual Studio Code and Microsoft Word.

The option of using Microsoft Word is aimed at the goal of allowing customers to be more self-sufficient in handling quick, simple changes in format while requiring less technical expertise.

 The report development process for a Business Central report begins with a data definition in Visual Studio Code. All the data structure, working data elements, data flow, and AL logic are defined there. We must start in Visual Studio Code to create or modify report objects. Once all of the elements of the dataset definition and request page are in place, the development work proceeds to the SQL Report Builder, Visual Studio, or Word, where the display layout work is done, including any desired dynamic options.

When a report layout is created, SQL Report Builder or Visual Studio (whichever tool you are using) builds a definition of the report layout in the XML-structured **Report Definition Language Client-Side (RDLC)**. If Word is used to build a Business Central report layout, the result is a custom XML part that is used to map the data into a report at runtime.

Business Central allows us to create reports of many types with different *look and feel* attributes. The consistency of the report's look and feel does not have the same level of design importance as it has for pages. Patterns may have been developed that relate to reports, so before starting a new format of report, it is best to check if there is an applicable pattern.

Good design practice dictates that enhancements should integrate seamlessly, both in process and appearance, unless there is an overwhelming justification for being different. There are still many opportunities for reporting creativity. The tools that are available within Business Central to access and manipulate data for reports are very powerful. Of course, there is always the option to output report results to other processing and presentation tools, such as Excel or third-party products. Outputting a report to Excel allows the user to take advantage of the full Excel toolset to further manipulate and analyze the reported data.

Business Central report types

The standard Business Central application uses only a few of the possible report styles, most of which are in a relatively basic format. The following are the types of reports that are included in Business Central:

- **List**: This is a formatted list of data. A standard list is the **Inventory - List** report (report 701):

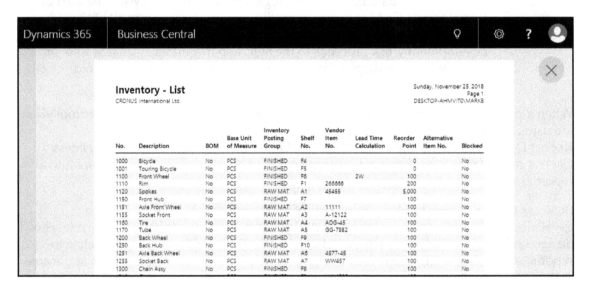

- **Document**: This is formatted similarly to a pre-printed form, where a page (or several pages) contains a header, detail, and footer section with dynamic content. Examples of document reports include customer invoice, packing list (even though it's called a list, it's a document report), purchase order, and accounts payable cheque. The following screenshot is a customer **Sales-Invoice** document report preview:

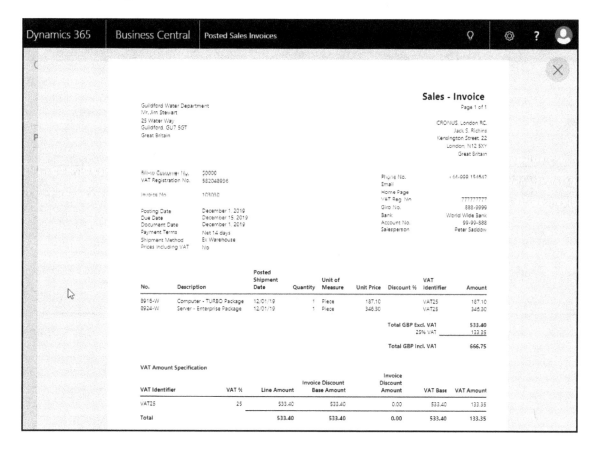

List and document report types are defined based on their layouts. The following three report types are defined based on their usage rather than their layouts, and are as follows:

- **Transaction**: This provides a list of ledger entries for a particular master table. For example, a Transaction list of Item Ledger entries for all of the items matching a particular criteria, or a list of General Ledger entries for some specific accounts, as shown in the following screenshot:

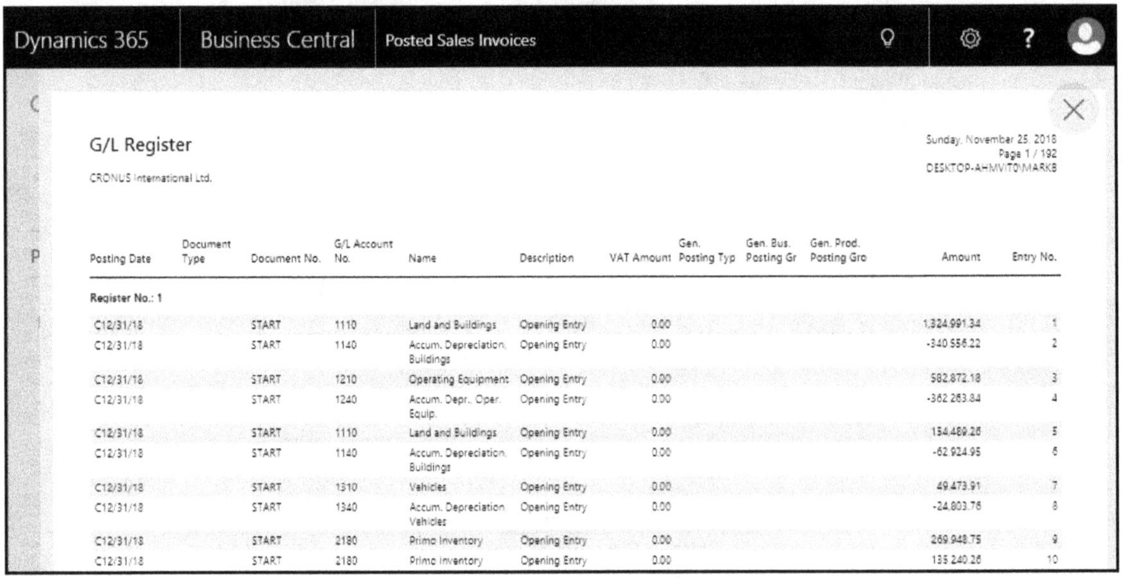

- **Test**: These reports are printed from journal tables prior to posting the transactions. Test reports are used to pre-validate data before it's posted. The following screenshot is a **Test** report for a **General Journal - Test** batch:

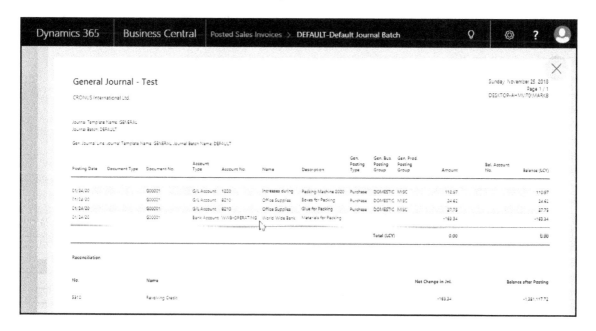

- **Posting**: These reports are printed as an audit trail as part of a post and print process. Posting report printing is controlled by the user's choice of either a **Posting Only** option or a **Post and Print** option. The posting portions of both options work the same. Post and print runs a report that is selected in the application's setup (in the applicable Templates page in columns that are hidden by default). This type of posting audit trail report, which is often needed by accountants, can be regenerated completely and accurately at any time.

The default setup uses the same report that you would use as a transaction (history) report, similar in format to the **G/L Register** that's shown in the following screenshot:

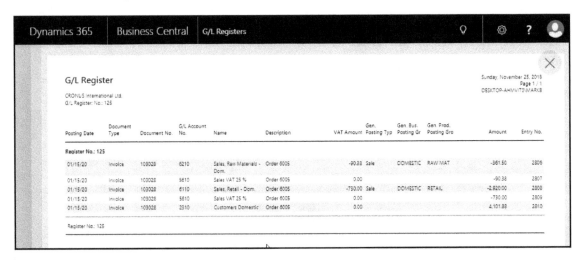

Report types summarized

The following table describes the different basic types of reports that are available in Business Central:

Type	Description
List	This is used to list volumes of similar data in a tabular format, such as a list of Sales Order Lines, a list of Customers, or a list of General Ledger Entries.
Document	This is used in *record-per-page header* plus *line item detail* dual layout situations, such as a Sales Invoice, a Purchase Order, a Manufacturing Work Order, or a Customer Statement.
Transaction	This generally presents a list of transactions in a nested list format, such as a list of General Ledger Entries grouped by G/L Account, Physical Inventory Journal Entries grouped by Item, or Salesperson To-Do List by Salesperson.
Test	This prints in a list format as a pre-validation test and data review, prior to a Journal Posting run. A Test Report option can be found on any Journal page, such as the General Journal, Item Journal, or the Jobs Journal. Test reports show errors that must be corrected prior to posting.

Posting	This prints in a list format as a record of which data transactions were posted into permanent status, that is, moved from a journal to a ledger. A posting report can be archived at the time of original generation or regenerated as an audit trail of posting activity.
Processing only	This type of report only processes data and does not generate a report output. It has the `ProcessingOnly` report property set to `Yes`.

Many reports in the standard system don't fit neatly within the preceding categories, but are variations or combinations. Of course, this is also true of many custom reports.

Report naming

Simple reports are often named the same as the table with which they are primarily associated, plus a word or two describing the basic purpose of the report. Common key report purpose names include the words Journal, Register, List, Test, and Statistics. Some examples include **General Journal - Test, G/L Register,** and **Customer - Order Detail**.

When there are conflicts between naming based on the associated tables and naming based on the use of the data, the usage context should take precedence in naming reports, just as it does with pages. One absolute requirement for names is that they must be unique; no duplicate names are allowed for a single object type. Remember, the **caption** (what shows on the printed report heading) is not the same as the **name** (the internal name of the report object). Each one is a different report property.

Report components – overview

What we generally refer to as the report or report object that's created with SQL Server Report Builder or Visual Studio Report Designer is technically referred to as an **RDLC Report**. (From here on out, we will focus on the Visual Studio report layout tool. The tools are somewhat different, but the end results are basically the same.) An RDLC Report includes information that describes the logic to be followed when processing the data (the data model), the dataset structure that is generated by Visual Studio Code, and the output layout that's designed with Visual Studio. RDLC Reports are stored in the Business Central database. Word report XML layouts are also stored in the Business Central database. Business Central allows there to be multiple RDLC and Word formats for a single report. We will use the term "report" when we are referring to the output, the description, or the object.

Reports share some attributes with pages, including aspects of the designer, features of various controls, some of the triggers, and even some of the properties. Where those parallels exist, we should take notice of them. Where there is consistency in the Business Central toolset, it is easier to learn and use.

Report structure

The overall structure of a Business Central RDLC Report consists of the following elements:

- Report properties
- Report triggers
- Request page:
    - Request page properties
    - Request page triggers
    - Request page controls:
        - Request page control triggers

- DataItems:
    - DataItem properties
    - DataItem triggers
    - Data columns:
        - Data column properties

- SSRB (RDLC) layout:
    - SSRB (RDLC) controls:
        - SSRB (RDLC) control properties

- Word layout:
    - Word layout template
    - Word controls:
        - Word control properties

Report data overview

Report components, report properties and triggers, request page properties and triggers, and DataItems and their properties and triggers define the data flow and overall logic for processing the data. Another set of components, Data Fields and working storage, are defined as being subordinate to the DataItems (or request page). These are all designed and defined in Visual Studio Code.

 Data Fields are defined in this book as the fields that are contained in the DataItems (application tables). Working Storage (also referred to as working data or variables) fields are defined in this book as the data elements that are defined within a report (or other object) for use in that object. The contents of working storage data elements aren't permanently stored in the database. All of these are collectively referred to in the Business Central *Help* as columns.

These components define the data elements that are made available to Visual Studio as a dataset, which will be used in the layout and delivery of results to the user. In addition, labels (text literals) for display can be defined separately from any DataItem, but are also included in the dataset that's passed to Visual Studio. Labels must be **Common Language Specification** (**CLS**) compliant names, which means labels can contain only alpha, decimal, and underscore characters, and must not begin with an underscore. If the report is to be used in a multi-language environment, the `CaptionML` label must be properly defined to support the alternate languages.

 Visual Studio cannot access any data elements that are not defined within the Report Designer. Each data element that's passed in the dataset, whether it's a Data Field or working data, must be associated with a DataItem (except for labels).

The **Report Request** page displays when a report is invoked. Its purpose is to allow users to enter information to control the report. Control information that's entered through a request page may include filters, control dates, other parameters and specifications, as well as formatting or processing options to use for this report run. The request page appears once at the beginning of a report, at runtime.

The following screenshot shows a sample request page, the one associated with the
CUSTOMER LIST (report 101):

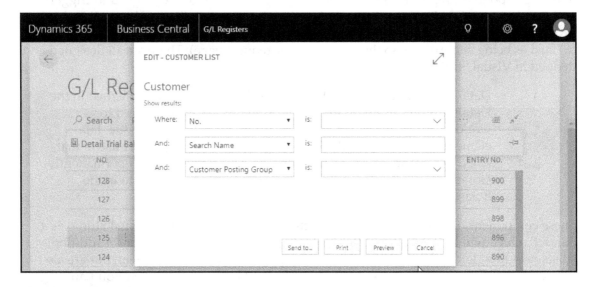

Report layout overview

The report layout is designed in Microsoft Word using data elements that are defined in
dataset DataItems by the Report Designer, and then made available to Microsoft Word. The
report layout includes the page header, body, and page footer.

Within the report body, there can be none, one, or more detail rows. There can also be
header and footer rows. The detail rows are the definition of the primary, repeating data
display.

All of the report formatting is controlled in Microsoft Word. The font, field positioning, and
graphics are all defined as part of the report layout. The same is true for pagination control,
headings and footers, some totaling, column-width control, color, and many other display
details.

Of course, if the display target changes dramatically, for example, from a desktop
workstation display to a browser on a phone, the appearance of the report layout will
change dramatically as well. One of the advantages of the Business Central reporting layout
toolset is to support the required flexibility. Because we must expect significant variability
in our user's output devices (desktop video, browser, tablet, phone), we should design and
test accordingly.

Report data flow

One of the principal advantages of the Business Central report is its built-in data flow structure. At the beginning of any report, we will define the DataItems (the tables) that the report will process. We can create a processing-only report that has no DataItems (if no looping through database data is required), but that situation often calls for a code unit to be used. In a report, Business Central automatically creates a data flow process for each DataItem or table reference. This automatically-created data flow provides specific triggers and processing events for each DataItem, as follows:

- Preceding the DataItem
- After reading each record of the DataItem
- Following the end of the DataItem

The underlying **black-box** report logic (the part we can't see or affect) automatically loops through the named tables, reading and processing one record at a time. Therefore, any time we need a process that steps through a set of data one record at a time, it is often easier to use a report object.

The reference to a database table in a report is referred to as a DataItem. The report data flow structure allows us to nest DataItems to create a hierarchical grandparent, parent, and child structure. If `DataItem2` is nested within `DataItem1`, and related to `DataItem1`, then for each record in `DataItem1`, all of the related records in `DataItem2` will be processed.

The following example uses tables from our WDTU system. The design is for a report to list all the scheduled instances of a `Radio Show Playlist` DataItem grouped by `Radio Show`, which in turn is grouped by `Radio Show Type`. Thus, `Radio Show Type` is the primary table (`DataItem1`). For each `Radio Show Type`, we want to list all the Radio Shows of that type (`DataItem2`). And for each `Radio Show`, we want to list all the scheduled instances of that show that have been recorded in the `Playlist Header` (`DataItem3`).

Open Visual Studio Code and create a new file with the `.al` extension called `Report 50102 "Demo"`. In Object Designer, select the `Report` object type and click the **New** button. On the **Report Dataset Designer** screen, we will first enter the table name, `Radio Show Type` (or table number `50101`), as we can see in the following screenshot. The DataItem `Name`, to which the AL code will refer to, is `DataItem1` in our example. Then, we will enter the second table, `Radio Show`, which is automatically indented relative to the DataItem above it, that is, the superior or parent DataItem. This indicates the nesting of the processing of the indented (child) DataItem within the processing of the superior (parent) DataItem.

For our example, we have renamed the DataItems to better illustrate report data flow. The normal behavior would be for the Name in the right column to default to the table name shown in the left column (for example, the name for Radio Show would be <Radio Show> by default). This default DataItem name would only need to be changed if the same table appeared twice within the DataItem list. If there were a second instance of Radio Show, for example, we could simply give it the name RadioShow2, but it would be much better to give it a name describing its purpose in context.

For each record in the parent DataItem, the indented DataItem will be fully processed, dependent on the filters and the defined relationships between the superior and indented tables. In other words, the visible indentation is only part of the necessary parent-child definition.

For our example, we will enter a third table, Playlist Header, and our example name of DataItem3, as shown in the following screenshot:

```
1    report 50102 "Demo"
2    {
3        dataset {
4            dataitem(DataItem1; "Radio Show Type") {
5                dataitem(DataItem2; "Radio Show") {
6                    dataitem(DataItem3; "Playlist Header") { }
```

The following diagram shows the data flow for the preceding DataItem structure. The chart boxes are intended to show the nesting that results from the indentation of the DataItems in the preceding screenshot. The Radio Show DataItem is indented under the Radio Show Type DataItem. This means that for every processed Radio Show Type record, all of the selected Radio Show records will be processed. The same logic applies to the Playlist Header records and Radio Show records, that is, for each Radio Show record processed, all selected Playlist Header records are processed:

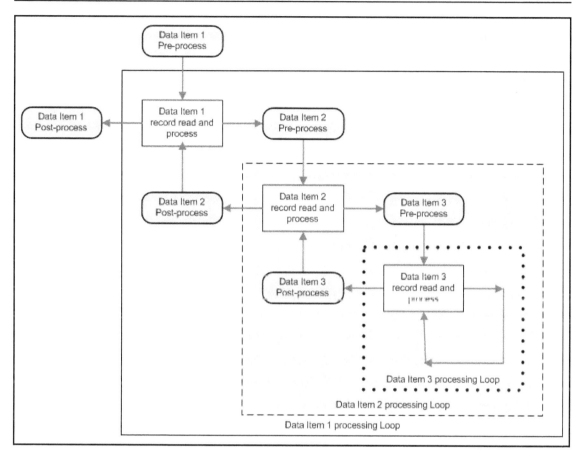

The blocks visually illustrate how DataItem nesting controls the data flow. As we can see, the full range of processing for **Data Item 2** occurs for each **Data Item 1** record. In turn, the full range of processing for **Data Item 3** occurs for each **Data Item 2** record.

In Business Central, report processing occurs in two separate steps: the first tied primarily to what has been designed in Visual Studio Code, and the second tied to what has been designed in Microsoft Word. The data processing that's represented in the preceding diagram all occurs in the first step, yielding a complete dataset that contains all the data that is to be rendered for output.

Report components – detail

Earlier, we reviewed a list of the components of a report object. Now, we'll review detailed information about each of those components. Our goal here is to understand how the pieces of the report puzzle fit together.

Report properties

A subset of the Report Designer's report properties are shown in the following screenshot. Some of these properties have essentially the same purpose as similarly named properties in pages and other objects:

```
 1     report 50102 "Demo"
 2    {
 3         AccessByPermission      AccessByPermission property ⓘ
 4         ApplicationArea
 5         Caption
 6         CaptionML                                              }
 7         DefaultLayout
 8         Description
 9         EnableExternalAssemblies
10         EnableExternalImages
11         EnableHyperlinks
12         PaperSourceDefaultPage
13         PaperSourceFirstPage
14         PaperSourceLastPage
15           {
```

The properties in the preceding screenshot are defined as follows:

- `Caption`: This is the name that is displayed for this report; `Caption` defaults to `Name`.
- `CaptionML`: This is the `Caption` translation for a defined alternative language.
- `Description`: This is for internal documentation.
- `UseRequestPage`: This can either be `Yes` or `No`, and controls whether or not the report will begin with a Request Page so that user parameters can be entered.
- `UseSystemPrinter`: This determines whether the default printer for the report should be the defined system printer, or whether Business Central should check for a setup-defined user/report printer definition. More on user/report printer setup can be found in the Business Central application help.

- `EnableExternalImages`: If `Yes`, this allows links to external (non-embedded) images on the report. Such images can be outside the Business Central database.
- `EnableHyperLinks`: If `Yes`, this allows links to other URLs, including other reports or pages.
- `EnableExternalAssemblies`: If `Yes`, this allows for the use of external custom functions as part of the report.
- `ProcessingOnly`: This is set to `Yes` when the report object is being used only to process data and no reporting output is to be generated. If this property is set to `Yes`, then that overrides any other property selections that would apply in a report-generating situation.
- `ShowPrintStatus`: If this property is set to `Yes` and the `ProcessingOnly` property is set to `No`, then a **Report Progress** window, including a **Cancel** button, is displayed. When `ProcessingOnly` is set to `Yes`, if we want a **Report Progress** window, we must create our own dialog box.
- `TransactionType`: This can be in one of four basic options: `Browse`, `Snapshot`, `UpdateNoLocks`, and `Update`. These control the record locking behavior that will be applied in this report. The default is `UpdateNoLocks`. This property is generally only used by advanced developers.
- `Permissions`: This provides report-specific setting of permissions, which are the rights to access data tables, subdivided into `Read`, `Insert`, `Modify`, and `Delete`. This allows the developer to define report and processing permissions that override the user-by-user permissions security setup.
- `PaperSourceFirstPage`, `PaperSourceDefaultPage`, and `PaperSourceLastPage`: These give us a choice of paper source tray.
- `PreviewMode`: This specifies the choice of the default **Normal** or **Print Layout**, causing the report to open in either the interactive view, allowing for manipulation, or in the fixed format, on which it will appear on a printer.
- `DefaultLayout`: This specifies whether the report will default to using either the Word or the RDLC layout.
- `WordMergeDataItem`: This defines the table on which the outside processing loop will occur for a Word layout, which is equivalent to the first DataItem's effect on an RDLC layout.
- `PDFFontEmbedding`: This specifies whether the font will be embedded in generated PDF files from the report.

Microsoft Word – report properties

The Word properties window is available from the ribbon on top of the screen:

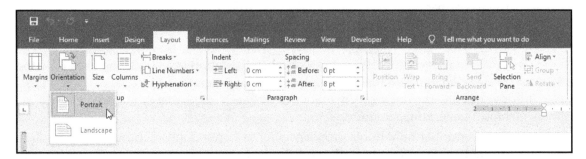

In the **Layout** ribbon, we can set **Margins**, **Orientation**, and paper **Size**. Other properties such as **Font**, styles, and effects can be set directly from the **Home** ribbon:

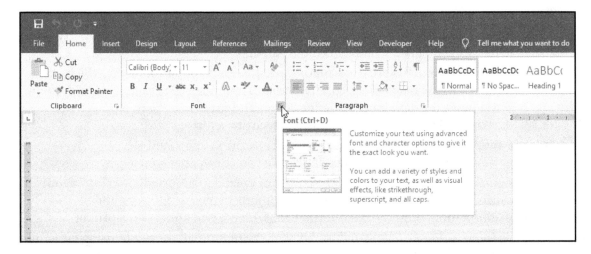

Another way to access property details is to highlight the element of interest, and then right-click and select the **Properties** option for that element. This opens up a control-specific **Properties** window that includes a menu of choices of property categories to access. In the following screenshot, the **Font** properties are open, and the available options for the **Font** properties are displayed:

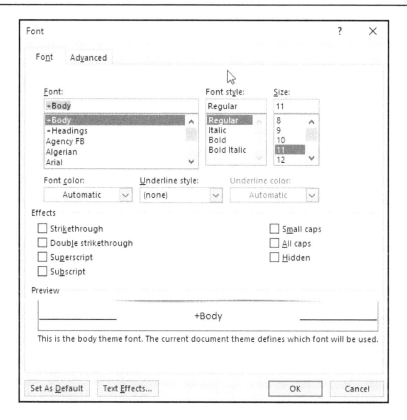

Some may feel it's easier to find and change all of the properties' options here.

Report triggers

The following screenshot shows the Report Designer's report triggers, all of which are available in a report:

```
1    report 50102 "Demo"
2    {
3        trigger OnInitReport()
4        begin
5        end;
6
7        trigger OnPreReport()
8        begin
9        end;
10
11       trigger OnPostReport()
12       begin
13       end;
14
```

Descriptions for the report triggers are as follows:

- `OnInitReport()`: This executes once when the report is opened.
- `OnPreReport()`: This executes once after the request page completes. All the DataItem processing follows this trigger.
- `OnPostReport()`: This trigger executes once at the end of all of the other report processing, if the report completes normally. If the report terminates with an error, this trigger does not execute. All of the DataItem processing precedes this trigger.

Request page properties

The request page properties are a subset of page properties, which are covered in detail in `Chapter 4`, *Pages – The Interactive Interface*. Usually, most of these properties are not changed, simply because the extra capability is not needed. An exception is the `SaveValues` property which, when set to `Yes`, causes entered values to be retained and redisplayed when the page is invoked another time. A screenshot of a subset of the request page properties follows:

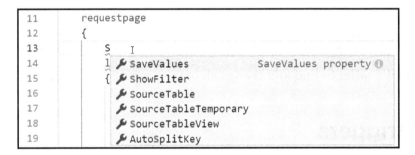

Request page triggers

Request pages have a full complement of triggers, thus allowing complex pre-report processing logic. Because of their comparatively simplistic nature, request pages seldom need to take advantage of these trigger capabilities. The following screenshot shows the triggers of a request page:

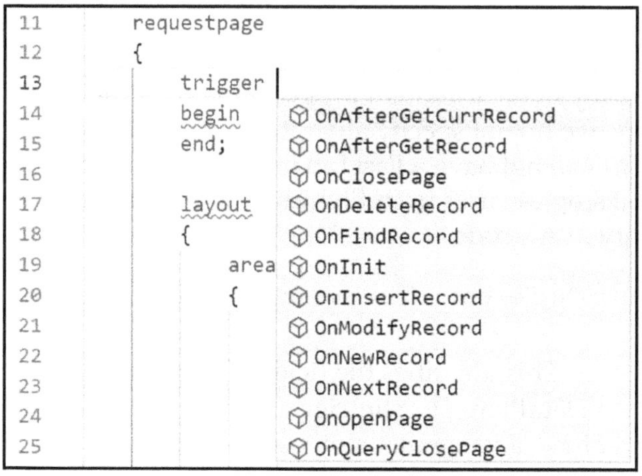

```
11        requestpage
12        {
13            trigger |
14            begin        ⊙ OnAfterGetCurrRecord
15            end;         ⊙ OnAfterGetRecord
16                         ⊙ OnClosePage
17            layout       ⊙ OnDeleteRecord
18            {            ⊙ OnFindRecord
19                area     ⊙ OnInit
20                {        ⊙ OnInsertRecord
21                         ⊙ OnModifyRecord
22                         ⊙ OnNewRecord
23                         ⊙ OnNextRecord
24                         ⊙ OnOpenPage
25                         ⊙ OnQueryClosePage
```

DataItem properties

The following screenshot shows the properties of a report DataItem:

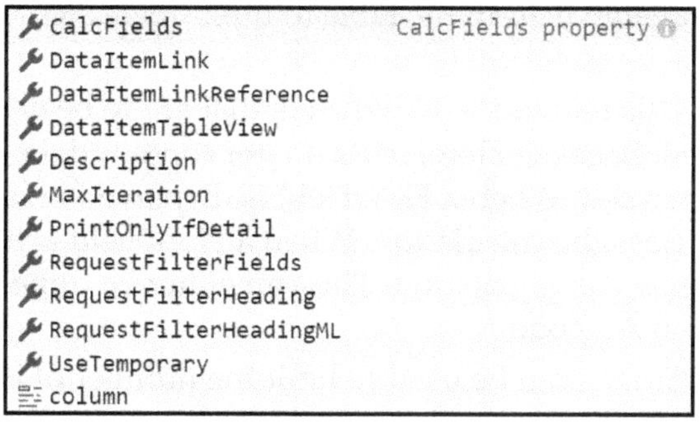

```
🔧 CalcFields                  CalcFields property ⓘ
🔧 DataItemLink
🔧 DataItemLinkReference
🔧 DataItemTableView
🔧 Description
🔧 MaxIteration
🔧 PrintOnlyIfDetail
🔧 RequestFilterFields
🔧 RequestFilterHeading
🔧 RequestFilterHeadingML
🔧 UseTemporary
▤ column
```

The following are descriptions of frequently used report DataItem properties:

- `DataItemTableView`: This is the definition of the fixed limits to be applied to the DataItem (the key, ascending or descending sequence, and what filters to apply to this field).

If we don't define a key in `DataItemTableView`, then the users can choose a key to control the data sequence during processing. If we do define a key in the DataItem properties and, in the `ReqFilterFields` property, we do not specify any filter Fieldnames to be displayed, this DataItem will not have a FastTab displayed as part of the Request Page. This will stop the user from filtering this DataItem, unless we provide the capability in AL code.

- `DataItemLinkReference`: This names the parent DataItem to which this one is linked.
- `DataItemLink`: This identifies the field-to-field linkage between this DataItem and its parent DataItem. That linkage acts as a filter because only the records in this table that have a value that matches with the linked field in the parent DataItem will be processed. If no field linkage filter is defined, all the records in the child table will be processed for each record that's processed in its parent table.
- `ReqFilterFields`: This property allows us to choose certain fields to be named in the report request page to make it easier for the user to access them as filter fields. So long as the report request page is activated for a DataItem, the user can choose any available field in the table to filter, regardless of what is specified here.
- `CalcFields`: This names the FlowFields that are to be calculated for each record that's processed. Because FlowFields do not contain data, they have to be calculated to be used. When a FlowField is displayed on a page, Business Central automatically does the calculation. When a FlowField is to be used in a report, we must instigate the calculation. This can either be done here in this property or explicitly within AL code.
- `MaxIteration`: This can be used to limit the number of iterations the report will make through this DataItem. For example, we would set this to 7 to make the virtual date table process one week's data.
- `PrintOnlyIfDetail`: This should only be used if this DataItem has a child DataItem, that is, one indented/nested below it. If `PrintOnlyIfDetail` is `Yes`, then controls associated with this DataItem will only print when data is processed for the child DataItem.
- `UseTemporary`: This specifies that a temporary table is supplying the dataset to populate the columns for this DataItem.

DataItem triggers

Each DataItem has the following triggers available:

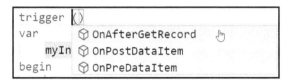

The DataItem triggers are where most of the flow logic is placed for a report. Developer defined functions may be freely added but, generally, they will be called from within the following three triggers:

- `OnPreDataItem()`: This is the logical place for any preprocessing to take place that can't be handled in report or DataItem properties or in the two report preprocessing triggers.
- `OnAfterGetRecord()`: This is the data *read and process* loop. The code that's placed here has full access to the data of each record, one record at a time. This trigger is repetitively processed until the logical end of table is reached for this DataItem. This is where we would typically access data in related tables. This trigger is represented on our report data flow diagram as any one of the boxes labeled `Data Item processing Loop`.
- `OnPostDataItem()`: This executes after all the records in this DataItem are processed, unless the report is terminated by means of a user canceled by execution of an AL `BREAK` or `QUIT` function, or by an error.

Creating a report in Business Central

Because our Business Central report layouts will all be developed in Microsoft Word, our familiarity with Visual Studio Code will only get us part way to having Business Central report development expertise. We've covered most of the basics of the Visual Studio Code part of Business Central report development. Now, we need to dig into the Microsoft Word part. If you are already a Microsoft Word expert, you won't need to spend much time on this part of the book. If you know little or nothing about the Microsoft Word layout tools, you will need to experiment and practice.

Learn by experimentation

One of the most important learning tools available is experimentation. Report development is one area where experimentation will be extremely valuable. We need to know which Report layouts, control settings, and field formats work well for our needs and which do not. The best way to find out is by experimentation.

Create a variety of test reports, beginning with the very simple, and make them progressively more complex. Document what you learn as you make discoveries. You will end up with your own personal report development *Help* documentation. Once we've created a number of simple reports from scratch, we should modify test copies of some of the standard reports that are part of the Business Central system.

 We must always make sure that we are working on test copies, not the originals!

Some reports will be relatively easy to understand, and others that are very complex will be difficult to understand. The more we test, the better we will be able to determine which standard Business Central report designs can be borrowed for our work, and where we are better off starting from scratch. Of course, we should always check to see if there is a pattern that is applicable to the situation that we are working on.

Report building – phase 1

Our goal is to create a report for our WDTU data that will give us a list of all the scheduled radio show instances that have been organized within Radio Show by Radio Show Type, as shown in the following screenshot:

```
1    report 50101 "Shows by Type"
2  ⊟ {
3        dataset
4  ⊟    {
5            dataitem(RadioShowType; "Radio Show Type")
6  ⊟        {
7                dataitem(RadioShow; "Radio Show")
8  ⊟            {
9                    dataitem(PlaylistHeader; "Playlist Header")
```

An easy way to recreate the preceding screenshot is to simply use IntelliSense. Type the letter D in the **Code** window, enter a name, and then the target table name (in this case, `Radio Show Type`, then `Radio Show`, and then `Playlist Header`).

Before we go any further, let's make sure we've got some test data in our tables. To enter data, we can use the pages we built earlier. The specifics of our test data aren't critical. We simply need a reasonable distribution of data so that our report test will be meaningful. The following triple screenshot provides an example minimal set of data:

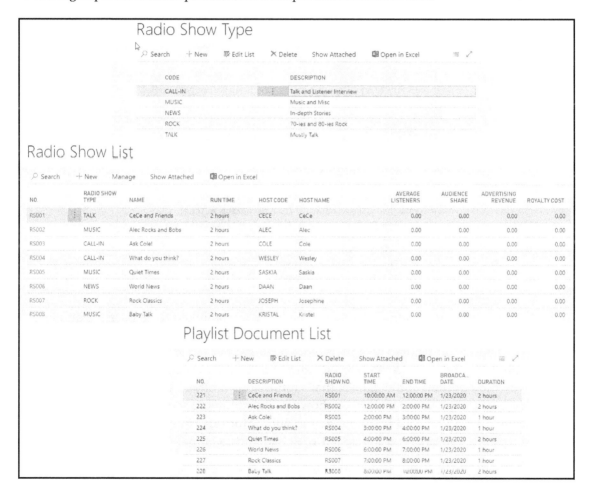

Since the Visual Studio Code part of our report design is relatively simple, we can do it as part of our phase 1 effort. It's simple because we aren't building any processing logic, and we don't have any complex relationships to address. We just want to create a nice, neat, nested list of data.

The next step is to define the data fields we want to be available for processing and outputting by Microsoft Word:

```
Report 50101 Shows by Type.al  ●
1    report 50101 "Shows by Type"
2    {
3        WordLayout = './Shows by Type.docx';
4    |
5        dataset            I
6        {
7            dataitem(RadioShowType; "Radio Show Type")
8            {
9                column(UserComment; UserComment) { }
10               column(Code_RadioShowType; Code) { IncludeCaption = true; }
11               column(Description_RadioShowType; Description) { IncludeCaption = true; }
12               dataitem(RadioShow; "Radio Show")
13               {
14                   column(No_RadioShow; "No.") { IncludeCaption = true; }
15                   column(Name_RadioShow; Name) { IncludeCaption = true; }
16                   column(RunTime_RadioShow; "Run Time") { IncludeCaption = true; }
17                   dataitem(PlaylistHeader; "Playlist Header")
18                   {
19                       column(PostingDate_PlaylistHeader; "Broadcast Date") { IncludeCaption = true; }
20                       column(StartTime_PlaylistHeader; "Start Time") { IncludeCaption = true; }
```

Each of the subordinate nested DataItems must be properly linked to its parent DataItem. The `Playlist Header` DataItem is joined to the `Radio Show` DataItem by the "Radio Show No." and "No." fields. The `Radio Show` DataItem is joined to the `Radio Show Type` DataItem by the "Radio ShowType" and `Radio Show Type` fields, that is, "Code". The `Radio Show` portion of the dataset that's returned is limited by setting the `PrintOnlyIfDetail` value to `true`, as shown in the following screenshot. This choice will cause the `Radio Show` record to not be sent to output for reporting if no subordinate `Playlist Header` records are associated with that `Radio Show`:

```
11          column(Description_RadioShowType; Description) { IncludeCaption = true; }
12          dataitem(RadioShow; "Radio Show")
13          {
14              DataItemLink = "Radio Show Type" = FIELD (Code);
15              DataItemTableView = SORTING ("Radio Show Type");
16              PrintOnlyIfDetail = true;
17              column(No_RadioShow; "No.") { IncludeCaption = true; }
18              column(Name_RadioShow; Name) { IncludeCaption = true; }
19              column(RunTime_RadioShow; "Run Time") { IncludeCaption = true; }
20              dataitem(PlaylistHeader; "Playlist Header")
21              {
22                  DataItemLink = "Radio Show No." = FIELD ("No.");
23                  DataItemTableView = SORTING ("No.");
24                  column(PostingDate_PlaylistHeader; "Broadcast Date") { IncludeCaption
25                  column(StartTime_PlaylistHeader; "Start Time") { IncludeCaption = tru
```

The other data that we can pass to Microsoft Word are the labels. Labels will be used later as captions in the report and are enabled for multi-language support. Let's create a title label that we will hand over the fence to Microsoft Word. Go to the end of the `.al` file and type `L` or use *Ctrl* + *spacebar*:

```
54      labels
55      {
56          ReportTitle = 'Show Schedule by Type';
57      }
```

Now that we have our AL dataset definition completed, we should compile, build, and publish our work before doing anything else. Then, before we begin our Microsoft Word work, it's a good idea to check that we don't have some hidden error that will get in our way later. The easiest way to do that is just to run what we have now. What we expect to see is a basic **Request Page** display, allowing us to run a report with no layout defined.

Report building – phase 2

As we mentioned earlier, there are several tools we can use for Business Central report layout development. The specific screen appearance depends somewhat on which tool is being used.

To begin our report development work in Microsoft Word, we must build our AL dataset definition. Then, we need to navigate to the generated Word document and use the right mouse button to select **Open Externally** to open up Microsoft Word. We will see the following screen:

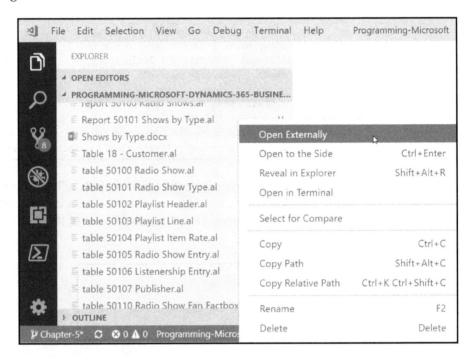

To design reports with Microsoft Word, the **Developer** tab needs to be exposed, as explained in Chapter 1, *Introduction to Business Central*.

On the right-hand side of the screen is the **XML Mapping**, which can be activated from the **Developer** ribbon:

Let's start by adding the report name to our layout. Expand **NavWordReportXMLPart** and then expand labels. Right-click on the **ReportTitle** menu and then click on **Insert Content Control**, as shown in the following screenshot:

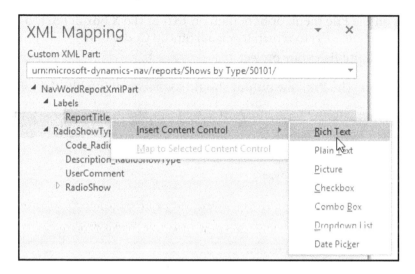

Next, we will add some fields to the page header. First, we will expand two of the categories in the **XML Mapping** panel, which is on the right-hand side of our layout screen. The two categories we want to expand are RadioShowType and RadioShow, which contain the data elements that are passed from our report dataset, as shown in the following screenshot:

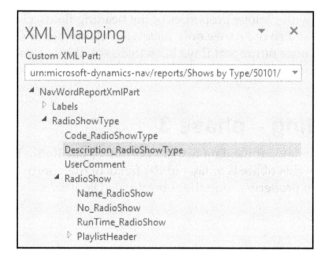

At this point, it's a good time to save our work and test to see what we have done so far:

1. Click on the top-left **File** menu option, the disc icon, or *Ctrl + S* to save the design as a Word file.
2. Click on the **File** menu option, then on **Exit** or the **X** box at the top-right of the screen (or *Alt + F4*) to return to Visual Studio Code.
3. Build and publish your project.

Now, **Run** the report. The **Preview** output should look something like the following:

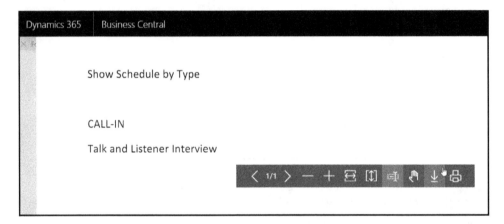

This isn't especially impressive, but it's not bad if this is your first try at creating a Business Central report.

We could experiment with various properties of the heading fields, choosing different fonts, bolding, colors, and so on. As we only have a small number of simple fields to display (and could recreate our report if we have to do so), this is a good time to learn more about some of the report appearance capabilities that Microsoft Word provides.

Report building – phase 3

Finally, we are ready to lay out the data display portion of our **Radio Shows by Type** report. The first step of this phase is to lay out the fields of our controlling DataItem data in such a way that we can properly group the subordinate DataItems' data.

Once again, open the Microsoft Word layout from Visual Studio Code. Put the cursor on a new row at the end of the document and insert a table with two rows and a few columns, as shown in the following screenshot:

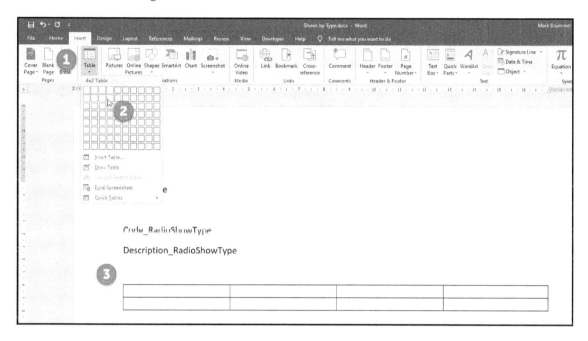

Select the second row in the Microsoft Word table and make it a repeater by clicking on the RadioShow DataItem in the XML Mapping pane and selecting **Repeating**:

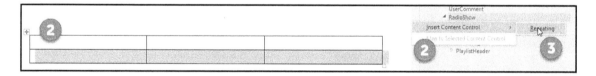

In the second-row columns, we will select the fields from **XML Mapping**, as shown in the following screenshot:

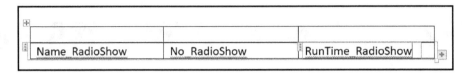

In the first-row columns, we will add captions. If you want to, you can make the table look nicer by using the design options in the Microsoft Word ribbon:

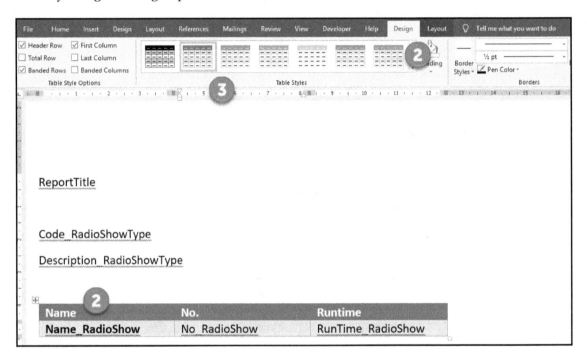

If we save the Word document and publish our solution, we can run the report. The result should look as follows:

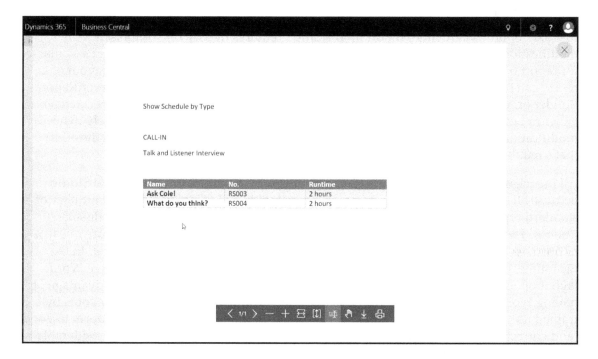

Modifying an existing report with Report Designer or Word

The basic process we must follow to modify an existing report is the same, regardless of whether the report is one of the standard reports that comes with Business Central or a custom report that we are enhancing in some way. An important discipline to follow in all cases where we are modifying a report that has been in production is *not* to work on the original, but on a copy. In fact, if this is a standard report we are customizing, we should leave the original copy alone and do all our work on a copy. Not only is this safer because we will eliminate the possibility of creating problems in the original version, but it will make upgrading easier later on. Even when working on a new custom report, it is good practice to save intermediate copies for backup. This allows you to return to a previous working step should the next development step not go as planned.

While it is certainly possible to add a new layout to an existing dataset without disturbing the original material in Business Central, the potential for a mistake to occur when creating a production problem is why best practice dictates working on a copy, not the original.

Just like report construction, report modification requires the use of two toolsets. Any modification that is done to the processing logic or the definition of the data that's available for report output must be done using Visual Studio Code. Modification to the layout of a report can be done using Visual Studio, just like we've been doing, the SQL Server Report Builder or, when a Word layout is available, using Microsoft Word. Each report can have either or both an RDLC and a Word layout, but for those reports that are unlikely to need modification by a non-programmer, a Word layout will probably not be worth the effort that's required to create it.

All Business Central report layouts can be modified by a developer using Visual Studio because all standard reports have been developed with RDLC layouts. A small number of standard reports also have Word layouts available in the initial distribution of Business Central. These include reports 1304, 1305, 1306, and 1307. It is likely that future releases of Business Central will have additional report layouts available in Word format. In the meantime, if we want other reports, whether they be standard or custom, to have Word layout options available, we will have to create those ourselves. The primary advantage of having Word layout options for reports is to allow for the modification of the layouts by a trained user or developer using only Word. As the modifications must still conform to good (and correct) report layout practices, appropriate training, careful work, and considerable common sense are needed to make such modifications, even though the tool is Microsoft Word.

Request page

A request page is a page that is executed at the beginning of a report. Its presence or absence is under the developer's control. A request page looks similar to what's shown in the following screenshot, which is based on one of the standard system reports, that is, the **CUSTOMER - ORDER DETAIL** report, report 108:

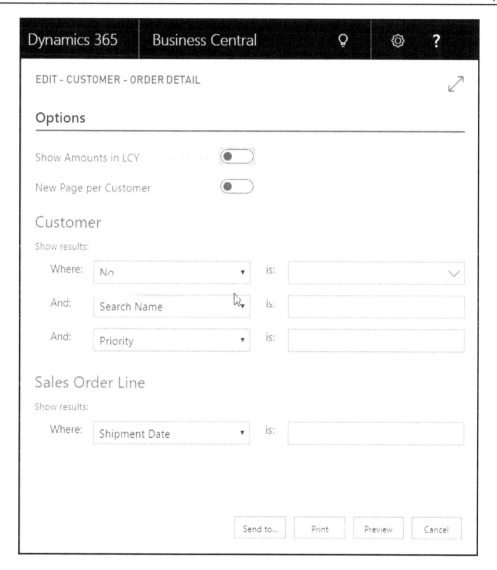

There are three FastTabs in this page. The **Customer** and **Sales Order Line** FastTabs are tied to the data tables associated with this report. These FastTabs allow the user to define both data filters and flow filters to control report processing. The **Options** FastTab exists because the software developer wanted to allow some additional user options for this report.

Adding a request page option

Because we have defined the default sort sequences (`DataItemTableView`), except for the first DataItem, and we have not defined any requested filters (`ReqFilterFields`), the default request page for our report has only one DataItem FastTab. Since we have not defined any processing options that would require user input before the report is generated, we have no **Options** FastTab.

Our goal now is to allow the user to optionally input text that will be printed at the top of the report. This could be a secondary report heading, instructions on interpreting the report, or some other communications to the report reader. To add this capability, perform the following steps:

1. Open `Report 50101` in Visual Studio Code.
2. Add a global variable named `UserComment` with a data type of `Text`. We will not define the `Length` field, as shown in the following screenshot; this will allow the user to enter a comment of any length:

```
66
67          var
68              UserComment: Text;
69
70      }                           I
```

3. Add this variable as a data `column` to be passed to Visual Studio. The `column` must be a subordinate of the DataItem. We do not need a caption defined as we will use the variable name for this field in the report layout, as shown in the following screenshot:

```
1    report 50101 "Shows by Type"
2    {
3        DefaultLayout = Word;
4        WordLayout = './Shows by Type.docx';
5        UsageCategory = ReportsAndAnalysis;
6
7        dataset
8        {
9            dataitem(RadioShowType; "Radio Show Type")
10            {
11                column(UserComment; UserComment) { }
12                column(Code_RadioShowType; Code) { IncludeCaption = true; }
13                column(Description_RadioShowType; Description) { IncludeCap
```

4. Add the request page to the report, as displayed in the following screenshot:

```
33      requestpage
34      {
35          layout
36          {
37              area(content)
38              {
39                  group(Options)
40                  {
41                      field(UserComment; UserComment)
42                      {
43                          ApplicationArea = Basic;
44                          Caption = 'User Comment';
45                      }
46                  }
```

5. Access Microsoft Word through **Open Externally**.
6. Add a text box to the layout design surface, just below the report title, stretching the box out as far as the report layout allows.
7. Expand the **XML Mapping** in the **Developer** ribbon.
8. Add the `UserComment` field to the new space, as shown in the following screenshot:

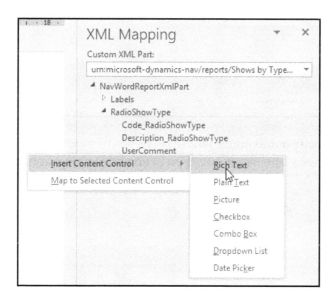

9. Save the Word document and exit Microsoft Word. Then, publish the project.
10. Run **Report 50101**.

In the request page, the user can enter their comment, as shown in the following screenshot:

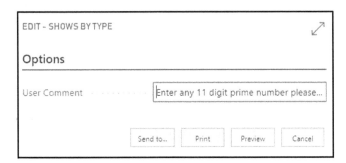

The report heading then shows the comment in whatever font, color, or other display attribute the developer has defined:

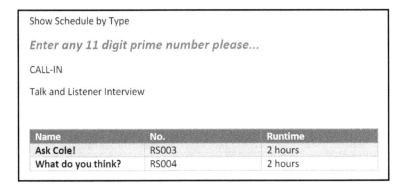

Because we didn't specify a maximum length on our `UserComment` field, we can type in as much information as we want. Try it out; type in an entire paragraph for a test.

Processing-only reports

One of the report properties we reviewed earlier was **ProcessingOnly**. If that property is set to `Yes`, then the report object will not output a dataset for displaying or printing—it will simply process the data we program it to process. The beauty of this capability is that we can use the built-in processing loop of the Business Central report object, along with its sorting and filtering capabilities, to create a variety of data updating routines with minimal programming. Use of report objects also gives us access to the request page to allow user input and guidance for the run. We could create the same functionality using code unit objects and by programming all of the loops, filtering, user interface request pages, and so on, ourselves. However, with a **processing-only** report, Business Central gives us a lot of help, and makes it possible to create some powerful routines with minimal effort.

At the beginning of the run of a processing-only report, there is very little user interface variation compared to a normal printing report. The processing-only request page looks much like it would for a printing report, except that the choices to **Print** and **Preview** are not available. Everything else looks the same. Of course, we have the big difference of no visible output at the end of processing.

Creative report plagiarism and patterns

In the same fashion as we discussed regarding pages in `Chapter 4`, *Pages – The Interactive Interface*, when we want to create a new report of a type that we haven't made recently (or at all), it's a good idea to find another report that is similar in an important way and study it. We should also check if there is a Business Central pattern defined for an applicable category of report. As the minimum, in both of these investigations, we will learn how the developers of Business Central solved a data flow, totaling, or filtering challenge. In the best case, we will find a model that we can follow closely, respectfully plagiarizing (copying) a working solution, thus saving ourselves much time and effort.

Often, it is useful to look at two or three of the standard Business Central reports for similar functions to see how they are constructed. There is no sense in reinventing the design for a report of a particular type when someone else has already invented a version of it. Not only that, but they have provided us with the plans and given us the AL code, as well as the complete structure of the existing report object.

When it comes to modifying a system such as Business Central, plagiarism is a very effective research and design tool. In the case of reports, our search for a model may be based on any of several key elements. We may be looking for a particular data flow approach and find that the Business Central developers used the Integer table for some DataItems (as many reports do).

We may need a way to provide some creative filtering, similar to what is done in an area of the standard product. We might want to provide user options to print either detailed or a couple of different levels of totaling, with a layout that looks good, no matter which choice the user makes. We may be dealing with all three of these design needs in the same report. In such a case, it is likely that we are using multiple Business Central reports as our models: one for this feature, another for that feature, and so forth.

If we have a complicated, application-specific report to create, we may not be able to directly model our report on a model that already exists. However, often, we can still find ideas in standard reports that we can apply to our new design. We will almost always be better off using a model rather than inventing a totally new approach.

If our design concept is too big a leap from what was done previously, we should consider what we might change in our design so that we can build on the strengths of AL and existing Business Central routines. Creating entirely new approaches may be very satisfying (when it works) but, too often, the extra costs exceed the incremental benefits.

Summary

In this chapter, we focused on the structural and layout aspects of Business Central report objects. We studied the primary structural components, data, and format, along with the request page. We also experimented with some of the tools and modestly expanded our WDTU application.

In the next chapter, we will begin exploring the key tools that pull the pieces of the Visual Studio Code developer experience and the AL programming language together.

Questions

1. The following are defined in Visual Studio Code (choose three):
   - DataItems
   - Field display editing
   - Request Page
   - Database updating

2. Reports can be set to `ProcessingOnly` status dynamically by AL code. True or false?

3. Reports are fixed displays of data that's extracted from the system, designed only for hardcopy output. True or false?

4. Business Central report data flow includes a structure that makes "child" DataItems fully processed for each record that's processed in the "parent" DataItem. What is the visible indication that this structure exists in a report Dataset Designer form (choose one)?
   - Nesting
   - Indentation
   - Linking

5. Queries can be designed to directly feed the Visual Studio Report Designer. True or false?

6. Union Joins are available using a special setup parameter. True or false?

7. A report that only does processing and generates no printed output can be defined. True or false?

8. Which of the following are properties of queries (choose two)?
   - `TopNumberOfRows`
   - `FormatAs`
   - `OrderBy`
   - `FilterReq`

9. Business Central has four Report Designers. Reports can be created using any one of these by itself. True or false?

10. Business Central queries can directly generate OData and CSV files and are cloud compatible. True or false?

11. Which of the following are Business Central Report Types (choose three)?
    - List
    - Document
    - Invoice
    - Posting

12. Queries cannot have multiple DataItems on the same indentation level. True or false?

13. Report formatting in Word has all the capabilities of report formatting in Visual Studio. True or false?

14. Business Central reports can be run for testing directly from Visual Studio with *Alt* + *R*. True or false?

15. Repeater rows are used in Microsoft Word tables to display multiple records from a dataset. True or false?

16. Queries are used to support what items (choose two)?
    - Charts
    - Pages
    - Cues
    - Data Sorting

17. Most reports can be initially created using the Report Wizard. True or false?

18. Interactive capabilities that are available after a report is displayed include what (choose two)?
    - Font definition
    - Data Show/Hide
    - Sorting by columns
    - Data filtering

19. DataItem parent-child relationships that are defined in Visual Studio Code must also be considered in the SQL Server Report Builder in order to have data display properly in a parent-child format. True or false?

20. Users can create Word report layouts based on an existing dataset and put them into production without having access to a Developer's license. True or false?

Introduction to AL 6

"Programs must be written for people to read, and only incidentally for machines to execute."

– Harold Abelson and Julie Sussman

"The details are not the details. They make the design."

– Charles Eames

So far, we have reviewed the basic objects of Business Central, such as tables, data fields, pages, queries, and reports. For each of these, we reviewed triggers in various areas, the purpose of which are to be containers for AL code. When triggers are fired (invoked), the AL code within is executed.

In this chapter, you'll start learning the AL programming language, though many of the things we will cover you should already know about from your experience programming in other languages. Some of the basic AL syntax and procedure definitions can be found in the Business Central help, as well as in Microsoft Docs for Microsoft Dynamics 365 Business Central.

As with most programming languages, we have considerable flexibility to define our own model for our code structure. However, when we are inserting new code within the existing code, it's always a good idea to utilize the model and follow the structure that exists in the original code.

The goal of this chapter is to help us to productively use the development tools and be comfortable in AL. We'll focus on the tools and processes that we will use the most often. We will also review concepts that we can apply to more complex tasks down the road. In this chapter, we will cover the following topics:

- Understanding Visual Studio Code
- AL syntax, operators, and built-in procedures
- AL naming conventions
- Input/output procedures
- Creating custom procedures
- Basic process flow structures

Understanding Visual Studio Code

With a few exceptions, all of the development for Business Central applications takes place within Visual Studio Code. Exceptions include the use of Microsoft Word (or Microsoft SQL Server) for reporting, as we saw in `Chapter 5`, *Queries and Reports*, plus the work we may do in the JavaScript language to create compatible add-ins. While it is possible, development using a text editor is only appropriate for special cases, such as making modifications to existing objects, which is done by an advanced developer.

As an **Integrated Development Environment** (**IDE**), Visual Studio Code provides us with a rich set of tools for our AL development work. While Visual Studio Code is not as fully featured as Microsoft's Visual Studio, it is intended to be a cross-platform, modern development toolkit. Most importantly, Visual Studio Code is the most popular IDE and chances are you are already familiar with it.

Explorer

All Business Central object development work starts from within Visual Studio Code in the **EXPLORER**. After opening a project folder, you should be able to see the following screen:

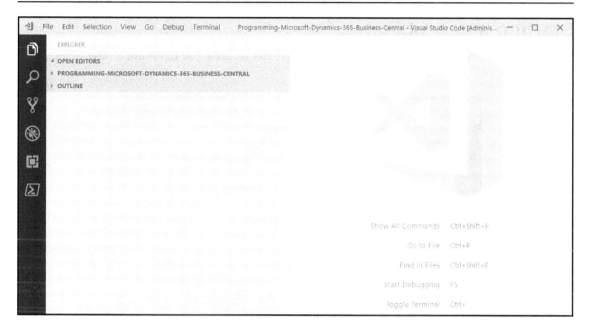

The type of object that we'll be working on is chosen by the object definition, which we can view by clicking on one of the files in the menus, as shown in the following screenshot:

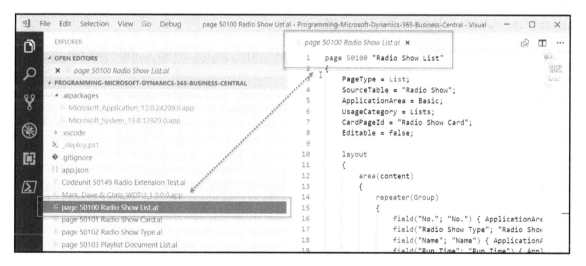

It is considered a best practice to apply logical naming to your files so that you can see which object type and ID is used without having to open each individual file.

Starting a new object

When we select **New File** from the **File** menu, we get a blank file to create a new object, as shown in the following screenshot:

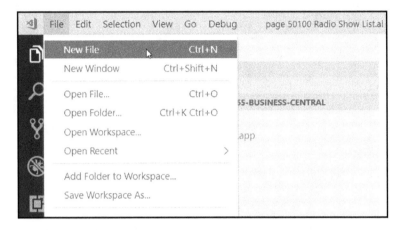

The fastest way to define a skeleton object is to use snippets. To enable the snippets, we must first save our new file using the .al file extension.

This forces us to think about file naming before defining the object, but we can always rename the file after the object's declaration is done.

To start using snippets after saving the file, we simply type the letter t and wait for IntelliSense to show the list of available snippets:

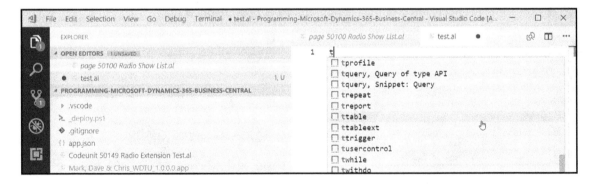

Once we select a snippet, the cursor automatically takes us to the first variable we have to populate. We can use the *Tab* key to move through the fields one by one:

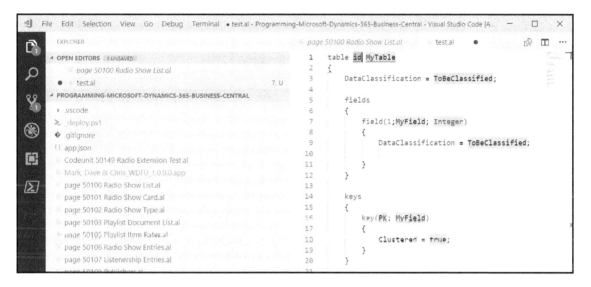

Object designer navigation

In many places in the various designers within Visual Studio Code, there are standard keyboard shortcuts available. Some of these are as follows:

- *Ctrl* + *N* to create a new empty file
- *Ctrl* + *O* to open an existing file
- *Ctrl* + spacebar to access AL IntelliSense, which shows us what we can do for the object that we are working on
- *F5* to publish the project
- *Ctrl* + *Shift* + *B* to do an on-the-fly build (very useful for error checking as we go)
- *Ctrl* + / to comment or uncomment code and properties
- *Ctrl* + *X*, *Ctrl* + *C*, and *Ctrl* + *V* in normal Windows mode for deletion (or cut), copy, and paste, respectively

We can cut, copy, and paste AL code—even procedures—relatively freely within an object, from object to object, or to a text-friendly tool (for example, Word or Excel) much as if we were using a text editor. The source and target objects don't need to be of the same type.

The easiest way to copy a complete object is to create a new version. You can do this as follows: open the object that you're working on. Click on **File** | **Save As** for the object, assign a new object number, and change the object name (no duplicate object names are allowed). A quick (mouseless) way to do a **Save As** is by pressing *Alt + F*, then pressing the *A* key—continuously hold down the *Alt* key while pressing first *F* and then *A*.

Some AL naming conventions

In the previous chapters, we discussed naming conventions for tables, pages, and reports. In general, the naming guidelines for Business Central objects and AL encourage consistency, common sense, and readability. Use meaningful names. These make the system more intuitive to the users and more self-documenting.

When we name variables, we must try to keep the names as self-documenting as possible. We should differentiate between similar, but different, variable meanings, such as `Cost` (cost from the vendor) and `Amount` (selling price to the customer). Embedded spaces, periods, or other special characters should be avoided (even though we find some violations of this in the base product). If we want to use special characters for the benefit of the user, we should put them in the caption, not in the name. If possible, we will stick to letters and numbers in our variable names. We should always avoid Hungarian naming styles (see `https://docs.microsoft.com/en-us/previous-versions/visualstudio/visual-studio-6.0/aa260976(v=vs.60)`); keep names simple and descriptive.

There are a number of reasons to keep variable names simple. Other software products that we may interface with may have limitations on variable names. Some special characters have special meanings to other software or in another human language. In Business Central, symbols such as `?` and `*` are wildcards and must be avoided in variable names. The `$` symbol has a special meaning in other software. SQL Server adds its own special characters to Business Central names, and the resultant combinations can get quite confusing (not just to us, but to the software). The same can be said for the names that are constructed by the internal RDLC generator, which replaces spaces and periods with underscores.

When we are defining multiple instances of a table, we should either differentiate clearly by name (for example, `Item` and `NewItem`) or by a descriptive suffix (for example, `Item`, `ItemForVarient`, and `ItemForLocation`). In the very common situation where a name is a compound combination of words, begin each abbreviated word with a capital letter (for example, `NewCustBalDue`).

Avoid creating variable names that are common words that might be reserved words (for example, `Page`, `Column`, `Number`, and `Integer`). Visual Studio Code will sometimes not warn us that we have used a reserved word, and we may find our logic and the automatic logic working at very mysterious cross purposes.

Do not start variables with a prefix, x, which is used in some automatically created variables, such as `xRec`. We should make sure that we can clearly differentiate between working storage variable names and the field names originating in tables. Sometimes, Visual Studio Code will allow us to have a global name, local name, and/or record variable name, all with the same literal name. If we do this, we are practically guaranteeing a variable misidentification bug where the compiler uses a different variable than what we intended to be referenced.

When defining a temporary table, preface the name logically, for example, with `Temp`. In general, use meaningful names that help in identifying the type and purpose of the item being named. When naming a new procedure, we should be reasonably descriptive. Don't name two procedures that are located in different objects with the same name. It will be too easy to get confused later.

In short, be careful, be consistent, be clear, and use common sense.

Variables

As we've gone through examples showing various aspects of Visual Studio Code and AL, we've seen and referred to variables in a number of situations. Some of the following are obvious, but for clarity's sake, we'll summarize them here.

In Chapter 3, *Data Types and Fields*, we reviewed various data types for variables that are defined within objects (referred to in Chapter 3, *Data Types and Fields*, as working storage data). Working storage consists of all of the variables that are defined for use within an object, but whose contents disappear when the object closes. Working storage data types, as discussed in Chapter 3, *Data Types and Fields*, are those that can be defined in either the AL global variables or AL local variables tabs. Variables can also be defined in several other places in a Business Central object.

AL Globals

Global variables are defined on the `var` section of each object in AL.

 Global variables should be avoided. Dynamics Business Central legacy code has inherited many of them from the MS-DOS era of the product (called Navision or Navigator) when local variables were not available.

Global text constants are defined as variables. The primary purpose of the text constants area is to allow for easier translation of messages from one language to another. By putting all message text in this one place in each object, a standardized process can be defined for language translation.

Procedures are most often defined at the end of an AL file. The following screenshot provides an example of this:

```
procedure CreateRadioShows()
begin
    HelperCreateRadioShow('RS001', 'TALK', 'CeCe and Friends', 020000T - 000000T, 'CECE', 'CeCe');
    HelperCreateRadioShow('RS002', 'MUSIC', 'Alec Rocks and Bobs', 020000T - 000000T, 'ALEC', 'Alec
    HelperCreateRadioShow('RS003', 'CALL-IN', 'Ask Cole!', 020000T - 000000T, 'Cole', 'Cole');
    HelperCreateRadioShow('RS004', 'CALL-IN', 'What do you think?', 020000T - 000000T, 'WESLEY',
    HelperCreateRadioShow('RS005', 'MUSIC', 'Quiet Times', 020000T - 000000T, 'SASKIA', 'Saskia');
    HelperCreateRadioShow('RS006', 'NEWS', 'World News', 020000T - 000000T, 'DAAN', 'Daan');
    HelperCreateRadioShow('RS007', 'ROCK', 'Rock Classics', 020000T - 000000T, 'JOSEPH', 'Josephine
    HelperCreateRadioShow('RS008', 'MUSIC', 'Baby Talk', 020000T - 000000T, 'KRISTAL', 'Kristel');
end;
```

AL Locals

Local identifiers only exist if they're defined within the range of a procedure or trigger. This is true if the trigger is a developer-defined procedure, one of the default system triggers, or a standard application-supplied procedure.

Procedure-local identifiers and return values are declared in the definition of the procedure.

The **Variables** and **Text Constants** tabs for **AL Locals** are the same in use to the **AL Globals** when using the `var` keyword. The declaration of the **AL Locals** form can be seen in the following screenshot:

```
procedure HelperCreateShowType("Code": Code[10]; Descr: Text):Boolean
var
    RadioShowType: Record "Radio Show Type";
begin
    RadioShowType.Code := Code; I
    RadioShowType.Description := Descr;
    RadioShowType.Insert;
end;
```

Special working storage variables

Some working storage variables have additional attributes to be considered.

Temporary tables

Temporary tables were discussed in `Chapter 2`, *Tables*. Let's take a quick look at how one is defined. Defining a temporary table begins just like any other variable definition of the `Record` data type. To make it temporary, we add the `temporary` keyword after the table name, as shown in the following screenshot:

```
procedure HelperCreateShowType("Code": Code[10]; Descr: Text):Boolean
varI
    RadioShowType: Record "Radio Show Type" temporary;
begin
    RadioShowType.Code := Code;
    RadioShowType.Description := Descr;
    RadioShowType.Insert;
end;
```

We can use a temporary table just as though it were a permanent table, with some specific differences:

- The table only contains the data we add to it during this instance of the object in which it resides.
- We cannot change any aspect of the definition of the table, except by changing the permanent table.

- Processing for a temporary table is done wholly in the client system, in a user-specific instance of the business logic. It is, therefore, inherently a single user.
- A properly utilized temporary table reduces network traffic and eliminates any locking issues for that table. It is often much faster than processing the same data in a permanent database-resident table because both data transmission and physical storage I/O are significantly reduced.

> In some cases, it's a good idea to copy the database table data into a temporary table for repetitive processing within an object. This can give us a significant speed advantage for a particular task by updating data in the temporary table, then copying it back out to the database table at the end of processing.
>
> When using temporary tables, we need to be very careful that references from the AL code in the temporary table, such as data validations, don't inappropriately modify permanent data elsewhere in the database. We must also remember that, if we forget to properly mark the table as temporary, we will likely corrupt production data with our processing.

Arrays

Arrays of up to 10 dimensions containing up to a total of 1,000,000 elements in a single variable can be created in a Business Central object. Defining an array is done simply by setting the Array keyword of a variable. An example is shown in the following screenshot, which defines a record array of three rows, with 99 elements in each row:

```
I procedure HelperCreateShowType("Code": Code[10]; Descr: Text):Boolean
  var
      RadioShowType: Array[3,99] of Record "Radio Show Type";
  begin
      RadioShowType[1,1].Code := Code;
      RadioShowType[1,1].Description := Descr;
      RadioShowType[1,1].Insert;
  end;
```

The comma separates the dimensions of the array. The numbers indicate the maximum number of elements of each of the dimensions. An array variable such as TotalCountArray is referred to in AL as follows:

- The 15th entry in the first row is TotalCountArray[1,15]
- The last entry in the last row is TotalCountArray[3,99]

An array of a complex data type, such as a record, may behave differently than a single instance of the data type, especially when passed as a parameter to a procedure. In such a case, we must make sure that the code is thoroughly tested so that we aren't surprised by unexpected results.

Initialization

When an object is initiated, the variables in that object are automatically initialized. Booleans are set to `False`. Numeric variables are set to zero. Text and code data types are set to the empty string. Dates are set to `0D` (the undefined date) and times are set to `0T` (the undefined time). The individual components of complex variables are appropriately initialized. The system also automatically initializes all system-defined variables.

Of course, once the object is active, through our code and property settings, we can do whatever additional initialization we wish. If we wish to initialize variables at intermediate points during processing, we can use any of several approaches. First, we will reset a `Record` variable (for example, the `TempRadioShowLedger` temporary table defined in the preceding example) with the `RESET` procedure, then initialize it with the `INIT` procedure in statements in the form, as follows:

```
TempRadioShowLedger.RESET;
TempRadioShowLedger.INIT;
```

The `RESET` procedure makes sure that all of the previously set filters on this table are cleared. The `INIT` procedure makes sure that all of the fields, except those in the primary key, are set either to their `InitValue`, property value or to their data type default value. The primary key fields must be explicitly set by the AL code.

For all types of data, including complex data types, we can initialize fields with the `CLEAR` or `CLEARALL` procedure in a statement in the following form:

```
CLEAR(TotalArray[1,1]);
CLEAR(TotalArray);
CLEAR("Shipment Code");
```

The first example would clear a single element of the array—the first element in the first row. Since this variable is an `Integer` data type, the element would be set to `Integer` zero when cleared. The second example would clear the entire array. In the third example, a variable defined as a `Code` data type would simply be set to an empty string.

System-defined variables

Business Central also provides us with some variables automatically, such as `Rec`, `xRec`, `CurrPage`, `CurrReport`, and `CurrXMLport`. What variables are provided is dependent on the object that we are operating on. Descriptions of some of these can be found in the help titled *System-Defined Variables* (`https://docs.microsoft.com/en-us/dynamics-nav/system-defined-variables`).

AL programming

Many of the things that we do during development in Visual Studio Code might not be called programming by some people as it doesn't involve writing AL code statements. However, so long as these activities contribute to the definition of the object and affect the processing that occurs, we'll include them in our broad definition of AL programming.

These activities include setting properties at the object and DataItem levels, creating request pages in reports, defining controls and their properties, defining report data structures and their properties, creating source expressions, defining procedures, and, of course, writing AL statements in all of the places where we can put AL. We will focus on programming primarily as it relates to tables, reports, and codeunits.

We will touch on programming for pages and XMLports. In the case of reports, AL statements can reside only in the components that are developed within the report designer.

Business Central objects are generally consistent in structure. Most have some properties and triggers. Pages and reports have controls, though the tools that define the controls in each are specific to the individual object type. Reports have a built-in DataItem looping logic. XMLports also have DataItem looping logic, but those are structured differently from reports; for example, reports can have multiple DataItems at 0 level and XMLports can only have one node at 0 level. All of the object types that we are considering can contain AL code in one or more places. All of these can contain procedure definitions that can be called either internally or externally (if not marked as local). Remember, good design practice says that any procedures designed as a *library* or reusable procedures that are called from a variety of objects should be placed in a codeunit or, in some circumstances, in the primary table.

 Don't forget that our fundamental coding work should focus on tables and procedure libraries as much as possible, as these are the foundation of the Business Central system.

Non-modifiable procedures

A procedure is a defined set of logic that performs a specific task. Similar to many other programming languages, AL includes a set of prewritten procedures that are available to us to perform a wide variety of different tasks. The underlying logic for some of these procedures is hidden and not modifiable. These non-modifiable procedures are supplied as part of the AL programming language. Some simple examples of non-modifiable procedures are as follows:

- `DATE2DMY`: Supply a date to this procedure and, depending on a calling parameter, it will return the integer value of the day, month, or year of that date
- `STRPOS`: Supply a string variable and a string constant to this procedure and it will return the position of the first instance of that constant within the variable, or a zero, if the constant is not present in the string that's contained in the variable
- `GET`: Supply a value and a table to this procedure and it will read the record in the table with a primary key value equal to the supplied value if a matching record exists
- `INSERT`: This procedure will add a record to a table
- `MESSAGE`: Supply a string and optional variables and this procedure will display a message to the operator

Such procedures are the heart of AL tools. There are over one hundred of them. On the whole, they are designed around the essential purpose of a Business Central system—business and financial applications data processing. These procedures are not modifiable; they operate according to their predefined rules. For development purposes, they act as basic language components.

Modifiable procedures

In addition to the prewritten `language component` procedures, there are a large number of prewritten `application component` procedures. The difference between the two types is that the code implementing the latter is visible and modifiable through cloning, though we should be extremely cautious about making such clones.

An example of an application component procedure might be one to handle the task of processing a customer's shipping address to eliminate empty lines and standardize the layout based on user-defined setup parameters. Such a procedure would logically be placed in a codeunit and hence made available to any routine that needs this capability.

In fact, this procedure exists. It is called `SalesHeaderShipTo` and is located in the `Format Address` codeunit. We can explore the following codeunits for some procedures we might find useful to use or that we can borrow logic from. This is not an all-inclusive list, as there are many procedures in other codeunits that we may find useful in a future development project, either to be used directly or as templates to design our own, similar procedure. Many library codeunits have the words `Management` or `Mgt` in their name:

Object number	Name
356	DateComprMgt
358	DateFilter-Calc
359	PeriodFormManagement
365	Format Address
397	Mail
5052	AttachmentManagement
5054	WordManagement
6224	XML DOM Management

The prewritten application procedures, generally, have been provided to address the needs of the Business Central developers working at Microsoft. However, we can use them too. Our challenge will be to find out whether they exist and to understand how they work. There is very little documentation of these `application component` procedures. A feature has been added to the AL editor to help us in our review of such procedures. If we highlight the procedure reference in the in-line code and right-click it, we are given the option to **Go to definition**. This allows us to easily find the procedure's code and review it.

One significant aspect of these application procedures is the fact that they are written in AL, and their construction is totally exposed. In theory, they can be cloned, though this is not advisable. If we decide to change one of these procedures, we should choose events.

If no events exist, we can either request events or, much better, clone them into our own library codeunit, creating a new version and making any modifications to the new version while leaving the original untouched.

Custom procedures

We can also create our own custom procedures to meet any need. The most common reason to create a new procedure is to provide a single, standardized instance of logic to perform a specific task. When we need to use the same logic in more than one place, we should consider creating a callable procedure.

We should also create a new procedure when we're modifying standard Business Central processes through events. Our procedure then becomes an event subscriber.

If a new procedure is going to be used in several objects, it should be housed in our library codeunit (we may choose to have multiple library codeunits for the purpose of clarity or project management). If a new procedure is only for use in a single object, then it can be resident in that object. This latter option also has the advantage of allowing the new procedure direct access to the global variables within the object being modified, if necessary.

Creating a procedure

Let's take a quick look at how a procedure can be created. We'll use the small date formula app we created in `Chapter 3`, *Data Types and Fields*, and add a new codeunit, `Codeunit 50141`. We will call it `Date Formula Management`.

When working on projects with larger teams, creating more codeunits is advised so that you have a better chance of each developer working on separate objects.

We will create our new codeunit by simply clicking on **New File** in the **File** menu, then choosing **File | Save As**, and entering `Codeunit 50141 Date Formula Mgt`. We will select the codeunit snippet and populate the variables.

Now comes the important part—designing and coding our new procedure. When we had the procedure operating as a local procedure inside the table where it was called, we didn't worry about passing data back and forth. We simply used the data fields that were already present in the table and treated them as global variables, which they were. Now that our procedure will be external to the object that it was called from, we have to pass data values back and forth. Here's the basic calling structure of our procedure:

```
Output := Procedure (Input Parameter1, Input Parameter2)
```

In other words, we need to feed two values into our new callable procedure and accept a `Return` value on completion of the procedure being processed.

The result of the function should be similar to the following:

```
0 references
procedure CalculateNewDate(DateFormulaToTest: DateFormula; ReferenceForDateCalc: Date): Date
begin
    exit(CalcDate(DateFormulaToTest, ReferenceForDateCalc));
end;
```

Press *Ctrl* + *Shift* + *B* to check whether we have a clean build. If we get an error, we must do the traditional programmer thing: find it, fix it, and rebuild. Repeat until we get a clean build.

Finally, we will return `Table 50140` to our test to complete the changes that are necessary so that we can use the external procedure rather than the internal procedure. We have two obvious choices for doing this. One is to replace the internal formula in our existing internal procedure with a call to our external procedure. This approach results in fewer object changes.

The other choice is to replace each of our internal procedure calls with a call to the external procedure. This approach may be more efficient at runtime because, when we need the external procedure, we will invoke it in one step rather than two. We will walk through the first option here and then you should try the second option on your own.

Which option is the best? It depends on our criteria. Such a decision comes down to a matter of identifying the best criteria on which to judge the design options, then applying that criteria. Remember, whenever feasible, simple is good.

For the first approach (calling our new codeunit resident procedure), we must add our new `Codeunit 50141 Date Formula Mgt` variable to `Table 50140`. After designing the table, navigate to the procedure and add a new line between the procedure declaration and the `Begin` keyword. Add the `local` variable, as shown in the following screenshot (it's good practice to define variables as local unless global access is required):

```
2 references
local procedure CalculateNewDate()
var
    DateFormMgt: Codeunit "Date Formula Mgt.";
begin
    "Date Result" := CalcDate("Date Formula to Test", "Reference for Date Calculation");
end;
```

The two lines of code that called the internal procedure, `CalculateNewDate`, must be changed to call the external procedure. The syntax for that call is as follows:

```
Global/LocalVariable :=
Global/LocalObjectName.ProcedureName(Parameter1,Parameter2,...).
```

Based on that, the new line of code should be as follows:

```
"Date Result" := DateFormMgt.CalculateNewDate("Date Formula to
Test","Reference Date for Calculation");
```

If all has gone well, we should be able to build our application. When that step works successfully, we can run the page and experiment with different reference dates and date formulas, just like we did back in `Chapter 3`, *Data Types and Fields*. We should get the same results for the same entries that we saw before.

When you try out the other approach of replacing each of the calls to the internal procedure by directly calling the external procedure, you will want to do the following:

- Either define the `Date Formula Management` codeunit as a global variable or as a local variable for each of the triggers where you are calling the external procedure
- Delete the now unused internal `CalculateNewDate` procedure

We should now have a better understanding of the basics of constructing both internal and external procedures and some of the optional design features that are available to us for building procedures.

AL syntax

AL syntax is relatively simple and straightforward. The basic structure of most AL statements is essentially similar to what you learned with other programming languages. AL is modeled on Pascal and tends to use many of the same special character and syntax practices as Pascal.

Assignment and punctuation

Assignment is represented with a colon followed by an equal sign, the combination being treated as a single symbol. The evaluated value of the expression, to the right of the assignment symbol, is assigned to the variable on the left-hand side, as shown in the following line of code:

```
"Phone No." := '312-555-1212';
```

All statements are terminated with a semicolon. Multiple statements can be placed on a single program line, but that makes the code hard for others to read.

Fully qualified data fields are prefaced with the name of the record variable that they are a part of (see the preceding code line as an example of where the `record` variable is named `Phone No.`). The same structure applies to fully qualified procedure references; the procedure name is prefaced with the name of the object that they are defined in.

Single quotes are used to surround string literals (see the phone number string in the preceding line of code).

Double quotes are used to surround an identifier (for example, a variable or a procedure name) that contains any character other than numerals or upper and lowercase letters. For example, the `Phone No.` field name in the preceding line of code is constructed as `"Phone No."` because it contains a space and a period. Other examples would be `"Post Code"` (contains a space), `"E-Mail"` (contains a dash), and `"No."` (contains a period).

Parentheses are used much the same as in other language—to indicate sets of expressions that will be interpreted according to their parenthetical groupings. The expressions are interpreted in sequence, first by the innermost parenthetical group, then the next level, and so forth. The expression *(A / (B + (C * (D + E))))* would be evaluated as follows:

1. Summing *(D + E)* into `Result1`.
2. Multiplying `Result1` times *C*, yielding `Result2`.
3. Adding `Result2` to *B*, yielding `Result3`.
4. Dividing *A* by `Result3`.

Brackets [ ] are used to indicate the presence of subscripts for indexing array variables. A text string can be treated as an array of characters, and we can use subscripts with the string name to access individual character positions within the string, but not beyond the terminating character of the string. For example, `Address[1]` represents the leftmost character in the `Address` text variable contents.

Brackets are also used for `IN` (in range) expressions, as shown in the following code snippet:

```
Boolean := SearchValue IN[SearchTarget]
```

In this line, `SearchValue` and `SearchTarget` are text variables.

Statements can be continued on multiple lines without any special punctuation; however, we can't split a variable or literal across two lines. Because the AL code editor limits lines to 132 characters long, this capability is often used. The following example shows two instances that are interpreted in exactly the same manner by the compiler:

```
ClientRec."Phone No." := '312' + ' ' + '555' + '-' + '1212';
ClientRec."Phone No." := '312' +
  '-' + '555' +
  '-' + '1212';
```

Expressions

Expressions in AL are made up of four elements—constants, variables, operators, and procedures. We could include a fifth element, expressions, because an expression may include a subordinate expression within it. As we become more experienced in coding AL, we will find that the capability of nesting expressions can be both a blessing and a curse, depending on the specific use and readability of the result.

We can create complex statements that will conditionally perform important control actions and operate in much the same way that a person would think about a task. We can also create complex statements that are very difficult for a person to understand. These are tough to debug and sometimes almost impossible to deal with in a modification.

One of our responsibilities is to be able to tell the difference so that we can write code that makes sense in operation, but is also easy to read and understand.

According to the Business Central Docs, an AL expression
(`https://msdn.microsoft.com/en-us/library/dd301381(v=nav.90).aspx`) is a group of
characters (data values, variables, arrays, operators, and procedures) that can be evaluated
with the result that has an associated data type. The following are two code statements that
accomplish the same result in slightly different ways. They each assign a literal string to a
text data field. In the first one, the right-hand side is a literal data value. In the second, the
right-hand side of the `:=` assignment symbol is an expression:

```
ClientRec."Phone No." := '312-555-1212';
ClientRec."Phone No." := '312' + '-' + '555' + '-' + '1212';
```

Operators

Now, we'll review AL operators grouped by category. Depending on the data types we are
using with a particular operator, we may need to know the type conversion rules by
defining the allowed combinations of operator and data types for an expression. The
Business Central docs provides good information on type conversion rules. Search for the
phrase `type Conversion` to learn more.

Before we review the operators that can be categorized, let's discuss some operators that
don't fit well into any of the categories. These include the following:

Other Operators	
Symbol	**Evaluation**
.	Member of: Fields in Records Controls in Forms Controls in Reports Functions in Objects
()	Grouping of elements
[]	Indexing
::	Scope
..	Range
@	Case-insensitive

Explanations regarding the use of the operator symbols in the preceding table are as follows:

- The symbol represented by a single dot or period doesn't have a given name in the Business Central documentation, so we'll call it the member symbol or dot operator (as it is referred to in the MSDN Visual Basic Developer documentation). It indicates that a field is a member of a table (`TableName.FieldName`), a control is a member of a page (`PageName.ControlName`) or report (`ReportName.ControlName`), or a procedure is a member of an object (`Objectname.ProcedureName`).

- Parentheses `( )` and brackets `[ ]` can be considered operators based on the effect their use has on the results of an expression. We discussed their use in the context of parenthetical grouping and indexing using brackets, as well as with the `IN` procedure earlier. Parentheses are also used to enclose the parameters in a procedure call, as shown in the following code snippet:

```
Objectname.ProcedureName(Param1,Param2,Param3);
```

- The scope operator is a two character sequence consisting of two colons in a row, `::`. The scope operator is used to allow AL code to refer to a specific option value using the text descriptive value rather than the integer value that is actually stored in the database. For example, in our AL database table, `Radio Show`, we have an option field defined, called `Frequency`, with option string values of `(blank)`, `Hourly`, `Daily`, `Weekly`, and `Monthly`. Those values will be stored as integers 0, 1, 2, 3, or 4, but we can use the strings to refer to them in code, which makes our code more self-documenting. The scope operator allows us to refer to `Frequency::Hourly` (rather than 1) and `Frequency::Monthly` (rather than 4). These constructs are translated by the compiler as 1 and 4, respectively. If we want to type fewer characters when entering code, we could enter just enough of the option string value to be unique, letting the compiler automatically fill in the rest when we next save, compile, close, and reopen the object. In a similar fashion, we can refer to objects in the `[Object Type::"Object Name"]` format to be translated into the object number, as shown in the following code snippet:

```
PAGE.RUN(PAGE::"Bin List"); is equivalent to  PAGE.RUN(7303);
```

- The range operator is a two character sequence, "..", with two dots in a row. This operator is very widely used in Business Central, not only in AL code (including CASE statements and IN expressions), but also in filters that are entered by users. The English lowercase alphabet can be represented by the range *a..z*, the set of single digit numbers by the range -9..9 (that is, minus 9 dot dot 9), and all of the entries starting with the letter *a* (lowercase) by a..a*. Don't underestimate the power of the range operator.

Arithmetic operators and procedures

The arithmetic operators include the following set of operators:

Arithmetic Operators		
Symbol	**Action**	**Data Types**
+	Addition	Numeric, Date, Time, Text and Code (concatenation),
-	Subtraction	Numeric, Date, Time
*	Multiplication	Numeric
/	Division	Numeric
DIV	Integer Division (provides only the integer portion of the quotient of a division calculation)	Numeric
MOD	Modulus (provides only the integer remainder of a division calculation)	Numeric

As we can see, in the **Data Types** column, these operators can be used on various data types. Numeric types include Integer, Decimal, Boolean, and Character data types. Text and Code are both String data.

Sample statements using DIV and MOD are shown in the following code, where BigNumber is an integer containing 200:

```
DIVIntegerValue := BigNumber DIV 60;
```

The contents of DIVIntegerValue, after executing the preceding statement, will be 3:

```
MODIntegerValue := BigNumber MOD 60;
```

The contents of `MODIntegerValue`, after executing the preceding statement, will be `20`.

The syntax for these `DIV` and `MOD` statements is as follows:

```
IntegerQuotient := IntegerDividend DIV IntegerDivisor;
IntegerModulus := IntegerDividend MOD IntegerDivisor;
```

Boolean operators

`Boolean` operators only operate on expressions that can be evaluated as `Boolean`. These are shown in the following table:

Boolean Operators	
Symbol	Evaluation
NOT	Logical NOT
AND	Logical AND
OR	Logical OR
XOR	Exclusive Logical OR

The result of an expression based on a `Boolean` operator will also be `Boolean`.

Relational operators and procedures

The relational operators are listed in the following screenshot. Each of these is used in an expression of the following format:

```
Expression RelationalOperator Expression
```

An example is *(Variable1 + 97) > ((Variable2 * 14.5) / 57.332)*. The following operators can be used:

Relational Operators	
Symbol	Evaluation
<	Less than
>	Greater than
<=	Less than or Equal to
>=	Greater than or Equal to
=	Equal to
<>	Not equal to
IN	IN Valueset

We will spend a little extra time on the `IN` operator, because this can be very handy and is not documented elsewhere. The term `Valueset` in the **Evaluation** column for `IN` refers to a list of defined values. It would be reasonable to define `Valueset` as a container of a defined set of individual values, expressions, or other value sets. Some examples of `IN`, as used in the standard Business Central product code, are as follows:

```
GLEntry."Posting Date" IN [0D,WORKDATE]

Description[I+2] IN ['0'..'9']

"Gen. Posting Type" IN ["Gen. Posting Type"::Purchase, "Gen. Posting
Type"::Sale]

SearchString IN ['','=><']

No[i] IN ['5'..'9']

"FA Posting Date" IN [01010001D..12312008D]
```

Here is another example of what the `IN` operator, as used in an expression, might look like:

```
TestString IN ['a'..'d','j','q','l'..'p'];
```

If the value of `TestString` were a or m, then this expression would evaluate to `TRUE`. If the value of `TestString` were z, then this expression would evaluate to `FALSE`. Note that the data type of the search value must be the same as the data type of `Valueset`.

Precedence of operators

When expressions are evaluated by the AL compiler, the parsing routines use a predefined precedence hierarchy to determine what operators to evaluate first, what to evaluate second, and so forth. This precedence hierarchy is provided in the Business Central Docs section, *C/AL Operators – Operator Hierarchy* (`https://msdn.microsoft.com/en-us/dynamics-nav/c-al-operators`), but for convenience, the information is repeated here:

C/AL Operator Precedence Hierarchy		
Sequence	**Symbols**	
1	.	Member (Fields in Records, etc)
	[ ]	Indexing
	( )	Parenthetical Grouping
	::	Scope
	@	Case-insensitive
2		Unary instances of:
	NOT	Logical Not
	+	Positive value
	-	Negating value
3	*	Multiplication
	/	Division
	DIV	Integer division
	MOD	Modulus
	AND	Logical AND
	XOR	Logical Exclusive OR
4	+	Addition or Concatenation
	-	Subtraction
	OR	Logical OR
5	>	Greater than
	<	Less than
	>=	Greater than or equal to
	<=	Less than or equal to
	<>	Not equal to
	IN	IN Valueset
6	..	Range

For complex expressions, we should always freely use parentheses to make sure that the expressions are evaluated the way we intend them to be.

Frequently used AL procedures

It's time to learn about more of the standard procedures that are provided by Microsoft. We will focus on the following short list of frequently used procedures: MESSAGE, ERROR, CONFIRM, and STRMENU.

There is a group of procedures in AL called `Dialog` procedures. The purpose of these procedures is to allow communication, that is, dialog, between the system and the user. In addition, the `Dialog` procedures can be useful for quick and simple testing/debugging. To make it easier for us to proceed with our next level of AL development work, we'll take time now to learn about these four dialog procedures. None of these procedures will operate if the AL code is running on the Business Central job queue as it has no GUI available. To handle that situation in previous versions of Business Central, the `Dialog` procedure statements had to be conditioned with the `GUIALLOWED` procedure to check whether or not the code was running in a GUI allowed environment. If the code was being used in a web service or API, it would not be `GUIALLOWED`. However, in Business Central, API and web services simply ignore `Dialog` procedures.

In each of these procedures, data values can be inserted through the use of a substitution string. The substitution string is the `%` (percent sign) character, followed by numbers `1` through `10`, located within a message text string. This could look like the following code snippet, assuming that the local currency was defined as USD:

```
MESSAGE('A message + a data element to display = %1', "OrderAmount");
```

If the `OrderAmount` value was `$100.53`, the output from the preceding code would be as follows:

```
A message + a data element to display = $100.53
```

We can have up to ten substitution strings in one dialog procedure. The use of substitution strings and their associated display values is optional. We can use any one of the dialog procedures simply to display a completely predefined text message with nothing that is variable. Use of text constant for the message is recommended as it makes maintenance and multi-language enabling easier.

The MESSAGE procedure

`MESSAGE` is easy to use for the display of transient data and can be placed almost anywhere in our AL code. All it requires of the user is acknowledgement that the message has been read. The disadvantage of messages is that they are not displayed until either the object completes its run or pauses for some other external action. Plus, if we inadvertently create a situation that generates hundreds or thousands of messages, there is no graceful way to terminate their display once they are displaying.

It's common to use MESSAGE as the elementary trace tool. We can program the display of messages to occur only under particular circumstances and use them to view either the flow of processing (by outputting simple identifying codes from different points in our logic) or to view the contents of particular data elements through multiple processing cycles.

To display information to the user without interrupting them in their work, notifications can be used. You can learn more about notifications via the following MSDN article:
`https://msdn.microsoft.com/en-us/dynamics-nav/notifications-deve loping`.

MESSAGE has the a syntax of MESSAGE (String [, Value1] , ...]), where there are as many ValueX entries as there are %X substitution strings (up to ten).

Here is a sample debugging message:

```
MESSAGE('Loop %1, item No. %2',LoopCounter,"Item No.");
```

The display would look as follows (when the counter was 14 and the Item No. was BX0925):

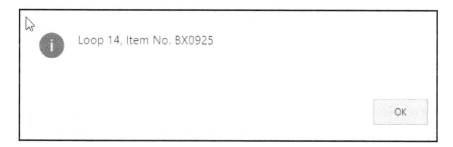

When MESSAGE is used for debugging, make sure that all messages are removed before releasing the object to production.

The ERROR procedure

When an ERROR procedure is invoked, the execution of the current process terminates, the message is immediately displayed, and the database returns to the status it had following the last (implicit or explicit) COMMIT procedure as though the process that was calling the ERROR procedure had not run at all.

We can use the ERROR procedure in combination with the MESSAGE procedure to assist in repetitive testing. MESSAGE procedures can be placed in code to show what is happening with an ERROR procedure that's been placed just prior to where the process would normally complete. Because the ERROR procedure rolls back all database changes, this technique allows us to run through multiple tests against the same data without any time-consuming backup and restoration of our test data. The enhanced testing procedurality that's built into Business Central can accomplish the same things in a much more sophisticated fashion, but sometimes there's room for a temporary, simple approach.

An ERROR procedure call is formatted almost exactly like a MESSAGE call. ERROR has the syntax, ERROR(String [, Value1] ,...]), where there are as many ValueX entries as there are %X substitution strings (up to ten). If the preceding MESSAGE call was an ERROR procedure instead, the code line would be as follows:

```
ERROR('Loop %1, Item No. %2',LoopCounter,"Item No.");
```

The display would look as follows:

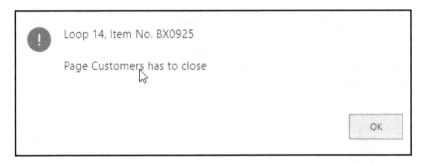

We can increase the ease of ERROR message recognition by including the word ERROR in our message, as shown in the following screenshot:

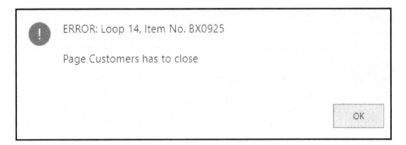

Even in the best of circumstances, it is difficult for a system to communicate clearly with users. Sometimes, our tools, in their effort to be flexible, make it too easy for developers to take the easy way out and communicate poorly or not at all. For example, an ERROR statement of the ERROR('') form will terminate the run and roll back all data processing without even displaying a message at all. An important part of our job, as developers, is to ensure that our systems communicate clearly and completely.

The CONFIRM procedure

A third dialog procedure is the CONFIRM procedure. A CONFIRM procedure call causes processing to stop until the user responds to the dialog. In CONFIRM, we will include a question in our text because the procedure provides **Yes** and **No** button options. The application logic can then be conditioned on the user's response.

 We can also use CONFIRM as a simple debugging tool to control the path the processing will take. Display the status of data or processing flow and then allow the operator to make a choice (**Yes** or **No**) that will influence what happens next. Execution of a CONFIRM procedure will also cause any pending MESSAGE procedure output values to be displayed before the CONFIRM procedure displays. Combined with MESSAGE and ERROR, creative use of CONFIRM can add to our elementary debugging/diagnostic toolkit.

CONFIRM has the following syntax:

```
BooleanValue := CONFIRM(String [, Default]  [, Value1]  ,...)
```

When we do not specify a value for Default, the system will choose FALSE (which displays as **No**). We should almost always choose the Default option as it will do no damage if accepted inadvertently by an inattentive user. The Default choice is FALSE, which is often the safest choice (but TRUE may be specified by the programmer). There are as many ValueX entries as there are %X substitution strings (up to ten).

If we just code OK := CONFIRM(String), the default choice will be False.

A CONFIRM procedure call with a similar content to the preceding examples might look like the following sample for the code and the display:

```
Answer := CONFIRM('Loop %1, Item No. %2\OK to
continue?',TRUE,LoopCounter,"Item No.");
```

The output screen is shown in the following screenshot:

In typical usage, the CONFIRM procedure is part of, or is referred to, by a conditional statement that uses the Boolean value that's returned by the CONFIRM procedure.

An additional feature for on-screen dialogs is the use of the backslash (\) that's embedded in the text. This forces a new line in the displayed message. This works throughout Business Central screen display procedures.

To display a backslash on-screen, we must put two of them in our message text string, (\\).

The STRMENU procedure

A fourth dialog procedure is the STRMENU procedure. A STRMENU procedure call also causes processing to pause while the user responds to the dialog. The advantage of the STRMENU procedure is its ability to provide several choices, rather than just two (**Yes** or **No**). A common use is to provide an option menu in response to the user pressing a command button.

STRMENU has the following syntax:

```
IntegerValue := STRMENU(StringVariable of Options separated by commas
[, OptionDefault][, Instruction])
```

`IntegerValue` will contain the user's selection entry, and `OptionDefault` is an integer representing which option will be selected by default when the menu displays. If we do not provide an `OptionDefault` value, the first option that's listed will be used as the default. `Instruction` is a text string that will display the preceding list of options. If the user responds with **Cancel** or presses the *Esc* key, the value that's returned by the procedure is 0.

Use of the `STRMENU` procedure eliminates the need to use a `Page` object when asking the user to select from a limited set of options. It can also be utilized from within a report or codeunit when calling a page would restrict processing choices.

If we phrase our instruction as a question rather than simply an explanation, then we can use `STRMENU` as a multiple choice inquiry to the user.

Here is an example of `STRMENU` with the instruction phrased as a question:

```
OptionNo := STRMENU('Blue,Plaid,Yellow,Hot Pink,Orange,Unknown',6,
                    'Which of these is not like the others?');
```

The output screen is shown in the following screenshot:

Setting the default to 6 caused the sixth option (**Unknown**) to be the active selection when the menu is displayed.

Record procedures

Now, we will review some of the procedures that we commonly use in record processing.

The SETCURRENTKEY procedure

The syntax for `SETCURRENTKEY` is as follows:

```
[BooleanValue :=] Record.SETCURRENTKEY(FieldName1,[FieldName2], ... )
```

Because Business Central is based on the SQL Server database, `SETCURRENTKEY` simply determines the order in which the data will be presented for processing. The actual choice of the index to be used for the query is made by the SQL Server Query Analyzer. For this reason, it is very important that the data and resources available to the SQL Server Query Analyzer are well maintained. This includes maintaining the statistics that are used by the Query Analyzer, as well as making sure that efficient index options have been defined. Even though SQL Server picks the actual index, the developer's choice of the appropriate `SETCURRENTKEY` parameter can have a major affect on performance.

 The fields that are used in the `SETCURRENTKEY` command do not have to match a key in the table definition. You can also use `FlowFields` as fields for `SETCURRENTKEY`, but expect slower performance when doing this.

The indexes that are defined in the SQL Server do not have to be the same as those defined in the AL table definition. For example, we can add additional indexes in the SQL Server and not in AL, disable indices in the SQL Server but leave the matching keys enabled in AL, and so on. Any maintenance of the SQL Server indices should be done through the Business Central table designer using the Business Central keys and properties, not directly in SQL Server. Even though the system may operate without a problem, any mismatch between the application system and the underlying database system makes maintenance and upgrades more difficult and error-prone.

Business Central-defined keys are no longer required to support SIFT indexes because SQL Server can dynamically create the required indices. However, depending on dynamic indices for larger datasets, they can lead to bad performance. Good design is still our responsibility as developers.

The SETRANGE procedure

The SETRANGE procedure provides the ability to set a simple range filter on a field. The SETRANGE syntax is as follows:

```
Record.SETRANGE(FieldName [,From-Value] [,To-Value]);
```

Prior to applying its range filter, the SETRANGE procedure removes any filters that were previously set for the defined field (filtering procedures are defined in more detail in the next chapter). If SETRANGE is executed with only one value, that one value will act as both the From and To values. If SETRANGE is executed without any From or To values, it will clear the filters on the field. This is a common use of SETRANGE. Some examples of the SETRANGE procedure in code are as follows:

- Clear the filters on Item.No.:

```
Item.SETRANGE("No.");
```

- Filter to get only Items with No. from 1300 through 1400:

```
Item.SETRANGE("No.",'1300','1400');
```

- Alternatively, you can use the variable values from LowVal through HiVal:

```
Item.SETRANGE("No.",LowVal,HiVal);
```

To be effective in a query, SETRANGE must be called before the OPEN, SAVEASXML, and SAVEASCSV procedures.

The SETFILTER procedure

SETFILTER is similar to, but much more flexible than, the SETRANGE procedure because it supports the application of any of the supported Business Central filter procedures to table fields. The SETFILTER syntax is as follows:

```
Record.SETFILTER(FieldName, FilterExpression [Value],...);
```

The `FilterExpression` consists of a string (text or code) in standard Business Central filter format, including any of the operators (<, >, *, &, |, and =) in any legal combination. Replacement fields (`%1, %2, ..., %9`) are used to represent the values that will be inserted into `FilterExpression` by the compiler to create an operating filter that's formatted as though it were entered from the keyboard. Just like `SETRANGE`, prior to applying its filter, the `SETFILTER` procedure clears any filters that were previously set for the defined field, as in the following example:

- Filter to get only items with `No.` from `1300` through `1400`:

```
Item.SETFILTER("No.",'%1..%2','1300','1400');
```

- Alternatively, you can do this with any of the variable values of `LowVal`, `MedVal`, or `HiVal`:

```
Item.SETFILTER"No.",'%1|%2|%3',LowVal,MedVal,HiVal);
```

To be effective in a query, `SETFILTER` must be called before the `OPEN`, `SAVEASXML`, and `SAVEASCSV` procedures.

The GET procedure

`GET` is the basic data retrieval procedure in AL. `GET` retrieves a single record based on the primary key only. It has the following syntax:

```
[BooleanValue :=] Record.GET ( [KeyFieldValue1] [,KeyFieldValue2] ,...)
```

The parameter for the `GET` procedure is the primary key value (or all of the values, if the primary key consists of more than one field).

Assigning the `GET` procedure result to `BooleanValue` is optional. If the `GET` procedure is not successful (no record found) and the statement is not part of an `IF` statement, the process will terminate with a runtime error. Typically, therefore, the `GET` procedure is encased in an `IF` statement, which is structured like so:

```
IF Customer.GET(NewCustNo) THEN ...
```

GET data retrieval is not constrained by filters, except for security filters (see help, *How to: Set Security Filters* at
`https://msdn.microsoft.com/en-us/library/hh166853(v=nav.90).aspx`). If there is a matching record in the table, GET will retrieve it.

FIND procedures

The FIND family of procedures is the general purpose data retrieval procedure in AL. It is much more flexible than GET, and therefore more widely used. GET has the advantage of being faster as it operates only on unfiltered direct access through the primary key, looking for a single uniquely keyed entry. There are two forms of FIND procedures in AL, one a remnant from a previous database structure and the other designed specifically to work efficiently with SQL Server. Both are supported, and we will find both in standard code.

The older version of the FIND procedure has the following syntax:

```
[BooleanValue :=] RecordName.FIND ( [Which] ).
```

The newer SQL Server-specific members of the FIND procedure family have slightly different syntax, as we will see shortly.

Just like the GET procedure, assigning the FIND procedure result to a Boolean value is optional. However, in almost all of the cases, FIND is embedded in a condition that controls subsequent processing appropriately. Either way, it is important to structure our code to handle the instance where FIND is not successful.

FIND differs from GET in several important ways, some of which are as follows:

- FIND operates under the limits of whatever filters are applied on the subject field.
- FIND presents the data in the sequence of the key that is currently selected by default or by AL code.
- When FIND is used, the index that's used for the data reading is controlled by the SQL Server Query Analyzer.
- Different variations of the FIND procedure are designed specifically for use in different situations. This allows coding to be optimized for better SQL Server performance. All of the FIND procedures are described further in the help section, *C/AL Database Functions and Performance on SQL Server*, at `https://msdn.microsoft.com/en-us/library/dd355237.aspx`.

The forms of FIND are as follows:

- FIND('-'): This finds the first record in a table that satisfies the defined filter and current key.
- FINDFIRST: This finds the first record in a table that satisfies the defined filter and defined key choice. Conceptually, it is equivalent to FIND('-') for a single record read but better for SQL Server when a filter or range is applied.
- FIND('+'): This finds the last record in a table that satisfies the defined filter and defined key choice. Often, this is not an efficient option for SQL Server because it causes it to read a set of records when, many times, only a single record is needed. The exception is when a table is to be processed in reverse order. Then, it is appropriate to use FIND('+') with SQL Server.
- FINDLAST: This finds the last record in a table that satisfies the defined filter and current key. It is conceptually equivalent to FIND('+') but, often, much better for SQL Server as it reads a single record, not a set of records.
- FINDSET: This is the most efficient way to read a set of records from SQL Server for sequential processing within a specified filter and range. FINDSET allows you to define the standard size of the read record cache as a setup parameter but, normally, it defaults to reading 50 records (table rows) for the first server call. The syntax includes two optional True/False parameters, as follows:

```
FINDSET([ForUpdate][, UpdateKey]);
```

- The first parameter controls whether or not the read is in preparation for an update and the second parameter is TRUE when the first parameter is TRUE and the update is of key fields. FINDSET clears any FlowFields in the records that are read.

FIND ([Which]) options and the SQL Server alternatives

Let's review the FIND procedure option's syntax variations:

```
[BooleanValue :=] RecordName.FIND ( [Which] )
```

The [Which] parameter allows you to specify which record is searched for, relative to the defined key values. The defined key values are the set of values currently in the fields of the active key in the memory-resident record of the RecordName table.

The following table lists the `Which` parameter options and prerequisites:

FIND "which" parameter	FIND action	Search and primary key value prerequisite before FIND
=	Match the search key values exactly	All must be specified
>	Read the next record with key values larger than the search key values	All must be specified
<	Read the next record with key values smaller than the search key values	All must be specified
>=	Read the first record found with key values equal to or larger than the search key values	All must be specified
<=	Read the next record with key values equal to or smaller than the search key values	All must be specified
-	Read the first record in the selected set. If used with SQL Server, reads a set of records	No requirement
+	Read the last record in the selected set. If used with SQL Server, reads a set of records	No requirement

The second table lists the `FIND` options, which are specific to SQL Server, as follows:

FINDxxxx options	FINDxxx action	Search and primary key value prerequisite before FINDxxx
FINDFIRST	Read the first record in a table based on the current key and filter. Used only for access to a single record, not in a read loop.	All must be specified
FINDLAST	Read the last record in a table based on the current key and filter. Used only for access to a single record, not in a read loop.	All must be specified
FINDSET	Read the record set specified. Syntax is `Record.FINDSET([ForUpdate][,UpdateKey])` Set `ForUpdate = True` if data to be updated Set `ForUpdate = True` and `UpdateKey = True` if a key field is to be updated If no parameter specified, both default to False	All must be specified

For all `FIND` options, the results always respect the applied filters.

The FIND('-') procedure is sometimes used as the first step of reading a set of data, such as reading all of the sales invoices for a single customer. In such a case, the NEXT procedure is used to trigger all subsequent data reads after the sequence is initiated with FIND('-'). Generally, FINDSET should be used rather than FIND('-'); however, FINDSET only works to read forward, not in reverse. We should use FINDFIRST if only the first record in the specified range is of interest.

One form of the typical C/SIDE database read loop is as follows:

```
IF MyData.FIND('-') THEN
  REPEAT
    Processing logic here
  UNTIL MyData.NEXT = 0;
```

The same processing logic using the FINDSET procedure is as follows:

```
IF MyData.FINDSET THEN
  REPEAT
    Processing logic here
  UNTIL MyData.NEXT = 0;
```

We will discuss the REPEAT-UNTIL control structure in more detail in the next chapter. Essentially, it does what it says; *repeat the following logic until the defined condition is true.* For the FIND-NEXT read loop, the NEXT procedure provides both the definition of how the read loop will advance through the table and when the loop is to exit.

When DataTable.NEXT = 0, it means there are no more records to be read. We have reached the end of the available data, based on the filters and other conditions that apply to our reading process.

The specific syntax of the NEXT procedure is DataTable.NEXT(Step). DataTable is the name of the table being read. Step defines the number of records Business Central will move forward (or backward) per read. The default Step is 1, meaning that Business Central moves ahead one record at a time, reading every record. A Step of 0 works the same as a Step of 1. If the Step is set to 2, Business Central will move ahead two records at a time and the process will only be presented with every other record.

Step can also be negative, in which case Business Central moves backward through the table. This would allow us to execute a FIND('+') procedure for the end of the table, then a NEXT(-1) procedure to read backwards through the data. This is very useful if, for example, we need to read a table sorted ascending by date and want to access the most recent entries first.

Conditional statements

Conditional statements are the heart of process flow structure and control.

The BEGIN-END compound statement

In AL, there are instances where the syntax only allows the use of a single statement. However, a design may require the execution of several (or many) code statements.

AL provides at least two ways to address this need. One method is to have the single statement call a procedure that contains multiple statements.

However, inline coding is often more efficient to run and understand. So, AL provides a syntax structure to define a compound statement or block of code. A compound statement containing any number of statements can be used in place of a single code statement.

A compound statement is enclosed by the reserved words BEGIN and END. The compound statement structure looks like this:

```
BEGIN
  <Statement 1>;
  <Statement 2>;
  ..
  <Statement n>;
END
```

The AL code contained within a BEGIN-END block should be indented by two characters, as shown in the preceding pseudocode snippet, to make it obvious that it is a block of code.

IF-THEN-ELSE statement

IF is the basic conditional statement of most programming languages. It operates in AL much the same as how it works in other languages. The basic structure is as follows: IF a conditional expression is true, THEN execute Statement-1 or (if condition is not true) execute Statement-2. The ELSE portion is optional. The syntax is as follows:

```
IF <Condition> THEN <Statement-1> [ ELSE <Statement-2> ]
```

Note that the statements within an IF statement do not have terminating semicolons, unless they are contained in a BEGIN-END framework. IF statements can be nested so that conditionals are dependent on the evaluation of other conditionals. Obviously, you need to be careful with such constructs, because it is easy to end up with convoluted code structures that are difficult to debug and difficult for the developers following us to understand. In the next chapter, we will review the CASE statement that can make some complicated conditionals much easier to format and understand.

As we work with Business Central AL code, we will see that, often, <Condition> is really an expression built around a standard AL procedure. This approach is frequently used when the standard syntax for the procedure is Boolean value, procedure expression. Some examples are as follows:

- `IF Customer.FIND('-') THEN... ELSE...`
- `IF CONFIRM('OK to update?',TRUE) THEN... ELSE...`
- `IF TempData.INSERT THEN... ELSE...`
- `IF Customer.CALCFIELDS(Balance,Balance(LCY)) THEN...`

Indenting code

Since we have just discussed the BEGIN-END compound statements and the IF conditional statements, which also are compound (that is, containing multiple expressions), this seems like a good time to discuss indenting code.

In AL, the standard practice for indenting subordinate, contained, or continued lines is relatively simple. Always indent such lines by two characters, except where there are left and right parentheses to be aligned.

 To indent a block of code two characters at a time with the Business Central AL code editor, select them and click on the *Tab* key. To remove the indentation one character at a time, select the code and click on *Shift + Tab*.

In the following examples, the parentheses are not required in all of the instances, but they don't cause any problems and can make the code easier to read.

Some examples are as follows:

```
IF (A <> B) THEN
   A := A + Count1
ELSE
  B := B + Count2;
```

Or here's another:

```
IF (A <> B) THEN
   A := A + Count1;
```

Or check out this example:

```
IF (A <> B)THEN BEGIN
  A := A + Count1;
  B := A + Count2;
   IF (C > (A * B)) THEN
     C := A * B;
END ELSE
   B := B + Count2;
```

Some simple coding modifications

Now, we'll add some AL code to objects we've created for our WDTU application.

Adding field validation to a table

In Chapter 4, *Pages – The Interactive Interface*, we created the 50110 "Radio Show Fan" table. We've decided that we want to be able to use this list for promotional activities, such as having drawings for concert tickets. Of course, we want to send the tickets to the winners at their mailing addresses. We didn't include these fields originally in our table design, so we must add them now.

To keep our design consistent with the standard product, we will model these fields after the equivalent ones in the `18 - Customer` table. Our updated table, `50110`, will look as follows:

```
1    table 50110 "Radio Show Fan"
2    {
3        DataClassification = ToBeClassified;
4
5        fields
6        {
7            field(1; "No."; Code[20]) { }
8            field(10; "Radio Show No."; Code[20]) { }
9            field(20; Name; Text[50]) { }
10           field(30; "E-Mail"; Text[250]) { }
11           field(40; "Last Contacted"; Date) { }
12           field(60; Address; Text[50]) { }
13           field(70; "Address 2"; Text[50]) { }
14           field(80; City; Text[50]) { }
15           field(90; "Country/Region Code"; Code[10]) { }
16           field(100; "Post Code"; Code[20]) { }
```

Part of modeling our `50110 "Radio Show Fan"` table fields on those in the `18 - Customer` table is faithfully copying the applicable properties. For example, the `TableRelation` property for the `Post Code` field in table `18` contains the following lines of code, which we should include for the `Post Code` field in table `50010`:

```
PostCode.ValidatePostCode(City, "Post Code", County, "Country/Region Code",
(CurrFieldNo <> 0) AND GUIALLOWED);
```

When a `Radio Show Fan` record is added or the `Post Code` field is changed, we would like to update the appropriate address information. We will see that `PostCode` is a reference to the record, that is, the `Post Code` table. To learn as much as we can about how this procedure works, how we should call it, and what information is available from the `Post Code` table (table `225`), we will look at the `Post Code` table field list.

First, here's the field list in table `225` `"Post Code"`:

```
table 225 "Post Code"
t
  fields
  {
    field(1;Code;Code[20])
    {
    }
    field(2;City;Text[30])
    {
    }
    field(3;"Search City";Code[30])
    {
    }
    field(4;"Country/Region Code";Code[10])
    {
    }
    field(5;County;Text[30])
    {
    }
  }
  keys
  {
    key("Code,City";Code, City)
```

Here's the signature for the `ValidatePostCode` procedure:

```
field(100; "Post Code"; Code[20])
{
    trigger OnValidate()
    var           procedure ValidatePostCode(var City: Text[30], var PostCode: Co
        PostCode: de[20], var County: Text[30], var CountryCode: Code[10], UseDia
    begin         log: Boolean)
        PostCode.ValidatePostCode(City, "Post Code", County, "Country/Region Code",
    end;
```

By doing some analysis of what we have dissected, we can see that the `ValidatePostCode` procedure call uses five calling parameters. There is no return value. The procedure avoids the need to a return value by passing four of the parameters *by reference* (not *by value*), as we can tell by the `var` keyword on the parameters.

We conclude that we can just copy the code from the `Post Code` table `OnValidate` trigger in the `Customer` table into the equivalent trigger in our `Fan` table. This will give us the `Post Code` maintenance we want. The result looks as follows (the `CurrFieldNo` variable is a system-defined variable left over from previous versions and has been retained for compatibility reasons):

```
field(100; "Post Code"; Code[20])
{
    trigger OnValidate()
    var
        PostCode: Record "Post Code";
    begin
        PostCode.ValidatePostCode(City, "Post Code", County, "Country/Region Code",
            (CurrFieldNo <> 0) AND GUIALLOWED);
    end;
}
```

We can test our work by running the `50111 Radio Show Fans` page. All we need to do is add the fields to the page and move to the `Post Code` field, click on it, and choose an entry from the displayed list of codes. The result should be the population of the `Post Code` field, the `Country/Region Code` field, and the `City` field. If we fill in the new data fields for some `Fan` records, our `Radio Show Fan` table should look as follows:

We've accomplished our goal. The way we've done it may seem disappointing. It didn't feel like we really designed a solution or wrote any code. What we did was find where in Business Central the same problem had already been solved, figured out how that solution worked, cloned it into our object, and we were done.

Each time we start this approach, we should look at the defined patterns (https://community.dynamics.com/nav/w/designpatterns/105.nav-design-patterns-repository.aspx) to see whether any patterns fit our situation. The benefit of starting with a pattern is that the general structural definition is defined for how this procedure should be done within Business Central. Whether you find a matching pattern or not, the next step is to find and study applicable AL code within Business Central.

Obviously, this approach doesn't work every time. However, every time it does work, it is a small triumph of efficiency. This helps us to keep the structure of our solution consistent with the standard product and allows us to reuse existing code constructs and minimize the debugging effort and chances of production problems. In addition, our modifications are more likely to work, even if the standard base application procedure changes in a future version.

Adding code to a report

Most reports require some embedded logic to process user selected options, calculate values, or access data in related tables. To illustrate some possibilities, we will extend our WDTU application to add a new report.

To support promotions giving away posters, concert tickets, and so on, we must further enhance the `Radio Show Fan` table and create a new report to generate mailing information from it. Our first step is to create a new dataset in the Visual Studio Code IDE. We should define the data fields we want to include for mailings (including a global variable of `CountryName`), then save and compile the result as a report called `50102 "Fan Promotion List"`, as shown in the following screenshot:

```
report 50102 "Fan Promotion List"
{
    DefaultLayout = Word;
    WordLayout = './FanPromotionList.docx';
    UsageCategory = ReportsAndAnalysis;
    ApplicationArea = Basic;

    dataset
    {
        dataitem(DataItemName; "Radio Show Fan")
        {
            column(Name; Name) { }
            column(Address; Address) { }
            column(Address_2; "Address 2") { }
            column(City; City) { }
            column(Post_Code; "Post Code") { }
            column(Country_Region_Code; "Country/Region Code") { }
        }
    }
}
```

Laying out the new Report Heading

Next, we will begin the design of the report layout in Microsoft Word. If we build our application, a Word template will be created, which we can open externally.

We will add a report header by simply creating it with a default style, as shown in the following screenshot:

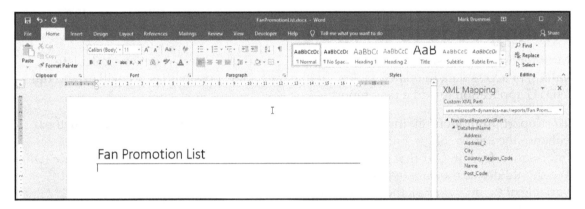

Saving and testing

At this point, it's time to save and test what we've done so far. Exit from Microsoft Word. Save the report layout changes. Build and publish your application and run the report using the search.

This first test is very simple (assuming it works). The **Report Request Page** will appear in the web client. Click on **Preview** to see the report display on-screen. The layout shown in the preceding screenshot will result in the following report page (or something similar):

Lookup-related table data

Once we have a successful test of the report (heading only), we'll move on to laying out the body of the report. As we think through the data, we will want to include a mailing address, such as name, address, a second address, city, country name, and post code, and realize that our table data includes country code, not country name. So, we will look up the country name from the `Country/Region` table (table 9). Let's take care of that now.

First, we'll add a couple of global variables to our report. One of them will allow us to access the `Country/Region` table, and the other will act as a holding place for the country name data we get from that table, as shown in the following screenshot:

```
    }
var
    CountryRegion: Record "Country/Region";
    CountryName: Text;
}
```

Each time we read a Radio Show Fan record, we'll look up the country name for that fan and store it in `CountryName` by entering the following code snippet:

```
        column(Country_Region_Code; "Country/Region Code") { }

        trigger OnAfterGetRecord()
        begin
            CountryRegion.Get("Country/Region Code");
            CountryName := CountryRegion.Name;
        end;
    }
```

Now, we can add the `CountryName` variable to the list of data elements attached to the DataItem Radio Show Fan so that it will be included in the data that's passed to Microsoft Word and, when the report is run, to the report viewer.

While what we've done will probably work most of the time, how could it be made better? For one thing, shouldn't we handle the situation where there is no `Country/Region` code in the fan record? Do we really need to move the country name to a global variable instead of simply reporting it directly from the `Country/Region` record?

Both of these issues could be handled better. Look up the GET procedure in help to see what should be done in terms of error handling. Additionally, after we work through the report as we're doing so here, we can enhance it by eliminating use of the CountryName global variable. For now, let's just move on and complete an initial version of our report by creating the rest of our report layout in Microsoft Word.

Laying out the new report Body

Open the report layout in Microsoft Word. From the ribbon, we'll grab a table and drag it into the layout work area for the report body. The table should contain five columns and two rows.

We will add the data fields from the XML mapping into each of the data row text boxes (the bottom row). In the top row, we will type captions. We will make the second row a repeating row:

Saving and testing

After we lay out, save and exit, update, and save and build, it's time to do another test run of our report in process. If we simply preview it without doing any filtering, we should see all of our test data address information (complete with country name), as shown in the following screenshot:

Handling user entered report options

Part of our report design includes allowing the user to choose fans based on some simple demographic data, such as age and gender. We'll need to add two more fields to our Radio Show Fan table definition, one for Gender and the other for Birth Date, from which we can calculate the fan's age, as shown in the following screenshot:

```
table 50110 "Radio Show Fan"
{
    DataClassification = ToBeClassified;

    fields
    {
        field(1; "No."; Code[20]) { }
        field(10; "Radio Show No."; Code[20]) { }
        field(20; Name; Text[50]) { }
        field(30; "E-Mail"; Text[250]) { }
        field(40; "Last Contacted"; Date) { }
        field(60; Address; Text[50]) { }
        field(70; "Address 2"; Text[50]) { }
        field(80; City; Text[50]) { }
        field(90; "Country/Region Code"; Code[10]) { }
        field(95; County; Text[30]) { }
        field(100; "Post Code"; Code[20])
        { ...
        }
        field(110; Gender; Option) { OptionMembers = ,Male,Female; }
        field(120; "Birth Date"; Date) { }
```

This back and forth process of updating one object, then a different one, then yet another, is typical of the Business Central development process most of the time. Exceptions are those cases where either the task is so simple we think of everything the first time through, or the cases where we create a completely documented, full-featured design before any development starts (but nobody thinks of everything, there are always changes; our challenge is to keep the changes under control).

An advantage to the more flexible approach we are following is that it allows us to view (and share with others) intermediate versions of the application as it is developed. Design issues can be addressed as they come up, and overlooked features can be considered midstream. Two downsides are the very real possibility of scope creep (the project growing uncontrollably) and poorly organized code. Scope creep can be controlled by good project management. If the first pass through results in poorly organized code, then a thoughtful refactoring is appropriate, cleaning up the code while retaining the design.

For the user to choose which Fan demographics will be used to filter the Fan data for a particular promotion, we will have to create a request page for entry of the desired criteria. This, in turn, requires the definition of a set of global variables in our Report object to support the request page data entry fields and as working variables for the age calculation and Fan selection. We've decided that, if Fan fits any of the individual criteria, we will include them. This makes our logic simpler. Our final global variable list in report 50102 looks as follows:

```
var
    CountryRegion: Record "Country/Region";
    CountryName: Text;
    Age12orLess: Boolean;
    Age13to18: Boolean;
    Age19to34: Boolean;
    Age35to50: Boolean;
    AgeOver50: Boolean;
    Male: Boolean;
    Female: Boolean;
    SelectThisFan: Boolean;
    FanAge: Integer;
}
```

Defining the Request Page

Now, let's define the `requestpage`. Click on **View** | **Request Page** and make the entries necessary to describe the page's contents, as shown in the following screenshot:

```
requestpage
{
    layout
    {
        area(content)
        {
            group(Options)
            {
                field(Age12orLess; Age12orLess) { ApplicationArea = Basic; Caption = 'Age 12 or less'; }
                field(Age13to18; Age13to18) { ApplicationArea = Basic; Caption = 'Age 13 to 18'; }
                field(Age19to34; Age19to34) { ApplicationArea = Basic; Caption = 'Age 19 to 34'; }
                field(Age35to50; Age35to50) { ApplicationArea = Basic; Caption = 'Age 34 to 50'; }
                field(AgeOver50; AgeOver50) { ApplicationArea = Basic; Caption = 'Age over 50'; }
                field(Male; Male) { ApplicationArea = Basic; Caption = 'Male'; }
                field(Female; Female) { ApplicationArea = Basic; Caption = 'Female'; }
```

Finishing the processing code

Next, we will create the AL code to calculate a fan's age (in years) based on their birth date and the current `WORKDATE`. The logic is simple—subtract the birthdate from the `WORKDATE`. This gives a number of days. So, we will divide by 365 (not worrying about leap years) and round down to integer years (if someone is 25 years, 10 months, and 2 days old, we will just consider them 25). In the following code, we did the division as though the result were a decimal field. However, because our math is done in integers, we could have used the simpler expression:

```
FanAge := ((WORKDATE - "Birth Date") DIV 365);
```

Finally, we'll write the code to check each `Fan` record data against our selection criteria, determining whether we want to include that fan in our output data (`SelectThisFan` set to `True`). This code will select each fan who fits any of the checked criteria; there is no combination logic here.

The following is our commented AL code for report `50102`:

```
trigger OnAfterGetRecord()
begin
    //Look up the Country Name using the Country/Region Code
    CountryRegion.Get("Country/Region Code");
    CountryName := CountryRegion.Name;

    //Calculate the fan's age
    FanAge := ROUND(((WORKDATE - "Birth Date") / 365), 1.0, '<');

    //Select Fans to receive promotional material
    SelectThisFan := FALSE;
    IF Age12OrLess AND (FanAge <= 12) THEN
        SelectThisFan := TRUE;
    IF Age13to18 AND (FanAge > 12) AND (FanAge < 19) THEN
        SelectThisFan := TRUE;
    IF Age19to34 AND (FanAge > 18) AND (FanAge < 35) THEN
        SelectThisFan := TRUE;
    IF Age35to50 AND (FanAge > 34) AND (FanAge < 51) THEN
        SelectThisFan := TRUE;
    IF AgeOver50 AND (FanAge > 50) THEN
        SelectThisFan := TRUE;
    IF Male AND (Gender = Gender::Male) THEN
        SelectThisFan := TRUE;
    IF Female AND (Gender = Gender::Female) THEN
        SelectThisFan := TRUE;

    //If this Fan not selected, skip this Fan record on report
    IF SelectThisFan <> TRUE THEN
        CurrReport.SKIP;
end;
```

After this version of the report is successfully tested, enhance it. Make the report support choosing any of the options (as it is now) or, at the user option, choose a combination of age range plus gender. Hint: add additional check boxes to allow the user to control which set of logic will be applied. We should also change the code to use CASE statements (rather than IF statements). CASE statements often provide an easier to understand view of the logic.

Testing the completed report

After we save and compile our report, we'll run it again. Now, we will get an expanded request option page. After this, we check-marked a couple of the selection criteria, as shown in the following screenshot:

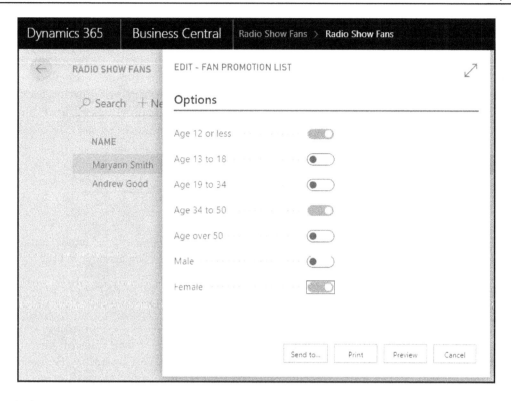

Now, let's preview our report. Using the sample data we previously illustrated, our report output shows two records in the following screenshot; one selected on the basis of Gender and the other on Age:

At this point, we have a report that runs and is useful. It can be enhanced to support more complex selection criteria. As usual, there are a number of different ways to accomplish essentially the same result. Some of those paths would be significantly different for the developer, but nearly invisible to the user. Some might not even matter to the next developer who has to work on this report. What is important at this point is that the result works reliably, provides the desired output, operates with reasonable speed, and does not cost too much to create or maintain. If all of these goals are met, most of the other differences are usually not very important.

Summary

"Furniture or gold can be taken away from you, but knowledge and a new language can easily be taken from one place to the other, and nobody can take them away from you."

– David Schwarzer

In this chapter, we covered Visual Studio Code navigation. We covered a number of AL language areas, including procedures and how they may be used, variables of various types (both development and system), basic AL syntax, expressions, and operators. Some of the essential AL procedures that we covered included user dialogs, SETRANGE filtering, GET, variations of FIND, and BEGIN-END for code structures, plus IF-THEN for basic process flow control. Finally, we got some hands-on experience by adding validation code to a table and creating a new report that included embedded AL code and a request page.

In the next chapter, we will expand our exploration and practice using AL. We will learn about additional AL procedures, flow control structures, input/output procedures, and filtering.

Questions

1. All Business Central objects can contain AL code—true or false?
2. Which object type has to be designed outside of Visual Studio Code? Choose one:

    - Page
    - XmlPort
    - Table
    - Report

3. All AL Assignment statements include the symbol—true or false?

4. One setting defines how parameters are passed to procedures, that is, whether a parameter is passed by reference or by value. Choose that one setting identity:

   - `DataType`
   - `Subtype`
   - `Var`
   - `Value`

5. In Visual Studio Code, we can use wizards to get started with object definitions—true or false?

6. The AL code cannot be inserted into the RDLC generated by the Visual Studio Report Designer (or the SQL Server Report Builder)—true or false?

7. When a table definition is changed, the fields should always be added to all pages—true or false?

8. Object numbers and names are so flexible that we can (and should) choose our own approach to numbering and naming—true or false?

9. `BEGIN-END` are always required in `IF` statements—true or false?

10. All Business Central development work starts from Visual Studio Code—true or false?

11. Modifiable procedures include which of the following? Choose two:

    - Application management
    - `DATE2MDY`
    - `Mail`
    - `STRLEN`

12. Report heading text can either be typed in manually or brought into Word through label parameters—true or false?

13. Whenever possible, the controlling logic to manage data should be resident within the tables—true or false?

14. Filter wildcards include which three of the following?

    - ?
    - : :
    - *
    - ^
    - @

15. Choice of the proper version of the `FIND` statement can make a significant difference in processing speed—true or false?

16. When we are working in Visual Studio Code to change AL code, the object designer automatically backs up our work every few minutes so that we don't have to—true or false?

17. When an `ERROR` statement is executed, the user is given the choice to terminate processing, cause a rollback, or to ignore the error and continue processing—true or false?

18. Arithmetic operators and procedures include which of the following? Choose two:

    - *
    - >
    - =
    - /

Intermediate AL 7

"You need to "listen deeply"—listen past what people say they want to hear to what they need."

– Jon Meads

"People's behavior makes sense if you think about it in terms of their goals, needs, and motives."

– Thomas Mann

In the previous chapter, you learned enough AL to create a basic operational set of code. In this chapter, you will learn more AL functions and pick up a few more good habits along the way. If you are getting started as a professional Business Central developer, the built-in AL functions represent a significant portion of the knowledge that you will need on a day-to-day basis. If you are a manager or consultant needing to know what Business Central can do for your business or your customer, an understanding of these functions will help you too.

Our goal is to competently manage I/O, create moderately complex program logic structures, and understand data filtering and sorting as handled in Business Central and AL. Because the functions and features in AL are designed for business and financial applications, we can do a surprising amount of ERP work in Business Central with a relatively small number of language constructs.

Keep in mind that anything discussed in this chapter relates only indirectly to those portions of Business Central objects that contain no AL, for example, Microsoft **SQL Server Report Builder (SSRB)** and Microsoft Word report layouts. This chapter's goals are to accomplish the following:

- Review some AL development basics
- Learn about a variety of useful (and widely used) AL functions
- Better understand filtering
- Apply what you've learned to expand your WDTU application using some of the AL development tools

As described in `Chapter 1`, *Introduction to Business Central*, all internal Business Central logic development is done in AL and all AL development is done in Visual Studio Code. Some user interface design is done using Microsoft Word. It is also possible to integrate JavaScript objects for a variety of purposes.

IntelliSense

As an IDE, Visual Studio Code contains a number of tools designed to make our AL development effort easier. One of these is IntelliSense. When we are in one of the areas where AL code is supported, the IntelliSense menu window can be accessed via *Ctrl +* spacebar:

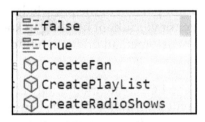

IntelliSense is a very useful multi-purpose tool for the developer. It serves the following purposes:

- As a quick reference to the available AL functions
- Documentation of the syntax of those functions
- Access Microsoft Docs for more information on those functions
- As a source of variable names or function structures to paste into our code

The use of IntelliSense for reference purposes is especially helpful, not only when we are a beginning AL developer, but also after we have become experienced developers. It is a guide to the inventory of available code tools with some very handy built-in programming aids.

The second use of IntelliSense is as a symbol table. The symbol table for our object is visible in the left column of IntelliSense's display. The displayed symbol set (the variable set) is context sensitive. It will include all system-defined symbols, and all our global and local symbols from the function that had focus at the time we accessed IntelliSense. Although it would be useful, there is no way within the symbol menu to see all local variables in one view. The local symbols will be at the top of the list, but we have to know the name of the first global symbol to determine the scope of a particular variable (that is, if an entry appears in the symbol list before the first global, it is a local variable; otherwise, it's global).

The third use for IntelliSense is as a code template with a paste function option available, as well as a list of available snippets. The snippets start with the letter t and can most often be found at the end of the list or simply by pressing the letter t.

Internal documentation

When we are creating or modifying software, we should always document what we have done. It is often difficult for developers to spend much time (time equals money) on documentation because many don't enjoy doing it, and the benefits to customers are difficult to quantify in advance. A reasonable goal is to provide enough documentation so that a knowledgeable person can later understand what we have done, as well as the reasons why.

If we choose good variable names, the AL code will tend to be self-documenting. If we lay our code out neatly, use indentation consistently, and localize logical elements in functions, then the flow of our code should be easy to read. We should also include comments that describe the functional reason for the change. This will help the next person working in this code not only be able to follow the logic of the code, but to understand the business reasons for that code.

In the case of a brand-new function, a simple statement of purpose is often all that is necessary. In the case of a modification, it is extremely useful to have comments providing a functional definition of what the change is intended to accomplish, as well as a description of what has been changed. If there is external documentation of the change, including a design specification, the comments in the code should refer back to this external documentation.

In any case, the primary focus should be on the functional reason for the change, not just the technical reason. Any good programmer can study the code and understand what changed, but without the documentation describing why the change was made, the task of the next person to maintain or upgrade that code will be made much more difficult.

Inline comments can be done in two ways. The most visible way is to use a // character sequence (two forward slashes). The text that follows the slashes on that line will be treated as a comment by the compiler—it will be ignored. If the comment spans multiple physical lines, each line of the comment must also be preceded by two forward slashes.

In the following screenshot, we have used // to place comments inline to identify a change:

```
begin
    //Look up the Country Name using the Country/Region Code
    CountryRegion.Get("Country/Region Code");
    CountryName := CountryRegion.Name;

    //Calculate the fan's age
    FanAge := ROUND(((WORKDATE - "Birth Date") / 365), 1.0, '<');

    //Select Fans to receive promotional material
    SelectThisFan := FALSE;
    IF Age12OrLess AND (FanAge <= 12) THEN
        SelectThisFan := TRUE;
```

A second way to place a comment within code is to surround the comment with a matched pair of braces { }. As braces are less visible than the slashes, we should use // when our comment is relatively short. If we decide to use { }, it's a good idea to insert a // comment, at least at the beginning and end of the material inside the braces to make the comments more visible. It is also highly recommended to put each of the braces on a separate line to make them more obvious. Some experienced developers recommend using // on all removed code lines to make the deletions easier to spot later.

Consider the following lines of code as an example:

```
{//CDM.07.02 start deletion -------------
//CDM.07.02 Replace validation with a call to an external function
...miscellaneous AL validation code
//CDM.07.02 end deletion ------------ }
```

If, as part of a modification, we delete code that is part of the original distribution, we should leave the original statements in place, but commented out so that the old code is inoperative (an exception to this may apply if a source code control system that tracks all changes is in use). The same concept applies when we change the existing code; leave the original code in place commented out with the new version being inserted, as shown in the following screenshot. This approach does not necessarily apply to the code that we created originally:

```
procedure SetStyle():Text
begin
    if "News Required" then
        exit('Favorable');
    if "Weather Required" then
//  CDM 7.00.01
//          exit('Unfavorable');
        exit('Attention');
    if "Sports Required" then
        exit('Strong');
end;
```

Yet another approach, one that is especially suitable for modifications that exceed a small number of lines of code or that will be called from multiple places, is to create a new function for the modification. Name the function so that its purpose is obvious, and then call the function from the point of use. In this case, that function might be named something such as CheckDatePrizeLastWon. In this case, the function would only have one line of code (not a good example), and we would pass in the Last Prize Date value. The function would return a Boolean value, telling us whether the individual was eligible for a new prize.

Source code management

Instead of documenting within the code, many developers choose to use source code management tools, such as GitHub or Microsoft DevOps.

Tools such as these allow you to create change requests and connect changed code to these requests. Once the change is validated, it is connected to the documentation, automatically creating a knowledge database outside of the source code. This keeps the source code clean and readable.

Validation functions

AL includes a number of utility functions that are designed to facilitate data validation or initialization. Some of these functions are as follows:

- `TESTFIELD`
- `FIELDERROR`
- `INIT`
- `VALIDATE`

We will discuss these functions more in the following sections.

TESTFIELD

The `TESTFIELD` function is widely used in standard Business Central code. With `TESTFIELD`, we can test a variable value and generate an error message in a single statement if the test fails. The syntax is as follows:

```
Record.TESTFIELD (Field, [Value])
```

If `Value` is specified and the field does not equal that value, the process terminates with an error condition, and an error message is issued.

If no `Value` is specified, the field contents are checked for values of zero or blank. If the field is zero or blank, then an error message is issued.

The advantage of `TESTFIELD` is ease of use and consistency in code, and in the message displayed. The disadvantage is the error message is not as informative as a careful developer would provide.

The following screenshot of the `TESTFIELD` function usage is from `Table 18 - Customer`. This code checks to make sure that the **Sales Order** field's `Status` is equal to the option value `Open` before allowing the value of the **Sell-to Customer No.** field to be entered:

```
TESTFIELD(State,Status::Open);
```

An example of the error message that is generated when attempting to change the **Sell-to Customer No.** field when `Status` is not equal to the option value `Open` is as follows:

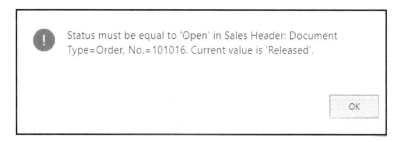

Status must be equal to 'Open' in Sales Header: Document Type=Order, No.=101016. Current value is 'Released'.

OK

FIELDERROR

Another function, which is very similar to the `TESTFIELD` function, is `FIELDERROR`. However, where `TESTFIELD` performs a test and terminates with either an error or an OK result, `FIELDERROR` presumes that the test was already performed and the field failed the test. `FIELDERROR` is designed to display an error message and then terminate the process. This approach is followed in much of the standard Business Central logic, especially in the posting codeunits (for example, codeunits `12`, `80`, and `90`). The syntax is as follows:

```
TableName.FIELDERROR(FieldName[,OptionalMsgText]);
```

If we include our own message text by defining a text constant in the variable section (so that the message can be multilingual), we will have the following line of code:

```
Text001     must be greater than Start Time
```

Then, we can reference the text constant in code as follows:

```
IF Rec."End Time" <- "Start Time" THEN
Rec.FIELDERROR("End Time",Text001);
```

The result is an error message from `FIELDERROR`, as shown in the following screenshot:

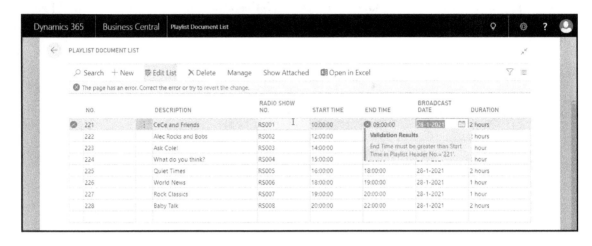

An error message that simply identifies the data field, but does not reference a message text, is as follows, with the record key information displayed:

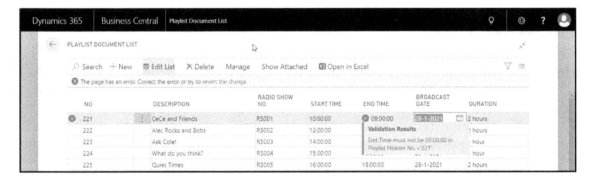

Because the error message begins with the name of the field, we will need to be careful that our text constant is structured to make the resulting error message easy to read.

If we don't include our own message text, the default message comes in two flavors. The first instance is the case where the referenced field is not empty. Then, the error message presumes that the error is due to a wrong value, as shown in the previous screenshot. In this case, where the referenced data field is empty, the error message logic presumes that the field should not be empty, as shown in the following screenshot:

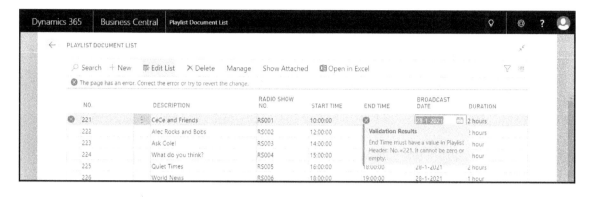

INIT

The `INIT` function initializes a record in preparation for its use, typically in the course of building a record entry to insert in a table. The syntax is as follows:

```
Record.INIT;
```

All the data fields in the record are initialized as follows:

- Fields that have an `InitValue` property defined are initialized to the specified value.
- Fields that do not have a defined `InitValue` are initialized to the default value for their data type.
- Primary key fields and timestamps are not automatically initialized. If they contain values, those will remain. If new values are desired, they must be assigned in code.

VALIDATE

The syntax of the `VALIDATE` function is as follows:

```
Record.VALIDATE (Field [, Value])
```

`VALIDATE` will fire the `OnValidate` trigger of `Record.Field`. If we have specified a `Value`, it is assigned to the field and the field validations are invoked.

If we don't specify a `Value`, then the field validations are invoked using the field value that already exists in the field. This function allows us to easily centralize our code design around the table—one of Business Central's strengths.

For example, if we were to code and change `Item."Base Unit of Measure"` from one unit of measure to another, the code should make sure that the change is valid. We should get an error if the new unit of measure has any quantity other than 1, because quantity equals 1 is a requirement of the `Base Unit of Measurement` field. Making the unit of measure change with a simple assignment statement would not catch a quantity value error.

The following are two forms of using VALIDATE that give the same end result:

- `Item.VALIDATE("Base Unit of Measure",'Box')`
- `Item."Base Unit of Measure" := 'Box';`
- `Item.VALIDATE("Base Unit of Measure");`

Date and time functions

Business Central provides a considerable number of date and time functions. In the following sections, we will cover several of those that are more commonly used, especially in the context of accounting date-sensitive activity:

- `TODAY`, `TIME`, and `CURRENTDATETIME` functions
- `WORKDATE` function
- `DATE2DMY`, `DATE2DWY`, `DMY2DATE`, `DWY2DATE`, and `CALCDATE` functions

TODAY, TIME, and CURRENTDATETIME

`TODAY` retrieves the current system date, as set in the operating system. `TIME` retrieves the current system time, as set in the operating system. `CURRENTDATETIME` retrieves the current date and time in the `DATETIME` format, which is stored in UTC international time (formerly referenced as **GMT** or **Greenwich Mean Time**) and then displayed in local time. If we are using the Windows client, these use the time setting in the Business Central client. If the system operates in multiple time zones at one time, search `Microsoft Dynamics Business Central Help` on the time zone for several references on how to deal with multiple time zones.

The syntax for each of these is as follows:

```
DateField := TODAY;
TimeField := TIME;
DateTimeField := CURRENTDATETIME;
```

These are often used for date- and time-stamping transactions or for filling in default values in fields of the appropriate data type. For data-entry purposes, the current system date can be entered by simply typing the letter T or the word TODAY in the date-entry field (this is not a case-sensitive entry). Business Central will automatically convert that entry into the current system date.

The undefined date in Business Central is represented by the earliest valid DATETIME in SQL Server, which is January 1, 1753 00:00:00:000. The undefined date in Business Central is represented as *0D* (zero *D*, as in days), with subsequent dates handled through December 31, 9999. A date outside this range will result in a runtime error.

The Microsoft Dynamics Business Central undefined time (*0T*) is represented by the same value as an undefined date (*0D*) is represented.

If a two-digit year is entered or stored as a date and has a value of 30 to 99, it is assumed to be in the 1900s. If the two-digit date is in the range of 00 to 29, then it is treated as a 2000s date.

WORKDATE

Many standard Business Central routines default dates to the work date rather than to the system date. When a user logs into the system, the work date is initially set equal to the system date. However, at any time, the operator can set the work date to any date by accessing the application menu and clicking on **Set Work Date...**, and then entering the new work date:

The user can also click on the **Work Date** displayed in the status bar at the bottom of the RTC. The following screenshot shows how to set the work date:

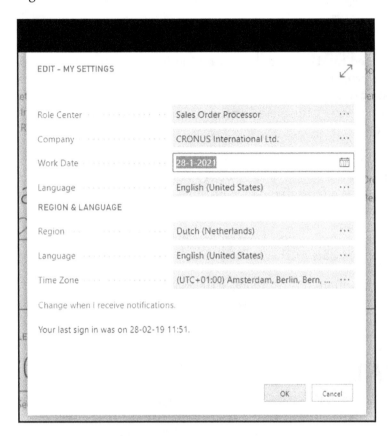

For data-entry purposes, the current work date can be entered by the operator by simply typing the letter w or W or the word WORKDATE in the date entry field. Business Central will automatically convert that entry into the current work date.

The syntax to access the current WorkDate value from within AL code is as follows:

```
DateField := WORKDATE;
```

The syntax to set the WORKDATE to a new date from within AL code is as follows:

```
WORKDATE(newdate);
```

DATE2DMY function

`DATE2DMY` allows us to extract the sections of a date (day of the month, month, and year) from a `Date` field. The syntax is as follows:

```
IntegerVariable := DATE2DMY ( DateField, ExtractionChoice )
```

`IntegerVariable` and `DateField` are just as their names imply. The `ExtractionChoice` parameter allows us to choose which value (day, month, or year) will be assigned to the `IntegerVariable` field. The following table provides the `DATE2DMY` extraction choices:

DATE2DMY extraction choice	Integer value result
1	2-digit day (1–31)
2	2-digit month (1–12)
3	4-digit year

DATE2DWY function

`DATE2DWY` allows us to extract the sections of a date (day of the week, week of the year, and year) from a `DateField` in exactly the same fashion as `DATE2DMY`. The `ExtractionChoice` parameter allows us to choose which value (day, week, or year) will be assigned to `IntegerVariable`, as shown in the following table:

DATE2DWY extraction choice	Integer value result
1	2-digit day (1–7 for Monday to Sunday)
2	2-digit week (1–53)
3	4-digit year

DMY2DATE and DWY2DATE functions

`DMY2DATE` allows us to create a date from integer values (or defaults) representing the day of the month, month of the year, and the four-digit year. If an optional parameter (`MonthValue` or `YearValue`) is not specified, the corresponding value from the system date is used. The syntax is as follows:

```
DateVariable := DMY2DATE ( DayValue [, MonthValue] [, YearValue] )
```

The only way to have the function use work date values for month and year is to extract those values and then use them explicitly. An example is as follows:

```
DateVariable := DMY2DATE(22,DATE2MDY(WORKDATE,2),DATE2MDY(WORKDATE,3))
```

 This example also illustrates how expressions can be built up of nested expressions and functions. We have WORKDATE within DATE2MDY within DMY2DATE.

DWY2DATE operates similarly to DMY2DATE, allowing us to create a date from integer values representing the day of the week (from 1 to 7 representing Monday to Sunday), week of the year (from 1 to 53), followed by the four-digit year. The syntax is as follows:

```
DateVariable := DWY2DATE ( DayValue [, WeekValue] [, YearValue] )
```

An interesting result can occur for week 53 because it can span two years. By default, such a week is assigned to the year in which it has four or more days. In that case, the year of the result will vary, depending on the day of the week in the parameters (in other words, the year of the result may be one year greater than the year specified in the parameters). This is a perfect example of why thorough testing of our code is always appropriate.

CALCDATE

CALCDATE allows us to calculate a date value that's been assigned to a date data type variable. The calculation is based on DateExpression that's been applied to a base date (reference date). If we don't specify BaseDateValue, the current system date is used as the default date. We can specify BaseDateValue either in the form of a variable of data type date or as a date constant.

The syntax for CALCDATE is as follows:

```
DateVariable := CALCDATE ( DateExpression [, BaseDateValue])
```

There are a number of ways in which we can build a DateExpression. The rules for the CALCDATE function, DateExpression, are similar to the rules for DateFormula, which are described in Chapter 3, *Data Types and Fields*.

If there is a CW, CM, CP, CQ, or CY (current week, current month, current period, current quarter, or current year, respectively) parameter in an expression, then the result will be evaluated based on the BaseDateValue. If we have more than one of these in our expression, the results are unpredictable. Any such expression should be thoroughly tested before being released to users.

If `DateExpression` is stored in a `DateFormula` variable (or a text or code variable with the `DateFormula` property set to `Yes`), then the `DateExpression` will be language independent. Also, if we create our own `DateExpression` in the form of a string constant within our inline AL code, surrounding the constant with `<  >` delimiters as part of the string, it will make the constant language independent. Otherwise, the `DateExpression` constant will be language dependent.

Regardless of how we have constructed our `DateExpression`, it is important to test it carefully and thoroughly before moving on. Incorrect syntax will result in a runtime error. One easy way to test it is by using a report whose sole task is to evaluate our expression and display the result. If we want to try different base dates, we can use the request page, accept the `BaseDateValue` as input, then calculate and display the `DateVariable` in the `OnValidate` trigger.

Some sample `CALCDATE` expression evaluations are as follows:

- `('<CM>',031017D)` will yield `03/31/2017`, that is, the last day of the current month for the date 3/10/2017
- `('<-WD2>',031216D)` will yield `03/08/2016`, that is, the `WeekDay #2` (the prior Tuesday) before the date 3/12/2016
- `('<CM+1D>',BaseDate)`, where `BaseDate` equals `03/10/17`, will yield `04/01/2017`, that is, the last day of the month of the base date plus one day (the first day of the month following the base date)

Data conversion and formatting functions

Some data-type conversions are handled in the normal process flow by Business Central without any particular attention on part of the developer, such as code to text and character to text. Some data-type conversions can only be handled through AL functions. Formatting is included because it can also include a data-type conversion. Rounding does not do a data-type conversion, but it does result in a change in format (the number of decimal places). Let's review the following functions:

- `ROUND` function
- `FORMAT` function
- `EVALUATE` function

ROUND

The ROUND function allows us to control the rounding precision for a decimal expression. The syntax for the ROUND function is as follows:

```
DecimalResult := ROUND (Number [, Precision] [, Direction] )
```

Here, Number is rounded, Precision spells out the number of digits of decimal precision, and Direction indicates whether to round up, round down, or round to the nearest number. Some examples of Precision values are shown in the following table:

Precision value	Rounding effect
100	To a multiple of 100
1	To an integer format
01	To two decimal places (the US default)
0.01	Same as .01
.0001	To four decimal places

If no Precision value is specified, the rounding default is controlled by a value set in General Ledger **Setup** in the **Appln. Rounding Precision** field on the **Application** tab. If no value is specified, rounding will default to two decimal places. If the precision value is, for example, .04 rather than .01, the rounding will be done to multiples of 4 at the number of decimal places specified.

The options available for the direction value are shown in the following table:

Direction value (a text value)	Rounding effect
'='	Round to the nearest (mathematically correct and the default)
'>'	Round up
'<'	Round down

Consider the following statement:

```
DecimalValue := ROUND (1234.56789,0.001,'<')
```

This would result in a `DecimalValue` containing `1234.567`. Let's check out the following statements:

```
DecimalValue := ROUND (1234.56789,0.001,'=')
DecimalValue := ROUND (1234.56789,0.001,'>')
```

These both result in a `DecimalValue` containing `1234.568`.

FORMAT function

The `FORMAT` function allows you to convert an expression of any data type (for example, `integer`, `decimal`, `date`, `option`, `time`, `Boolean`) into a formatted string. The syntax is as follows:

```
StringField := FORMAT( ExpressionToFormat [, OutputLength]
[, FormatString or FormatNumber])
```

The formatted output of the `ExpressionToFormat` will be assigned to the output of `StringField`. The optional parameters control the conversion according to a complex set of rules. These rules can be found in Microsoft Docs for the `FORMAT` function and `FORMAT` property. Whenever possible, we should always apply `FORMAT` in its simplest form. The best way to determine the likely results of a `FORMAT` expression is to test it through a range of the values to be formatted. We should make sure that we include the extremes of the range of possible values in our testing.

The optional `OutputLength` parameter can be zero (the default), a positive integer, or a negative integer. The typical `OutputLength` value is either zero, in which case the defined format is fully applied, or it is a value designed to control the maximum character length and padding of the formatted string result.

The last optional parameter has two mutually exclusive sets of choices. One set, represented by an integer `FormatNumber`, allows the choice of a particular predefined (standard) format, of which there are four to nine choices depending on the `ExpressionToFormat` data type. The format parameter of the number 9 is used for XMLport data exporting. Use of the optional number 9 parameter will convert AL format data types into XML standard data types. The other set of choices allows us to build our own format expression.

The Microsoft Docs information for the FORMAT property provides a relatively complete description of the available tools from which we can build our own format expression.

Even though the FORMAT function is non-executable, an erroneous FORMAT function will result in a runtime error that will terminate the execution of the process. Thus, to avoid production crashes, it is very important that we thoroughly test any code where FORMAT is used.

EVALUATE function

The EVALUATE function is essentially the reverse of the FORMAT function, allowing for the conversion of a string value into the defined data type. The syntax of the EVALUATE function is as follows:

```
[ BooleanVariable := ] EVALUATE ( ResultVariable,
StringToBeConverted [, 9]
```

The handling of a runtime error can be done by specifying BooleanVariable or including EVALUATE in an expression to deal with an error, such as an IF statement. The ResultVariable data type will determine what data conversion the EVALUATE function will attempt. The format of the data in StringToBeConverted must be compatible with the data type of ResultVariable; otherwise, a runtime error will occur.

The optional parameter, number 9, is only used for XMLport data exporting. Use of the optional number 9 parameter will convert Business Central format data types into XML standard data types. This deals with the fact that several equivalent XML data types are represented differently at the base system level, that is, under the covers. The Business Central data types for an EVALUATE result can include decimal, Boolean, DateTime, date, time, integer, and duration.

FlowField and SumIndexField functions

In Chapter 3, *Data Types and Fields*, we discussed SumIndexFields and FlowFields in the context of table, field, and key definition. To recap briefly, SumIndexFields are defined in the screen where the table keys are defined. They allow for the very rapid calculation of values in filtered data. In most ERP and accounting software systems, the calculation of group totals, periodic totals, and so on requires time consuming-processing of all the data to be totaled.

SIFT allows a Business Central system to respond almost instantly with totals in any area where the `SumIndexField` was defined and is maintained. In fact, use of SIFT totals combined with Business Central's retention of detailed data supports totally flexible ad hoc queries of the form "`What were our sales for red widgets between the dates of November 15th through December 24th?`". And the answer is returned almost instantly! `SumIndexFields` are the basis of FlowFields that have a method of `Sum` or `Average`; such a FlowField must refer to a data element that is defined as `a SumIndexField`.

When we access a record that has a `SumIndexField` defined, there is no visible evidence of the data sum that `SumIndexField` represents. When we access a record that contains FlowFields, the FlowFields are empty virtual data elements until they are calculated. When a FlowField is displayed in a page or report, it is automatically calculated by Business Central; the developer doesn't need to do so. However, in any other scenario, the developer is responsible for calculating FlowFields using the `CALCFIELDS` function.

FlowFields are one of the key areas where Business Central systems are subject to significant processing bottlenecks. Even with the improved design, it is still critical that the table keys used for the `SumIndexField` definition are designed with efficient processing in mind. Sometimes, as part of a performance tuning effort, it's necessary to revise existing keys or add new keys to improve FlowField performance.

 Note that even though we can manage indexes in SQL Server independently of the Business Central key definitions, having two different definitions of keys for a single table may make our system more difficult to support in the long run because the SQL Server resident changes aren't always readily visible to the Business Central developer.

In addition to being careful about the SIFT-key structure design, it is also important not to define any `SumIndexFields` that are not necessary. Each additional `SumIndexField` adds additional processing requirements and, thus, adds to the processing load of the system.

 Including `SumIndexFields` in a list page display is almost always a bad idea, because each `SumIndexField` instance must be calculated as it is displayed. Applicable functions include `CALCFIELDS`, `CALCSUMS`, and `SETAUTOCALCFIELDS`.

CALCFIELDS function

The syntax for `CALCFIELDS` is as follows:

```
[BooleanField := ] Record.CALCFIELDS ( FlowField1 [, FlowField2] ,...)
```

Executing the `CALCFIELDS` function will cause all the specified FlowFields to be calculated. Specification of the `BooleanField` allows us to handle any runtime error that may occur. Any runtime errors for `CALCFIELDS` usually result from a coding error or a change in a table key structure.

The FlowField calculation takes into account the filters (including FlowFilters) that are currently applied to the record (we need to be careful not to overlook this). After the `CALCFIELDS` execution, the included FlowFields can be used similarly to any other data fields. The `CALCFIELDS` must be executed for each cycle through the subject table.

Whenever the contents of a `BLOB` field are to be used, `CALCFIELDS` is used to load the contents of the `BLOB` field from the database into memory.

When the following conditions are true, `CALCFIELDS` uses dynamically maintained SIFT data:

- The Business Central key contains the fields that are used in the filters that were defined for the FlowField
- The `SumIndexFields` on the operative key contain the fields that are provided as parameters for calculation
- The `MaintainSIFTIndex` property on the key is set to `Yes`; this is the default setting

If all these conditions are not true and `CALCFIELDS` is invoked, we will not get a runtime error, but SQL Server will calculate the requested totals the hard way – by reading all the necessary records. This could be very slow and inefficient, and should not be used for frequently processed routines or large datasets. On the other hand, if the table does not contain a lot of data or the SIFT data will not be used very often, it may be better to have the `MaintainSIFTIndex` property set to `No`.

SETAUTOCALCFIELDS function

The syntax for SETAUTOCALCFIELDS is as follows:

```
[BooleanField := ] Record.SETAUTOCALCFIELDS
( FlowField1 [, FlowField2] [, FlowField3]...)
```

When SETAUTOCALCFIELDS for a table is inserted in code in front of record retrieval, the specified FlowFields are automatically calculated as the record is read. This is more efficient than performing CALCFIELDS on the FlowFields after the record has been read.

If we want to end the automatic FlowField calculation to a record, call the function without any parameters:

```
[BooleanField := ] Record.SETAUTOCALCFIELDS()
```

An automatic FlowField calculation equivalent to SETAUTOCALCFIELDS is automatically set for the system record variables, Rec and xRec.

CALCSUMS function

The CALCSUMS function is conceptually similar to CALCFIELDS for the calculation of Sums only. However, CALCFIELDS operates on FlowFields and CALCSUMS operates directly on the record where the SumIndexFields are defined for the keys. This difference means that we must specify the proper key, plus any filters to apply when using CALCSUMS (the applicable key and filters to apply are already defined in the properties for the FlowFields).

The syntax for CALCSUMS is as follows:

```
[ BooleanField := ] Record.CALCSUMS ( SumIndexField1 [,SumIndexField2]
,...)
```

Prior to a statement of this type, we should specify a key that has the SumIndexFields defined (to maximize the probability of good performance). Before executing the CALCSUMS function, we also need to specify any filters that we want to apply to the Record from which the sums are to be calculated. The SumIndexFields calculations take into account the filters that are currently applied to the record.

Executing the CALCSUMS function will cause the specified SumIndexFields totals to be calculated. Specification of the BooleanField allows us to handle any runtime error that may occur. Runtime errors for CALCSUMS usually result from a coding error or a change in a table key structure. If possible, CALCSUMS uses the defined SIFT. Otherwise, SQL Server creates totals on the fly.

Before the execution of CALCSUMS, SumIndexFields contain only the data from the individual record that was read. After the execution of CALCSUMS, the included SumIndexFields contain the totals that were calculated by the CALCSUMS function (these totals are only in memory, not in the database). These totals can then be used the same as data in any field; however, if we want to access the individual record's original data for that field, we must either save a copy of the record before executing the CALCSUMS or we must reread the record. The CALCSUMS must be executed for each read cycle through the subject table.

Comparing CALCFIELDS and CALCSUMS

In the Sales Header record, there are FlowFields defined for Amount and "AmountIncludingVAT". These FlowFields are all based on Sums of entries in the SalesLine table. The CalcFormula for Amount is
Sum("SalesLine".AmountWHERE(DocumentType=FIELD(DocumentType),DocumentNo.=FIELD(No.))).

CALCSUMS can be used on any integer, big integer, or decimal field with any filter on any table, but for larger datasets, creating a key with a SumIndexField is recommended.

To calculate a TotalOrderAmount value while referencing the Sales Header table, the code can be as simple as this:

```
"Sales Header".CALCFIELDS (Amount);
```

To use TotalOrderAmount := "Sales Header".Amount; to calculate the same value from code directly referencing the Sales Line table, the required code is similar to the following (assuming a Sales Header record has already been read):

```
"Sales Line".SETRANGE("Document Type","Sales Header"."Document Type");
"Sales Line".SETRANGE("Document No.","Sales Header"."No.");
"Sales Line".CALCSUMS(Amount);
TotalOrderAmount := "Sales Line".Amount;
```

Flow control functions

Process flow control functions are the functions that execute the decision-making and resultant logic branches in executable code. IF-THEN-ELSE, as discussed in Chapter 6, *Introduction to AL*, is also a member of this class of functions. Here, we will discuss the following:

- REPEAT-UNTIL
- WHILE-DO
- FOR-TO and FOR-DOWNTO
- CASE-ELSE
- WITH-DO
- QUIT, BREAK, EXIT, and SKIP

REPEAT-UNTIL

REPEAT-UNTIL allows us to create a repetitive code loop, which REPEATs a block of code UNTIL a specific conditional expression evaluates to TRUE. In that sense, REPEAT-UNTIL defines a block of code, operating somewhat like the BEGIN-END compound statement structure that we covered in Chapter 6, *Introduction to AL*. REPEAT tells the system to keep reprocessing the block of code, while the UNTIL serves as the exit doorman, checking whether the conditions for ending the processing are true. Because the exit condition is not evaluated until the end of the loop, a REPEAT-UNTIL structure will always process at least once through the contained code.

REPEAT-UNTIL is very important in Business Central because it is often part of the data input cycle, along with the FIND-NEXT structure, which will be covered shortly.

Here is an example of the REPEAT-UNTIL structure to process and sum data in the 10-element array CustSales:

```
LoopCount := 0;
REPEAT
  LoopCount := LoopCount + 1;
  TotCustSales := TotCustSales + CustSales[LoopCount];
UNTIL LoopCount = 10;
```

WHILE-DO

A WHILE-DO control structure allows us to create a repetitive code loop that will DO (execute) a block of code WHILE a specific conditional expression evaluates to TRUE. WHILE-DO is different from REPEAT-UNTIL, both because it may need a BEGIN-END structure to define the block of code to be executed repetitively (REPEAT-UNTIL does not), and because it has different timings for the evaluation of the exit condition.

The syntax of the WHILE-DO control structure is as follows:

```
WHILE <Condition> DO <Statement>
```

The Condition can be any Boolean expression that evaluates to TRUE or FALSE. The Statement can be simple or the most complex compound BEGIN-END statement. Most WHILE-DO loops will be based on a BEGIN-END block of code. The Condition will be evaluated at the beginning of the loop. When it evaluates to FALSE, the loop will terminate. Thus, a WHILE-DO loop can be exited without processing.

A WHILE-DO structure to process data in the 10-element array CustSales is as follows:

```
LoopCount := 0;
WHILE LoopCount < 10
DO BEGIN
  LoopCount := LoopCount + 1;
  TotCustSales := TotCustSales + CustSales[LoopCount];
END;
```

In Business Central, REPEAT-UNTIL is much more frequently used than WHILE-DO.

FOR-TO or FOR-DOWNTO

The syntax for FOR-TO and FOR-DOWNTO control statements are as follows:

```
FOR <Control Variable> := <Start Number> TO <End Number> DO <Statement>
FOR <Control Variable> := <Start Number> DOWNTO <End Number> DO <Statement>
```

A FOR control structure is used when we wish to execute a block of code a specific number of times.

The `Control Variable` is an integer variable. `Start Number` is the beginning count for the `FOR` loop and `End Number` is the final count for the loop. If we wrote the `FOR LoopCount := 5 TO 7 DO [block of code]` statement, then `[block of code]` would be executed three times.

`FOR-TO` increments the `Control Variable`. `FOR-DOWNTO` decrements the `Control Variable`.

We must be careful not to manipulate the `Control Variable` in the middle of our loop. Doing so will likely yield unpredictable results.

CASE-ELSE statement

The `CASE-ELSE` statement is a conditional expression, which is very similar to `IF-THEN-ELSE`, except that it allows more than two choices of outcomes for the evaluation of the controlling expression. The syntax of the `CASE-ELSE` statement is as follows:

```
CASE <ExpressionToBeEvaluated> OF
  <Value Set 1> : <Action Statement 1>;
  <Value Set 2> : <Action Statement 2>;
  <Value Set 3> : <Action Statement 3>;
  ...
  ...
  <Value Set n> : <Action Statement n>;
 [ELSE <Action Statement n + 1>;
END;
```

The `ExpressionToBeEvaluated` must not be a record. The data type of the `Value Set` must be able to be automatically converted into the data type of the `ExpressionToBeEvaluated`. Each `Value Set` must be an expression, a set of values, or a range of values. The following example illustrates a typical instance of a `CASE-ELSE` statement:

```
CASE Customer."Salesperson Code" OF
  '2','5','9': Customer."Territory Code" := 'EAST';
  '16'..'20': Customer."Territory Code" := 'WEST';
  'N': Customer."Territory Code" := 'NORTH';
  '27'..'38': Customer."Territory Code" := 'SOUTH';
 ELSE Customer."Territory Code" := 'FOREIGN';
END;
```

In the preceding code example, we can see several alternatives for the Value Set. The first line (EAST) Value Set contains a list of values. If "Salesperson Code" is equal to '2', '5', or '9', the EAST value will be assigned to Customer."Territory Code". The second line, (WEST) Value Set, is a range, any value from '16' through '20'. The third line, (NORTH) Value Set, is just a single value ('N'). If we look through the standard Business Central code, we will see that a single value is the most frequently used CASE structure in Business Central. In the fourth line of our example (SOUTH), the Value Set is again a range ('27'..'38'). If nothing in any Value Set matches ExpressionToBeEvaluated, the ELSE clause will be executed, which sets Customer."TerritoryCode" equal to 'FOREIGN'.

An example of an IF-THEN-ELSE statement equivalent to the preceding CASE-ELSE statement is as follows:

```
IF Customer."Salesperson Code" IN ['2','5','9'] THEN
  Customer."Territory Code" := 'EAST'
   ELSE IF Customer."Salesperson Code" IN ['16'..'20'] THEN
     Customer."Territory Code" := 'WEST'
    ELSE IF Customer."Salesperson Code" = 'N' THEN
      Customer."Territory Code" := 'NORTH'
     ELSE IF Customer."Salesperson Code" IN ['27'..'38'] THEN
       Customer."Territory Code" := 'SOUTH'
       ELSE Customer."Territory Code" := 'FOREIGN';
```

The following is a slightly less intuitive example of the CASE-ELSE statement. In this instance, ExpressionToBeEvaluated is a simple TRUE and the Value Set statements are all conditional expressions. The first line containing a Value Set expression that evaluates to TRUE will be the line whose Action Statement is executed. The rules of execution and flow in this instance are the same as in the previous example:

```
CASE TRUE OF Salesline.Quantity < 0:
 BEGIN
  CLEAR(Salesline."Line Discount %");
  CredTot := CredTot - Salesline.Quantity;
 END;
  Salesline.Quantity > QtyBreak[1]:
   Salesline."Line Discount %" := DiscLevel[1];
  Salesline.Quantity > QtyBreak[2]:
   Salesline."Line Discount %" := DiscLevel[2];
  Salesline.Quantity > QtyBreak[3]:
   Salesline."Line Discount %" := DiscLevel[3];
  Salesline.Quantity > QtyBreak[4]:
   Salesline."Line Discount %" := DiscLevel[4];
```

```
  ELSE
    CLEAR(Salesline."Line Discount %");
END;
```

WITH-DO statement

When we are writing code referring to fields within a record, the most specific syntax for field references is the fully qualified [RecordName.FieldName] reference. When referring to the City field in the Customer record, use the Customer.City reference.

In many AL instances, the record name qualifier is implicit because the compiler assumes a default record qualifier based on code context. This happens automatically for variables within a page bounded to a table. The bound table becomes the implicit record qualifier for fields referenced in the page object. In a table object, the table is the implicit record qualifier for fields referenced in the AL in that object. In report and XMLport objects, the DataItem record is the implicit record qualifier for the fields referenced within the triggers of that DataItem, such as OnAfterGetRecord and OnAfterImportRecord.

In all other AL code, the only way to have an implicit record qualifier is to use the WITH-DO statement. WITH-DO is widely used in the base product in codeunits and processing reports. The WITH-DO syntax is as follows:

```
WITH <RecordQualifier> DO <Statement>
```

Typically, the DO portion of this statement will be followed by a BEGIN-END code block, thus allowing a compound statement. The scope of the WITH-DO statement is terminated by the end of the DO statement.

When we execute a WITH-DO statement, RecordQualifier becomes the implicit record qualifier that's used by the compiler until the end of that statement or until that qualifier is overridden by a nested WITH-DO statement. A fully qualified syntax would require the following form:

```
Customer.Address := '189 Maple Avenue';
Customer.City := 'Chicago';
```

The WITH-DO syntax takes advantage of the implicit record qualification, making the code easier to write and, hopefully, easier to read; for example, take a look at the following lines of code:

```
WITH Customer DO
BEGIN
  Address := '189 Maple Avenue';
```

```
    City := 'Chicago';
  END;
```

Best practice says that WITH-DO statements should only be used in functions within a codeunit or a report.

WITH-DO statements nested one within another are legal code, but are not used in standard Business Central. They are also not recommended because they can easily confuse the developer, resulting in bugs. The same comments apply to nesting a WITH-DO statement within a function where there is an automatic implicit record qualifier, such as in a table, report, or XMLport.

Of course, wherever the references to record variables other than the implicit one occur within the scope of WITH-DO, we must include the specific qualifiers. This is particularly important when there are variables with the same name (for example, City) in multiple tables that might be referenced in the same set of AL logic.

Some developers maintain that it is always better to use fully qualified variable names to reduce the possibility of inadvertent reference errors. This approach also eliminates any possible misinterpretation of variable references by a maintenance developer who works on this code later.

QUIT, BREAK, EXIT, and SKIP functions

This group of AL functions also controls process flow. Each acts to interrupt flow in different places and with different results. To get a full appreciation for how these functions are used, we should review them in code in Business Central.

QUIT function

The QUIT function is the ultimate processing interrupt for report or XMLport objects. When QUIT is executed, processing immediately terminates, even for the OnPostObject triggers. No database changes are committed. QUIT is often used in reports to terminate processing when the report logic determines that no useful output will be generated by further processing.

The syntax of the QUIT function is as follows:

```
CurrReport.QUIT;
CurrXMLport.QUIT;
```

BREAK function

The BREAK function terminates the DataItem in which it occurs. BREAK can only be used in DataItem triggers in reports and XMLports. It can be used to terminate the sequence of processing one DataItem segment of a report while allowing subsequent DataItem processing to continue.

The BREAK syntax is as follows:

```
CurrReport.BREAK;
CurrXMLport.BREAK;
```

EXIT function

EXIT is used to end the processing within an AL trigger. EXIT works the same, regardless of whether it is executed within a loop. It can be used to end the processing of the trigger or to pass a return value from a local function. A return value cannot be used for system-defined triggers or local functions that don't have a return value defined. If EXIT is used without a return value, a default return value of zero is returned.

The syntax for EXIT is as follows:

```
EXIT([<ReturnValue>])
```

SKIP function

When executed, the SKIP function will skip the remainder of the processing in the current record cycle of the current trigger. Unlike BREAK, it does not terminate the DataItem processing completely. It can be used only in the OnAfterGetRecord trigger of a report or XMLport object. In reports, when the results of processing in the OnAfterGetRecord trigger are determined not to be useful for output, the SKIP function is used to terminate that single iteration of the trigger, without interfering with any subsequent processing.

The SKIP syntax can be either of the following:

```
CurrReport.SKIP;
CurrXMLport.SKIP;
```

Input and output functions

In the previous chapter, you learned about the basics of the FIND function. You learned about FIND('-') to read from the beginning of a selected set of records, FINDSET to read a selected set of records, and FIND('+') to begin reading at the far end of the selected set of records. Now we will review additional functions that are generally used with FIND functions in typical production code. While we are designing code that uses the MODIFY and DELETE record functions, we need to consider possible interactions with other users on the system. There might be someone else modifying and deleting records in the same table that our application is updating.

We may want to utilize the LOCKTABLE function to gain total control of the data briefly while updating it. We can find more information on LOCKTABLE in the online *AL Reference Guide* help (https://docs.microsoft.com/en-us/dynamics365/business-central/dev-itpro/developer/devenv-dev-overview). The SQL Server database supports **record level locking**. There are a number of factors that we should consider when coding data locking in our processes. It is worthwhile reading all of the AL reference guide material that's found by doing a search for LOCKTABLE, particularly, *Locking in Microsoft SQL Server*.

NEXT function with FIND or FINDSET

The syntax defined for the NEXT function is as follows:

```
IntegerValue := Record.NEXT ( ReadStepSize )
```

The full assignment statement format is rarely used to set an IntegerValue. In addition, there is no documentation for the usage of a non-zero IntegerValue. When IntegerValue goes to zero, it means a NEXT record was not found.

If the ReadStepSize value is negative, the table will be read in reverse; if ReadStepSize is positive (the default), then the table will be read forward. The size of the value in ReadStepSize controls which records should be read. For example, if ReadStepSize is 2 or -2, then every second record will be read. If ReadStepSize is 10 or -10, then every tenth record will be read. The default value is 1, in which case, every record will be read and the read direction will be forward.

In a typical data-read loop, the first read is a FIND or FINDSET function, followed by a REPEAT-UNTIL loop. The exit condition is the UNTILRecord.NEXT=0; expression. The AL for FINDSET and FIND('-') are structured alike.

The full AL syntax for this typical loop looks as follows:

```
IF CustRec.FIND('-') THEN
REPEAT
  <Block of AL logic>
UNTIL CustRec.NEXT = 0;
```

INSERT function

The purpose of the INSERT function is to add new records to a table. The syntax for the INSERT function is as follows:

```
[BooleanValue :=] Record.INSERT ( [ TriggerControlBoolean ] )
```

If BooleanValue is not used and the INSERT function fails (for example, if the insertion would result in a duplicate primary key), the process will terminate with an error. Generally, we should handle a detected error in code using the BooleanValue and supplying our own error-handling logic, rather than allow a default termination.

The TriggerControlBoolean value controls whether or not the table's OnInsert trigger fires when the INSERT occurs. The default value is FALSE. If we let the default FALSE control, we run the risk of not performing error checking that the table's designer assumed would be run when a new record was added.

When we are reading a table, and we also need to INSERT records into that same table, the INSERT should be done to a separate instance of the table. We can use either a global or local variable for that second instance. If we INSERT into the same table we are reading, we run the risk of reading the new records as part of our processing (likely a very confusing action). We also run the risk of changing the sequence of our processing unexpectedly due to the introduction of new records into our dataset. While the database access methods are continually improved by Microsoft, and this warning may be overcautious, it is better to be safe than sorry.

MODIFY function

The purpose of the MODIFY function is to modify (update) existing data records. The syntax for MODIFY is as follows:

```
[BooleanValue :=] Record.MODIFY ( [ TriggerControlBoolean ] )
```

If BooleanValue is not used and MODIFY fails, for example, if another process changes the record after it was read by this process, then the process will terminate with an error statement. The code should either handle a detected error or gracefully terminate the process. The TriggerControlBoolean value controls whether the table's OnModify trigger fires when this MODIFY occurs. The default value is FALSE, which would not perform any OnModify processing. MODIFY cannot be used to cause a change in a primary key field. In that case, the RENAME function must be used.

System-based checking can be performed to make sure that a MODIFY is done using the current version of the data record. This is done by making sure that another process hasn't modified and committed the record after it was read by this process. Our logic should refresh the record using the GET function, then change any values, and then call the MODIFY function.

Rec and xRec

In the Table and Page objects, the system automatically provides us with the system variables, Rec and xRec. Until a record has been updated by MODIFY, Rec represents the current record data in process and xRec represents the record data before it was modified. By comparing field values in Rec and xRec, we can determine whether changes have been made to the record in the current process cycle. Rec and xRec records have all the same fields in the same structure as the table to which they relate.

DELETE function

The purpose of the DELETE function is to delete existing data records. The syntax for DELETE is as follows:

```
[BooleanValue :=] Record.DELETE ( [ TriggerControlBoolean ] )
```

If DELETE fails and the BooleanValue option is not used, the process will terminate with an error statement. Our code should handle any detected error or terminate the process gracefully, as appropriate.

The TriggerControlBoolean value is TRUE or FALSE, and it controls whether the table's OnDelete trigger fires when this DELETE occurs. The default value is FALSE. If we let the default FALSE prevail, we run the risk of not performing error checking that the table's designer assumed would be run when a record was deleted.

In Business Central, there is check to make sure that a DELETE is using the current version of the record and to make sure that another process hasn't modified and committed the record after it was read by this process.

MODIFYALL function

MODIFYALL is the high-volume version of the MODIFY function. If we have a group of records in which we wish to modify one field in all of these records to the same new value, we should use MODIFYALL. It is controlled by the filters that are applied at the time of invoking. The other choice for doing a mass modification would be to have a FIND-NEXT loop in which we modified each record, one at a time. The advantage of MODIFYALL is that it allows the developer and the system to optimize code for the volume update. Any system optimization will be a function of what SQL statements are generated by the AL compiler.

The syntax for MODIFYALL is as follows:

```
Record.MODIFYALL (FieldToBeModified, NewValue
[,TriggerControlBoolean ] )
```

The TriggerControlBoolean value, a TRUE or FALSE entry, controls whether the table's OnModify trigger fires when this MODIFY occurs. The default value is FALSE, which would result in the OnValidate field trigger not being executed. In a typical situation, a filter or series of filters would be applied to a table, followed by the MODIFYALL function. A simple example where we will reassign all Territory Code for a particular Salesperson to NORTH is as follows:

```
Customer.RESET ;
Customer.SETRANGE("Salesperson Code",'DAS');
Customer.MODIFYALL("Territory Code",'NORTH',TRUE);
```

DELETEALL function

DELETEALL is the high-volume version of the DELETE function. If we have a group of records that we wish to delete, use DELETEALL. The other choice would be a FIND-NEXT loop, in which we delete each record, one at a time. The advantage of DELETEALL is that it allows the developer and the system to optimize code for the volume deletion. Any system optimization will be a function of what SQL statements are generated by the AL compiler.

The syntax for DELETEALL is as follows:

```
Record.DELETEALL ( [,TriggerControlBoolean] )
```

The TriggerControlBoolean value, a TRUE or FALSE entry, controls whether the table's OnDelete trigger fires when this DELETE occurs. The default value is FALSE. If the TriggerControlBoolean value is TRUE, then the OnDelete trigger will fire for each record that's deleted. In that case, there is little to no speed advantage for DELETEALL versus the use of a FIND-DELETE-NEXT loop.

In a typical situation, a filter or series of filters would be applied to a table, followed by the DELETEALL function, similar to the preceding example. Like MODIFYALL, DELETEALL respects the filters that are set and does not do any referential integrity error checking.

Filtering

Few other systems have filtering implemented as comprehensively as Business Central, nor do they have it tied so neatly to the detailed retention of historical data. The result of Business Central's features is that even the most basic implementation of Business Central includes very powerful data analysis capabilities that are available to the end user.

As developers, we should appreciate the fact that we cannot anticipate every need of any user, let alone anticipate all the needs of all users. We know we should give the users as much freedom as possible to allow them to selectively extract and review data from their system. Wherever feasible, users should be given the opportunity to apply their own filters so that they can determine the optimum selection of data for their particular situation. On the other hand, freedom, here as everywhere, is a double-edged sword. With the freedom to decide just how to segment our data, comes the responsibility for figuring out what constitutes a good segmentation to address the problem at hand.

As experienced application software designers and developers, we have presumably considerable insight into good ways to analyze and present the data. On that basis, it may be appropriate for us to provide some predefined selections. In some cases, constraints of the data structure allow only a limited set of options to make sense. In such a case, we should provide specific accesses to data (through pages and/or reports). However, we should allow more sophisticated users to access and manipulate the data flexibly on their own.

When applying filters using any of these options, be very conscious of the table key that will be activated when the filter takes effect. In a table containing a lot of data, filtering on a field that is not very high in the currently active key (in other words, near the beginning of the key field sequence) may result in poor (or even very poor) response time for the users. In the same context, in a system suffering from a poor response time during processing, we should first investigate the relationships of active keys to applied filters, as well as how the keys are maintained. This may require SQL Server expertise, in addition to Business Central expertise.

Both the SETCURRENTKEY and SETRANGE functions are important in the context of data filtering. These were reviewed in Chapter 6, *Introduction to AL*, so we won't review them again here.

The SETFILTER function

SETFILTER allows us to define and apply any filter expression that could be created manually, including various combinations of ranges, AL operators, and even wild cards. The SETFILTER syntax is as follows:

```
Record.SETFILTER ( Field, FilterString [, FilterValue1], . . . ] );
```

SETFILTER also can be applied to Query objects with similar syntax:

```
Query.SETFILTER ( ColumnName, FilterString
[, FilterValue1], . . . ] );
```

FilterString can be a literal, such as '1000..20000' or 'A*|B*|C*', but this is not good practice. Optionally (and preferably), we can use variable tokens in the form of %1, %2, %3, and so forth, representing variables (but not operators) such as FilterValue1, FilterValue2, and so forth to be substituted in the filter string at runtime. This construct allows us to create filters whose data values can be defined dynamically at runtime. A new SETFILTER replaces any previous filtering in the same filter group (this will be discussed in more detail shortly) on that field or column prior to setting the new filter.

A pair of SETFILTER examples are as follows:

```
Customer.SETFILTER("Salesperson Code",'KKS'|'RAM'|'CDS');
Customer.SETFILTER("Salesperson Code",'%1|%2|%3',SPC1,SPC2,SPC3);
```

If SPC1 equals 'KKS', SPC2 equals 'RAM', and SPC3 equals 'CDS', these two examples would have the same result. Obviously, the second option allows a degree of flexibility which is not provided by the first option because in the second option, the variables could be assigned other values.

The COPYFILTER and COPYFILTERS functions

These functions allow you to copy the filters of a single field or all the filters on a record (table) and apply those filters to another record. Their syntax is as follows:

```
FromRecord.COPYFILTER(FromField, ToRecord.ToField)
```

The From and To fields must be of the same data type. The From and To tables do not have to be of the same format:

```
ToRecord.COPYFILTERS(FromRecord)
```

Note that the COPYFILTER field-based function begins with the FromRecord variable, while the COPYFILTERS record-based function begins with the ToRecord variable. ToRecord and FromRecord must be different instances of the same table.

The GETFILTER and GETFILTERS functions

These functions allow us to retrieve the filters on a single field or all the filters on a record (table) and assign the result to a text variable. Their syntax is as follows:

```
ResultString := FilteredRecord.GETFILTER(FilteredField)
ResultString := FilteredRecord.GETFILTERS
```

Similar functions exist for query objects. Those syntaxes are as follows:

```
ResultString := FilteredQuery.GETFILTER(FilteredColumn)
ResultString := FilteredQuery.GETFILTERS
```

The text contents of the `ResultString` will contain an identifier for each filtered field and the currently applied value of the filter. `GETFILTERS` is often used to retrieve the filters on a table and print them as part of a report heading. The `ResultString` will look similar to the following:

```
Customer:.No.: 10000..999999, Balance: >0
```

The FILTERGROUP function

The `FILTERGROUP` function can change or retrieve the filter group that is applied to a table. A filter group contains a set of filters that were previously applied to the table by the `SETFILTER` or `SETRANGE` functions, or as table properties defined in an object. The `FILTERGROUP` syntax is as follows:

```
[CurrentGroupInteger ] := Record.FILTERGROUP ([NewGroupInteger])
```

Using just the `Record.FILTERGROUP([NewFilterGroupInteger])` portion sets the active filter group.

Filter groups can also be used to filter query DataItems. All the currently defined filter groups are active and apply in combination (in other words, they are logically ANDed, resulting in a logical intersection of the sets). The only way to eliminate the effect of a filter group is to remove the filters in a group.

The default filter group for Business Central is 0 (zero). Users have access to the filters in this filter group. Other filter groups, numbered up through 6, have assigned Business Central uses. We should not redefine the use of any of these filter groups, but use higher numbers for any custom filter groups in our code.

 Check out Microsoft Docs for `FILTERGROUP function` and `Understanding Query Filters` for more information (https://docs.microsoft.com/en-us/dynamics365/business-central/dev-itpro/developer/methods-auto/recordref/recordref-filtergroup-method)

One use of a filter group is to assign a filter that the user cannot see is operative and cannot change. Our code could change the filter group, set a special filter, and then return the active filter group to its original state. The following lines of code are an example of this:

```
Rec.FILTERGROUP(42);
Rec.SETFILTER(Customer."Salesperson Code",MySalespersonID);
Rec.FILTERGROUP(0);
```

This could be used to apply special application-specific permissions to a particular system function, such as filtering out access to customers by salesperson so that each salesperson can only examine data for their own customers.

The MARK function

A mark on a record is an indicator that disappears when the current session ends and which is only visible to the process that is setting the mark. The MARK function sets the mark. The syntax is as follows:

```
[BooleanValue := ] Record.MARK ( [SetMarkBoolean] )
```

If the optional BooleanValue and assignment operator (:=) are present, the MARK function will give us the current MARK status (TRUE or FALSE) of the record. If the optional SetMarkBoolean parameter is present, the record will be marked (or unmarked) according to that value (TRUE or FALSE). The default value for SetMarkBoolean is FALSE. The MARK functions should be used carefully, and only when a simpler solution is not readily available. Marking records can cause significant performance problems on large datasets.

CLEARMARKS function

CLEARMARKS clears all the marks from the specified record, that is, from the particular instance of the table in this instance of the object. The syntax is as follows:

```
Record.CLEARMARKS
```

The MARKEDONLY function

MARKEDONLY is a special filtering function that can apply a mark-based filter.

The syntax for MARKEDONLY is as follows:

```
[BooleanValue := ] Record.MARKEDONLY
( [SeeMarkedRecordsOnlyBoolean] )
```

If the optional `BooleanValue` parameter is defined, it will be assigned a `TRUE` or `FALSE` value to tell us whether the special `MARKEDONLY` filter is active. Omitting the `BooleanValue` parameter, `MARKEDONLY` will set the special filter, depending on the value of `SeeMarkedRecordsOnlyBoolean`. If that value is `TRUE`, it will filter to show only marked records; if that value is `FALSE`, it will remove the marked filter and show all records. The default value for `SeeMarkedRecordsOnlyBoolean` is `FALSE`.

Although it may not seem logical, there is no option to see only the unmarked records.

 For additional information on the `MARKEDONLY` function, refer to the following blog entry: `https://marijebrummel.blog/2014/03/07/tip-36-using-mark-and-markedonly-in-the-role-tailored-client/`.

The RESET function

This function allows us to `RESET`, that is, clear, all filters that are currently applied to a record. `RESET` also sets the current key back to the primary key, removes any marks, and clears all internal variables in the current instance of the record. Filters in `FILTERGROUP 1` are not reset. The syntax is `FilteredRecord.RESET;`.

InterObject communication

There are several ways for communicating between objects during Business Central processing. We will review some of the more commonly used ways in the following sections.

Communicating through data

The most widely used and simplest communication method is through data tables. For example, the `No. Series` table is the central control for all document numbers. Each object that assigns numbers to a document (for example, order, invoice, shipment, and so on) uses codeunit `396`, `NoSeriesManagement`, to access the `No. Series` table for the next number to use, and then updates the `No. Series` table so that the next object needing to assign a number to the same type of document will have the updated information.

Communicating through function parameters

When an object calls a function in another object, information is generally passed through the calling and return parameters. The calling and return parameter specifications are defined when the function is developed. The generic syntax for a function call is as follows:

```
[ReturnValue := ] FunctionName ( [ Parameter1 ] [ ,Parameter2 ] ,...)
```

The rules for including or omitting the various optional fields are specific to the local variables that are defined for each individual function. As developers, when we design the function, we define the rules and thereby determine just how communications with the function will be handled. It is obviously important to define complete and consistent parameter passing rules prior to beginning a development project.

Communication via object calls

Sometimes, we need to create an object, which in turn calls other objects. We may simply want to allow the user to be able to run a series of processes and reports, but only enter the controlling parameters once. Our user interface object will be responsible for invoking the subordinate objects after having communicated setup and filter parameters.

An important set of standard functions has been designed for various modes and circumstances of invoking other objects. Examples of these functions are SETTABLEVIEW, SETRECORD, and GETRECORD (there are others as well). There are also instances where we will need to build our own data-passing function.

To properly manage these relatively complex processes, we need to be familiar with the various versions of the RUN and RUNMODAL functions. We will also need to understand the meaning and effect of a single instance or multiple instances of an object. Briefly, key differences between invoking a page or report object from within another object through RUN versus RUNMODAL are as follows:

- RUN will clear the instance of the invoked object every time the object completes, which means that all of the internal variables are initialized. This clearing behavior does not apply to a codeunit object; state will be maintained across multiple calls to RUN.

- RUNMODAL does not clear the instance of the invoked object, so internal global variables are not reinitialized each time the object is called. The object can be reinitialized using CLEAR(Object).
- RUNMODAL does not allow any other object to be active in the same user session while it is running, whereas RUN allows another object instance to run in parallel with the object instance initiated by RUN.

Covering these topics in more detail is too advanced for this book, but once you have mastered the material covered here, you should study the information in the Microsoft Docs section relative to this topic. There is also pattern documentation on this topic, which is defined at
https://community.dynamics.com/nav/w/designpatterns/108.posting-routine-select-behaviour.

Enhancing the WDTU application

Now that we have some new tool to work with, let's enhance our WDTU application. This time, our goal is to implement functionality to allow the program manager to plan the playlist schedules for radio shows. The process, from the user's point of view, will essentially be as follows:

1. Call up Playlist document page that displays header, details, and FactBox workspaces.
2. Enter Playlist Header using the Radio Show table data.
3. Enter Playlist Line using the resource table DJ data; the Radio Show table data for news, weather, or sports shows; and the Item table data for music, PSAs, and advertisements.
4. The FactBox will display the required program-element fields from Radio Show/Playlist Header. These will include news (yes or no), weather (yes or no), sports (yes or no), and Number of required PSAs and advertisements.
5. The FactBox will also track each of the five possible required elements.

Since this development effort is an exercise to learn more about developing Business Central applications, we have some specific Business Central AL components we want to use so that we can learn more about them. Among those are the following:

- Create a CASE statement as well as a multipart IF statement for contrast
- Add code to the OnValidate trigger of fields in a table
- Implement a lookup into a related table to access needed data

- Cause FlowFields to be processed for display
- Implement a FactBox to display `Radio Show` requirements for news, sports, weather, PSAs, and advertisements
- Create a new function, passing a parameter in and getting results passed back

As with any application enhancement, there will be a number of auxiliary tasks we'll have to accomplish to get the job done. These include adding some new fields to one or more tables. Not surprisingly, adding new data fields often leads to adding the new fields to one or more pages for maintenance or display. We'll have to create some test data in order to test our modifications. It's not unusual in the course of an enhancement to also find that other changes are needed to support the new functionality.

Modifying table fields

Because we want the Business Central tables to be the core of the design and to host as much of the processing as makes sense, we will start our enhancement work with table modifications.

The first table modification is to add the data fields to the `Playlist Header`, as shown in the following screenshot, to support the definition and tracking of various program segment requirements. In the `Radio Show` table, each show has requirements defined for a specific number of PSAs and advertisements, and for the presence of news, sports, and weather spots. The `Playlist Header` needs this requirement information stored, along with the associated TSA and advertisement counts for this show instance. We will obtain the news, sports, and weather line counts by means of a function call:

```
table 50100 "Radio Show"
{
    fields
    {
        field(1; "No."; Code[20]) { }
        ...
        field(1010; "PSAs Required"; Boolean) { }
        field(1011; "PSA Count"; Integer) { }
        field(1020; "Ads Required"; Boolean) { }
        field(1021; "Ads Count"; Integer) { }
        field(1030; "News Required"; Boolean) { }
        field(1050; "Sports Required"; Boolean) { }
        field(1070; "Weather Required"; Boolean) { }
    }
}
```

Because `Playlist Line` includes an `Option` field that identifies the PSA and advertisement records, we will use a FlowField to calculate the counts for each of those line types. We will construct the FlowField definition for the `PSA Count` field, starting in the properties section of the field:

```
field(1011; "PSA Count"; Integer)
{
    FieldClass = FlowField;
    CalcFormula = count ("Playlist Line" where
        ("No." = field ("No."), Type = const (Item), "Data Format" = const (PSA)));
    Editable = false;
}
field(1020; "Ads Required"; Boolean) { }
field(1021; "Ads Count"; Integer)
{
    FieldClass = FlowField;
    CalcFormula = count ("Playlist Line" where
        ("No." = field ("No."), Type = const (Item), "Data Format" = const (Advertisement)));
    Editable = false;
}
```

Go through the same sequence for the `Ads Count` field.

The only additional change we want to make to the `Playlist Line` table is to ensure that the `Duration` field is not editable. We do this so that the `Start Time` and `End Time` entries define `Duration` rather than the other way around. Making the `Duration` field non-editable is done by simply setting the field's `Editable` property to `false`:

```
table 50103 Playlist Line.al  ●
15                 }
16                 field(30; "Data Format"; Option) { OptionMembers
17                 field(40; "Publisher Code"; Code[10]) { }
18                 field(50; Description; Text[50]) { }
19                 field(60; Duration; Duration)
20                 {
21                     Editable = false;
22                 }
23                 field(70; "Start Time"; Time) { }
24                 field(80; "End Time"; Time) { }
```

Adding validation logic

We need validation logic for both our `Playlist` tables, that is, `Header` and `Line`. We will start with `Playlist Header` validation.

Playlist Header validation

The `Playlist Header` data fields are as follows:

- `No.`: This is the ID number for this instance of a radio show; its contents are user-defined
- `Radio Show No.`: This is selected from the `Radio Show` table
- `Description`: This is displayed by means of a FlowField from the `Radio Show` table
- `Broadcast Date`: This is the show's scheduled broadcast date; it also serves as the posting date for any data analysis filtering
- `Start Time`: This is the show's scheduled broadcast start time
- `End Time`: This is the show's scheduled broadcast end time
- `Duration`: This is the show's broadcast length, displayed by means of a FlowField from the `Radio Show` table
- `PSAs Required` and `Ads Required`: These show whether PSAs and advertisements are required for broadcast during the show; they are copied from the `Radio Show` table, but are editable by the user
- `News Required`, `Sports Required`, and `Weather Required`: This checks whether each of these program segments are required during the show; they are copied from the `Radio Show` table, but are editable by the user

When the user chooses the `Radio Show` to be scheduled, we want the five different feature requirements fields in the `Playlist Header` to be filled in by AL logic, as shown in the following screenshot:

```
table 50102 Playlist Header.al  ●
 6          field(10; "Radio Show No."; code[20])
 7          {
 8              trigger OnValidate()
 9              var
10                  RadioShow: Record "Radio Show";
11              begin
12                  if RadioShow.Get("Radio Show No.") then begin
13                      "PSAs Required" := RadioShow."PSAs Required";
14                      "Ads Required" := RadioShow."Ads Required";
15                      "News Required" := RadioShow."News Required";
16                      "Sports Required" := RadioShow."Sports Required";
17                      "Weather Required" := RadioShow."Weather Required";
18                  end else begin
19                      "PSAs Required" := false;
20                      "Ads Required" := false;
21                      "News Required" := false;
22                      "Sports Required" := false;
23                      "Weather Required" := false;
24                  end;
25              end;
26          }
```

Even though the `Radio Show No.` was entered in the data field, our validation code needs to read the `Radio Show` record (here, defined as the local variable `RadioShow`). Once we have read the `Radio Show` record, we can assign all five show feature requirements fields from the `Radio Show` record into the `Playlist Header` record.

Then, because two fields in the `Playlist Header` record are lookup FlowFields, we need to `Update` the page after the entry of the `Radio Show No.`. The update is done through a `CurrPage.UPDATE` command, as shown in the following screenshot:

```
field("Radio Show No."; "Radio Show No.")
{
    ApplicationArea = Basic;
    trigger OnValidate()
    begin
        CurrPage.Update;
    end;
}
```

The next validation we need is to calculate the End Time show as soon as the Start Time is entered. The calculation is simple: add the length of the show to the Start Time. We have defined the Duration field in the Playlist Header to be a lookup reference to the source field in the Radio Show record. As a result, to calculate with that field, we would need to use a CALCFIELDS function first. Instead, we'll obtain the show length from the Radio Show record:

```
field(50; "Start Time"; Time)
{
    trigger OnValidate()
    var
        RadioShow: Record "Radio Show";
    begin
        RadioShow.Get("Radio Show No.");
        "End Time" := "Start Time" + RadioShow."Run Time";
    end;
```

Now we can see that we have one of those situations that we sometimes encounter when developing a modification. It might have been better to have the Duration field of Playlist Header be a Normal data field rather than a FlowField. If this is the only place where we will use Duration from Playlist Header for calculation or assignment, then the current design is fine. Otherwise, perhaps we should change the Duration field to a Normal field and assign Run Time from RadioShow to it at the same time the several requirements fields are assigned. At this point, though, for the purposes of our WDTU scenario, we will stick with what we have already created.

Creating the Playlist subpage

In Chapter 2, *Tables*, a homework assignment was to create the 50003 Playlist Document page. We should have used the snippet to create that page, giving us something such as this:

```
page 50104 Playlist Document.al  ✕                                              ⌐
  1    page 50104 "Playlist Document"
  2    {
  3        PageType = Document;
  4        SourceTable = "Playlist Header";
  5        ApplicationArea = Basic;
  6        UsageCategory = Documents;
  7        layout
  8        {
  9            area(content)
 10            {
 11                group(Group)
 12                {
 13                    field("No."; "No.") { ApplicationArea = Basic; }
 14                    field(Description; Description) { ApplicationArea = Basic; }
 15                    field("Radio Show No."; "Radio Show No.")
 16  +                 { ···
 22                    }
 23                    field("Start Time"; "Start Time") { ApplicationArea = Basic; }
 24                    field("End Time"; "End Time") { ApplicationArea = Basic; }
 25                    field("Broadcast Date"; "Broadcast Date") { ApplicationArea = Basic; }
 26                    field(Duration; Duration) { ApplicationArea = Basic; }
 27                }
 28            }
 29        }
 30    }
```

Another necessary part of a document page is the subpage. Our subpage can be created using the snippet based on table 50003, Playlist Line. The result will be as follows:

```
page 50109 Playlist Subpage.al  ●
  1    page 50109 "Playlist Subpage"
  2    {
  3        PageType = ListPart;
  4        SourceTable = "Playlist Line";
  5
  6        layout
  7        {
  8            area(Content)
  9            {
 10                repeater(Group)
 11                {
 12                    field(Type; Type) { ApplicationArea = All; }
 13                    field("No."; "No.") { ApplicationArea = All; }
 14                    field("Data Format"; "Data Format") { ApplicationArea = All; }
 15                    field(Description; Description) { ApplicationArea = All; }
 16                    field(Duration; Duration) { ApplicationArea = All; }
 17                    field("Start Time"; "Start Time") { ApplicationArea = All; }
 18                    field("End Time"; "End Time") { ApplicationArea = All; }
 19                }
 20            }
 21        }
```

To make the document work the way we are used to having Business Central document forms work, we will need to set some properties for this new page. See the bold properties circled in the following screenshot:

```
page 50109 Playlist Subpage.al  ●
1    page 50109 "Playlist Subpage"
2    {
3        PageType = ListPart;
4        SourceTable = "Playlist Line";
5        AutoSplitKey = true;
6        DelayedInsert = true;
7        layout
8        {
```

We have set the `DelayedInsert` and `AutoSplitKey` properties to `true`. These settings will allow the `Playlist Line` to not be saved until the primary key fields are all entered (`DelayedInsert`), and will support the easy insertion of new entries between two existing lines (`AutoSplitKey`).

Finally, we will need to connect our new `Playlist` subpage `ListPart` page 50109 to the `Playlist` document page 50104 to give us a basic and complete document page. All we need to do to accomplish that is add a new `Part` line to page 50104, as shown in the following screenshot:

```
page 50104 Playlist Document.al  ●
1    page 50104 "Playlist Document"
2    {
3        PageType = Document;
4        SourceTable = "Playlist Header";
5        ApplicationArea = Basic;
6        UsageCategory = Documents;
7        layout
8        {
9            area(content)
10           {
11               group(Group)
12 ⊞            { ···
27               }
28               part(lines; "Playlist Subpage")
29               {
30                   SubPageLink = "Document No." = FIELD ("No.");
31                   SubPageView = SORTING ("Document No.", "Line No.");
32
```

Playlist Line validations

The Playlist Line data fields are as follows:

- Document No.: This is the automatically assigned link to the No. field in the parent Playlist record (the automatic assignment is based on the page, Playlist Subpage properties, which we'll take care of when working on the Playlist pages)
- Line No.: This is an automatically assigned number (based on page properties), and the rightmost field in the Playlist Line primary key
- Type: This is a user-selected Option that defines whether this entry is a Resource, such as an announcer; a Show, such as a news show; or an Item, such as a recording to play on the air
- No.: This is the ID number of the selected entry in its parent table
- DataFormat: This is information from the Item table for a show or recording
- Description: This is assigned from the parent table, but can be edited by the user
- Duration, Start Time and End Time: This is information about a show or recording that indicates the length and its position within the schedule of this Radio Show

The source of contents of the No., DataFormat, Description, and time-related fields of the record depend on the Type field. If the Type is Resource, the fields are filled in from the Resource table; for Item, from the Item table; for Show, from the Radio Show table. To support this, our OnValidate code looks at the Type entry and uses a CASE statement to choose which set of actions to take.

First, we will build the basic CASE statement, as shown in the following code screenshot, and compile it. That way, we can ensure that we've got all the components of the structure in place and only need to fill in the logic for each of the option choices:

```
field("No."; "No.")
{
    ApplicationArea = All;
    trigger OnValidate()
    begin
        case Type of
            Type::Resource:
                begin
                end;
            Type::Item:
                begin
                end;
            Type::Show:
                begin
                end;
        end;
    end;
}
```

Next, we must add a variable for each of the tables from which we will pull the data Resource, Item, and Show. The use of IntelliSense makes it much easier to find the correct field names for each of the variables we want to select to assign to the Playlist Line record fields:

```
trigger OnValidate()
var
    Res: Record Resource;
    Item: Record item;
    RadioShow: Record "Radio Show";
begin
    case Type of
        Type::Resource:
            begin
                res.|
            end;           AssistEdit  procedure AssistEdit(OldRes
        Type::Item        CheckResourcePrivacyBlocked
            begin         CreateTimeSheets
            end;          DisplayMap
        Type::Show        GetUnitOfMeasureFilter
            begin         ValidateShortcutDimCode
            end;          Address
    end;                  "Address 2"
```

When we are all done constructing the CASE statement, it should look like this:

```
field("No."; "No.")
{
    ApplicationArea = All;
    trigger OnValidate()
    var
        Res: Record Resource;
        Item: Record item;
        RadioShow: Record "Radio Show";
    begin
        case Type of
            Type::Resource:
                begin
                    Res.Get("No.");
                    Description := Res.Name;
                end;
            Type::Item:
                begin
                    Item.Get("No.");
                    Description := item.Description;
                    "Data Format" := item."Data Format";
                    Duration := item.Duration;
                end;
            Type::Show:
                begin
                    RadioShow.Get("No.");
                    Description := RadioShow.Name;
```

The last set of OnValidate code we need to add is to calculate the End Time from the supplied Start Time and Duration (or Start Time from the End Time and Duration), as shown in the following screenshot:

```
field(70; "Start Time"; Time)
{
    trigger OnValidate()
    begin
        if Duration <> 0 then
            "End Time" := "Start Time" + Duration;
    end;
}
field(80; "End Time"; Time)
{
    trigger OnValidate()
    begin
        if "Start Time" <> 0T then
            Duration := "End Time" - "Start Time";
    end;
}
```

Obviously, the design could be expanded to have the `Duration` value be user editable, along with an appropriate change in the AL logic. After our initial work on the `Playlist` functionality is completed, making that change would be a good exercise for you, as would be the addition of the "housekeeping" commands to clear out fields that are not used by the assigned record `Type`, such as clearing the `DataFormat` field for a `RadioShow` record.

Creating a function for our FactBox

For this application, we want our FactBox to display information relating to the specific radio show we are scheduling. The information to be displayed includes the five show segment requirements and the status of fulfillment (counts) of those requirements by the data that's entered into date. The requirements come from the `Playlist Header` fields: PSAs required, advertisements required, news required, sports required, and weather required. The counts come from summing up data in the `Playline Line` records for a show. We can use the `Playlist Header` field's PSA count and ad count for those two counts. These counts can be obtained through the FlowField property definitions we defined earlier for these two fields.

For the other three counts, we must read through the `Playlist Line` and sum up each of the counts. To accomplish that, we'll create a function that we can call from the FactBox page. Since our new function is local to the `Playlist Header` and `Playlist Line` tables, we will define the function in the `Playlist Header` (table 50102).

The logic of our counting process is described in the following pseudocode:

1. Filter the `Playlist Line` table for `Radio Show` we are scheduling and for segment entries (`Playlist Line`) that represent shows
2. Look up the `Radio Show` record for each of those records
3. Using the data from the `Radio Show` record, look up the `Radio Show Type` code
4. In the `Radio Show Type` record, use the news, weather, or sports fields to determine which `Playlist Line` counter should be incremented

Based on this logic, we must have local variables defined for the three tables: `Playlist Line`, `Radio Show`, and `Radio Show Type`.

Translating our pseudocode into executable AL, our function looks as follows:

```
table 50103 Playlist Line.al  ●       table 50102 Playlist Header.al  ●

55  |         procedure NWSRequired(Category: Option ,News,Weather,Sports): Integer
56  |         var
57  |             PlaylistLine: Record "Playlist Line";
58  |             RadioShow: Record "Radio Show";
59  |             RadioShowType: Record "Radio Show Type";
60  |             Cnt: Integer;
61  |         begin
62  |             PlaylistLine.SetRange("Document No.", "No.");
63  |             PlaylistLine.SetRange(Type, PlaylistLine.Type::Show);
64  |             if PlaylistLine.FindSet then repeat
65  |                 RadioShow.get(PlaylistLine."No.");
66  |                 RadioShowType.get(RadioShow."Radio Show Type");
67  |                 case Category of
68  |                     Category::News:
69  |                         if RadioShowType.Code = 'News' then
70  |                             Cnt += 1;
71  |                     Category::Weather:
72  |                         if RadioShowType.Code = 'Weather' then
73  |                             Cnt += 1;
74  |                     Category::Sports:
75  |                         if RadioShowType.Code = 'Sports' then
76  |                             Cnt += 1;
77  |                 end;
78  |             until PlaylistLine.Next = 0;
79  |         end;
80  }
```

In the process of writing this code, we noticed another design flaw. We defined the type of Radio Show with code that allows users to enter their choice of text strings. We just wrote code that depends on the contents of that text string being specific values. A better design would be to have the critical field be an Option data type so that we can depend on the choices being members of a predefined set. However, the Code field is our primary key field, and we probably shouldn't use an Option field as the primary key. We will continue with our example with the design as is, but you should consider how to improve it. Making that improvement will be excellent practice.

Creating a FactBox page

All the hard work is now done. We just have to define a FactBox page and add it to the `Playlist` page. We can create a FactBox page using the snippet to define a `CardPart`:

```
page 50112 "Playlist Factbox"
{
    PageType = Card;
    Application 🔧 API
    UsageCatego 🔧 Card
    SourceTable 🔧 CardPart
                🔧 ConfirmationDialog
}
```

Our FactBox will contain the fields from the `Playlist Header` that relate to two of the five required show segments, that is, the **PSA Count** and **Ad Count** fields, as shown in the following screenshot:

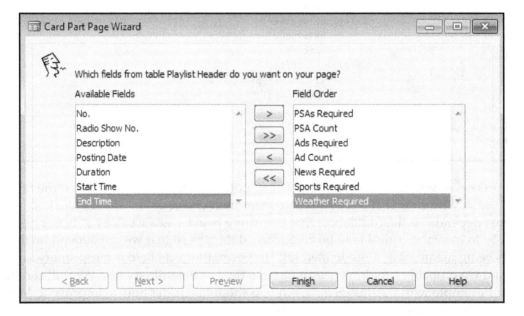

Once we exit the **Card Part Page Wizard** and go into the page designer, we will have a page layout that looks as follows:

```
page 50112 Playlist factbox.al ●
1    page 50112 "Playlist Factbox"
2    {
3        PageType = CardPart;
4        ApplicationArea = All;
5        UsageCategory = Administration;
6        SourceTable = "Playlist Header";
7
8        layout
9        {
10           area(Content)
11           {
12               group(GroupName)
13               {
14                   field("PSAs Required"; "PSAs Required") { ApplicationArea = All; }
15                   field("PSA Count"; "PSA Count") { ApplicationArea = All; }
16                   field("Ads Required"; "Ads Required") { ApplicationArea = All; }
17                   field("Ads Count"; "Ads Count") { ApplicationArea = All; }
18                   field("News Required";"News Required") { ApplicationArea = All;}
19                   field("Weather Required";"Weather Required") { ApplicationArea = All;
20                   field("Sports Required";"Sports Required") { ApplicationArea = All;
21               }
```

At this point, we will need to add the logic to take advantage of the NWSRequired function that we created earlier. This function is designed to return the count of the segment type that's identified in the calling parameter. Since a line on a page can be an expression, we can simply code the function calls right on the page lines with an appropriate caption defined, as we can see in the following screenshot. We will intersperse the Count lines for a consistent appearance on the page, as shown in the following screenshot:

```
group(GroupName)
{
    field("PSAs Required"; "PSAs Required") { ApplicationArea = All; }
    field("PSA Count"; "PSA Count") { ApplicationArea = All; }
    field("Ads Required"; "Ads Required") { ApplicationArea = All; }
    field("Ads Count"; "Ads Count") { ApplicationArea = All; }
    field("News Required"; "News Required") { ApplicationArea = All; }
    field("Weather Required"; "Weather Required") { ApplicationArea = All;
    field("Sports Required"; "Sports Required") { ApplicationArea = All; }
    field(NewsCount; NWSRequired(1)) { ApplicationArea = All; }
    field(WeatherCount; NWSRequired(2)) { ApplicationArea = All; }
    field(SportsCount; NWSRequired(3)) { ApplicationArea = All; }
}
```

We will save the new FactBox page as page `50112`, named `Playlist` FactBox.

One final development step is required. We must connect the new FactBox Card Part to `Playlist Document`. All that is required is to define the FactBox area and add our FactBox as an element in that area:

```
page 50104 Playlist Document.al ●
1    page 50104 "Playlist Document"
2    {
3        PageType = Document;
4        SourceTable = "Playlist Header";
5        ApplicationArea = Basic;
6        UsageCategory = Documents;
7        layout
8        {
9            area(content)
10           {
11               group(Group)
12  ⊞           { ···
27               }
28               part(lines; "Playlist Subpage")
29  ⊞           { ···
33               }
34           }
35           area(FactBoxes)
36           {
37               part(factbox;"Playlist Factbox")
38               {
39                   SubPageLink = "No." = FIELD ("No.");
40               }
41           }
42       }
43   }
```

Multiple FactBoxes can be part of a primary page. If we look at page `21` – **Customer Card**, we will see a FactBox area with eight FactBoxes, of which two are system parts.

The end result of our development effort is shown in the following screenshot when we run page `50104`—`Playlist` with some sample test data, which we entered by running the various tables:

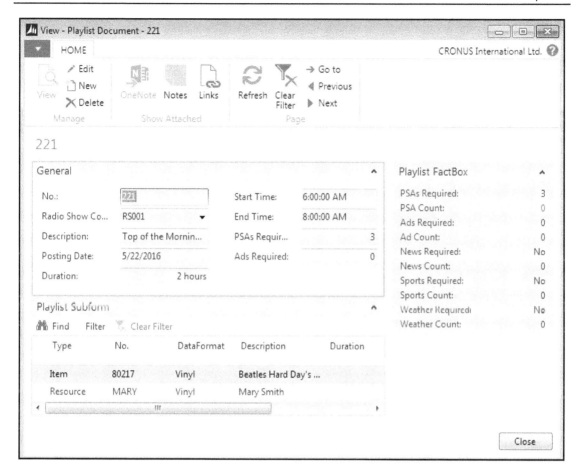

Summary

In this chapter, we covered a number of practical tools and topics regarding AL coding and development. We started by reviewing methods and then we dived into a long list of functions that we will need on a frequent basis.

We covered a variety of selected data-centric functions, including some for computation and validation, some for data conversion, and others for date handling. Next, we reviewed functions that affect the flow of logic and the flow of data, including FlowFields and SIFT, processing flow control, input and output, and filtering. Finally, we put a number of these to work in an enhancement for our WDTU application.

In the next chapter, we will move from the details of the functions to the broader view of AL development integration into the standard Business Central code, as well as debugging techniques.

Questions

1. Which three of the following are valid date-related Business Central functions?
   - DATE2DWY
   - CALCDATE
   - DMY2DATE
   - DATE2NUM

2. RESET is used to clear the current sort key setting from a record. True or false?

3. Which functions can be used to cause FlowFields to be calculated? Choose two:
   - CALCSUMS
   - CALCFIELDS
   - SETAUTOCALCFIELDS
   - SUMFLOWFIELD

4. Which of the following functions should be used within a report's OnAfterGetRecord trigger to end processing just for a single iteration of the trigger? Choose one:
   - EXIT
   - BREAK
   - QUIT
   - SKIP

5. The WORKDATE value can be set to a different value from the system date. True or false?

6. Only one FactBox is allowed on a page. True or false?

7. Braces {} are used as a special form of a repeating CASE statement. True or false?

8. Which of the following is not a valid AL flow control combination? Choose one:
   1. REPEAT-UNTIL
   2. DO-UNTIL
   3. CASE-ELSE
   4. IF-THEN

9. A `FILTERGROUP` function should not be used in custom code. True or false?

10. The `REPEAT – UNTIL` looping structure is most often used to control data reading processes. True or false?

11. Which of the following formats of `MODIFY` will cause the table's `OnModify` trigger to fire? Choose one:
    - `MODIFY`
    - `MODIFY(TRUE)`
    - `MODIFY(RUN)`
    - `MODIFY(READY)`

12. Marking a group of records creates a special index; therefore, marking is especially efficient. True or false?

13. A `CASE` statement structure should never be used in place of a nested `IF` statement structure. True or false?

14. An average FlowField requires which of the following?
    - A record key
    - SQL Server database
    - An integer variable
    - A decimal variable

15. The `TESTFIELD` function can be used to assign new values to a variable. True or false?

16. The `VALIDATE` function can be used to assign new values to a variable. True or false?

17. The AL Symbol Menu can be used for several of the following purposes. Choose two:
    - Find applicable functions
    - Test coded functions
    - Use entries as a template for function syntax and arguments
    - Translate text constants into a support language

18. Documentation cannot be integrated into in-line AL code. True or false?

19. If `MAINTAINSIFTINDEX` is set to `NO` and `CALCFIELDS` is invoked, the process will terminate with an error. True or false?

20. `SETRANGE` is often used to clear all filtering from a single field. True or false?

8
Advanced AL Development Tools

Quality isn't something you lay on top of subjects and objects like tinsel on a Christmas tree. Quality must be in the heartwood.

Robert Pirsig, paraphrased

Often when you think you're at the end of something, you're at the beginning of something else.

– Fred Rogers

Business Central is extremely flexible and suitable for addressing many types of problems, there are a lot of choices for advanced Business Central topics. We'll try to cover those that will be most helpful in an effort to put together a complete implementation.

First, we will review the overall structure of Business Central as an application software system, aiming for a basic understanding of the process flow of the system, along with some of the utility functions built into the standard product. Before designing modifications for Business Central, it is important to have a good understanding of the structural *style* of the software, so that our enhancements are designed for a better fit.

Secondly, we will review some special components of the Business Central system that will allow us to accomplish more at a lower cost. These resources include features such as XMLports and web services that we can build on, and they will help us use standard interface structures to connect with the world outside of the Business Central system. Fortunately, Business Central has a good supply of such features.

The topics we will cover in this chapter include the following:

- Role Center pages
- The Search and Action menus
- XMLports
- Web services and OData

Business Central process flow

Primary data, such as sales orders, purchase orders, production orders, and financial transactions, flow through the Business Central system, as follows:

- **Initial setup**: This is where the essential master data, reference data, and control and setup data is entered. Most of this preparation is done when the system (or a new application) is prepared for production use.
- **Transaction entry**: Transactions are entered into documents and then transferred as part of a posting sequence into a `Journal` table, or data may be entered directly into a `Journal` table. Data is preliminarily validated as it is entered, with master and auxiliary data tables being referenced as appropriate. The entry can be via manual keying, an automated transaction generation process, or an import function that brings in transaction data from another system.
- **Validate**: This step provides for additional data validation processing of a set of one or more transactions, often in batches, prior to submitting it to `Posting`.
- **Post**: This step posts a `Journal` batch that includes completing transaction data validation, adding entries to one or more `Ledger` tables, and perhaps also updating a `Register` table and document history.
- **Utilize**: This is where we access the data via pages, queries, and/or reports, including those that feed web services and other consumers of data. At this point, total flexibility exists. Whatever tools are appropriate for users' needs should be used, whether internal to Business Central or external (external tools are often referred to as **Business Intelligence (BI)** tools). Business Central's built-in capabilities for data manipulation, extraction, and presentation should not be overlooked.
- **Maintenance**: This is the continued maintenance of all Business Central data, as appropriate.

The following diagram provides a simplified picture of the flow of application data through a Business Central system:

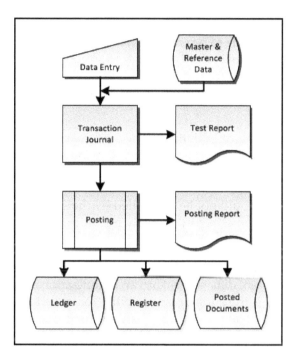

As you can see, many of the transaction types include additional reporting, multiple ledgers to update, and even auxiliary processing. However, this represents the basic data flow in Business Central whenever a `Journal` table and a `Ledger` table are involved.

When we enhance an existing Business Central functional area, such as Jobs or Service Management, we may need to enhance related process flow elements by adding new fields to journals, ledgers, posted documents, and so on.

When we create a new functional area, we will likely want to replicate the standard Business Central process flow in some form for the new application's data. For example, for our WDTU application, we will handle the entry of playlists in the same fashion as `Journal` is entered. A day's playlists would be similar to a `Journal` batch in another application. After a day's shows have been broadcast, the completed playlist will be posted into the `Radio Show` ledger as a permanent record of the broadcasts.

Initial setup and data preparation

Data must be maintained as new master data becomes available or when various system operating parameters and other elements change. The standard approach for Business Central data entry allows records to be entered that have just enough information to define the primary key fields, but not necessarily enough to support processing. This allows for a great deal of flexibility in the timing and responsibility for entry and completeness of new data. This approach applies to both setup data entry and ongoing production transaction data entry.

For example, a sales person might initialize a new customer entry with a name, address, and phone number, just entering the data to which they have easy access. At this point, there is not enough information recorded to process orders for this new customer. At a later time, someone in the accounting department can set up posting groups, payment terms, and other control data that should not be controlled by the sales department. With this additional data, the new customer record is ready for production use.

The Business Central data entry approach allows the system to be updated on an incremental basis as the data arrives, providing an operational flexibility many systems lack. This works because often, data comes into an organization on a piecemeal basis. The other side of this flexibility is the added responsibility for users to ensure that partially updated information is completed in a timely fashion. For a user organization that can't manage this, it may be necessary to create special procedures, or even system customizations that enforce the necessary discipline.

Transaction entry

Transactions are entered into a `Journal` table. Data is preliminarily validated as it is entered; master and auxiliary data tables are referenced as appropriate. Data validation is one of more powerful existing feature in Business Central like FlowFields. Validations are based on the evaluation of the individual transaction data, plus the related master records and associated reference tables; for example, lookups being satisfied, application or system setup parameter constraints being met, and so on.

Testing and posting the Journal batch

Any additional validations that are needed to ensure the integrity and completeness of the transaction data prior to being posted are done either in pre-post routines or directly in the posting processes. The actual posting of a `Journal` batch occurs after the transaction data is completely validated.

Depending on the specific application, when `Journal` transactions don't pass muster during this final validation stage, either the individual transaction is bypassed while acceptable transactions are posted, or the entire `Journal` batch is rejected until the identified problem is resolved.

The posting process adds entries to one or more ledgers, and sometimes to a document history table. When a `Journal Entry` is posted to a ledger, it becomes part of the permanent accounting record. Most data cannot be changed or deleted once it resides in a ledger (an example exception would be the due date on a payable).

Register tables may also be updated during posting, recording the ID number ranges of ledger entries posted, when they are posted, and in what batches. This adds to the transparency of the Business Central application system for audits and analysis.

In general, Business Central follows the standard accounting practice of requiring ledger revisions to be made by posting reversing entries, rather than by deletion of problem entries. The overall result is that Business Central is a very auditable system, a key requirement for a variety of government, legal, and certification requirements for information systems.

Utilizing and maintaining the data

The data in a Business Central system can be accessed by means of pages, queries, and/or reports, providing total flexibility. Whatever tools are available to the developer or the user, and are appropriate, should be used. There are some very good tools in Business Central for data manipulation, extraction, and presentation. Among other things, these include the SIFT/FlowField functionality, the pervasive filtering capability (including the ability to apply filters to subordinate data structures), and the `Navigate` function. Business Central includes the ability to create page parts for graphing, with a wide variety of predefined chart page parts included as part of the standard distribution. We can also create our own chart parts using tools delivered with the system or available from blogs or MSDN.

The Business Central database design approach could be referred to as a **rational normalization**. Business Central isn't constrained by a rigid normalized data structure, where every data element appears only once. The Business Central data structure is normalized, so long as that principle doesn't get in the way of processing speed. Where processing speed or user convenience is improved by duplicating data across tables, Business Central does so. In addition, the duplication of master file data into transactions allows for the one-time modification of data when appropriate, such as a ship-to address in a Sales Order. That data duplication often greatly simplifies data access for analysis.

Data maintenance

As with any database-oriented application software, the ongoing maintenance of master data, reference data, and setup and control data is required. In Business Central, the maintenance of data uses many of the same data preparation tools that were initially used to set up the system.

Role Center pages

One of the key features of Business Central is the Role Tailored user experience, centered on Role Centers tied to user work roles. The Role Tailored approach provides a single point of entry and access into the system for each user through their assigned Role Center. Each user's Role Center acts as their home page. Each Role Center focuses on the tasks needed to support its users' jobs throughout the day. Primary tasks are front and center, while the **ACTIONS** ribbon and **Search** menu provide easy access to other functions, making them only a click or two away.

The standard Business Central distribution from Microsoft contains more than two dozen different Role Center pages, identified for user roles such as Bookkeeper, Sales Manager, Shop Supervisor, Purchasing Agent, and so on (page 9011 is identified as Foundation, rather than as a **Role Center**, or **RC**). Some localized Business Central distributions may have additional Role Center pages included. It is critical to realize that the Role Centers supplied out of the box are not generally intended to be used directly out of the box.

The Role Center pages should be used as templates for custom Role Centers tailored to the specific work role requirements of the individual customer implementation.

One of the very critical tasks of implementing a new system is to analyze the work flow and responsibilities of the system's intended users and configure Role Centers to fit the users. In some cases, the supplied Role Centers can be used with minimal tailoring. Sometimes, it will be necessary to create completely new Role Centers. Even then, we will often be able to start with a copy of an existing Role Center page, which we will modify as required. In any case, it is important to understand the structure of the Role Center page and how it is built.

Role Center structure

The following screenshot shows page 9006—Order Processor Role Center:

The components of the Role Center highlighted in the preceding screenshot are as follows:

1. Action ribbon
2. Navigation pane
3. Activity pane
4. Headlines (headline is introduced from Business Central and is not available in previous versions)
5. Cues (in Cue Groups)
6. Page parts
7. System part

We need to understand the construction of a Role Center page so that we are prepared to modify an existing Role Center or create a new one. First, we'll take a look at page 9006 "Order Processor Role Center" in the Page Designer:

```
1    page 9006 "Order Processor Role Center"
2    {
3        Caption = 'Sales Order Processor', Comment='{Dependency=Match,"ProfileDescription_ORDERPROCESSOR"}';
4        PageType = RoleCenter;
5
6        layout
7        {
8            area(rolecenter)
9            {
10               part(Control104;"Headline RC Order Processor")
11 ⊞           { ...
13               }
14               part(Control19018515308;"SO Processor Activities")
15 ⊞           { ...
18               }
19               part(Control1907692008;"My Customers")
```

The Role Center page layout should look familiar, because it's very similar in structure to the pages we've designed previously. What is specific to a Role Center page? There is a container control of the rolecenter area. This is required for a Role Center page.

Note that the PageType is rolecenter, and there is no SourceTable.

Role Center headlines page

We'll take a quick look at the first `part` control's properties. The `part` property is `page 1441 "Headline RC Order Processor"`:

```
1    page 1441 "Headline RC Order Processor"
2    {
3        Caption = 'Headline';
4        PageType = HeadlinePart;
5        RefreshOnActivate = true;
6        SourceTable = "Headline RC Order Processor";
7
8        layout
9        {
10           area(content)
11           {
12               group(Control2)
13               {
14                   ShowCaption = false;
15                   Visible = UserGreetingVisible;
16                   field(GreetingText;GreetingText)
17                   {
18                       ApplicationArea = Basic,Suite;
19                       Caption = 'Greeting headline';
20                       Editable = false;
21                       Visible = UserGreetingVisible;
22                   }
```

Headline pages are used to show KPI information to the users and they are the first thing the users see when opening Business Central.

There is a special `PageType` property called `HeadLinePart`, and the `RefreshOnActivate` property is used to make sure new information is displayed when the Role Center updates.

 More information can be found on Microsoft Docs, at `https://docs. microsoft.com/en-us/dynamics365/business-central/dev-itpro/ developer/devenv-create-role-center-headline`.

Role Center activities page

We'll take a quick look at the next part control's properties. The `page` property is `page 9060 "SO Processor Activities"`:

```
1   page 9060 "SO Processor Activities"
2   {
3       Caption = 'Activities';
4       PageType = CardPart;
5       RefreshOnActivate = true;
6       SourceTable = "Sales Cue";
7
8       layout
9       {
10          area(content)
11          {
12              cuegroup("For Release")
13              {
```

In the previous screenshot, you can see the various properties of the `part` control.

Cue groups and cues

Now, we'll focus on page `9060`—`SO Processor Activities`. Designing that page, we see the following layout. Comparing the controls we see there to those of the Role Center, we can see that this page `part` is the source of the **Activities** section of the Role Center page.

In the properties of the `SO Processor Activities` page, we can see that this is a `PageType` property of `CardPart` tied to `SourceTable`, which is `Sales Cue`.

There are three `cuegroup` controls—`ForRelease`, `Sales Orders Released Not Shipped`, and `Returns`. In each `cuegroup` control, there are the `field` controls for the individual cues:

```
 8      layout
 9      {
10          area(content)
11          {
12              cuegroup("For Release")
13              {
14                  Caption = 'For Release';
15                  CueGroupLayout = Wide;
16                  field("Sales Quotes - Open";"Sales Quotes - Open")
17                  {
18                      ApplicationArea = Basic,Suite;
19                      DrillDownPageID = "Sales Quotes";
20                      ToolTip = 'Specifies the number of sales quotes that are not yet converted to invoices or orders.';
21                  }
22                  field("Sales Orders - Open";"Sales Orders - Open")
23                  {
24                      ApplicationArea = Basic,Suite;                               I
25                      DrillDownPageID = "Sales Order List";
26                      ToolTip = 'Specifies the number of sales orders that are not fully posted.';
27                  }
28
29                  actions
30 ⊞              { …
48                  }
49              }
50              cuegroup("Sales Orders Released Not Shipped")
51 ⊞          { …
108             }
109             cuegroup(Returns)
110 ⊞          { …
144             }
145             cuegroup("Document Exchange Service")
146 ⊞          { …
161             }
```

An individual cue is displayed as an iconic shortcut to a filtered list through a FlowField, or to a query or other data source through a Normal field. The stack of papers in the cue icon resulting from a filtered value represents an idea of the number of records in that list. The actual number of entries is also displayed next to the icon (see the **Sales Orders - Open** example in the following screenshot).

 The Stack image is the default icon for a Cue and changes automatically, based on the data. If required, the icon can be changed into any of several hundred other images. A very useful tool for finding these images can be found on Mibuso,
at `https://mibuso.com/downloads/dynamics-nav-image-library`.

The purpose of this type of cue is to provide a single-click point of access to a specific user task. The set of these cues is intended to represent the full set of primary activities for a user, based on their work role:

Business Central provides another cue format (like the **AVERAGE DAYS DELAYED** cue in the preceding screenshot), which is based on a calculated value stored in a Normal field.

Next, we want to design the referenced table, `Sales Cue`, to see how it is constructed:

```
1   table 9053 "Sales Cue"
2   {
3       Caption = 'Sales Cue';
4
5       fields
6       {
7           field(1;"Primary Key";Code[10])
8  ⊞      { …
10          }
11          field(2;"Sales Quotes - Open";Integer)
12 ⊞      { …
19          }
20          field(3;"Sales Orders - Open";Integer)
21 ⊞      { …
29          }
30          field(4;"Ready to Ship";Integer)
31 ⊞      { …
41          }
42          field(5;Delayed;Integer)
43 ⊞      { …
54          }
55          field(6;"Sales Return Orders - Open";Integer)
56 ⊞      { …
64          }
65          field(7;"Sales Credit Memos - Open";Integer)
66 ⊞      { …
73          }
74          field(8;"Partially Shipped";Integer)
75 ⊞      { …
86          }
87          field(9;"Average Days Delayed";Decimal)
88 ⊞      { …
93          }
94          field(10;"Sales Inv. - Pending Doc.Exch.";Integer)
95 ⊞      { …
100         }
101         field(12;"Sales CrM. - Pending Doc.Exch.";Integer)
102 ⊞     { …
107         }
```

As you can see in the preceding screenshot, there is a simply structured table, with an integer field for each of the action cues and a decimal field for the information cue, all of which were displayed in the Role Center we are analyzing. There is also a key field, two fields identified as date filters, and a field identified as a Responsibility Center filter.

> The design pattern used for cue tables is the Singleton Pattern, which can be found on the Microsoft Design Patterns Wiki (https://community.dynamics.com/nav/w/designpatterns/282.cue-table).

When we display the properties of one of these integer fields, `Sales Orders - Open`, we find it is a FlowField providing a count of `Sales Orders` with a status of `Open`:

```
field(3;"Sales Orders - Open";Integer)
{
    AccessByPermission = TableData "Sales Shipment Header"=R;
    CalcFormula = Count("Sales Header" WHERE ("Document Type"=FILTER(Order),
                                              Status=FILTER(Open),
                                              "Responsibility Center"=FIELD("Responsibility Center Filter")));
    Caption = 'Sales Orders - Open';
    Editable = false;
    FieldClass = FlowField;
```

If we inspect each of the other integer fields in this table, we will find a similar FlowField setup. Each is defined to fit the specific cue to which it's tied. If we think about what the cues show (a count) and how FlowFields work (a calculation based on a range of data records), we can see this is a simple, direct method of providing the information necessary to support cue displays. Clicking on the action cue (the count) opens up the list of records being counted. The information cue is tied to a decimal field, which is computed by means of a function, as shown in the following screenshot, in the cue table that is invoked from the Role Center page when the cue is displayed:

```
procedure CalculateAverageDaysDelayed() AverageDays: Decimal
var
    SalesHeader: Record "Sales Header";
    SumDelayDays: Integer;
    CountDelayedInvoices: Integer;
begin
    FilterOrders(SalesHeader,FieldNo(Delayed));
    if SalesHeader.FindSet then begin
      repeat
        SumDelayDays += MaximumDelayAmongLines(SalesHeader);
        CountDelayedInvoices += 1;
      until SalesHeader.Next = 0;
      AverageDays := SumDelayDays / CountDelayedInvoices;
    end;
end;
```

This brings us to the end of the Role Center structure. Next, we will discuss the system part.

System part

Now that we have covered the components of the **Activities** portion of the Role Center page, let's take a look at the other components.

Returning to page 9006 in the Page Designer, we can examine the properties of the system part control. This page part property is the one that incorporates a view of the user's notes data into the Role Center. Take a look at the following screenshot:

```
part(Control21;"Report Inbox Part")
{
    AccessByPermission = TableData "Report Inbox"=R;
    ApplicationArea = Suite;
}
systempart(Control1901377608;MyNotes)
{
    ApplicationArea = Basic,Suite;
}
}
}
```

Looking at this control's properties, we see a PartType of systempart and a link to MyNotes, which displays as My Notifications.

Page parts

Let's look at the second group in page 9006, the group that defines the column appearing in the Role Center page:

```
1    page 9006 "Order Processor Role Center"
2    {
3        Caption = 'Sales Order Processor', Comment='{Dependency=Match,"ProfileDescription_ORDERPROCESSOR"}';
4        PageType = RoleCenter;
5
6        layout
7        {
8            area(rolecenter)
9            {
10               part(Control104;"Headline RC Order Processor")
11               {…
13               }
14               part(Control1901851508;"SO Processor Activities")
15               {…
18               }
19               part(Control1907692008;"My Customers")
20               {…
22               }
23               part(Control14;"Team Member Activities")
24               {…
26               }
27               part(Control13;"Power BI Report Spinner Part")
28               {
29                   ApplicationArea = Basic,Suite;
30               }
31               part(Control1;"Trailing Sales Orders Chart")
32               {…
35               }
36               part(Control4;"My Job Queue")
37               {…
40               }
41               part(Control1905989608;"My Items")
42               {…
45               }
46               part(Control21;"Report Inbox Part")
47               {…
50               }
51               systempart(Control1901377608;MyNotes)
52               {…
```

As you can see, there are nine page parts and a system part defined.

Page parts not visible

If we look at the display of the Role Center page generated by this layout again, we will see a chart (Trailing Sales Orders), followed by two list parts (My Items and Report InBox). The My Job Queue page part does not appear. This page part is defined by the developer, with the Visible property equal to FALSE:

```
part(Control4;"My Job Queue")
{
    ApplicationArea = Basic,Suite;
    Visible = false;
}
```

This causes it not to display unless the Role Center page is customized by the user (or an administrator or a developer) and the part is added to the visible part list.

Page parts for user data

Three of the page parts in Role Center page 9006 provide data that is specific to the individual user. They track My data, information important to the user who is logged in. When we design any one of the pages, we can open the page properties to find out what table the page is tied to. Then, viewing any of those tables in the table designer, we will see that a highly ranked field is User ID. An example is the My Item table, which is shown here:

```
table 9152 "My Item"
{
    Caption = 'My Item';

    fields
    {
        field(1;"User ID";Code[50])
        { ...
        }
        field(2;"Item No.";Code[20])
        { ...
        }
        field(3;Description;Text[100])
        { ...
        }
        field(4;"Unit Price";Decimal)
        { ...
        }
        field(5;Inventory;Decimal)
        { ...
```

The `User ID` allows the data to be filtered to present user-specific information to each user. In some cases, this data can be updated directly in the Role Center page part; for example, in `My Customers` and `My Items`. In other cases, such as `My Job Queue`, the data is updated elsewhere and is only viewed in the Role Center page part. If our users need to track other information in a similar manner, such as `My Service Contracts`, we can readily plagiarize the approach used in the standard page parts.

Navigation pane and action menus

The last major Role Center page components we'll review are the navigation pane and the action ribbon. Even though there are two major parts of the Role Center page that provide access to action choices, they both are defined in the **Action Designer** section of the **Page Designer**.

The display of Action Controls in a Role Center page is dependent on a combination of the definition of the controls in the Action Designer, certain properties of the page, and the configuration/personalization of the page. Many of the default Role Centers provided with the product are configured as examples of possibilities of what can be done. Even if one of the default Role Centers seems to fit our customer's requirements exactly, we should create a copy of that Role Center page as another page object and reconfigure it. This way, we can document how that page was set up and make any necessary tweaks.

We'll start with Role Center page `9006` because it is used as the default Role Center and is used in so many other examples. Copy page `9006` into page `50020—WDTU Role Center` by using the copy/paste utility from **Go To Definition** | **Save As...**, and with a new page object ID of `50020` and an object name of `WDTU` Role Center.

Once we have the new page saved, in order to use this page as a Role Center, we must create a profile for the page. This is done within the RTC and is typically a system administrator task. Invoke the RTC and click on the **Departments** menu button in the navigator pane. Then, click on **Administrator: Application Setup** | **Role Tailored Client** | **Lists: Profiles**.

Click on the **New** icon and create a new profile, like this one:

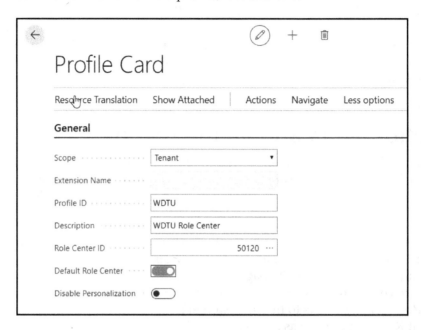

For the purpose of easy access to this Role Center for testing, we could also checkmark the **Default Role Center** box. Then, when we invoke the client, our test Role Center will be the one that displays (if no other profile is assigned to this user). Another approach to testing is to assign our user ID to use this profile. In order to test all of the aspects of the Role Center page, we must launch it as the assigned Role Center for the active user.

A major area where action choices are presented in a Role Center (and also in other page types) is the ribbon. The ribbon for the standard page 9006—Order Processor Role Center, as delivered from Microsoft, looks like the following screenshot:

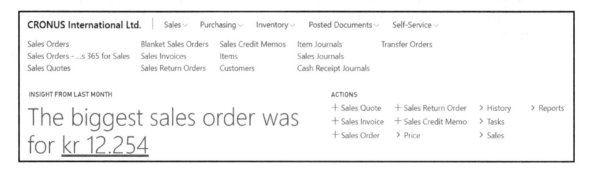

We can see the different action choices present in the ribbon.

Action Designer

The actions for a page are defined and maintained in the `action` section. Open our new page 50120—`WDTU Role Center` in the Page Designer, then search for `action` to view the current set of actions defined for this page.

For our newly created page 50120, cloned from page 9006, the Action Designer contents look like the following screenshot:

```
actions
{
    area(embedding)
    {
        ToolTip = 'Manage sales processes, view KPIs, and access your favorite items and customers.';
        action(SalesOrders)
        { ...
        }
        action(SalesOrdersShptNotInv)
        { ...
        }
        action(SalesOrdersComplShtNotInv)
        { ...
        }
        action(Items)
        { ...
        }
        action(Customers)
        { ...
        }
        action("Item Journals")
        { ...
        }
        action(SalesJournals)
        { ...
        }
        action(CashReceiptJournals)
        { ...
        }
        action("Transfer Orders")
        { ...
        }
    }
    area(sections)
    {
        group(ActionGroup76)
        { ...
        }
        group(ActionGroup63)
```

Whether they are actually displayed, how they are displayed, and where they are displayed are all controlled by a combination of the following factors:

- The structure of the controls within the action list
- The properties of the individual actions
- The customizations/personalizations that have been applied by a developer, administrator, or user

Each action belongs to an area. In hierarchical order, the area can be `Embedding`, `Sections`, `Creation`, or `Processing`. The specific `area` entry of each `actions` entry determines the area, ribbon, or navigation pane in which the subordinate groups of actions will appear:

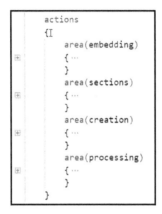

If the `area` entry is `embedding`, the indented subordinate actions will appear in the navigation pane. All the other areas will cause their subordinate actions to appear in the Role Center ribbon.

Creating a WDTU Role Center ribbon

If we were creating a Role Center to be used in a real production environment, we would likely be defining a new activities page, new cues, a new or modified cue table, new FactBoxes, and so on. However, since our primary purpose here is learning, we'll take the shortcut of piggybacking on the existing role center and simply add our WDTU actions to the foundation of that existing Role Center.

There are several steps to be taken to define our WDTU Role Center ribbon using the developer tools. The steps we need to take for our WDTU actions are as follows:

1. Define one or more new ribbon categories for the WDTU actions
2. Create the WDTU action controls in the Action Designer
3. Assign the WDTU action controls to the appropriate ribbon categories
4. Finalize any look and feel items

Let's add the following functions to the WDTU portion of the Action Ribbon:

- Radio Show list page
- Playlist page

To add an action, access the page—**Action Designer** screen, go the bottom of the list of existing actions, and add a new group for WDTU operations. Then, we add a line using the action snippet. Alternatively, we can copy/paste an existing action.

We connect the action to Page Radio Show List. Next, we will define the caption and image to represent this menu option. Let's do the same thing for one of the Playlist Document List pages, as shown in the following screenshot:

```
902        group(History)
903        {
904            Caption = 'History';
905            action("Navi&gate")
906            {
907                ApplicationArea = Basic, Suite;
908                Caption = 'Navi&gate';
909                Image = Navigate;
910                RunObject = Page Navigate;
911                ToolTip = 'Find all entries and documents that
912            }
913        }
914        group(WDTUOperations)
915        {
916            Caption = 'WDTU Operations';
917            action(RadioShows)
918            {
919                ApplicationArea = Basic, Suite;
920                Caption = 'Radio Shows';
921                Image = AddToHome;
922                RunObject = Page "Radio Show List";
923            }
924            action(Playlists)
925            {
926                ApplicationArea = Basic, Suite;
927                Caption = 'Playlists';
928                Image = PhysicalInventory;
929                RunObject = Page "Playlist Document List";
930            }
```

The resulting ribbon looks like the following screenshot:

Having gone over the Role Center pages, we will now discuss XMLports.

XMLports

XML (eXtensible Markup Language) is a structured text format developed to describe data to be shared by dissimilar systems. XML has become a standard for communications between systems. To make handling XML-formatted data simpler and more error resistant, Business Central provides XMLports, a data import/export object. In addition to processing XML-formatted data, XMLports can also handle a wide variety of other text file formats, including CSV files, generic flat files, and so on. XML-formatted data is text based, with each piece of information structured in one of two basic formats: elements or attributes. An element is the overall logical unit of information, while an attribute is a property of an element. They are formatted as follows:

- `<Tag>elementvalue</Tag>` (an **element** format)
- `<Tag AttribName="attribute datavalue">` (an **attribute** format))

Elements can be nested, but must not overlap. Element and attribute names are case-sensitive. Names cannot start with a number, punctuation character, or the letters `xml` (upper or lowercase), and cannot contain spaces. An attribute value must always be enclosed in single or double quotation marks. Some references suggest that elements should be used for data and attributes for metadata. Complex data structures are built of combinations of these two formats.

For example, let's consider the following code:

```
<Table Name='Sample XML format'>
    <Record>
        <DataItem1>12345</DataItem1>
        <DataItem2>23456</DataItem2>
    </Record>
    <Record>
        <DataItem1>987</DataItem1>
    </Record>
    <Record>
        <DataItem1>22233</DataItem1>
        <DataItem2>7766</DataItem2>
    </Record>
</Table>
```

In this instance, we have a set of data identified as `Table` with an attribute of `Name` equal to `'SampleXMLformat'`, which contains three `Record` instances, each `Record` containing data in one or two fields named `DataItem1` and `DataItem2`. The data is in a clearly structured text format, so it can be read and processed by any system prepared to read this particular XML format. If the field tags are well designed, the data is easily interpretable by humans, as well. The key to a successful exchange of data using XML is the sharing and common interpretation of the format between the transmitter and recipient.

XML is a standard format, in the sense that the data structure options are clearly defined. It is very flexible, in the sense that the identifying tag names (in < > brackets) and the related data structures are totally open-ended in how they can be defined and processed. The specific structure and the labels are whatever the communicating parties decide they should be. The rules of XML only determine how the basic syntax should operate.

XML data structures can be as simple as a flat file consisting of a set of identically formatted records or as complex as a sales order structure with headers containing a variety of data items, combined with associated detail lines containing their own assortments of data items. An XML data structure can be as complicated as the application requires.

XML standards are maintained by the W3C, whose website is at `www.w3.org`. There are many other useful websites for basic XML information.

XMLport components

Although in theory, XMLports can operate in both an import and an export mode, in practice, individual XMLport objects tend to be dedicated to either import or export. This allows the internal logic to be simpler. XMLports utilize a process of looping through and processing data, similar to that of report objects.

The components of XMLports are as follows:

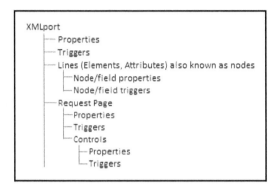

Let's take a look at the properties first.

XMLport properties

XMLport properties are shown in the following screenshot of the properties of the XMLport object 9170:

```
1    xmlport 9170 "Profile Import/Export"
2    {
3        Caption = 'Profile Import/Export';
4        Encoding = UTF8;
5        FormatEvaluate = Xml;
6
7        schema
8        {
9            textelement(Profiles)
```

Descriptions of the individual properties are as follows:

- `Caption`: This is the name that is displayed for the XMLport; it defaults to the contents of the `Name` property.
- `CaptionML`: The `Caption` translation for a defined alternative language.
- `Direction`: This defines whether this XMLport can only `Import`, `Export`, or `<Both>`; the default is `<Both>`.
- `DefaultFieldsValidation`: This defines the default value (`Yes` or `No`) for the `FieldValidate` property for individual XMLport data fields. The default for this field is `Yes`, which will set the default for individual field `FieldValidate` properties to `Yes`.
- `Encoding` (or `TextEncoding`): This defines the character encoding option to be used: UTF-8 (ASCII compatible), UTF-16 (not ASCII compatible), or ISO-8859-2 (for certain European languages written in Latin characters). UTF-16 is the default. This is inserted into the heading of the XML document.
- The `TextEncoding` option is only available if the `Format` property is Fixed Text or Variable Text. In this case, a character coding option of **MS-DOS** is available and is the default.
- `XMLVersionNo`: This defines to which version of XML the document conforms, `Version1.0` or `1.1`. The default is `Version1.0`. This is inserted into the heading of the XML document.
- `Format/Evaluate`: This can be C/SIDE `Format/Evaluate` (the default) or XMLFormat `Evaluate`. This property defines whether the external text data is (for imports) or will be (for exports) XML data types or C/SIDE data types. In each case, the default processing for all fields will be appropriate to the defined data type. If the external data does not fit in either of these categories, then the XML data fields must be processed through a temporary table. The temporary table processing approach reads the external data into text data fields, with data conversion logic done in C/AL into data types that can then be stored in the Business Central database. Very limited additional information on this is available in the online help in temporary property (XMLports).
- `UseDefaultNamespace` and `DefaultNamespace`: These properties are provided to support compatibility with other systems that require the XML document to be in a specific namespace, such as the use of a web service as a reference within Visual Studio. `UseDefaultNamespace` defaults to `No`. A default namespace in the form of **URN** (short for **Uniform Resource Name**, or, in this case, a **Namespace Identifier**), concluding with the object number of the XMLport, is supplied for the `DefaultNamespace` property. This property is only active if the `Format` property is XML.

- `Namespaces`: This property takes you to a new screen where you can set up multiple namespaces for the XMLport, including a prefix.
- `InlineSchema`: This property defaults to `No`. An inline schema allows the XML schema document (an XSD) to be embedded within the XML document. This can be used by setting the property to `Yes` when exporting an XML document, which will add the schema to that exported document. This property is only active if the `Format` property is XML.
- `UseLax`: This property defaults to `No`. Some systems may add information to the XML document, which is not defined in the XSD schema used by the XMLport. When this property is set to `Yes`, that extraneous material will be ignored, rather than resulting in an error. This property is only active if the `Format` property is XML.
- `Format`: This property has the options of `XML`, `Variable Text`, or `Fixed Text`. It defaults to XML. This property controls the import/export data format that the XMLport will process. Choosing `XML` means that the processing will only deal with a properly formatted XML file. Choosing `Variable Text` means that the processing will only deal with a file formatted with delimiters set up as defined in the `FieldDelimiter`, `FieldSeparator`, `RecordSeparator`, and `TableSeparator` properties, such as CSV files. Choosing `Fixed Text` means that each individual element and attribute must have its `Width` property set to a value greater than 0 (zero), and the data to be processed must be formatted accordingly. If enabled, these four fields can also be changed programmatically from within C/AL code.
- `FileName`: This can be filled with the predefined path and name of a specific external text data file, to be either the source (for `Import`) or target (for `Export`) for the run of the XMLport, or this property can be set dynamically. Only one file can be opened at a time, but the file in use can be changed during the execution of the XMLport (not often done).
- `FieldDelimiter`: This applies to `Variable Text` format external files only. It defaults to double quote (`<">`), the standard for so-called *comma-delimited* text files. This property supplies the string that will be used as the starting delimiter for each data field in the text file. If this is `Import`, then the XMLport will look for this string, and then use the string following as data until the next `FieldDelimiter` string is found, terminating the data string. If this is `Export`, the XMLport will insert this string at the beginning and end of each data field contents string.

- FieldSeparator: This applies to Variable Text format external files only. It defaults to a comma <,>, the standard for so-called comma delimited text files. This property supplies the string that will be used as the delimiter between each data field in the text file (looked for on Import or inserted on Export). See the help for this property for more information.

- RecordSeparator: This applies to VariableText or FixedText format external files only. This defines the string that will be used as the delimiter at the end of each data record in the text file. If this is Import, the XMLport will look for this string to mark the end of each data record. If this is Export, the XMLport will append this string at the end of each data record output. The default is <<NewLine>>, which represents any combination of **CR** (short for **carriage return**-ASCII value 13) and **LF** (short for **line feed**-ASCII value 10) characters. See the help for this property for more information.

- TableSeparator: This applies to Variable Text or Fixed Text format external files only. This defines the string that will be used as the delimiter at the end of each DataItem; for example, each text file. The default is <<NewLine><NewLine>>. See the help for this property for more information.

- UseRequestForm: This determines whether a request page should be displayed to allow the user choice of sort sequence, entry of filters, and other requested control information. The options are Yes and No. The default is <Yes>. An XMLport request page only has the **OK** and **Cancel** options.

- TransactionType: This property identifies the XMLport processing server transaction type as Browse, Snapshot, UpdateNoLocks, or Update. This is an advanced and seldom-used property. For more information, we can refer to the help files and SQL Server documentation.

- Permissions: This property provides report-specific setting of permissions, which are rights to access data, subdivided into Read, Insert, Modify, and Delete. This allows the developer to define permissions that override the user-by-user permissions security setup.

XMLport triggers

XMLport has a very limited set of triggers, which are as follows:

- Documentation() is for documentation comments.
- OnInitXMLport() is executed once, when the XMLport is loaded, before the table views and filters have been set.

- `OnPreXMLport()` is executed once, after the table views and filters have been set. Those can be reset here.
- `OnPostXMLport()` is executed once, after all the data is processed, if the XMLport completes normally.

XMLport data lines

An XMLport can contain any number of data lines. The data lines are laid out in a strict hierarchical structure, with the elements and attributes mapping exactly, one for one, in the order of the data fields in the external text file, the XML document.

XMLports should not be run directly from a navigation pane action command (due to conflicts with Business Central UX standards), but can be run either from ribbon actions on a Role Center or other page or by means of an object containing the necessary AL code. When running from another object (as opposed to running from an action menu entry), AL code calls the XMLport to stream data either to or from an appropriately formatted file (XML document or other text format). This calling code is typically written in a codeunit, but can be placed in any object that can contain C/AL code.

The following example code executes an exporting XMLport and saves the resulting file from the Business Central service tier to the client machine:

```
XMLfile.Create(TEMPORARYPATH + 'RadioShowExport.xml');
XMLfile.CreateOutStream(OutStream);
XMLPORT.Export(50000, OutStream);
FromFileName := XMLfile.Name;
ToFileName := 'RadioShowExport.xml';
XMLfile.Close();

//Need to call DOWNLOAD to move the xml file
//from the service tier to the client machine
Download(FromFileName, 'Downloading File...', 'C:', 'Xml
file(*.xml)|*.xml', ToFileName);

//Make sure to clean up the temporary file from the
//service tier
Erase(FromFileName);
```

Two text variables (the `FromFileName` and `ToFileName` variables), a `File` variable, and an `OutStream` variable are required to support the preceding code. Take a look at the following screenshot:

```
22        var
23            XMLFile: File;
24            OutStream: OutStream;
25            FromFileName: Text;
26            ToFileName: Variant;
27        }
```

Here, you can see the data variables defined.

The XMLport line properties

Different XMLport line properties are active on a line depending on the value of the `SourceType` property. The first four properties listed are common to all three `SourceType` values (`Text`, `Table`, or `Field`), and the other properties specific to each are listed after the screenshots, showing all the properties for each `SourceType`:

- `Indentation`: This indicates at what subordinate level in the hierarchy of the XMLport this entry exists. Indentation 0 is the primary level, parent to all higher-numbered levels. Indentation 1 is a child of indentation 0, indentation 2 is a child of 1, and so forth. Only one indentation 0 is allowed in an XMLport, so often, we will want to define the level 0 line to be a simple text element line. This allows for the definition of multiple tables at indentation level 1.

- `NodeName`: This defines the node name that will be used in the XML document to identify the data associated with this position in the XML document. No spaces are allowed in `NodeName`; we can use underscores, dashes, and periods, but no other special characters.

- `NodeType`: This defines if this data item is an element or an attribute.

- `SourceType`: This defines the type of data this field corresponds to in the Business Central database. The choices are `Text`, `Table`, and `Field`. `Text` means that the value in the `SourceField` property will act as a global variable, and typically, it must be dealt with by embedded C/AL code. `Table` means that the value in the `SourceField` property will refer to a Business Central table. `Field` means that the value in the `SourceField` property will refer to a Business Central field within the parent table previously defined as an element.

SourceType as text

A description of the text-specific properties is as follows:

- TextType: This defines the Business Central data type as Text or BigText. Text is the default.
- VariableName: This contains the name of the global variable, which can be referenced by C/AL code.

The Width, NamespacePrefix, MinOccurs, and MaxOccurs properties will be discussed later in this chapter.

SourceType as table

The descriptions of the table-specific properties are as follows:

- SourceTable: This defines the Business Central table being referenced.
- VariableName: This defines the name to be used in C/AL code for the Business Central table. It is the functional equivalent of the definition of a global variable.
- SourceTableView: This enables the developer to define a view by choosing a key and sort order or by applying filters on the table.
- ReqFilterHeading and ReqFilterHeadingML: These fields allow for the definition of the name of the request page filter definition tab that applies to this table.
- CalcFields: This lists the FlowFields in the table that are to be calculated automatically.
- ReqFilterFields: This lists the fields that will initially display on the request page filter definition tab.
- LinkTable: This allows for the linking of a field in a higher-level item to a key field in a lower-level item. If, for example, we were exporting all of the purchase orders for a vendor, we might link Buy-From Vendor No. in Purchase Header to No. in a vendor record. LinkTable, in this case, would be vendor and LinkField would be No.; therefore, LinkTable and LinkFields work together. The use of the LinkTable and LinkFields operates the same as applying a filter on the higher-level table data, so that only records relating to the defined lower-level table and field are processed. See the Help for more details.

- LinkTableForceInsert: This can be set to force insertion of the linked table data and execution of the related OnAfterInitRecord() trigger. This property is tied to the LinkTable and LinkFields properties. It also applies to Import.
- LinkFields: This defines the fields involved in a table + **Field** linkage.
- Temporary: This defaults to No. If this property is set to Yes, it allows for the creation of a Temporary table in working storage. Data imported into this table can then be evaluated, edited, and manipulated, before being written out to the database. This Temporary table has the same capabilities and limitations as a Temporary table defined as a global variable.
- AutoSave: If set to Yes (the default), an imported record will automatically be saved to the table. Either AutoUpdate or AutoReplace must also be set to Yes.
- AutoUpdate: If a record exists in the table with a matching primary key, all the data fields are initialized, and then all the data from the incoming record is copied into the table record.
- AutoReplace: If a record exists in the table with a matching primary key, the populated data fields in the incoming record are copied into the table record; all the other fields in the target record are left undisturbed. This provides a means to update a table by importing records with a limited number of data fields filled in.

The Width, NamespacePrefix, MinOccurs, and MaxOccurs properties are discussed later in this chapter.

SourceType as field

A description of the field-specific properties is as follows:

- SourceField: This defines the data field being referenced. It can be a field in any defined table.
- FieldValidate: This only applies to Import. If this property is Yes, then whenever the field is imported into the database, the OnValidate() trigger of the field will be executed.
- AutoCalcField: This applies to Export and FlowField data fields only. If this property is set to Yes, the field will be calculated before it is retrieved from the database. Otherwise, a FlowField will export as an empty field.

The details of the Width, NamespacePrefix, MinOccurs, and MaxOccurs properties will be in the next section.

Element or attribute

An element data item can appear many times, but an attribute data item can appear no more than once; the occurrence control properties differ based on the NodeType.

NodeType element data item

The element-specific properties are as follows:

- Width: When the XMLport Format property is Fixed Text, then this field is used to define the fixed width of this element's field.
- MinOccurs: This defines the minimum number of times this data item can occur in the XML document. This property can be Zero or Once (the default).
- MaxOccurs: This defines the maximum number of times this data item can occur in the XML document. This property can be Once or Unbounded. Unbounded (the default) means any number of times.
- NamespacePrefix: When an XMLport has multiple namespaces, this property allows you to select a specific one.

NodeType attribute data item

The attribute-specific property is Occurrence: this is either Required (the default) or Optional, depending on the text file being imported.

XMLport line triggers

There are different XMLport triggers, depending on whether the DataType is Text, Table, or Field.

DataType as text

The triggers for having the DataType as Text are as follows:

- Export::onBeforePassVariable(), for Export only: This trigger is typically used for manipulation of the text variable
- Import::OnAfterAssignVariable(), for Import only: This trigger gives us access to the imported value in a text format

DataType as Table

The triggers for having the `DataType` as `Table` are as follows:

- `Import::OnAfterInsertRecord()`, for `Import` only: This trigger is typically used when the data is being imported into temporary tables. This is where we would put the C/AL code to build and insert records for the permanent database tables.
- `Import::OnBeforeModifyRecord()`, for `Import` only: When `AutoSave` is `Yes`, this is used to update the imported data before saving it.
- `Import::OnAfterModifyRecord()`, for `Import` only: When `AutoSave` is `No`, this is used to update the data after updating.
- `Export::OnPreXMLItem()`, for `Export` only: This trigger is typically used for setting filters and initializing before finding and processing the first database record.
- `Export::OnAfterGetRecord()`, for `Export` only: This trigger allows for access to the data after the record is retrieved from the Business Central database. This trigger is typically used to allow manipulation of the table fields being exported.
- `Import::OnAfterInitRecord()`, for `Import` only: This trigger is typically used to check whether a record should be processed further or to manipulate the data.
- `Import::OnBeforeInsertRecord()`, for `Import` only: This is another place where we can manipulate data before it is inserted into the target table. This trigger is executed after the `OnAfterInitRecord()` trigger.

DataType as Field

The triggers for having the `DataType` as `Field` are as follows:

- `Import::OnAfterAssignField()`, for `Import` only: This trigger provides access to the imported data value for evaluation or manipulation before providing output to the database
- `Export::OnBeforePassField()`, for `Export` only: This trigger provides access to the data field value just before the data is exported

XMLport Request Pages

XMLports can also have a Request Page to allow the user to enter `Option` control information and filter the data being processed. The default filter fields that will appear on the Request Page are defined in the properties form for the XMLport line table.

Any desired options that are to be available to the user as a part of the Request Page must be defined in `RequestOptionsPageDesigner`. This Designer is accessed from the XMLport Designer through **View** | **Request Page**. The definition of the contents and layout of the Request Options page are essentially done in the same way as other pages are done. As with any other filter setup screen, the user has complete control of what fields are used for filtering and what filters are applied.

Web services

Web services are an industry standard software interface that allow software applications to interoperate by using standard interface specifications along with standard communications services and protocols. When Business Central publishes some web services, those functions can be accessed and utilized by properly programmed software residing anywhere on the web. This software does not need to be directly compatible with AL, or even .NET; it just needs to obey web services conventions and have security access to the Business Central web services.

Some benefits of Business Central web services are as follows:

- Very simple to publish, that is, to expose a web service to a consuming program outside of Business Central
- Provides managed access to Business Central data while respecting and enforcing the Business Central rules, logic, and design that already exist
- Uses Windows Authentication and respects Business Central data constraints
- Supports **SSL** (**Secure Socket Layer**)
- Supports both the SOAP interface (cannot access query objects) and the OData(4)/REST interface (cannot access codeunit objects)

Disadvantages of Business Central web services include the following:

- Allowing access to a system from the web requires a much higher level of security.
- The Business Central objects that are published generally need to be designed (or, at least, customized) to properly interface with this very different user interface.
- Access from the web complicates the system administrator's job of managing loads on the system.

There are several factors that should be considered in judging the appropriateness of an application being considered for web services integration. Some of these are as follows:

- What is the degree to which the functionality of the standard RTC interface is needed? A web services application should not try to replicate what would normally be done with a full client, but should be used for limited, focused functionality (remember, there is now a full-featured web client available for Business Central).
- What is the amount of data to be exchanged? Generally, web services are used remotely. Even if they are used locally, there are additional levels of security handshaking and intersystem communications required. These involve additional processing overhead. Web services should be used for low data volume applications.
- How public is the user set? For security reasons, the user set for direct connection to our Business Central system should generally be limited to known users, not the general public. Web services should not be used to provide internet exposure to the customer's Business Central system, but rather, for **intranet** access.

Because web services are intended for use by low-intensity users, there are separate license options available with lower costs per user than the full client license. This can make the cost of providing web services-based access quite reasonable, especially if by doing so, we increase the ability of our Business Central users to provide better service to their customers and to realize increased profits.

Exposing a web service

Three types of Business Central objects can be published as web services: pages, queries, and codeunits. The essential purposes are as follows:

- Pages provide access to the associated primary table. Use card pages for table access, unless there is a specific reason to use another page type.
- Codeunits provide access to the functions contained within each codeunit.
- Queries provide rapid, efficient access to data in a format that is especially compatible with a variety of other Microsoft products, as well as products from other vendors.

An XMLport can be exposed indirectly, as a codeunit parameter. This provides a very structured way of exposing Business Central data through a web service. (See AJ Kauffmann's blog series on XMLports in web services, at `http://kauffmann.nl/index.php/2011/01/15/how-to-use-xmlports-in-web-services -1/.) There is an example later in this chapter.`)

When a page has no special constraints, either via properties or permissions, there will normally be eleven methods available. They are as follows:

- `Create`: This creates a single record (similar to a Business Central `INSERT`).
- `CreateMultiple`: This creates a set of records (the passed argument must be an array).
- `Read`: This reads a single record (similar to a Business Central `GET`).
- `ReadMultiple`: This reads a filtered set of records, paged. The page size is a parameter.
- `Update`: This updates a single record (similar to a Business Central `MODIFY`).
- `UpdateMultiple`: This updates a set of records (the passed argument must be an array).
- `Delete`: This deletes a single record.
- `IsUpdated`: This checks if the record has been updated since it was read.
- `ReadByRecID`: This reads a record based on the record ID.
- `GetRecIDFromKey`: This gets a record ID based on the record key.
- `Delete_<PagePartName>` (`PagePartRecordKey`): This deletes a single record that is exposed by a page part of `TypePage`, such as the **Sales Order** subform page part of the **Sales Order** page.

Whatever constraints have been set in the page that we have published will be inherited by the associated web services. For example, if we publish a page that has the `Editable` property set to `No`, then only the `Read`, `ReadMultiple`, and `IsUpdated` methods will be available as web services. The other five methods will be suppressed by virtue of the `Editable` property which is equal to `No`.

Publishing a web service

Publishing a web service is one of the easiest things we will ever do in Business Central. However, as stated earlier, this doesn't mean that we will be able to simply publish existing objects without creating versions specifically tailored for use with web services. However, for the moment, let's just go through the basic publishing process.

The first column allows us to specify whether the object is a page, codeunit, or query. This is followed by the **OBJECT ID**, and then the **SERVICE NAME**. Finally, the **PUBLISHED** flag must be checked:

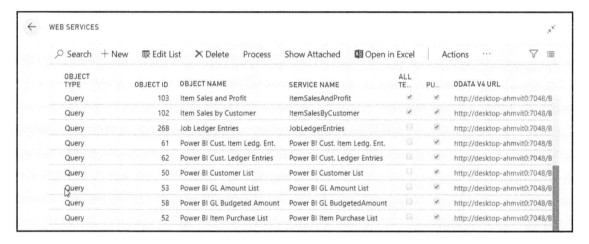

As you can see, at this point, the web services for that object are published.

Enabling web services

Prior to using web services, we must enable them from the Business Central administration application. In Business Central administration, we can see the checkboxes for enabling them. We can either enable SOAP Services, or OData Services, or both, as shown in the following screenshot:

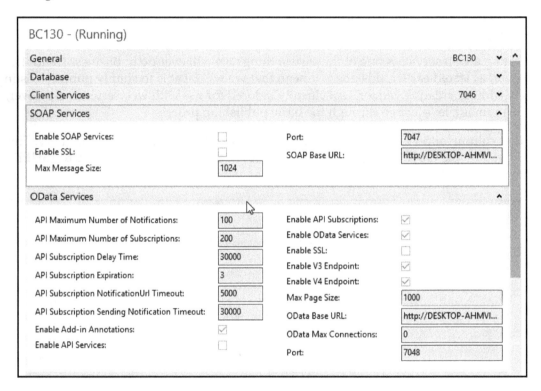

We have now enabled the services.

Determining what was published

Once an object has been published, we may want to see exactly what is available as a web service. As web services are intended to be accessed from the web, in the address bar of our browser, we will enter the following (all as one string):

```
http://<Server>:<WebServicePort>/<ServerInstance>/WS/
<CompanyName>/services
```

Some example URL addresses are as follows:

```
http://localhost:7047/DynamicsBusiness Central/WS/Services
http://Arthur:7047/DynamicsBusiness Central/WS/CRONUS International Ltd
/Services
```

 The company name is optional and case-sensitive.

When the correct address string is entered, our browser will display a screen similar to the following image. This screenshot is in an XML format of a data structure called **WSDL** (short for **Web Services Description Language**):

In this case, we can see that we have two Business Central SOAP services available: `Codeunit/Radio_Show_Management` and `Page/Radio_Show_Card`.

To see the methods (which are Business Central functions) that have been exposed as web services by publishing these two objects, we can enter other, similar URLs in our browser address bar. To see the web services exposed by our codeunit, we can change the URL used earlier to replace `Services` with `Codeunit/Radio_Show_Management`. We must also include the company name in the URL that lists the methods WSDL.

To see the OData services, change the URL to one in the form, as follows:

```
http://<Server>:<WebServicePort>/<ServerInstance>/OData
```

From that entry in our browser, we get information about what's available as OData. OData is structured like XML, but OData provides the full metadata (structural definition) of the associated data in the same file as the data. This allows OData to be consumed without the requirement of a lot of back and forth technical preplanning communication:

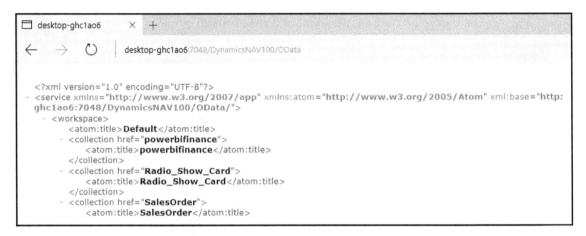

The actual consumption (meaning *use*) of a web service is also fairly simple, but that process occurs outside of Business Central, in any of a wide variety of off-the-shelf or custom applications not a part of this book's focus. Examples are readily available in the help, the MSDN library, the Business Central forums, and elsewhere.

Tools that can be used to consume Business Central web services include, among others, Microsoft Power BI, Microsoft Excel, Microsoft SharePoint, applications written in C#, other .NET languages, open source PHP, and a myriad of other application development tools. Remember, web services are a standard interface for dissimilar systems.

As with any other enhancement to the system functionality, serious thought needs to be given to the design of what data is to be exchanged and what functions within Business Central should be invoked for the application to work properly. In many cases, we will want to provide some simple routines to perform standard Business Central processing or validation tasks without exposing the full complexity of Business Central internals as web services.

Perhaps we want to provide just two or three functions from a codeunit that contains many additional functions. Or, we may want to expose a function that is contained within a report object. In each of these instances, and others, it will be necessary to create a basic library of AL functions, perhaps in a codeunit that can be published as web services (generally recognized as a best practice).

 The use of web services carries issues that must be dealt with in any production environment. In addition to delivering the required application functionality, there are security, access, and communications issues that need to be addressed. It is recommended that a Business Central web service not be directly exposed to external users, but Business Central data may be secured by limiting access through the use of custom, functionally limited, external software interfaces. While it's outside the scope of this text, proper attention to data security is critical to the implementation of a good quality solution.

XMLport – web services integration example for WDTU

WDTU subscribes to a service that compiles listenership data. This data is provided to subscribers in the form of XML files. The agency that provides the service has agreed to push that XML data directly to a web service exposed by our Business Central system. This approach will allow WDTU to have access to the latest listenership data as soon as it is released by the agency.

WDTU must provide access to the XMLport that fits the incoming XML file format. The handshaking response expected by the agency computer from our web service is a fixed XML file with one element (`Station ID`) and an attribute of the said element (`Frequency`).

The first step is to build our XMLport. We do this by using the `txmlport` snippet from a new AL file in Visual Studio Code. Define the new XMLport lines, as shown in the following screenshot:

```
1    XmlPort 50100 "Ratings Import"
2    {
3        UseDefaultNamespace = true;
4
5        schema
6        {
7            textelement(Root)
8            {
9                MaxOccurs = Once;
10               tableelement(ListenershipEntries; "Listernership Entry")
11               {
12                   MinOccurs = Zero;
13                   XmlName = 'RatingsData';
14                   fieldelement(EntryNo; ListenershipEntries."Entry No.") { }
15                   fieldelement(Date; ListenershipEntries.Date) { }
16                   fieldelement(StartTime; ListenershipEntries."Start Time") { }
17                   fieldelement(EndTime; ListenershipEntries."End Time") { }
18                   fieldelement(RadioShowID; ListenershipEntries."Radio Show No.") { }
19                   fieldelement(Listeners; ListenershipEntries."Listener Count") { }
20                   fieldelement(Audience; ListenershipEntries."Audience Share") { }
21                   fieldelement(Age; ListenershipEntries."Age Demographic") { }
22               }
23           }
24       }
```

Set the `Format/Evaluate` property to `XML Format/Evaluate`. This allows Visual Studio to automatically understand the data types involved, such as integer, decimal, and so on. Set `UseDefaultNamespace` to `Yes`, and `DefaultNamespace` to `urn:Microsoft-dynamics-nav/xmlports/x50000`, which is the default format, or `urn:Microsoft-dynamics-nav/xmlports/RatingsImport`.

Even though we are using the XMLport as an import-only object, make sure the `Direction` property stays at `<Both>`. When the value is set to either `Import` or `Export`, it is not possible to use the XMLport as a `Var` (by reference) parameter in the codeunit function, which we will expose as a web service.

The following is the XMLport `50100` properties screen, with those changes in place:

```
1    XmlPort 50100 "Ratings Import"
2    {
3        UseDefaultNamespace = true;
4        FormatEvaluate = Xml;
5        DefaultNamespace = 'urn:Microsoft dynamics nav/xmlports/RatingsImport';
6        Direction = Both;
7
8        schema
```

Set the `MaxOccurs` property to `Once`, as shown in the following screenshot:

```
textelement(Root)
{
    MaxOccurs = Once;
    tableelement(ListenershipEntries; "Listernership Entry")
    {
```

Set `MinOccurs` to `Zero`, and make sure `MaxOccurs` remains at the default value of `<Unbounded>`, as shown in the following screenshot:

```
tableelement(ListenershipEntries; "Listernership Entry")
{ I
    MinOccurs = Zero;
    XmlName = 'RatingsData';
    fieldelement(EntryNo; ListenershipEntries."Entry No.") { }
```

Now that we have our XMLport constructed, it's time to build the codeunit that will be published as a web service. In the C/AL Locals screen, enter the single parameter, `RatingsXML`, type `XmlPort`, and a subtype of `Ratings Import`. Make sure the `Var` column on the left is checked. The screen should then look like the following screenshot:

```
1  codeunit 50101 "WDTU Web Service"
2  {
3      procedure ImportRating(RatingsXML: XmlPort "Ratings Import"): Text
4      begin
5          RatingsXML.Import();
6          exit('<Root><Station Frequency="91.5">WDTU<Station></Root>');
7      end;
8
9  }
```

Now, we will publish the codeunit we just created.

Open the client and navigate to **WEB SERVICES**. Fill in an **OBJECT TYPE** of `Codeunit`, an **OBJECT ID** of `50001`, and a **SERVICE NAME** of `WDTU Ratings`, and check **PUBLISHED**:

Now, to test what we've done, we need to open a browser and enter a URL in the following format:

```
http://<Server>:<SOAPWebServicePort>/<ServerInstance>/WS/
<CompanyName>/services
```

More specifically, take the following URL as an example:

```
http://localhost:7047/BC130/WS/CRONUS/Codeunit/RatingWebService
```

For testing purposes, we could just click on the web icon on the right-hand end of our new entry in the web services screen, as shown in the preceding screenshot. The result in our browser screen should look like the following screenshot, showing that we can connect with our web service and that our XMLport contains all the fields for the data we plan to import:

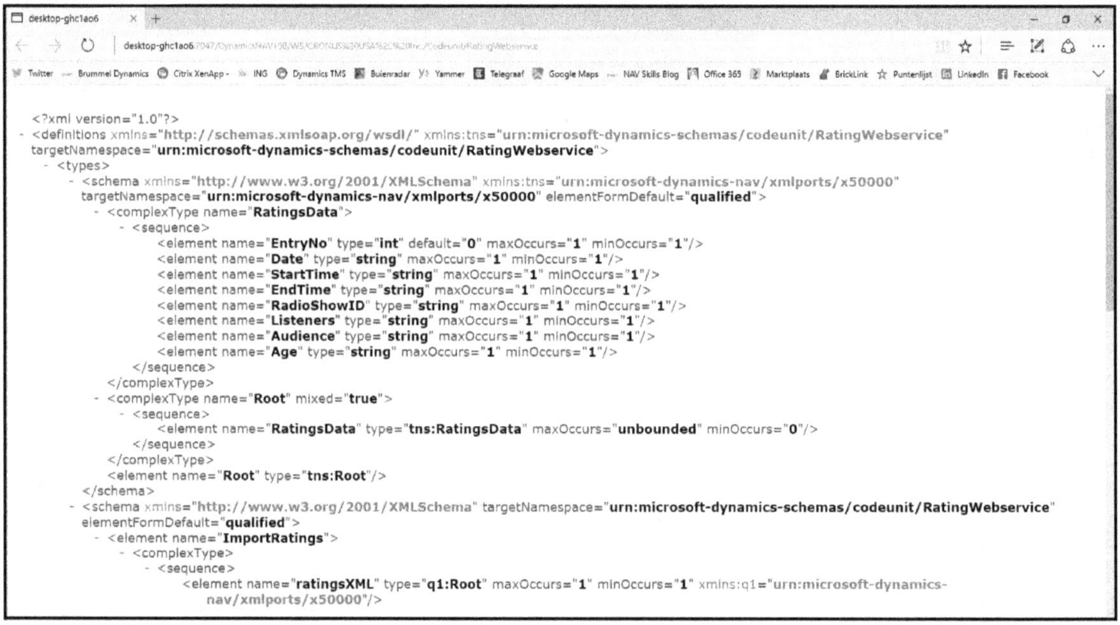

With this, we conclude our discussion of web services.

Summary

In this chapter, we reviewed some of the more advanced Business Central tools and techniques. By now, you should have a strong admiration for the power and flexibility of Business Central. Many of these subject areas will require more study and hands-on practice. We spent a lot of time on Role Center construction because that is the heart of the Role Tailored Experience. Much of what you learned about Role Center design and construction can be applied across the board, in role tailoring other components. We went over XMLports and web services, and then showed how the two capabilities can be combined to provide a simple but powerful method of interfacing with external systems. By now, you should almost be ready to begin your own development project. In the next chapter, we will cover the debugger, extensibility (adding non-AL controls to pages), and some additional topics.

Questions

1. Users cannot delete or modify database data through web services. True or false?

2. What source do the action items for the **Departments** button come from? Choose one of the following options:
   - Action Menu entries
   - Cue Group definitions
   - MenuSuite objects
   - Navigation Pane objects

3. Software external to Business Central that accesses Business Central web services must be .NET compatible. True or false?

4. Action Ribbons can be modified in which of the following ways? Choose three of the following options:
   - AL changes in the Action Designer
   - Dynamic AL code configuration
   - Implementer/administrator configuration
   - User personalization
   - Application of a profile template

5. XMLports cannot contain AL code: all data manipulation must occur outside of the XMLport object. True or false?

6. The default `PromotedActionCategoriesML` includes which of the following? Choose two:
    - Page
    - Report
    - Standard
    - New

7. Web services are an industry-standard interface defined by the World Wide Web Consortium. True or false?

8. Role Centers can have several components. Choose two of the following:
    - Activity pane
    - Browser part
    - Cues
    - Report Review pane

9. Web services are a good tool for publishing Business Central to be used as a public retail sales system on the web. True or false?

10. An action can appear in multiple places in a Role Center; for example, in the Home button of the Navigation Pane, in the Action Ribbon, and in a Cue Group. True or false?

11. Which of the following object types can be published as web services? Choose two of the following options:
    - Reports
    - Queries
    - XMLports
    - Pages

12. A Cue can be a shortcut to a filtered list supported by a field in a Cue table. True or false?

13. New system parts can be created by a Business Central developer using AL tools. True or false?

14. All new implementations should create new Role Centers based on the results of a detailed analysis of the intended users' work roles, using only the standard Role Centers as templates. True or false?

15. All web service data interfaces require the use of XML data files. True or false?

16. Role Center Cues can be tied to FlowFields, normal fields, or queries. True or false?

17. Actions in a ribbon are promoted so that they can be displayed in color. True or false?

18. Role Center components include which of the following options? Choose two:
    - Cues
    - Microsoft Office parts
    - Web services
    - Page parts

19. Once a Role Center layout has been defined by the developer, it cannot be changed by the users. True or false?

20. In the client, XMLports can only be used to process XML formatted files, and cannot process other text file formats. True or false?

Successful Conclusions **9**

Each update of Business Central includes new features and capabilities. **Microsoft Dynamics 365 Business Central** is no exception. It is our responsibility to understand how to apply these new features, use them intelligently in our designs, and develop them with both their strengths and limitations in mind. Our goal in the end is not only to provide workmanlike results but, if possible, to delight our users with the quality of the experience and the ease to use of our products.

In this chapter, we will cover the following topics:

- Reviewing Business Central objects that contain functions we can use directly or as templates in our solutions
- Reviewing some of the Visual Studio Code tools that help us debug our solutions
- Learning ways we can enhance our solutions using external controls that are integrated into Business Central
- Discussing design, development, and delivery issues that should be addressed in our projects

Creating new AL routines

Now that we have a good overall picture of how we enable users to access the tools we create, we are ready to start creating our own Business Central AL routines. It is important that you learn your way around the Business Central AL code in the standard product first. You may recall the advice in a previous chapter that the new code we create should be visually and logically compatible with what already exists. If we think of our new code as a guest being hosted by the original system, we will be doing what any thoughtful guest does: fitting smoothly into the host's environment.

An equally important aspect of becoming familiar with the existing code is to increase the likelihood; we can take advantage of the features and components of the standard product to address some of our application requirements. There are at least two types of existing Business Central AL code that we should make use of whenever appropriate.

One group is the callable functions that are used liberally throughout Business Central. Once we know about these, we can use them in our logic whenever they fit. There is no documentation for most of these functions, so we must either learn about them here or do our homework and study Business Central code. The second group includes the many code snippets we can copy when we face a problem similar to something the Business Central developers have already addressed.

The code snippets differ from the callable functions in two ways. First, they are not structured as coherent and callable entities. Second, they are likely to serve as models, code that must be modified to fit the situation by changing variable names, adding or removing constraints, and so on.

In addition to the directly usable AL code, we should also make liberal use of the Business Central Design Patterns Repository, located at
`https://community.dynamics.com/nav/w/designpatterns/105.nav-design-patterns-rep`
`ository.aspx`.

Business Central Design Patterns provide common definitions of how certain types of functions are implemented in Business Central. Some of the Pattern examples include the following:

- Copy Document
- Create Data from Templates
- No. Series

- Single-Record (Setup) Table
- Master Data

There are many other patterns, and new pattern definitions are frequently added.

Callable functions

Most of the callable functions in Business Central are designed to handle a very specific set of data or conditions and have no general-purpose use. For example, the routines to update Check Ledger entries during a posting process are likely to apply only to that specific function. If we are making modifications to a particular application area within Business Central, we may find functions that we can utilize, either as is or as models for our new functions.

There are also many functions within Business Central that are relatively general purpose. They either act on data that is common in many different situations, such as dates and addresses, or they perform processing tasks that are common to many situations, such as providing access to an external file. We will review a few such functions in detail, then list a number of others worth studying. If nothing else, these functions are useful as guides for showing you how such functions are used in Business Central. The various parameters in these explanations are named to assist with your learning, and aren't named the same as they are in the Business Central code (though all structures, data types, and other technical specifications match the Business Central code).

If we are using one of these functions, we must take care to clearly understand how it operates. In each case, we should study the function and test with it before assuming we adequately understand how it works. There is little or no documentation for most of these functions, so understanding their proper use is totally up to us. If we need customization, that must be done by making a copy of the target function and then modifying the copy.

Codeunit 358 – DateFilterCalc

This codeunit is a good example of how well-designed and well-written code has long term utility. Except for code changes that are required by Business Central structural changes, this codeunit has changed very little since it originated in Business Central (Navision) V3.00 in 2001. That doesn't mean it is out of date; it means it was well-thought out and complete from its beginning.

Codeunit 358 contains two functions we can use in our code to create filters based on the **Accounting Period Calendar**. The first is `CreateFiscalYearFilter`. If we are calling this from an object that has codeunit 358 defined as a global variable named `DateFilterCalc`, our call would use the following syntax:

```
DateFilterCalc,CreateFiscalYearFilter
  (Filter,Name,BaseDate,NextStep)
```

The calling parameters are `Filter` (text, length 30), `Name` (text, length 30), `BaseDate` (date), and `NextStep` (integer).

The second such function is `CreateAccountingPeriodFilter`, and has the following syntax:

```
DateFilterCalc.CreateAccountingPeriodFilter
  (Filter,Name,BaseDate,NextStep)
```

In the following code screenshot from page 151—`Customer Statistics`, we can see how Business Central calls these functions. Page 152—`Vendor Statistics`, page 223—`Resource Statistics`, and a number of other master table statistics pages also use this set of functions:

```
trigger OnAfterGetRecord()
var
    CostCalcMgt: Codeunit "Cost Calculation Management";
begin
    if CurrentDate <> WorkDate then begin
        CurrentDate := WorkDate;
        DateFilterCalc.CreateAccountingPeriodFilter(CustDateFilter[1],CustDateName[1],CurrentDate,0);
        DateFilterCalc.CreateFiscalYearFilter(CustDateFilter[2],CustDateName[2],CurrentDate,0);
        DateFilterCalc.CreateFiscalYearFilter(CustDateFilter[3],CustDateName[3],CurrentDate,-1);
    end;
```

As shown in the following code screenshot, Business Central uses the filters stored in the `CustDateFilter` array to constrain the calculation of a series of FlowFields for the `Customers Statistics` page:

```
for i := 1 to 4 do begin
  SetFilter("Date Filter",CustDateFilter[i]);
  CalcFields(
    "Sales (LCY)","Profit (LCY)","Inv. Discounts (LCY)","Inv. Amounts (LCY)","Pmt. Discounts (LCY)",
    "Pmt. Disc. Tolerance (LCY)","Pmt. Tolerance (LCY)",
    "Fin. Charge Memo Amounts (LCY)","Cr. Memo Amounts (LCY)","Payments (LCY)",
    "Reminder Amounts (LCY)","Refunds (LCY)","Other Amounts (LCY)");
```

When one of these functions is called, the `Filter` and `Name` parameters are updated within the function so that we can use them as `return` parameters, allowing the function to return a workable filter and a name for that filter. The filter is calculated from the `BaseDate` and `NextStep` we supply.

The returned filter is supplied back in the format of a range filter string, `'startdate..enddate'` (for example, `01/01/16..12/31/16`). If we call `CreateFiscalYearFilter`, the `Filter` parameter will be for the range of a fiscal year, as defined by the system's `Accounting Period` table. If we call `CreateAccountingPeriodFilter`, the `Filter` parameter will be for the range of a fiscal period, as defined by the same table.

The dates of the Period or Year filter returned are tied to the `BaseDate` parameter, which can be any legal date. The `NextStep` parameter says which period or year to use, depending on which function is called. A `NextStep=0` says to use the period or year containing the `BaseDate`, `NextStep=1` says to use the next period or year into the future, and `NextStep=-2` says to use the period or year before last (go back two periods or years).

The `Name` value that's returned is also derived from the `Accounting Period` table. If the call is to `CreateAccountingPeriodFilter`, then `Name` will contain the appropriate accounting period name. If the call is to `CreateFiscalYearFilter`, then `Name` will contain `'Fiscal Year yyyy'`, where `yyyy` will be the four-digit numeric year.

Codeunit 359 – Period Form Management

This codeunit contains three functions that can be used for date handling. These are `FindDate`, `NextDate`, and `CreatePeriodFormat`.

FindDate function

The description of the `FindDate` function is as follows:

- Calling parameters (`SearchString` (text, length 3), `Calendar` (date table), `PeriodType` (option, integer))
- Returns `DateFound` Boolean

The calling syntax for the `FindDate` function is as follows:

```
BooleanVariable := FindDate(SearchString,CalendarRec,PeriodType)
```

This function is often used in pages to assist with date calculation. The purpose of this function is to find a date in the virtual `Date` table based on the parameters that are passed. The search starts with an initial record in the `Calendar` table. If we pass in a record that has already been initialized by positioning the table at a date, that will be the base date; otherwise, the `Work Date` will be used.

The `PeriodType` is an options field with the option value choices of day, week, month, quarter, year, and accounting period. For ease of coding, we could call the function with the integer equivalent (0, 1, 2, 3, 4, 5), or set up our own equivalent `Option` variable. In general, it's a much better practice to set up an `Option` variable because the `Option` strings make the code self-documenting.

The `SearchString` allows us to pass in a logical control string containing =, >, <, <=, >=, and so on. `FindDate` will find the first date, starting with the initialized `Calendar` date, which satisfies the `SearchString` logic instruction and fits the `PeriodType` defined. For example, if the `PeriodType` is day, and the date 01/25/16 is used along with the `SearchString` of >, then the date 01/26/16 will be returned in the `Calendar`.

NextDate function

The description of the `NextDate` function is as follows:

- Calling parameters (`NextStep` (integer), `Calendar` (the `Date` table), `PeriodType` (`Option`, integer))
- Returns `Integer`

The calling syntax for the `NextDate` function is as follows:

```
IntegerVariable := NextDate(NextStep,CalendarRec,PeriodType)
```

`NextDate` will find the next date record in the `Calendar` table that satisfies the calling parameters. The `Calendar` and `PeriodType` calling parameters for `NextDate` have the same definition as they do for the `FindDate` function. However, for this function to be really useful, the `Calendar` must be initialized before calling `NextDate`. Otherwise, the function will calculate the appropriate next date from day 0. The `NextStep` parameter allows us to define the number of periods of `PeriodType` to move, so as to obtain the desired next date. For example, if we start with a `Calendar` table positioned on 01/25/16, a `PeriodType` of quarter (that is 3), and a `NextStep` of 2, the `NextDate` will move forward two quarters and return with `Calendar` focused on Quarter, 7/1/16 to 9/30/16.

CreatePeriodFormat function

The description of the `CreatePeriodFormat` function is as follows:

- Calling parameters (`PeriodType` (Option, integer), `Date` (date))
- Returns text, length 10

The calling syntax for the `CreatePeriodFormat` function is as follows:

```
FormattedDate := CreatePeriodFormat(PeriodType,DateData)
```

`CreatePeriodFormat` allows us to supply a date and specify which of its format options we want through the `PeriodType`. The function's return value is a ten-character formatted text value, for example, mm/dd/yy or ww/yyyy, mon/yyyy, qtr/yyyy, or yyyy.

Codeunit 365 – Format Address

The functions in the `Format Address` codeunit do the obvious—they format addresses in a variety of situations. The address data in any master record (Customer, Vendor, Sales Order Sell-to, Sales Order Ship-to, Employee, and so on) may contain embedded blank lines. For example, the Address 2 line may be empty. When we print out the address information on a document or report, it will look better if there are no blank lines. These functions take care of such tasks.

In addition, Business Central provides setup options for multiple formats of City—Post Code—County—Country combinations. The Format Address functions format addresses according to what was chosen in the setup, or was defined in the Countries/Regions page for different Postal areas.

There are over 60 data-specific functions in the `Format Address` codeunit. Each data-specific function allows us to pass a record parameter for the record containing the raw address data, such as a Customer record, a Vendor Record, a Sales Order, and so on, plus a parameter of a one-dimensional text array with eight elements of length up to 90 characters. Each function extracts the address data from its specific master record format and stores it in the array. The function then passes that data to a general-purpose function, which does the actual work of resequencing, according to the various setup rules, and compressing the data by removing blank lines.

The following code examples are of the function call format for the functions of `Company` and the Sales Ship-to addresses. In each case, `AddressArray` is Text, Length 90, and one-dimensional with eight elements:

```
"Format Address".Company(AddressArray,CompanyRec);
"Format Address". SalesHeaderSellTo (AddressArray,SalesHeaderRec);
```

The function's processed result is returned in the `AddressArray` parameter.

In addition to the data-specific functions in the `Format Address` codeunit, we can also directly utilize the more general-purpose functions contained there. If we add a new address structure as part of an enhancement, we may want to create our own data-specific address formatting function in our custom codeunit. However, we should design our function to call the general purpose functions that already exist (and are already debugged).

The primary general-purpose address formatting function (the one we are most likely to call directly) is `FormatAddr`. This is the function that does most of the work in this codeunit. The syntax for the `FormatAddr` function is as follows:

```
FormatAddr(AddressArray,Name,Name2,ContactName,Address1,Address2,
   City,PostCode,County,CountryCode)
```

The calling parameters of `AddressArray`, `Name`, `Name2`, and `ContactName` are all text, length 90. `Address1`, `Address2`, `City`, and `County` are all text, length 50. `PostCode` and `CountryCode` are data type code, length 20, and length 10, respectively.

Our data is passed into the function in the individual `Address` fields. The results are passed back in the `AddressArray` parameter for us to use.

There are two other functions in the `Format Address` codeunit that are often called directly. They are `FormatPostCodeCity` and `GeneratePostCodeCity`. The `FormatPostCodeCity` function serves the purpose of finding the applicable setup rule for `PostCode`, plus `City` plus `County` plus `Country` formatting. It then calls the `GeneratePostCodeCity` function, which does the actual formatting.

Codeunit 396 – NoSeriesManagement

Throughout Business Central, master records (for example Customer, Vendor, Item, and so on) and activity documents (Sales Order, Purchase Order, Warehouse Transfer Orders, and so on) are controlled by the unique identification number assigned to each one. This unique identification number is assigned through a call to a function within the NoSeriesManagement codeunit. That function is InitSeries. The calling format for InitSeries is as follows:

```
NoSeriesManagement.InitSeries(WhichNumberSeriesToUse,
LastDataRecNumberSeriesCode, SeriesDateToApply, NumberToUse,
NumberSeriesUsed)
```

The WhichNumberSeriesToUse parameter is generally defined on a Numbers Tab in the Setup record for the applicable application area. LastDataRecNumberSeriesCode tells the function what Number Series was used for the previous record in this table. The SeriesDateToApply parameter allows the function to assign ID numbers in a date-dependent fashion. NumberToUse and the NumberSeriesUsed are return parameters.

The following screenshot shows an example for **Table 18 Customer**:

```
trigger OnInsert()
begin
    if "No." = '' then begin
        SalesSetup.Get;
        SalesSetup.TestField("Customer Nos.");
        NoSeriesMgt.InitSeries(SalesSetup."Customer Nos.",xRec."No. Series",0D,"No.","No. Series");
    end;
```

The following screenshot shows a second example for **Table 36 Sales Header**. In this case, the call to NoSeriesMgt has been placed in a local function:

```
if not IsHandled then
    if "No." = '' then begin
        TestNoSeries;
        NoSeriesMgt.InitSeries(GetNoSeriesCode,xRec."No. Series","Posting Date","No.","No. Series");
    end;
```

With the exception of `GetNextNo` (used in assigning unique identifying numbers to each of a series of transactions) and, possibly, `TestManual` (used to test if manual numbering is allowed), we are not likely to use other functions in the `NoSeriesManagement` codeunit. The other functions are principally used either by the `InitSeries` function or other Business Central routines, whose job is to maintain number series control information and data.

There is also a Business Central Pattern for describing the use of number series in Business Central. It is entitled `No. Series` and can be found at `https://community.dynamics.com/nav/w/designpatterns/74.no-series`.

Function models to review and use

It is very helpful when creating new code to have a model that works and that we can study (or clone). This is especially true in Business Central, where there is little or no development documentation available for many of the different functions we would like to use. One of the more challenging aspects of learning to develop in the Business Central environment is learning how to handle issues in the Business Central way. Learning the Business Central way is very beneficial because then our code works better, is easier to maintain, and easier to upgrade. There is no better place to learn the strengths and subtle features of the product than to study the code written by the developers who are part of the inner circle of Business Central creation.

 If there is a choice, don't add custom functions to the standard Business Central codeunits. Well segregated customizations in clearly identified custom objects make both maintenance and upgrades easier. When we build functions modeled on Business Central functions, the new code should be in a customer licensed codeunit.

The following is a list of objects that contain functions we may find useful to use in our code or as models. We find these useful to study how it's done in Business Central ("it" obviously varies, depending on the function's purpose):

- **Codeunit 1—Application Management**: This is a library of utility functions that's widely used in the system
- **Codeunits 11, 12, 13, 21, 22, 23, 80, 81, 82, 90, 91, and 92**: These are the Posting sequences for Sales, Purchases, General Ledger, and Item Ledger, and they control the posting of journal data into the various ledgers
- **Codeunit 228—Test Report-Print**: Functions for printing Test Reports for user review prior to Posting data

- **Codeunit 229—Print Documents**: Functions for printing document formatted reports
- **Codeunits 397 and 400—Mail**: Functions for interfacing with Outlook and SMTP mail
- **Codeunit 408—Dimension Management**: Don't write your own; use these
- **Codeunit 419—File Management**: Functions including BLOB tasks, file uploading, and downloading between server and client systems
- **Codeunits 802**: Online Map interfacing
- **Codeunit 5054—Word Management**: Interfaces to Microsoft Word
- **Codeunit 5063—Archive Management**: Storing copies of processed documents
- **Codeunits 5300 through 5313**: More Outlook interfacing
- **Codeunits 5813 through 5819**: Undo functions
- **Codeunit 6224**: XML DOM Management for XML structure handling
- **Table 330—Currency Exchange Rate**: Contains some of the key currency conversion functions
- **Table 370—Excel Buffer**: Excel interfacing
- **Page 344—Navigate**: Home of the unique and powerful Navigate feature

Management codeunits

There are over 150 codeunits with the word `Management` (or the abbreviation `Mgt`) as part of their description name (filter the codeunit names using `*Management*|*Mgt*` – don't forget that such a filter is case-sensitive). Each of these codeunits contains functions whose purpose is the management of some specific aspect of Business Central data. Many are specific to a very narrow range of data. Some are more general because they contain functions we can reuse in another application area (for example, codeunit 396—`NoSeriesManagement`).

When we are working on an enhancement in a particular functional area, it is extremely important to check the Management codeunits that are utilized in that area. We may be able to use some existing standard functions directly. This will have the benefit of reducing the code we have to create and debug. Of course, when a new version is released, we will have to check to see if the functions on which we relied have changed in a way that affects our code.

If we can't use the existing material as is, we may find functions we can use as models for tasks in the area of our enhancement. And, even if that is not true, by researching and studying the existing code, you will learn more about how data is structured and processed in the flow of the standard Business Central system.

Multi-language system

The Business Central system is designed as a multi-language system, meaning it can interface with users in many languages. The base product is distributed with American English as the primary language, but each local version comes with one or more other languages ready for use. Because the system can be set up to operate from a single database, displaying user interfaces in several different languages, Business Central is particularly suitable for firms operating from a central system serving users in multiple countries. Business Central is used by businesses all over the world, operating in dozens of different languages. It is important to note that, when the application language is changed, it has no effect on the data in the database. The data is not multi-language unless we provide that functionality, by means of our own enhancements or data structure.

The basic elements that support the multi-language feature include the following:

- Multi-language captioning properties (for example, `CaptionML`) that support definitions of alternative language captions for all the fields, action labels, titles, and so on
- The Text Constants property, `ConstantValueML`, which is a supporting definition of alternative language messages

 For Business Central, Microsoft switched to translations using XLIFF files. At the time of publishing this book there is no consensus on efficiently managing these files.

Before embarking on an effort to create multi-language enabled modifications, review all the available documentation on this topic (search Help on the word language). It's wise to do some small scale testing to ensure that you understand what is required, and that your approach will work (such testing is required for any significant enhancement).

More information on translations can be found at `https://docs.microsoft.com/en-us/dynamics365/business-central/dev-itpro/developer/devenv-work-with-translation-files`.

Multi-currency system

Business Central was one of the first ERP systems to fully implement a multi-currency system. Transactions can start in one currency and finish in another. For example, we can create an order in US dollars and accept payment for the invoice in Euros or Bitcoin or Yen. For this reason, where there are money values, they are generally stored in the **local currency** (referenced as **LCY**), as defined in the setup. There is a set of currency conversion tools built into the applications, and there are standard (by practice) code structures to support and utilize those tools. Two examples of code segments from the `Sales Line` table illustrating the handling of money fields, are as follows:

```
GetSalesHeader;
if SalesHeader."Currency Code" <> '' then begin
  Currency.TestField("Unit-Amount Rounding Precision");
  "Unit Cost" :=
    Round(                                              I
      CurrExchRate.ExchangeAmLLCYToFCY(
        GetDate,SalesHeader."Currency Code",
        "Unit Cost (LCY)",SalesHeader."Currency Factor"),
      Currency."Unit-Amount Rounding Precision")
end else
  "Unit Cost" := "Unit Cost (LCY)";
```

In both cases, there's a function call to `ROUND` and use of the currency-specific `Currency.`
`"Amount Rounding Precision"` control value, as shown in the following code snippet
screenshot:

```
"Line Discount Amount" :=
  Round(
    Round(Quantity * "Unit Price",Currency."Amount Rounding Precision") *
    "Line Discount %" / 100,Currency."Amount Rounding Precision");
```

As we can see, before creating any modification that has money fields, we must familiarize ourselves with the Business Central currency conversion feature, the code that supports it, and the related setups. A good place to start is the AL code in table 37—`Sales Line`, table 39—`Purchase Line`, and table 330—`Currency Exchange Rate`.

Navigate

Navigate is an underappreciated tool for both the user and the developer. Our focus here is on its value to the developer. Navigate (page 344) finds and displays the counts and types of all the associated entries for a particular posting transaction. The term that's associated, in this case, is defined as those entries having the same Document Number and Posting Date. This is a handy tool for the developer as it can show the results of posting activity and provide the tools to drill into the detail of all those results. If we add new transactions and ledgers as part of an enhancement, our Navigate function should be enhanced to cover them, too.

Navigate can be called from the **Navigate** action, which appears in a number of places in the **Departments Tasks** menu and Role Center ribbons. From anywhere within Business Central, the easiest way to find Navigate is to type the word into the **Search** box (see the following screenshot):

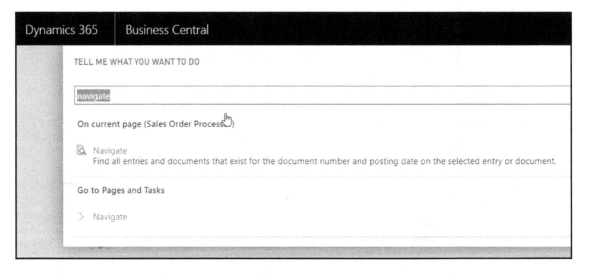

If we invoke the **Navigate** page using the menu action item, we must enter the **Posting Date** and **Document Number** for the entries we wish to find. Alternatively, we can enter a **Business Contact Type** (Vendor or Customer), a **Business Contact No.** (Vendor No. or Customer No.) and, optionally, an **External Document No.** There are occasions when this option is useful, but the **Posting Date** and **Document No.** option is more frequently useful.

Instead of seeking out a **Navigate** page and entering the critical data fields, it is much easier to call Navigate from a **Navigate** action on a page showing data. In this case, we can just highlight a record and click on **Navigate** to search for all the related entries. In the following example, a Posted Invoice is highlighted:

After clicking the **Navigate** action, the page will pop up filled in, as shown in the following screenshot:

Had we accessed the **Navigate** page through one of the menu entries we found through **Search**, we would have filled in the **Document No.** and **Posting Date** fields and clicked on **Find**. As we can see here, the **Navigate** page shows a list of related, posted entries (one of which will include the entry we highlighted when we invoked the Navigate function). If we highlight one of the lines in the **Related Entries** list, then click on the **Show Related Entries** icon at the top of the page, we will see an appropriately formatted display of the chosen entries.

If we highlight the **G/L Entry** table entries and click on **Show Related Entries**, we will see a result as shown in the following screenshot. Note that all the G/L Entry tables are displayed for the same **Posting Date** and **Document No.**, matching those specified at the top of the **Navigate** page:

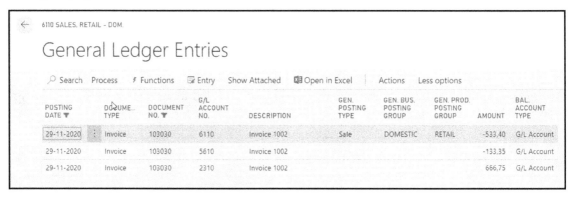

Modifying for Navigate

If our modification creates a new table that will contain posted data and the records contain both **Document No.** and **Posting Date** fields, we can include this new table in the **Navigate** function.

The AL Code for Navigate functionality based on **Posting Date** and **Document No.** is found in the `FindRecords` and `FindExtRecords` functions of page 344—**Navigate**. The following screenshot shows the segment of the Navigate `CASE` statement code for the `CheckLedgerEntry` table:

```
if CostEntry.ReadPermission then begin
  CostEntry.Reset;
  CostEntry.SetCurrentKey("Document No.","Posting Date");
  CostEntry.SetFilter("Document No.",DocNoFilter);
  CostEntry.SetFilter("Posting Date",PostingDateFilter);
  InsertIntoDocEntry(Rec,DATABASE::"Cost Entry",0,CostEntry.TableCaption,CostEntry.Count);
end;
OnAfterNavigateFindRecords(Rec,DocNoFilter,PostingDateFilter);
```

The code checks READPERMISSION. If that permission is enabled for this table, then the appropriate filtering is applied. Next, there is a call to the InsertIntoDocEntry function, which fills in the temporary table that is displayed in the **Navigate** page. If we wish to add a new table to the Navigate function, we must replicate this functionality for our new table.

In addition, we must add the code that will call up the appropriate page to display the records that Navigate finds. This code should be subscribing to the OnAfterNavigateFindRecords event publisher of the **Navigate** page, modeling on the applicable section of code in this function (that is, choose the code set that best fits our new tables). Making a change like this, when appropriate, will not only provide a powerful tool for our users, but also provide a powerful tool for us as developers.

Debugging in Business Central

In general, the processes and tools we use for debugging can serve multiple purposes. The most immediate purpose is always that of identifying the causes of errors and then resolving those errors. There are two categories of production errors, which may also occur during development, and **Business Central's debugger** module is very well-suited to addressing both of these. The Business Central debugger smoothly integrates developing in the Development Environment and testing in the **Role Tailored Client** (RTC).

The first category is the type that causes an error condition that terminates processing. In this case, the immediate goal is to find the cause and fix it as quickly as possible. The debugger is an excellent tool for this purpose. The second category is the type that, while running to completion successfully, gives erroneous results.

We often find that debugging techniques can be used to help us better understand how Business Central processes work. We may be working on the design of (or determination of the need for) a modification, or we may simply want to learn more about how a particular function is used or outcome is accomplished in the standard Business Central routines. It would be more appropriate to call these efforts analysis or self-education rather than debugging, even though the processes we use to dissect the code and view what it's doing are very similar. In the course of these efforts, less sophisticated approaches are sometimes useful in understanding what's going on. We'll quickly review some of those alternate approaches before studying the use of the Business Central debugger.

Dialog function debugging techniques

Sometimes, the simpler methods are more productive than the more sophisticated tools, because we can set up and test quickly, resolve the issue (or answer a question), and move on. All the simpler methods involve using one of the AL DIALOG functions, such as MESSAGE, CONFIRM, DIALOG, or ERROR. All of these have the advantage of working well in the RTC environment. However, we should remember that none of these techniques conform to the Testing Best Practices in the Help topic: *Testing the Application*. These should only be used when a quick one-time approach is needed, or when recommended testing practices simply won't easily provide the information needed and one of these techniques will do so.

Debugging with MESSAGE and CONFIRM

The simplest debug method is to insert MESSAGE statements at key points in our logic. This is very simple and, if structured properly, provides us with a simple trace of the code logic path. We can number our messages to differentiate them and display any data (in small amounts) as part of a message, like so:

```
MESSAGE('This is Test 4 for %1',Customer."No.");
```

A big disadvantage is that MESSAGE statements do not display until processing either terminates or is interrupted for user interaction. Also, if you create a situation that generates hundreds of messages, you will find it quite painful to click through them individually at process termination.

If we force a user interaction at some point, then our accumulated messages will appear prior to the interaction. The simplest way to force user interaction is to issue a CONFIRM message in the format, as follows:

```
IF CONFIRM ('Test 1',TRUE) THEN;
```

If we want to do a simple trace but want every message to be displayed as it is generated (that is, have the tracking process move at a very measured pace), we could use CONFIRM statements for all the messages. The operator must then respond to each one before our program will move on but, sometimes, that is what we want. However, if we make the mistake of creating the situation where hundreds of messages are generated, the operator will have to respond to each one individually in what could be a very time-consuming and inefficient process.

Debugging with DIALOG

Another tool that is useful for progress tracking is the DIALOG function. DIALOG is usually set up to display a window with a small number of variable values. As processing progresses, the values are displayed in real time. The following are a few ways we can use this:

- Simply tracking progress of processing through a volume of data. This is the same reason we would provide a DIALOG display for the benefit of the user. The act of displaying slows down processing somewhat, so we may want to update the DIALOG display occasionally, not on every record.
- Displaying indicators when processing reaches certain stages. This can be used as a very basic trace with the indicators showing the path taken, so we may gauge the relative speed of progress through several steps.
- We might have a six-step process to analyze. We could define six tracking variables and display all of them in the DIALOG. We would initialize each variable with values dependent on what we are tracking, such as A1, B2000, C300000, and so on. At each process step, update and display the current state of one or all of the variables. This can be a very helpful guide for how our process is operating. To slow things down, we could put a SLEEP(100) or SLEEP(500) after the DIALOG statement (the number is milliseconds of delay).

Debugging with text output

We can build a very handy debugging tool by outputting the values of critical variables or other informative indicators of progress, either to an external text file or to a table that's been created for this purpose. We need to either do this in single user mode or make it multi-user by including the USER ID on every entry.

This technique allows us to run a considerable volume of test data through the system, tracking some important elements while collecting data on the variable values, progress through various sections of code, and so on. We can even timestamp our output records so that we can use this method to look for processing speed problems.

Following the test run, we can analyze the results of our test more quickly than if we were using displayed information. We can focus on just the items that appear most informative and ignore the rest. This type of debugging is fairly easy to set up and to refine, as we identify the variables or code segments of most interest. We can combine this approach with the following approach using the ERROR statement, if we output to an external text file, then close it before invoking the ERROR statement so that its contents are retained following the termination of the test run.

Debugging with ERROR

One of the challenges of testing is maintaining repeatability. Quite often, we need to test several times using the same data, but the test changes the data. If we have a small database, we can always back up the database and start with a fresh copy each time. However, that can be inefficient and, if the database is large, impractical. If we are using the built-in Business Central Test functions, we can roll back any database changes so the tests are totally repeatable. Another alternative is to conclude our test with an ERROR function to test and retest with exactly the same data.

The ERROR function forces a runtime error status, which means the database is not updated (it is rolled back to the status at the beginning of the process). This works well when our debugging information is provided by using the debugger or any of the DIALOG functions we just mentioned prior to the execution of the ERROR function. If we are using MESSAGE to generate debugging information, we could execute a CONFIRM immediately prior to the ERROR statement and be assured that all of the messages are displayed. Obviously, this method won't work well when our testing validation is dependent on checking results using Navigate or our test is a multi-step process, such as order entry, review, and posting. In this latter case, only use of the built-in Test functions (creating test runner codeunits, and so on) will be adequate. However, in some situations, use of the ERROR function is a very handy technique for repeating a test with minimal effort.

When testing just the posting of an item, it often works well to place the test-concluding ERROR function just before the point in the applicable Posting codeunit where the process would otherwise be completed successfully. For the Rollback function to be effective, we must make sure there aren't any COMMIT statements included in the range of the code being tested.

The Business Central debugger

Debugging is the process of finding and correcting errors. Business Central uses the debugger from Visual Studio Code. The debugger can only be activated from Visual Studio Code.

Activating the debugger

Activating the debugger from the Development Environment is a simple matter of clicking on **Debug** | **Start Debugging** (or *Shift + Ctrl + F5*). The initial page that displays when the debugger is activated will look as follows (typically, with each session having a different **User ID**).

When we click on **Start Debugging**, an empty debugger page will open, awaiting the event that will cause a break in processing and the subsequent display of code detail (**Variables**), watched variables (**Watches**), and the **Call Stack**:

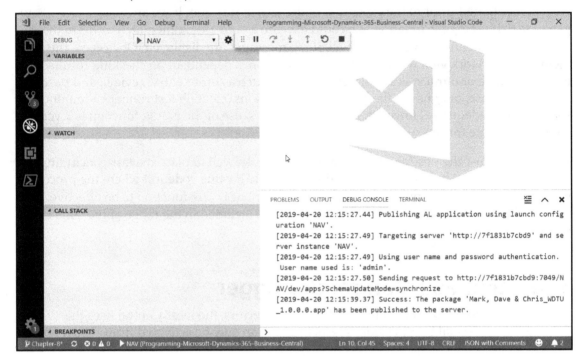

Creating break events

Once the debugger is activated and attached to a session, a break event must occur to cause the debug trace and associated data display to begin. Break events include (but are not limited to) the following:

- An error occurs that would cause object execution to be terminated
- A previously set breakpoint is reached during processing
- The record is read when the **Break on Record Write** break rule is active
- The Pause icon is clicked in the popup of the debugger page

Of the preceding events, the two most common methods of starting up a debug trace are the first two, an error, or reaching a previously set breakpoint. If, for example, an error condition is discovered in an operating object, the debugging process can be initiated by doing the following:

- Activating the debugger
- Running the process where the error occurs

When the error occurs, the page parts (**Variables**, **Watches**, and **Call Stack**) in the debug window will be populated, and we can proceed to investigate variable values, review code, and so forth.

Breakpoints are stopping points in an object that was set by the developer. Breakpoints can be set from Development Environment, in the **Debug | Toggle Breakpoint** option.

Active breakpoints are represented in code by a solid circle. An example is shown in the following code screenshot:

```
●    8        FromFileName  = XMLfile.Name;
     9        ToFileName := 'RadioShowExport.xml';
    10        XMLfile.Close();|
```

The debugger window

When viewing AL code in a Designer, breakpoints can be set, disabled, or removed by pressing the *F9* key. When viewing AL code in the Code window of the debugger, breakpoints can only be set or removed by pressing the *F9* key or clicking on the Toggle icon. Other debugger breakpoint controls are shown in the following screenshot:

The following are the ribbon actions that you can use:

- **Pause**: This breaks at the next statement
- **Step Over**: This is designed to execute a function without stopping, then break
- **Step Into**: This is designed to trace into a function
- **Step Out**: This is designed to complete the current function without stopping, and then break.

- **Restart**: Stop current session and republish the extension
- **Stop**: This stops the current activity but leaves the debugging session active

VARIABLES displays the Debugger Variable List where we can examine the status of all variables that are in scope. Additional variables can be added to the Watch list here, as shown in the following screenshot:

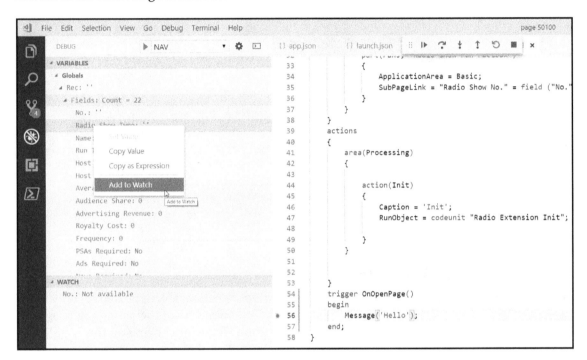

 Variables can be removed from the Watch list in the Debugger Watches page.

Visual Studio Code test-driven development

Business Central includes the enhanced AL Testability feature set, that's designed to support AL test-driven development. **Test-driven development** is an approach where the application tests are defined prior to the development of the application code. In an ideal situation, the code supporting application tests is written prior to, or at least at the same time as, when the code implementing the target application function is written.

Advantages of test-driven development include the following:

- Designing testing processes in conjunction with functional design
- Finding bugs early
- Preventing bugs reaching production
- Enabling regression testing, which prevents changes from introducing new bugs into previously validated routines

The AL Testability feature provides test-specific types of codeunits: test codeunits and test running codeunits. Test codeunits contain test methods, UI handlers, and AL code to support Test methods, including the `AssertError` function. Test runner codeunits are used to invoke Test codeunits for test execution management, automation, and integration. Test runner codeunits have two special triggers, each of which run in separate transactions so that the test execution state and results can be tracked. The two triggers are as follows:

- `OnBeforeTestRun`: This is called before each test. It allows you to define, via a Boolean, whether or not the test should be executed.
- `OnAfterTestRun`: This is called when each test completes and the test results are available. It allows the test results to be logged, or otherwise processed via AL code.

Among the ultimate goals of the AL Testability feature are the following:

- The ability to run suites of application tests both in automated mode and in regression tests:
    - **Automated** means that a defined series of tests could be run and the results recorded, all without user intervention
    - **Regression testing** means that the test can be run repeatedly as part of a new testing pass to make sure that the features that were previously tested are still in working order
- The ability to design tests in an atomic way, matching the granularity of the application code. In this way, the test functions can be focused and simplified. This allows for relatively easy construction of a suite of tests and, in some cases, reuse of test codeunits (or at least reuse of the structure of previously created test codeunits).
- The ability to develop and run the test and test runner codeunits within the familiar Visual Studio Code environment. The code for developing these testing codeunits is AL.

- The `TestIsolation` property of test runner codeunits allow tests to be run, then all database changes are rolled back so that no changes are committed. After a test series in this mode, the database is the same after the test as it was before the test.
- Once the testing codeunits have been developed, the actual testing process should be simple and fast in order to run and evaluate results.

Both positive and negative testing is supported. **Positive testing** looks for a specific result, a correct answer. **Negative testing** checks that errors are presented when expected, especially when data or parameters are out of range. The testing structure is designed to support the logging of test results, both failures and success, to tables for review, reporting, and analysis.

A function property defines functions within test codeunits to be `Test`, `Handler`, or `Normal`. Another function property, `TestMethodType`, allows the definition of a variety of Test Function types to be defined. `TestMethodType` property options include the following handlers, which are designed to handle user interface events without the need for a user to intervene:

- **MessageHandler**: This handles the `MESSAGE` statement
- **ConfirmHandler**: This handles `CONFIRM` dialogs
- **StrMenuHandler**: This handles `STRMENU` menu dialogs
- **PageHandler**: This handles pages that are not run modally
- **ModalPageHandler**: This handles pages that are run modally
- **ReportHandler**: This handles reports
- **RequestPagetHandler**: This handles the Request Page of a specific Report
- **FilterPageHandler**: This handles Filter Pages generated by a `FilterPageBuilder` data type
- **HyperlinkHandler**: This handles hyperlinks that are passed to the `HYPERLINK` function
- **SendNotificationHandler**: This handles the new Business Central Notifications
- **RecallNotificationHandler**: This handles the recall of the new Business Central Notifications

The Visual Studio Code test-driven development approach should proceed as follows:

1. Define an application function specification
2. Define the application technical specification
3. Define the testing technical specification, including both Positive and Negative tests
4. Develop test and test running codeunits (frequently; only one or a few test running codeunits will be required)
5. Develop Application objects
6. As soon as possible, run Application object tests by means of the test running codeunits, and log test results for historical and analytical purposes
7. Continue the development-testing cycle, updating the tests and the application as appropriate throughout the process
8. At the end of the successful completion of development and testing, retain all the test and test running codeunits for use in regression testing the next time the application must be modified or upgraded

With the latest product media, Microsoft released a full set of approximately 16,000 regression tests that were written by Microsoft for Business Central 2017 using the Business Central Testability tools. These are the tests that the Business Central product developers used to validate their work. The number of tests that apply to a specific situation depends on the local version and specific features involved. Make sure your license is updated, too.

Included are the regression tests and various tools to manage and execute tests that have been built on top of the testability features that were released for Microsoft Dynamics Business Central. Also included is a coverage tool and guidance documentation to create our own tests and integrate those with the Microsoft provided tests. This allows us to do full regression testing for large modifications and ISV solutions.

Other interfaces

Some Business Central systems must communicate with other software or even with hardware. Sometimes, that communication is Inside-Out (that is, initiated by Business Central) and sometimes, it is Outside-In (that is, initiated by the outside connection). It's not unusual for system-to-system communications to be a two-way street, a meeting of peers. To supply, receive, or exchange information with other systems (hardware or software), we will need at least a basic understanding of the interface tools that are part of Business Central.

Because of Business Central's unique data structures and the critical business logic embedded therein, it is very risky for an external system to access Business Central data directly via SQL Server without using AL-based routines as an intermediary.

Business Central has a number of methods of interfacing with the world outside its database. We will review those very briefly here. To learn more about these, we should begin by reviewing the applicable material in the online Developer and IT Pro Help material, plus any documentation available with the software distribution. We should also study sample code, especially that in the standard system, as represented by the **CRONUS Demonstration Database**. And, of course, we should take advantage of any other resources that are available, including the Business Central-oriented internet forums and blogs.

Client Add-ins

The Business Central Client Add-in API (also known as Client Extensibility) provides the capability to extend the client through the integration of external non-Business Central controls. The Client Add-in API uses .NET interfaces as the binding mechanism between a control add-in and the Business Central framework. Different interfaces and base classes are available to use, or a custom interface can be created. Controls can be designed to raise events that call on the `OnControlAddin` trigger on the page field control that hosts the add-in. They can also add events and methods that can be called from within AL.

Contrary to the limitations on other integration options, Client add-ins can be graphical and appear on the client display as part of, or mingled with, native Business Central controls. The following are a few simple examples of how Client add-ins might be used to extend client UI behavior:

- A Business Central text control that looks normal but offers a special behavior, but when the user double-clicks on it, the field's contents will display in a popup screen, accompanied by other related information or even a graphical display.
- A dashboard made up of several dials or gauges showing the percentage of chosen resources relative to target limits or goals. The dials are defined to support click and drill into the underlying Business Central detail data.
- An integrated sales call mapping function displays customer locations on a map and creates a sequenced call list with pertinent sales data from the Business Central database.

- Interactive visualization of a workflow or flow of goods in a process, showing the number of entries at each stage, and supports filtering to display selected sets of entries.
- Entry and storage of a written document signature on a touch screen.

Client Add-in comments

To take advantage of the Client Add-in capabilities, we will need to develop minimal JavaScript programming skills. Care will have to be taken when designing add-ins that their user interface style complements, rather than clashes with, the UI standards of the Business Central client.

Client Add-ins are a major extension of the Dynamics Business Central system. This feature allows ISVs to create and sell libraries of new controls and new control-based micro-applications. It allows vertically focused partners to create versions of Business Central that are much more tailored to their specific industries. This feature allows for the integration of third-party products, software, and hardware, at an entirely new level.

The Client add-in feature is very powerful. If you learn how to use it, you will have another flexible tool in your kit, and your users will benefit from it.

Business Central development projects – general guidance

Now that we understand the basic workings of the Business Central Visual Studio Code development environment and AL, we'll review the process of software design for Business Central enhancements and modifications.

When we start a new project, the goals and constraints for the project must be defined. The degree to which we meet these will determine our success. Some examples are follows:

- What are the functional requirements and what flexibility exists within these?
- What are the user interface standards?
- What are the coding standards?
- What are the calendar and financial budgets?
- What existing capabilities within Business Central will be used?

Knowledge is key

Designing for Business Central requires more forethought and knowledge of the operating details of the application than was needed with traditional models of ERP systems. As we have seen, Business Central has unique data structure tools (SIFT and FlowFields), quite a number of Business Central-specific functions that make it easier to program business applications, and a software data structure (journal, ledger, and so on) that is inherently an accounting data structure. The learning curve to become an expert in the way Business Central works is not easy. Business Central has a unique structure, and the primary documentation from Microsoft is limited to the embedded Help, which improves with every release of the product. The Business Central books published by Packt can be of great help, as are the Business Central Development Team blogs, the blogs from various Business Central experts around the world, and the Business Central forums that were mentioned earlier.

Data-focused design

Any new application design must begin with certain basic analysis and design tasks. This is just as applicable whether our design is for new functionality to be integrated into Business Central or is for an enhancement/expansion of existing Business Central capabilities.

First, determine what underlying data is required. What will it take to construct the information the users need to see? What level of detail and in what structural format must the data be stored so that it may be quickly and completely retrieved? Once we have defined the inputs that are required, we must identify the sources of this material. Some may be input manually, some may be forwarded from other systems, some may be derived from historical accumulations of data, and some will be derived from combinations of all these, and more. In any case, every component of the information needed must have a clearly defined point of origin, schedule of arrival, and format.

Defining the required data views

Define how the data should be presented by addressing the following questions:

- How does it need to be "sliced and diced"?
- What levels of detail and summary are required?
- What sequences and segmentations are required?

- What visual formats will be used?
- What media will be used?
- Will the users be local or remote?

Ultimately, many other issues also need to be considered in the full design, including user interface specifications, data and access security, accounting standards and controls, and so on. Because there are a wide variety of tools available to extract and manipulate Business Central data, we can start relatively simply and expand as appropriate later. The most important thing is to assure that we have all the critical data elements identified and then captured.

Designing the data tables

Data table definition includes the data fields, the keys to control the sequence of data access and to ensure rapid processing, frequently used totals (which are likely to be set up as SumIndex fields), references to lookup tables for allowed values, and relationships to other primary data tables. We will not only need to do a good job of designing the primary tables, but also all those supporting tables containing lookup and setup data. When integrating a customization, we must consider the effects of the new components on the existing processing, as well as how the existing processing ties into our new work. These connections are often the finishing touch that makes the new functionality operate in a truly seamlessly integrated fashion with the original system.

Designing the user data access interface

The following are some of the principle design issues that need to be considered:

- Design the pages and reports to be used to display or interrogate the data.
- Define what keys are to be used or available to the users (though the SQL Server database supports sorting data without predefined Business Central AL keys).
- Define what fields will be allowed to be visible, what the totaling fields are, how the totaling will be accomplished (for example, FlowFields or on-the-fly processing), and what dynamic display options will be available.
- Define what type of filtering will be needed. Some filtering needs may be beyond the ability of the built-in filtering function and may require auxiliary code functions.

- Determine whether external data analysis tools will be needed and will therefore need to be interfaced.
- Design considerations at this stage often result in returning to the previous data structure definition stage to add additional data fields, keys, SIFT fields, or references to other tables.

Designing the data validation

Define exactly how the data must be validated before it is accepted upon entry into a table. There are likely to be multiple levels of validation. There will be a minimum level, which defines the minimum set of information required before a new record is accepted.

Subsequent levels of validation may exist for particular subsets of data, which, in turn, are tied to specific optional uses of the table. For example, in the base Business Central system, if the manufacturing functionality is not being used, the manufacturing-related fields in the Item Master table do not need to be filled in. However, if they are filled in, they must satisfy certain validation criteria.

As we mentioned earlier, the sum total of all the validations that are applied to data when it is entered into a table may not be sufficient to completely validate the data. Depending on the use of the data, there may be additional validations being performed during processing, reporting, or inquiries.

Data design review and revision

Perform these three steps (table design, user access, data validation) for the permanent data (Masters and Ledgers) and then for the transactions (Journals). Once all of the supporting tables and references have been defined for the permanent data tables, there are not likely to be many new definitions required for the Journal tables. If any significant new supporting tables or new table relationships are identified during the design of Journal tables, we should go back and reexamine the earlier definitions. Why? Because there is a high likelihood that this new requirement should have been defined for the permanent data and was overlooked.

Designing the Posting processes

First, define the final data validations, and then define and design all the ledger and auxiliary tables (for example, Registers, Posted Document tables, and so on). At this point, we are determining what the permanent content of the posted data will be. If we identify any new supporting table or table reference requirements at this point, we should go back to the first step to make sure that this requirement didn't need to be in the design definition.

Whatever variations in data are permitted to be posted, they must be acceptable in the final, permanent instance of the data. Any information or relationships that are necessary in the final posted data must be ensured to be present before posting is allowed to proceed.

Part of the posting design is to determine whether data records will be accepted or rejected individually or in complete batches. If the latter, we must define what constitutes a batch; if the former, it is likely that the makeup of a posting batch will be flexible.

Designing the supporting processes

Design the processes that are necessary to validate, process, extract, and format data for the desired output. In earlier steps, these processes can be defined as "black boxes" with specified inputs and required outputs, but without overdue regard for the details of the internal processes. This allows us to work on the several preceding definitions and design steps without being sidetracked into the inner workings of the output-related processes.

These processes are the cogs and gears of the functional application. They are necessary, but often not pretty. By leaving the design of these processes in the application design as late as possible, we increase the likelihood that we will be able to create common routines and standardize how similar tasks are handled across a variety of parent processes. At this point, we may identify opportunities or requirements for improvement in material that was defined in a previous design step. In that case, we should return to that step relative to the newly identified issue. In turn, we should also review the effect of such changes for each subsequent step's area of focus.

Double-check everything

Lastly, review all the defined reference, setup, and other control tables to make sure that the primary tables and all defined processes have all the information available when needed. This is a final design quality control step.

It is important to realize that returning to a previous step to address a previously unidentified issue is not a failure of the process; it is a success. An appropriate quote that's used in one form or another by construction people, the world over, is *Measure twice, cut once*. It is much cheaper and more efficient (and less painful) to find and fix design issues during the design phase rather than after the system is in testing or, worse yet, in production.

Designing for efficiency

Whenever we are designing a new modification, we will not only need to design to address the defined needs, but also to provide a solution that processes efficiently. An inefficient solution carries unnecessary ongoing costs. Many of the things that we can do to design an efficient solution are relatively simple:

- Properly configure system and workstation software (often overlooked)
- Make sure networks can handle the expected load (with capacity to spare)
- Have enough server memory to avoid using virtual memory, since virtual memory = disk
- Most of all, do everything reasonable to minimize disk I/O

Disk I/O

The slowest thing in any computer system is the disk I/O. Disk I/O almost always takes more time than any other system processing activity. When we begin concentrating our design efforts on efficiency, our focus first should be on minimizing disk I/O.

The most critical elements are the design of the keys, the number of keys, the design of the SIFT fields, the number of SIFT fields, the design of the filters, and the frequency of access of data (especially FlowFields). If our system will have five or ten users processing a few thousand order lines per day, and is not heavily modified, we probably won't have much trouble. However, if we are installing a system with one or more of the following attributes (any of which can have a significant effect on the amount of disk I/O), we will need to be very careful with our design and implementation:

- Large concurrent user count
- High transaction volumes, especially in data being Posted
- Large stored data volumes, especially resulting from customizations or setup option choices

- Significant modifications
- Very complex business rules

Locking

One important aspect of the design of an integrated system such as Business Central, that is often overlooked until it rears its ugly head after the system goes into production, is the issue of **locking**. Locking occurs when one process has control of a data element, record, or group of records (in other words, part or all of a table) for the purpose of updating the data within the range of the locked data and, at the same time, another process requests the use of some portion of that data but finds it to be locked by the first process.

If a deadlock occurs, there is a serious design flaw wherein each process has data locked that the other process needs, and neither process can proceed. One of our responsibilities as developers or implementers is to minimize locking problems and eliminate any deadlocks.

Locking interference between processes in an asynchronous processing environment is inevitable. There will always be points in the system where one process instance locks out another one momentarily. The secret to success is to minimize the frequency of these and the time length of each lock. Locking becomes a problem when the locks are held too long and the other locked out processes are unreasonably delayed.

You may be wondering, what is an unreasonable delay? For the most part, a delay becomes unreasonable when the users can tell that it's happening. If the users see stopped processes or experience counter-intuitive processing time lengths (that is, a process that seems like it should take 10 seconds actually takes two minutes), then the delays will seem unreasonable. Of course, the ultimate unreasonable delay is the one that does not allow the required work to get done in the available time.

The obvious question is, how can we avoid locking problems? The best solution is simply to speed up processing. That will reduce the number of lock conflicts that arise. Important recommendations for improving processing speed include the following:

- Restricting the number of active keys, especially on the SQL Server
- Restricting the number of active SIFT fields, eliminating them when feasible
- Carefully reviewing the keys, not necessarily using the **factory default** options
- Making sure that all disk access code is SQL Server optimized

Some additional steps that can be taken to minimize locking problems are as follows:

- Always process tables in the same relative order
- When a common set of tables will be accessed and updated, lock a standard master table first (for example, when working on orders, always lock the `Order Header` table first)
- Shift long-running processes to off-hours or even separate databases

In special cases, the following techniques can be used (if done very, very carefully):

- Process data in small quantities (for example, process 10 records or one order, then `COMMIT`, which releases the lock). This approach should be very cautiously applied.
- In long process loops, process a `SLEEP` command in combination with an appropriate `COMMIT` command to allow other processes to gain control (see the preceding caution).

Refer to the documentation with the system distribution in the Business Central forums.

Updating and upgrading

You must be able to differentiate between updating a system and upgrading a system. In general, most of the Business Central development work we will do is modifying individual Business Central systems to provide tailored functions for end user firms. Some of those modifications will be created by developers as part of an initial system configuration and implementation before the Business Central system is in production use. Other such modifications will be targeted at a system that is in day-to-day production to bring the system up to date with changes in business process or external requirements. We'll refer to these system changes as updating.

Upgrading is when we implement a new version of the base AL application code distributed by Microsoft and port all the previously existing modifications into that new version. First, we'll discuss updating, and then we'll discuss upgrading.

Design for updating

Any time we are updating a production system by applying modifications to it, a considerable amount of care is required. Many of the disciplines that should be followed in such an instance are the same for a Business Central system as for any other production application system. However, some disciplines are specific to Business Central and the Visual Studio Code environment.

Increasing the importance of designing for ease of updating is Microsoft's process of providing Business Central updates on a frequent basis so that systems can be kept more up to date with fixes and minor feature enhancements. Keeping up with these Microsoft-provided updates is especially important for multi-tenant systems running in the cloud, that is, systems serving multiple unrelated customers with the software and databases being resident on internet-based server systems.

Customization project recommendations

Even though there are new tools to help us update our Business Central systems, we should still follow good practices in our modification designs and the processes of applying updates. Some of these recommendations may seem obvious. This would be a measure of our personal store of experience and our own common sense. Even so, it is surprising the number of projects that go sour because one (or many) of the following are not considered in the process of developing modifications:

- One modification at a time
- Design thoroughly before coding
- Design the testing in parallel with the modification
- Use the AL Testability feature extensively
- Multi-stage testing:
    - Cronus for individual objects
    - Special test database for functional tests
    - Copy of production database for final testing as appropriate
    - Setups and implementation
- Testing full features:
    - User interface tests
    - System load tests
    - User Training
- Document and deliver in a predefined, organized manner
- Follow up, wrap up, and move on

One change at a time

It is important to make changes to objects in a very well-organized and tightly-controlled manner. In most situations, only one developer at a time will make changes to an object. If an object needs to be changed for multiple purposes, the first set of changes should be fully tested (at least through the development testing stage) before the object is released to be modified for a second purpose.

If the project is so large and complex or deadlines are so tight that this one modification at a time approach is not feasible, we should consider the use of software source management systems, such as the **Git** or **Team Foundation** systems, which can easily help you separate multi-modifications.

Similarly, we should only be working on one functional change at a time. As developers, we might be working on changes in two different systems in parallel, but we shouldn't be working on multiple changes in a single system simultaneously. It's challenging enough to keep all the aspects of a single modification to a system under control without having incomplete pieces of several tasks, all floating around in the same system.

If multiple changes need to be made simultaneously to a single system, one approach is to assign multiple developers, each with their own components to address. Another approach is for each developer to work on their own copy of the development database, with a project librarian assigned to resolve overlapping updates. We should learn from the past. In mainframe development environments, having multiple developers working on the same system at the same time was common. Coordination issues were addressed as a standard part of the project management process. Applicable techniques are well-documented in professional literature. Similar solutions still apply.

Testing

As we all know, there is no substitute for complete and thorough testing. Fortunately, Business Central provides some very useful tools, such as the ones we previously discussed, to help us to be more efficient than we might be in some other environment. In addition to the built-in testing tools, there are also some testing techniques that are Business Central-specific.

Database testing approaches

If the new modifications are not tied to previous modifications and specific customer data, then we may be able to use the **Cronus** database as a test platform. This works well when our target is a database that is not heavily modified in the area on which we are currently working. As the Cronus database is small, we will not get lost in large data volumes. Most of the master tables in Cronus are populated, so we don't have to create and populate this information. Setups are done and generally contain reasonably generic information.

If we are operating with an unmodified version of Cronus, we have the advantage that our test is not affected by other preexisting modifications. The disadvantage, of course, is that we are not testing in a wholly realistic situation. Because the data volume in Cronus is so small, we are not likely to detect a potential performance problem.

Even when our modification is targeted at a highly modified system, where those other modifications will affect what we are doing, it's often useful to test a version of our modification initially in Cronus. This may allow us to determine if our change has internal integrity before we move on to testing in the context of the fully modified copy of the production system.

If the target database for our modifications is an active customer database, then there is no substitute for doing complete and final testing in a copy of the production database using a copy of the customer's license. This way, we will be testing the compatibility of our work with the production setup, the full set of existing modifications, and, of course, live data content and volumes. The only way to get a good feeling for possible performance issues is to test in a recent copy of the production database.

 Final testing should always be done using the customer's license.

Testing in production

While it is always a good idea to thoroughly test before adding our changes to the production system, sometimes, we can safely do our testing inside the production environment. If the modifications consist of functions that do not change any data and can be tested without affecting any ongoing production activity, it may be feasible to test within the production system.

Examples of modifications that may be able to be tested in the live production system can range from a simple inquiry page, a new analysis report, or when exporting data that is to be processed outside the system to a completely new subsystem that does not change any existing data. There are also situations where the only changes to the existing system are the addition of fields to existing tables. In such a case, we may be able to test just a part of the modification outside production, and then implement the table changes to complete the rest of the testing in the context of the production system.

Finally, we can use the Testing functions to control tests so that any changes to the database are rolled back at the conclusion of the testing. This approach allows for testing inside a production database with less fear of corrupting live data.

Make sure not to run any test codeunit on its own as test isolation is only handled by the test runner codeunit.

Using a testing database

From a testing point of view, the most realistic testing environment is a current copy of an actual production database. There are sometimes apparently good excuses as to why it is just too difficult to test using a copy of the actual production database.

Don't give in to excuses—use a testing copy of the production database!

Remember, when we implement our modifications, they will receive the **test by fire** in the environment of production. We need to do everything within reason to assure success. Let's review some of the potential problems involved in testing with a copy of the production database and how to cope with them:

- **It's too big**: This is not a good argument relative to disk space. Disk space is so inexpensive that we can almost always afford plenty of disk space for testing. We should also make every possible useful intermediate stage backup. Staying organized and making lots of backups may be time-consuming, but when done well and done correctly, it is less expensive to restore from a backup than to recover from being disorganized or having to redo a major testing process. This is one of the many places where appropriate use of the AL Testability tools can be very helpful by allowing various approaches to repetitive testing.

This is a meaningful argument if we are performing file processing of some of the larger files, for example, Item Ledger, Value Entry, and so on. However, Business Central's filtering capabilities are so strong that we should relatively easily be able to carve out manageably sized test data groups with which to work.

- **There's no data that's useful**: This might be true. However, it would be just as true for a test database, unless it were created expressly for this set of tests. By definition, whatever data is in a copy of the production database is what we will encounter when we eventually implement the enhancements that we are working on. If we build useful test data within the context of a copy of the production database, our tests will be much more realistic and, therefore, of better quality. In addition, the act of building workable test data will help us define what will be needed to set up the production system to utilize the new enhancements.

- **Production data will get in the way**: This may be true. If it is especially true, then perhaps the database must be preprocessed in some way to begin testing, or testing must begin with some other database, such as Cronus or a special testing-only mockup. As we stated earlier, all the issues that exist in the production database must be dealt with when we put the enhancements into production. Therefore, we should test in that environment. Overcoming such challenges will prepare us to do a better job at the critical time of going live with the newly modified objects.

- **We need to test repeatedly from the same baseline** or **we must do regression testing**: These are both good points, but don't have much to do with the type of database we're using for testing. Both cases are addressed by properly managing the setup of our test data and keeping incremental backups of our pretest and post-test data at every step of the way. SQL Server tools can assist in this effort. In addition, the AL Testability Tools are explicitly designed to support regression testing.

Remember, doing the testing job well is much less expensive than implementing a buggy modification and repairing the problems during production.

Testing techniques

As experienced developers, we are already familiar with good testing practices. Even so, it never hurts to be reminded about some of the more critical habits to maintain.

Any modification greater than trivial should be tested in one way or another by at least two people. The people that are assigned should not be a part of the team that created the design or coded the modification. It would be best if one of the testers is an experienced user, because users seem to have a knack (for obvious reasons) of understanding how the modification operates compared to how the rest of the system acts in the course of day-to-day work. This helps us obtain meaningful feedback on the user interface before going into production.

One of the testing goals is to supply unexpected data and make sure that the modification can deal with it properly. Unfortunately, those who were involved in creating the design will have a very difficult time being creative in supplying the unexpected. Users often enter data that the designer or programmer didn't expect. For that reason, testing by experienced users is beneficial.

The AL Testability Tools provide features to support testing how system functions deal with problem data. If possible, it would be good to have users help us define test data, and then use the Testability Tools to assure that the modifications properly handle the data.

After we cover the mainstream issues (whatever it is that the modification is intended to accomplish), we need to make sure our testing covers all boundary conditions. Boundary conditions are the data items that are exactly equal to the maximum, minimum, or other range limit. More specifically, boundaries are the points at which input data values change from valid to invalid. Boundary condition checking in the code is where programmer logic often goes astray. Testing at these points is very effective for uncovering data-related errors.

Deliverables

Create useful documentation and keep good records of testing processes and results. Testing scripts, both human-oriented and AL Testability Tool-based, should be retained for future reference. Document the purpose of the modifications from a business point of view. Add a brief, but complete, technical explanation of what must be done from a functional design and coding point of view to accomplish the business purpose. Briefly record the testing that was done. The scope of the record keeping should be directly proportional to the business value of the modifications being made and the potential cost of not having good records. All investments are a form of insurance and preventive medicine. We hope they won't be needed, but we have to allow for the possibility that they might be needed.

More complex modifications should be delivered and installed by experienced implementers—perhaps even by the developers themselves. Small Business Central modifications may be transmitted electronically to the customer site for installation by a skilled super user. Any time this is done, all the proper and normal actions must occur, including those actions regarding backup before importing changes, user instructions (preferably written) on what to expect from the change, and written instructions on how to correctly apply the change. There must also be a plan and a clearly defined process to restore the system to its state prior to the change, in case the modification doesn't work correctly.

Finishing the project

Bring projects to conclusion, and don't let them drag on through inaction and inattention – open issues get forgotten and then don't get addressed. Get it done, wrap it up, and then review what went well and what didn't go well, both for remediation and for application to future projects.

Set up ongoing support services as appropriate and move on to the next project. With the flexibility of the Role Tailored Client allowing page layout changes by both super users (configuration) and users (personalization), the challenge of user support has increased. No longer can the support person expect to know what display the user is viewing today.

Consequently, support services will almost certainly require the capability of the support person to be able to view the user's display. Without that, it will be much more difficult, time-consuming, and frustrating for the two-way support of personnel-user communication to take place. If it doesn't already exist, this capability will have to be added to the partner's support organization toolset and practices. There may be communications and security issues that need to be addressed at both the support service and the user site.

Plan for upgrading

The ability to upgrade a customized system is a very important feature of Business Central. Most other complex business application systems are very difficult to customize at the database-structure and process-flow levels. Business Central readily offers this capability. This is a significant difference between Business Central and the competitive products in the market.

Complementing the ability to be customized is the ability to upgrade a customized Business Central system. While not a trivial task, at least it is possible with Business Central. In many other systems, the only reasonable path to an upgrade is often to discard the old version and reimplement with the new version, recreating all customizations. Not only is Business Central unusually accommodating to being upgraded, but with each new version of the system, Microsoft has enhanced the power and flexibility of the tools it provides to help us do upgrades.

We may say, why should a developer care about upgrades? There are at least two good reasons we should care about upgrades. First, because our design and the coding of our modifications can have a considerable impact on the amount of effort required to upgrade a system. Second, because as skilled developers doing Business Central customizations, we might well be asked to be involved in an upgrade project. Because the ability to upgrade is important, and because we are likely to be involved one way or another, we will review a number of factors that relate to upgrades.

Benefits of upgrading

To ensure that we are on common ground about why upgrading is important to both the client and the Business Central partner, the following is a brief list of some of the benefits available from an upgrade:

- Easier support of a more current version
- Access to new features and capabilities
- Continued access to fixes and regulatory updates
- Improvements in speed, security, reliability, and user interface
- Assured continuation of support availability
- Compatibility with necessary infrastructure changes, such as new operating system versions
- Opportunity to do needed training, data cleaning, and process improvement
- Opportunity to resolve old problems, to do postponed housekeeping, create a known system reference point

This list is not complete, and not every benefit will be realized in any one situation.

Coding considerations

The most challenging and important part of an upgrade is porting code and data modifications from the older version of a system to the new version. When the new version has major design or data structure changes in an area that we have customized, it is quite possible that our modification structure will have to be redesigned and, perhaps, even be recoded from scratch.

On the other hand, many times, the changes in the new product version of Business Central don't affect much existing code, at least in terms of the base logic. If our modifications are done properly, it's often not very difficult to port custom code from the older version into the new version. By applying what some refer to as low-impact coding techniques, we can make the upgrade job easier and, thereby, less costly.

Low-impact coding

We have already discussed most of these practices in other chapters, but will review them here, in the context of coding to make it easier to upgrade. We won't be able to follow each of these, but will have to choose the degree to which we can implement low-impact code and which of these approaches fit our situation (this list may not be all-inclusive):

- Separate and isolate new code
- Create functions for significant amounts of new code that can be accessed using single codeline function calls
- Either add independent codeunits as repositories of modification functions or, if that is overkill, place the modification functions within the modified objects
- Add new data fields; don't change the usage of existing fields
- When the functionality is new, add new tables rather than modifying existing tables
- For minor changes, modify the existing pages, or else copy and change the clone pages
- Copy, then modify the copies of reports and XMLports, rather than modifying the original versions in place
- Don't change field names in objects; just change captions and labels, as necessary

In any modification, we will have conflicting priorities regarding doing today's job in the easiest and least expensive way versus doing the best we can do to plan for future maintenance, enhancements, updates, and upgrades. The right decision is never a black and white choice, but must be guided by subjective guidelines as to which choice is really in the customer's best interest.

Supporting material

With every Business Central system distribution, there have been some reference guides. These are minimal in Business Central. There are previously published guides available but, sometimes, we have to search for them. Some were distributed with previous versions of the product, but not with the latest version. Some are posted at various locations on *PartnerSource*, or another Microsoft website. Some may be available on one of the forums or on a blog.

Be a regular visitor to websites for more information and advice on AL, Business Central, and other related topics. The `https://dynamicsuser.net/` and `https://mibuso.com/` websites are especially comprehensive and well attended. Other smaller or more specialized sites also exist. Some of those that are available at the time of writing this book are as follows:

- *Microsoft Dynamics Business Central Team Blog*: `https://community.dynamics.com/business/b/financials`
- *Marije Brummel Blog*: `https://marijebrummel.blog/2018/11/25/blogging-the-gap/`
- Dmitry Katson blog: `https://community.dynamics.com/nav/b/katsonsnavblog`
- Saurav Dhyany: `https://saurav-nav.blogspot.com/`
- Alex Chow: `http://www.dynamicsnavconsultant.com/`
- Vjekoslav Babic's Blog: `http://vjeko.com/`
- Gunnar Gestsson: `https://www.dynamics.is/`
- Luc van Vugt's blog: `https://dynamicsuser.net/nav/b/vanvugt`

There are also a number of other useful blogs available. Look for them and review them regularly. The good ideas that are posted by the members of the Business Central community in their blogs, and on the Business Central forums, are generously shared freely, and often.

Finally, there are a number of books that focus on various aspects of Dynamics that are Business Central, all of which have been published by *Packt Publishing* (`www.packtpub.com`). Even the books about older versions of Business Central have a lot of good information about developing with the Business Central tools and applying Business Central's functionality in a wide variety of application environments.

Summary

We have covered many topics in this book, with the goal of helping you become productive in AL development with Dynamics Business Central. Hopefully, you've found your time spent with us to be a good investment. From this point on, your assignments are to continue exploring and learning, enjoy working with Business Central, Visual Studio Code, and AL, and to treat others as you would have them treat you.

> *"We live in a world in which we need to share responsibility. It's easy to say "It's not my child, not my community, not my world, not my problem." There are those who see the need and respond. Those people are my heroes."*

> *– Fred Rogers*

> *"Be kind whenever possible. It is always possible."*

> *– Dalai Lama*

Questions

1. Which one of the following provides access to several libraries of functions for various purposes that are widely used throughout the NAV system? Choose one:
    - Codeunit 412—Common Dialog Management
    - Codeunit 408—Dimension Management
    - Codeunit 396—NoSeriesManagement
    - Codeunit 1—Application Management

2. The Help files for Business Central cannot be customized by partner or ISV developers. True or false?

3. Which of the following are good coding practices? Choose three:
    - Careful naming
    - Good documentation
    - Liberal use of wildcards
    - Design for ease of upgrading

4. Custom AL code is not allowed to call functions that exist in the base Microsoft that was created for Business Central objects. True or false?

5. Business Central's multi-language capability allows an installation to have multiple languages active at one time. True or false?

6. Designing to minimize disk I/O in Business Central is not important because SQL Server takes care of everything. True or false?

7. Which of the following defines the Client add-in feature? Choose one:
    - The ability to add a new client of your own design to Business Central
    - A tool to provide for extending the user interface behavior
    - A special calculator feature for the client
    - A new method for mapping Customers to Contacts

8. When planning a new Business Central development project, it is good to focus on the design of the data structure, required data accesses, validation, and maintenance. True or false?

9. The Navigate feature can be used for which of the following? Choose three:
    - Auditing by a professional accountant
    - User analysis of data processing
    - Reversing posting errors
    - Debugging

10. Business Central modifications should always be delivered to customers in the form of text files. True or false?

11. Both source code changes and setting debugger breaks can only be done in the AL Editor. True or false?

12. You can enhance the Navigate function to include new tables that have been added to the system as part of an enhancement. True or false?

13. The C/Side Testing tools allow the implementation of regression tests. True or false?

14. Client Add-ins must be written in what language? Choose one:
    - C#
    - VB.NET
    - JavaScript
    - AL.NET

15. The Business Central debugger allows the value of Watched Variables to be changed in the middle of a debugging session. True or false?

16. The Business Central debugger runs as a separate session. True or false?

17. The C/Side Testing tools support which of the following? Choose four:
    - Positive testing
    - Negative testing
    - Automated testing
    - C# test viewing
    - TestIsolation (rollback) testing

18. Business Central includes a flexible multi-currency feature that allows transactions to begin in one currency and conclude in a different currency. True or false?

19. Business Central does not support linked SQL Server databases. True or false?

20. Simple debugging can be done without the use of the debugger. True or false?

Assessments

Chapter 1

1. Manufacturing, Order processing, Planning, and General accounting
2. Tablet client, Document emailing, and Mandatory fields
3. True
4. Journal—Transaction entries, Ledger—History, Register—Audit trail, Document—Invoice, Posting—Validation process
5. True
6. Customizable and C# IDE
7. Table, Page, Report, Codeunit, Query, XMLport, and MenuSuite
8. False
9. True
10. Role Center
11. False
12. Report layout
13. False
14. True, but through use of a temporary table
15. True
16. 50,000 - 60,000 and 50,000 - 99,999
17. False
18. False
19. Reusable code and a proven way to solve a common problem
20. False

Chapter 2

1. A Business Central table is the definition of data structure and a Business Central table should implement many of the business rules of a system
2. False
3. `LinkedObject`
4. False
5. `OnInsert` and `OnRename`
6. False
7. False
8. False—50,000-99,999
9. Customer, User, and Item Ledger Entry
10. True
11. False
12. Date and Integer
13. True
14. `Read`, `Delete`, and `Modify`
15. True
16. False—except with a very advanced technical method
17. False
18. False
19. SQL indexed views
20. False

Chapter 3

1. False
2. In the primary key in the related table
3. `Normal`—1
4. GPS location
5. Median
6. True

7. False
8. CaptionML
9. OnValidate and OnLookup
10. Records, DateFormula, and Objects
11. False
12. False and false
13. True
14. True
15. True
16. False
17. *W* for week and *CM* for current month
18. False
19. False
20. Decimal and option
21. Question mark (?) and Asterisk (*)

Chapter 4

1. False
2. Ribbon and navigation pane
3. False
4. False
5. Chart part and system part
6. False
7. False
8. Departments and home
9. True
10. True
11. True
12. Can affect FastTab displays and applies to decimal fields only
13. False
14. Card, Document, and List

15. False
16. `Visible, HideValue, Editable`
17. `DelayedInput`
18. False
19. False
20. True

Chapter 5

1. DataItems, Request Page, and Database updating
2. False
3. False
4. Indentation
5. False
6. False
7. True
8. `TopNumberOfRows` and `OrderBy`
9. False
10. False
11. List, Document, and Invoice
12. True
13. False
14. False
15. True
16. Charts and cues
17. False
18. Data Show/Hide and Sorting by columns
19. True
20. True

Chapter 6

1. False
2. `Page`
3. True
4. `Var`
5. False
6. True
7. False
8. False
9. False
10. True
11. Application management and `Mail`
12. True
13. True
14. `?`, `*`, and `&`
15. True
16. False
17. False
18. `*` and `/`

Chapter 7

1. `DATE2DWY`, `CALCDATE`, and `DMY2DATE`
2. True
3. `CALCFIELDS` and `SETAUTOCALCFIELDS`
4. `SKIP`
5. True
6. False
7. False
8. `DO-UNTIL`
9. False
10. True
11. `MODIFY(TRUE)`

12. False
13. False
14. A decimal variable
15. False
16. True
17. Find applicable functions and use entries as a template for function syntax and arguments
18. False
19. False
20. True

Chapter 8

1. False
2. MenuSuite objects
3. False
4. AL changes in the Action Designer, implementer/administrator configuration, and user personalization
5. False
6. Report and new
7. True
8. Activity pane and cues
9. False
10. True
11. Queries and pages
12. True
13. False
14. True
15. False
16. True
17. False
18. Cues and page parts
19. False
20. False

Chapter 9

1. Codeunit 1—Application Management
2. False
3. Careful naming, good documentation, and design for ease of upgrading
4. False
5. True
6. False
7. A tool to provide for extending the user interface behavior
8. True
9. Auditing by a professional accountant, user analysis of data processing, and debugging
10. False
11. True
12. True
13. True
14. JavaScript
15. False
16. True
17. Positive testing, negative testing, automated testing, and TestIsolation (rollback) testing
18. True
19. False
20. True

Other Books You May Enjoy

If you enjoyed this book, you may be interested in these other books by Packt:

Implementing Microsoft Dynamics 365 Business Central On-Premise - Fourth Edition
Roberto Stefanetti, Alex Chow

ISBN: 978-1-78913-393-6

- Explore new features introduced in Microsoft Dynamics NAV 2018
- Learn abstract techniques for data analysis, reporting, and debugging
- Install, configure, and use additional tools for business intelligence, document management, and reporting
- Discover Dynamics 365 Business Central and several other Microsoft services
- Utilize different tools to develop applications for Business CentralExplore new features introduced in Microsoft Dynamics NAV 2018
- Migrate to Microsoft Dynamics NAV 2018 from previous versions

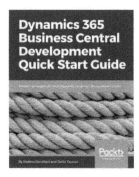

Dynamics 365 Business Central Development Quick Start Guide
Stefano Demiliani, Duilio Tacconi

ISBN: 978-1-78934-746-3

- Develop solutions for Dynamics 365 Business Central
- Create a sandbox for extensions development (local or on cloud)
- Use Docker with Dynamics 365 Business Central
- Create extensions for Dynamics 365 Business Central
- Handle dependencies, translations and reporting
- Deploy extensions on-premise and to the cloud
- Create serverless processes with Dynamics 365 Business Central
- Understand source code management for AL

Leave a review - let other readers know what you think

Please share your thoughts on this book with others by leaving a review on the site that you bought it from. If you purchased the book from Amazon, please leave us an honest review on this book's Amazon page. This is vital so that other potential readers can see and use your unbiased opinion to make purchasing decisions, we can understand what our customers think about our products, and our authors can see your feedback on the title that they have worked with Packt to create. It will only take a few minutes of your time, but is valuable to other potential customers, our authors, and Packt. Thank you!

Index

www.ingramcontent.com/pod-product-compliance
Lightning Source LLC
Chambersburg PA
CBHW060639060326
40690CB00020B/4449